What Educators and Parents Are Saying about The Spalding Method

"The strength of The Spalding Method is that children quickly learn the mechanics of reading, freeing them to enjoy the benefits of good literature at an early age. Spalding is effective because its principles and methods of instruction are well grounded in reading research."

Sylvia Richardson, M.D., L.L.D., Distinguished Professor of Communication Sciences and Disorders, Clinical Professor of Pediatrics, Emerita, University of South Florida, Tampa, Florida

"The Spalding Method was indispensable to me in home-schooling my four children over the last thirteen years. Simple and precise instruction in reading and writing the sounds of the alphabet paved the way for early fluent reading as well as accurate spelling and good penmanship. Guided practice in reading for content as well as reading for pleasure prepares students for comprehending even the most difficult material. Intensive student-teacher interaction makes The Spalding Method excellent for the home environment. I highly recommend *The Writing Road to Reading* to any parent seeking a meaningful and successful home-schooling experience."

Sim Gregory, Home-School Mother, Newcastle, Maine

"The Spalding Method is ideal for mainstream or learning disabled students because it is based on knowledge of how the brain works and on sound educational principles. Spalding gives students essential information about phonics and provides the comprehension strategies needed for proficient reading. Multisensory techniques are used to deliver comprehensive instruction in listening, speaking, spelling, reading, and writing. Thinking skills are developed in each lesson so students can meet new challenges with confidence. As one delighted student proudly wrote, 'There is nothing I am unable to do!'"

Carol Margeson, Ph.D., Clinical Psychologist, Sydney, Australia

"Romalda Spalding's *The Writing Road to Reading* is a total language arts method that captures all the richness and variety of the English language. For forty years, classroom teachers across America have found that it works . . . I enthusiastically endorse The Spalding Method because I know that if it were taught in every classroom, illiteracy would vanish."

Robert Sweet, Professional Staff Member, Committee on Education and the Workforce, United States House of Representatives

"The Spalding Method of teaching precise speech, legible handwriting, correct spelling, and fluent, accurate reading has done more to provide continuity and consistency for our entire curriculum than any other factor. It provides security for those who learn more slowly, while allowing others to progress rapidly. No program can compete with its effectiveness and economy. Our twenty-four years of Spalding has produced tremendous results by any standard of comparison and has led to the establishment of four Ben Franklin Schools based on The Spalding Method."

H. Marc Mason, Principal, Benjamin Franklin Elementary School, Mesa, Arizona

"The Spalding Method has been a godsend for my ESL [English as a second language] students. Many of them come to me with 'labels,' but I quickly discover that their only problem is, they have not been taught the alphabetic code. It is also delightful to observe the progress made by average and above-average ESL students who have lacked success but find it through Spalding. Spalding empowers students!"

Bertha Zapata, ESL Teacher, Broward Elementary School, Tampa, Florida

"I truly credit The Spalding Method with my success as a reading teacher of both regular and special education students. Not one of my master's courses in learning disabilities was able to help me teach my struggling readers what they most wanted to know—how to read. My students' new-found joy in reading for pleasure inspired me to learn all I could about this wonderful method and share it with as many others as possible."

Eileen Oliver, Teacher of the Year, 2001, former Special Reading Teacher, St. Charles Parish School, Boutte, Louisiana

"As superintendent of Village Christian Schools, a coeducational K–12 day school with a total enrollment of 1,950 students, I consider it a professional privilege to offer my strong endorsement of The Spalding Method. Over the past seven years, our standardized test scores have risen dramatically. However, the greatest gains have been in areas not covered by testing. Teacher enthusiasm, student self-esteem, and parent support for our school have all increased significantly. Our enrollment is roughly 30 percent minority, 5 percent to 8 percent have a variety of learning problems, and we have many families who do not speak English at home. . . . Thanks to Spalding, our students now do things in October that they were not doing until April. Would I consider changing to a different approach? Only if I were to find something more effective. To date, neither our faculty nor I have found anything more successful than this true multisensory, complete language arts program."

Ronald G. Sipus, Ph.D., Superintendent, Village Christian Schools, Sun Valley, California

"Spalding teaches children skills essential to precise speech, attentive listening and reading, and competent writing. In addition, teachers learn the content and techniques they need to teach children how the language works. The Spalding Method is the most effective language arts program I have worked with during my twenty-five years as a teacher, principal, and now curriculum director."

Jim Sexton, Director of Educational Services, ABS School Services, Phoenix, Arizona

"The language arts are considered foundational and paramount to all of the many academic skills taught at Fort Caspar Academy. The Spalding Method is a structured, thorough, and consistent way for students to learn all the language skills. As a result, student proficiency in reading, writing, spelling, and comprehension has risen dramatically. Parents are excited about the growth they see in their children's reading skills, and teachers are appreciative of the precise training available through Spalding Education International."

Norm Carrell, Principal, Snowy Range Academy, Laramie, Wyoming

THE WRITING ROAD
TO READING

THE *Writing* ROAD TO READING

The Spalding Method® for Teaching Speech, Spelling, Writing, and Reading

FIFTH REVISED EDITION

Romalda Bishop Spalding

Mary E. North, Ph.D., Editor

Collins

An Imprint of HarperCollinsPublishers

THE WRITING ROAD TO READING. © 1957, 1962, 1969, 1986, 1990, 2003 by Spalding Education International. All rights reserved. Printed in the United States of America. No part of this book may be used or reproduced in any manner whatsoever without written permission except in the case of brief quotations embodied in critical articles and reviews. For information address HarperCollins Publishers Inc., 10 East 53rd Street, New York, New York 10022.

HarperCollins books may be purchased for educational, business, or sales promotional use. For information please write to: Special Markets Department, HarperCollins Publishers Inc., 10 East 53rd Street, New York, New York 10022.

FIFTH EDITION

Designed by Oksana Kushnir

Library of Congress Cataloging-in-Publication Data
Spalding, Romalda Bishop.
The writing road to reading : the Spalding method for teaching speech, spelling, writing, and reading / Romalda Bishop Spalding ; Mary E. North, editor.—5th rev. ed.
    p.   cm.
Includes bibliographical references (p.) and index.
ISBN 0-06-052010-8
1. Reading—Phonetic method.   2. Language arts (Elementary)
3. English language—Study and teaching (Elementary)—United States.
I. North, Mary E. (Mary Elizabeth)   II. Title.
LB1573.3 .S6 2003
372.46'5—dc21   2002068465

10 11 12 13 WBC/CW 20 19 18 17 16 15 14 13 12

Contents

Foreword

By S. Farnham-Diggory*

Teach the child what is of use to a child, Rousseau said, *and you will find that it takes all his time.*

What is of use to a child interested in reading is explicit instruction in how the written language works—how it represents the sounds of speech, how it is produced with tools like pencils and chalk, how it signifies words and ideas. A program that provides such instruction—specifically, the Spalding program—absorbs children to an astonishing degree. It does indeed take all their time, or as much of it as teachers will allow.

This is perhaps the most impressive aspect of the Spalding program: its motivating power. This tells a psychologist like myself that Spalding has fully engaged the natural learning dispositions of the mind. We see this routinely in the child's devotion to the task of learning to talk. Learning to read by The Spalding Method inspires a similar devotion.

Reading ability is not, however, neurologically prewired the way spoken language ability is. A pervasive error in current reading instructional theory is that children will inductively discover the rules of the written language if they are immersed in a written language environment (Goodman and Goodman, 1979; Smith, 1971). Children do, of course, discover the rules of their spoken language through simple immersion—but that is because their brains are prewired for speech. Their brains are not prewired for reading. Left to their own inductive devices, the vast majority of children will not discover how the written language works. What they will discover is that they do not understand how it works. And, of course, they will think that is their own fault.

One of the most heartbreaking sights in American schools today is that of children—once so eager to read—discovering that they are not learning how. There comes over those sparkling eyes a glaze of listless despair. We are not talking here about a few children and scattered schools. We are talking about millions of children and every school in the nation. And the toll in young spirits is the least of it. The toll in the learning and thinking potential of our citizenry is beyond measure.

The reason for this catastrophe is straightforward: American citizens are not learning to read because they are not being taught how to read. The research evidence on this point is unequivocal.

*Dr. S. Farnham-Diggory is the former H. Rodney Sharp Professor of Educational Studies and Psychology and director of the Reading Study Center and of the Academic Study and Assistance Program, University of Delaware.

Fundamentally, the instructional disaster must be laid at the feet of the basal reader establishment, a billion-dollar industry that supplies every teacher and every pupil with a scheduled sequence of reading materials and lessons. The per-pupil costs and profits are astronomical. As in the case of many industries (the tobacco industry, for example), profits are not tied to healthful outcomes, they are tied to sales, and to anything legal that promotes sales. The fact that most people are not learning how to read does not deter basal sales. School systems simply switch basals, even on a statewide basis, which makes the sales game pretty exciting. But few systems have dared face the fact that none of the basals is effective.

This is not the place to present a detailed critique of the basals, but in summary, the problem is that they have lost touch with (1) the basic principles of skill acquisition and (2) the nature of the reading process. A pervasive problem, for example, is that basal programs do not provide sufficient practice. A reading assignment may not even incorporate a rule that was just taught. If you understand how skill development works, and how reading works, you can easily see where the basals go wrong and where the Spalding program does not. Let me explain what I mean.

Reading and Spelling Processes

Over the past fifteen years, theories of reading have rapidly evolved from simple stimulus-response notions to complex connectionist models that are represented as computer simulations (Gough, 1972; Rumelhart, 1977; Rumelhart and McClelland, 1986). In the early 1970s, we thought of reading as a linear process: See a letter (or a piece of a letter), put it together with other letters, formulate the word, recall the meaning of the word, hold that in mind, formulate another word, put all the words together, compute a new meaning, and so on. These theories were not very satisfactory, because it was intuitively obvious that reading did not work like that. Sometimes, for example, we see a word we expect to see instead of the word that is really there. By the end of the 1970s, reading theory had evolved from linear forms to parallel forms: Many processes are now considered to go on at the same time during reading. You are forming expectations, recalling earlier concepts, picking up print, organizing syntax, checking inferences, and so forth, more or less simultaneously. Reading is, in other words, now recognized as a *complex* skill—which means that it requires coordination of a number of subskills, just as piano-playing or basketball does.

The core reading subskill is forming connections between speech and print. More technically, this comes down to connections between specific speech units called phonemes and specific letters that represent them. For example, the letter *p* represents the phoneme /p/.

Spoken words are sequences of phonemes. Different words are made up of different sequences of phonemes. Since letters represent phonemes, a different sequence of phonemes will be represented by a different sequence of letters. That is the fundamental literary principle in all languages that use alphabetic systems, and it has to be thoroughly mastered.

However, a serious theoretical error currently pervades many American systems of reading instruction. It is that letter-phoneme correspondences cannot be or should not be taught in isolation because they do not exist in isolation. Phonemes change slightly from word to word. The phoneme /p/ as pronounced in the word *pot* will have more air behind it than the same phoneme as pronounced in the word *spot* or *top*. The phonemes would look different on a spectrograph. From this fact, the conclusion has incorrectly been drawn that isolated phonemes should not be taught as such because they do not exist in "pure" form.

As a result, many reading programs tell children something like this: "This letter *b* is the first sound in the word *boy.*" The teacher is instructed never to pronounce that phoneme in isolation. The results have been disastrous. It is simply not clear to most children what they are supposed to be learning. They do not know exactly what that letter *b* stands for, and the confusion increases as more and more phonemes are taught by this *implicit* (as it is called) method.

The children's confusion has given rise to a second theoretical error: the belief that children cannot hear phonemes in words—that they cannot analyze the sound pattern of a word. Of course, they can if they know what they are supposed to be listening *for.*

Analogous theoretical errors would arise if we never taught colors in isolation, on grounds that colors never exist in isolation, but are always a property of some object, and are slightly different in each case. You could point to the sky and say, "That is blue," and "Blue is what the rug is," and "Blue is what your mother's eyes are," and so on. You would soon have a thoroughly confused child, and you might well come to the erroneous conclusion that some children cannot *see* blue—they cannot analyze colors of objects.

In fact, it only takes children a minute or so to learn from a color chip what color is called *blue.* They can then easily categorize objects as blue, even though they never again see any blue as pure as the color chip, or, indeed, ever see any two blues that are exactly the same.

Similarly, children can easily learn isolated phonemes, and once they have learned them, they can easily identify them in words. Once they understand what they are supposed to be listening *for,* they can readily categorize a wide range of /p/ sounds as all being represented by the same letter *p.* The research evidence on this point is absolutely beyond dispute (Groff, 1977; Hohn and Ehri, 1983; Smith and Tager-Flusberg, 1982; Treiman, 1985; Treiman and Baron, 1983).

The fact is that human brains are prewired for categorizing sensory inputs. A sound does not have to be exactly like another sound for a child to recognize that the same symbol stands for it. We could not function on this planet if our brains did not have the ability to categorize a range of sensory inputs, and thus recognize that the same rule applies to them. Once you have heard one saber-toothed tiger growl, you had better believe you have heard them all.

This, then, is the core reading subskill. You have to learn which letters represent which phonemes in English. You do not have to learn every single letter-sound unit, but you need a substantial "working set." In every complex skill, there is a similar working set of basic units that have to be learned—feet positions in ballet, for example—out of which higher-order units can then be constructed. We can call the working set of letter-phoneme units the *first-order subskills* of literacy.

Second-order subskills refer to the fact that words are not random collections of letter-phoneme units. Some units are strongly associated with others; some units preclude the appearance of others; and so on. The skilled reader and speller knows these rules. A good instructor will teach them explicitly. It is true that second-order rules are implicit in words, and that if you simply memorized many words, you would ingest some second-order rules as well. But you would not have control of them.

One of the golden oldies of learning psychology is that rules are applied most extensively and efficiently if they are verbalizable. Once you can say what a rule is, you have maximally flexible use of it. The well-instructed literate will be able to articulate both first-order and second-order rules, as well as express them in behavior.

One interesting neurologically based difference between reading and spelling, however, is that the second-order subskills of spelling are different in *format* from those of reading. When you spell, you activate your rule knowledge sequentially. When you read, you activate it wholistically—you see a whole group of letters at once.

This means we want second-order-rule knowledge to be represented in both ways in the minds of students: We want them to know that certain sounds (and their associated letters) follow others, or are influenced by others, sequentially, and we also want them to know that certain letters (and their associated sounds) are grouped simultaneously with certain other letters. You will see how cleverly Spalding has charted a path through this instructional thicket.

There are also what we can call *third-order subskills* of literacy—involvement of learning and thinking processes. But these third-order subskills belong to a different stage of reading instruction, as will shortly be explained. The summary point at the moment is that the complex skills of reading and spelling require the coordination of a number of subskills, the most important being first-order subskills of pairing letters with phonemes, second-order subskills of grouping letter-phoneme units lawfully, and third-order subskills of thinking and learning.

Stages of Reading Acquisition

A helpful framework for organizing an instructional sequence for reading was provided by Jeanne Chall (1983a, 1983b), while director of the Reading Laboratory at Harvard University. According to Chall, we progress through six stages of reading skill development. Stage 0 is a prereading stage. Children are essentially discovering the world of print from billboards, cereal boxes, and the like. Stage 1 is the first stage of reading and is characterized by recognition of the alphabetic principle—namely, that letters represent speech sounds, or phonemes. Stage 2 is the expansion and consolidation of this principle, mastery to the point of automaticity, of the orthographic rules of the language. Stage 3 is the beginning of higher-order learning and thinking skill acquisition. As the saying goes, you are no longer learning to read, you are reading to learn. Essentially, you can now develop and embed comprehension subskills in the overall reading process. You can, for example, "flag" key concepts as important to remember while you're reading along. Stages 4 and 5 involve higher types of analytical and synthetic reasoning, as when you compare points of view or use new information to modify a personal theory—all during the ongoing process of reading.

Chall provided convincing evidence that reading skill acquisition does progress through these stages, in the order described.

Strategy Training Needs

A large number of college students lack Stage 3 skills, not to mention the higher-order Stage 4 and 5 skills that college is really about. In part, the deficiencies arise from the fact that the skills were never explicitly taught. It is a depressing fact, for example, that a youngster can go all the way through a biology course in high school without ever having once discussed the text material in class. Assignments are made, and students are expected to read them and comprehend them, as demonstrated by performance on so-called comprehension tests, but not once has there been a moment's training in the skills of understanding scientific text.

This is very serious, and I want to make clear that my current emphasis on Stage 1 and Stage 2 training doesn't mean that I think comprehension training is unimportant. The problem is that it cannot *begin* until Stage 2 decoding is automated, simply because a reader does not have available attentional capacity. The mind "frees up" for comprehension operations only after decoding operations become automatic. If you try to teach comprehension skills before then, you will generate a cycle of confusion: The attentional capacity necessary for mastering decoding will be drained by attempts to "remember the main idea," and capacity for comprehending will simultaneously be drained by decoding efforts. So neither Stage 2 nor Stage 3 mastery is achieved.

It is simply imperative to first consolidate and automate the Stage 2 decoding skills, which is what the Spalding program does, so that you can then go on to provide explicit instruction in higher-order reading routines. We turn now to the details of the Spalding system.

Why the Spalding Program Works

The program begins by teaching a set of letter-phoneme units that Spalding calls phonograms. There are seventy of these, the letters of the alphabet plus some multiple-letter units like *ea* and *ng*. These particular phonograms were selected by Anna Gillingham for Samuel Orton, the famous neurologist who later also asked her to develop a method for teaching reading to dyslexics. Spalding, after teaching a child for two and a half years under Orton's guidance, developed her own method for classroom teaching to prevent or remediate writing and reading problems. (Her method is also, in my judgment, far better for dyslexics than the Orton-Gillingham method.)

An important point about the Spalding phonograms is that they are correct by modern linguistic standards. That is, the letters represent minimal speech units (phonemes), *not* blends. In many of the basals, or in other collections of so-called phonics units, children have to learn excessive numbers of essentially arbitrary letter-sound units. This misses the point of the alphabetic system: Letters are supposed to represent the minimal sound units of the language, not larger units. If you specify larger units, you lose the very flexibility and parsimony that the alphabetic system optimizes.

Learning the phonograms is a straightforward paired-associates learning task that forms tight neural links between particular phonemes, particular letters, and particular motor (writing) movements. When you master the set, you have, in effect, stocked your long-term memory with a working sample of the orthographic units of English. You can access members of this set easily and flexibly, and you can output them in written or spoken form. Learning to do this is, amazingly, great fun for students of all ages. It does absolute wonders for the self-esteem of those wounded souls suffering from years of reading failure.

After the phonograms have been learned, instruction in spelling begins. Spalding uses a list of words compiled by frequency. Eight standardized tests that sample from this list are administered, and instruction is keyed to the threshold of a child's ability. This is strongly motivating. Easy words are boring; excessively difficult words are discouraging. Words that you can almost but not quite spell are fascinating, and discovering that you can actually figure out how to spell them is fair cause for jubilation—especially for a child with a history of spelling failure.

The spelling lesson "script" is exact. The teacher says a word and calls on the children to say the first syllable (or the first sound of a one-syllable word). The children write it, then the teacher writes it on the board. The children progress systematically through the word. If there is any difficulty, the class discusses the rule involved.

Over the course of spelling, children learn by example twenty-nine second-order rules, such as the five reasons why a silent *e* is attached to the end of a word. Given seventy phonograms and twenty-nine rules, you can spell about 80 percent of English words, and a higher percentage of the most frequent ones. The spelling words are written in notebooks. After second grade, some of the rules will be, too, and again with examples. Each child thus accumulates a personal list of hundreds of words for which the spelling has been worked out and repeatedly practiced. First graders and many kindergartners go at a pace of thirty words a week.

The personal spelling book has a remarkable psychological impact on children (not to mention parents), as most of their schoolwork usually disappears into teachers' files somewhere. The typical schoolchild never sees a cumulative record of daily accomplishments. A spelling book with hundreds and hundreds of correctly spelled words in it (words in the spelling book are checked to make sure all are spelled correctly) is a mighty impressive achievement. In addition, of course, the spelling book is a reference book, and children religiously use it as such. Thus, the spelling book serves as a practice, motivational, and reference device all at the same time.

In conjunction with the spelling, a simple marking system is taught. For example, both letters of a two-letter phonogram are underlined. This shows that they go together to form a unit. As another example, little numbers are used to indicate which sound is being used if there is more than one. Thus, *mother* is marked as

mo<u>th</u>² <u>er</u>

showing that *th* and *er* are units, and that the second (in order of frequency) *th* sound is active. There are five of these marking conventions. As soon as the class learns them (which is almost immediately), the students take turns marking the word they have just produced. In this way, spelling and marking works like a problem-solving seminar, with everyone deeply absorbed in doing some of the best analytical thinking of their lives.

Now you see how Spalding deals with the problem of representing second-order grouping rules both sequentially and wholistically. Once the letter-phoneme sequences have been produced (spelling), they are graphically coded. What goes into your visual memory, then, is a wholistic, graphic pattern that depicts lawful organizations of the first-order units.

When you see the word again (unmarked), it is that visual pattern, *not the sequence of sounds,* that will be activated. Thus, Spalding minimizes the risk of setting up "sounding-out" habits that interfere with wholistic word perception. Words are not sounded out while reading except rarely, when a difficult one is encountered, because they do not have to be. Structural analysis is not taught during reading, it is taught during spelling, when you have to do that sort of analysis anyway. The output of the analysis is then marked graphically, so the structure can be retrieved as a visual whole and will not have to be sounded out again.

When about 150 words are in the spelling notebooks, reading begins. A major shock for new Spalding teachers is that reading is never *taught*. It just begins. After hours of phonogram learning, sequential word analysis, and graphic marking, children can read. They simply pick up a book and start reading. (It is, of course, a pretty exciting day.) They fly right over the basal readers with their impoverished vocabularies and start in with good children's literature—like Sendak's *Where the Wild Things Are.* They also start right in thinking and reasoning about content. From the very first day of reading, the emphasis can be on ideas, information, forming inferences, tracing implications, and the like, because the emphasis doesn't have to be on word-attack. Stage 2 skills have been mastered. Attention is now available for mastering comprehension skills. In chapter 3, Spalding provides an overview of her approach to Stage 3 training.

By grade two, the children are reading such treasures as Thurber's *Many Moons* and Williams's *The Velveteen Rabbit.* Third graders polish off *Charlotte's Web* with aplomb. These are their *readers,* you understand. The children move quickly and deeply into the very best literature, and also into biography, poetry, and science. A list of fine writing is given for beginners through grade six in "Instructional Materials" (see pages 206–211).

But that is not the end of it. Spalding mentions that children work on her materials for three hours every day. Children in the Spalding system write stories, plays, poems, and research reports as intensively as they read.

It is very important to understand this and not to make the mistake of thinking that the richness of language arts is missing from the Spalding system. On the contrary, the richness far exceeds that found in the basal programs, because the children have the skills to participate fully in the literature culture and to pursue what interests them as fast and as far as they want to go.

When The Spalding Method is used in a remedial program, the leaps that children make can be downright alarming. Putting a logical system into the hands of intelligent children who have searched desperately for just such a system may enable them to run farther and faster with it than you dared to imagine. We have had children who were years below standard, reading at grade level in a matter of months—but, of course, they may be exceptions. Only time and more data will tell. (See page 198.)

Whatever the true success rate, it comes about because the Spalding system capitalizes on a body of psychological principles that are dead right in contemporary theoretical terms. Mrs. Spalding obviously had no way of anticipating that. Her own theoretical guidelines came from the teachings of William McCall at Columbia Teachers College, Orton's views of how the brain works, and the linguistics of the period. These theories have all been superseded in their respective fields, but the Spalding system can be recast in current theoretical frameworks because it was really derived from an intensive study of how children learn. (The same can be said of Montessori.) Of course, other good reading teachers have emphasized some of the same principles. In my collection of early readers is one published in 1855. It starts out with a list of phonograms and includes a simple marking system. These ideas have been around for a long time, but it remained for Spalding to combine them and forge them into a system of stunning efficiency.

A few words now of a more practical nature.

The Spalding Network

The system is currently spreading through a field network, rather than an academic network. Most elementary education faculty, the ones who teach teachers how to teach reading, have consultation contracts or other connections with the publishers of basal programs. It has therefore proved almost impossible to train teachers in The Spalding Method before they leave college. It is after they begin teaching, discover that their pupils aren't learning to read, and discover also that *they are accountable* for their pupils' failure that teachers begin searching for a system that works. A growing number of Spalding courses are therefore appearing on summer school and in-service rosters.

As an example of the type of field network that exists, consider Maricopa County, Arizona, which encompasses the Phoenix area. A number of school districts formed a loose consortium for the purpose of pooling information and promoting the training of teachers. Over a period of about five years, well over 1,000 teachers were trained in The Spalding Method, many by Spalding herself. The reading averages for their classes on the Iowa Tests were in the upper ninetieth percentile—and it should be emphasized that many of these schools were Chapter 1 schools, with large bilingual populations. Whether you are an experienced teacher or an inexperienced one (or a parent), you should take a Spalding course. It makes the procedures crystal clear and provides many tips you may miss in the textbook.

As the need for Spalding teachers grew, the Spalding Education Foundation (now Spalding Education International) was formed to certify Spalding instructors and perpetuate the method. To find courses throughout the United States and Australia, contact Spalding Education International (see page 201).

Preface

By Mary E. North, Ph.D.

Remarkable advances have occurred in reading research since the last edition of *The Writing Road to Reading*. Fortunately, Mrs. Spalding lived long enough to know that current research findings have validated the basic principles underlying her method. To perpetuate the method beyond her lifetime, she established a nonprofit 501(c)(3) corporation in 1986 and specified standards for instructor certification.

For over forty years, Mrs. Spalding inspired teachers and parents with her love of literature and her desire to help all children learn to speak precisely, spell accurately, write proficiently, and read fluently with comprehension. She often said that her dream was to prepare *all* children to become "lifelong learners," including those who needed challenge and those who needed more help with basic skills. It is not surprising then that her life exemplified what she intended. Every time Romalda Spalding tutored a child, taught a class, or instructed a group of teachers, she learned something to make The Spalding Method a little better. Teachers fortunate enough to be instructed by her realized that much of which was only inferred in her book became explicit in Mrs. Spalding's classrooms.

To ensure that her insights and classroom techniques not be lost after her death, the Spalding Education International (SEI) Board of Directors designated an editorial advisory board, consisting of individuals who had been instructed by her and who revered her method. They have prepared, with great respect and care, the fifth edition of *The Writing Road to Reading*. Their purpose is not to alter the well-proven Spalding Method but to explain more fully and in clearer detail its fundamentals. This edition also explains in simple terms why Spalding works—its theoretical foundations. Because the method is now being taught in other countries, this is the first international edition. Those familiar with earlier versions will find that the text has been reorganized in accordance with Romalda Spalding's desire to make her method as easy to use as possible. What Mrs. Spalding did in the classroom as an intuitive and experienced master teacher is made explicit in this edition.

Book Organization and Features

The book is divided into two parts: "Lessons, Procedures, and Why This Method Works," which describes the content and methodology of the program, and "Instructional Materials," for use in lesson planning and instruction. The text consists of a foreword, a preface, an introduction, and six chapters. Dr. Sylvia Farnham-Diggory provides an overview of The Spalding Method in the Foreword. The Preface explains the reason for the fifth edition and acknowledges those who made it possible. The Introduction sets forth essential elements of The Spalding Method and general statements of Mrs. Spalding's philosophy. Chapters 1, 2, and 3 describe in detail the content of the spelling, writing, and reading lessons. Chapter 4 summarizes research-based instructional components and explains how they are taught in The Spalding Method. Chapter 5 outlines essential steps to effective lesson planning. Chapter 6 presents the SEI mission and services and evidence of the method's effectiveness.

Each chapter begins with an overview, a visual layout of major sections. The body of the chapter consists of two to five main sections and a number of subsections. Each chapter in the text concludes with a summary, including key points and a few comments. New features in the text are instructional procedures with examples of teacher interactions—sample spelling, writing, and reading lesson dialogues designed to help teachers and parents implement the lessons.

"Instructional Materials" includes the essentials from the previous edition: an updated list of recommended children's literature, the seventy phonograms, the language rules, and a revised Extended Ayres Word List. New features include a section on syllable division, the Extended Ayres Word List given alphabetically and by parts of speech, a recommended language arts scope and sequence, and a framework for planning integrated language arts lessons.

Acknowledgments

I am deeply indebted to the Spalding Education International Board of Directors for their encouragement and patience during the five-year development process and to the SEI Editorial Advisory Board: This task could not have been accomplished without their insight, dedication, and experience as classroom teachers, Spalding certified teacher instructors, and principals of Spalding schools. The editorial advisory board was guided by and grateful for the valuable suggestions and comments received from Spalding Certified Teachers and Teacher Instructors, and from many classroom teachers, parents, and other professionals in the field.

For indefatigable assistance, I thank Marcia Sielaff, SEI editor, whose twelve-year experience as an editorial writer for the *Phoenix Gazette* enabled us to make a committee document readable and succinct. A special note of thanks to Jane LaGrone for extensive research on high-frequency words and to Candace Diehl for creating the manuscript and cursive handwriting samples in the primary and intermediate notebooks. Teachers, parents, and children will benefit from her excellent examples of Spalding handwriting. I am also grateful to the Australian Certified Teacher Instructors for their help with British pronunciations of the Extended Ayres Words.

My special thanks to Dr. Sylvia Farnham-Diggory for her thoughtful analysis of The Spalding Method and to Dr. Sylvia Richardson for her insightful suggestions and comments on the theoretical and lesson planning chapters.

I am grateful for the patience and expert assistance of senior editor Toni Sciarra, design director Leah Carlson-Stanisic, senior production editor Lisa Healy, copy editor Annette Corkey, and many others at HarperCollins Publishers who assisted in the publication of this new edition.

Finally, my heartfelt thanks to Warren North, SEI president, for his analytical review of the entire manuscript and his dedication to keeping the fifth edition faithful to the intent, methodology, and vision of Mrs. Spalding.

Part One

LESSONS, PROCEDURES, AND WHY THIS METHOD WORKS

INTRODUCTION TO
THE SPALDING METHOD

By Romalda B. Spalding

ENGLISH has become an international means of communication. Scholars estimate that English is spoken by over 1 billion people. It is a required study in the schools of most countries, and its use is expanding rapidly. This is basically because English has the richest and largest vocabulary, simple inflections, and no genders, and is, except for its spelling, the easiest language to learn. The ability to convey and receive information through this rich medium takes on added importance in democratic nations, whose preservation depends on a literate people.

Civilization is not inherited; its advance depends upon the ability of each generation to fully communicate and teach its children the recorded wisdom of past ages. Teaching language to children is therefore the highest profession in every age.

All schoolchildren deserve the most effective teaching of the basic skills of writing and reading that can be devised. Without these skills, the development of the mind, mental self-discipline and self-education, and a real appreciation of our cultural heritage are not possible. Nothing in all nature compares with the potential learning capacity of a young child. Teachers in kindergarten and the primary grades have an immense responsibility to the future of civilization.

The best teaching method is therefore of vital importance, and the best method is one that directly teaches all elements of the language. The Spalding Method does just that from the beginning, in kindergarten or first grade. Children spell words by writing their sounds, and read aloud their own writing, thus the title of the book, *The Writing Road to Reading*. Their manuscript writing of letters is almost identical with what they see on the printed page. Inattention, even from the first day, is seldom a problem, because the whole class participates in speaking and writing. In both spelling and reading, children use their knowledge of phonics and their minds instead of rote memorization.

The Writing Road to Reading presents in full working detail this method for rapidly teaching children, or adults, accurate speech, writing, spelling, and reading. I developed and used it exclusively over forty years of teaching in all elementary grades, in tutoring hundreds of individuals, and in presenting my course to thousands of teachers. Experience shows that any child qualified to enter school at the age of five or six is able, willing, and eager to write and read if taught by this logical approach to language.

The Spalding Method is direct and so organized that children use only paper and pencil *and* their *minds*. The direct use of their minds to work and learn, and to produce on paper, is far more interesting and instructive to all children than dittos and workbooks. Adults tend to greatly underestimate the mental abilities of children.

Essential Elements

There are four essential elements in The Spalding Method: spelling, writing, reading, and the educational philosophy. The philosophy is based on principles that provide consistency in teacher decision making, lesson planning, and teaching. The classroom teacher needs to be given two to three hours each day for teaching spelling, writing, and reading. These may be divided into separate thirty-minute periods. In each lesson, the interest and attention of all the class are captured because students participate with the teacher at all times.

The Spelling Lesson

English is a phonetic language. Phonics instruction, analysis of sounds, and composition of words properly belong in the spelling lesson. The *core* of the method is teaching the *saying* with the *writing* of the sounds used in spoken English. The relationship of each sound to the written symbol (phonogram) that represents it is thus made clear. Precise techniques for good, easy handwriting and for accurate pronunciation are taught from the beginning. Soon the child learns to combine these sounds into familiar words to pronounce a written or spoken word. Learning the spelling of words by writing them connects at once the spoken sounds to the written symbols. Students learn phonograms and words by writing them directly from hearing and saying them aloud (not by copying them). High-frequency words are taught so children can quickly become independent readers. These are only a small number of the words students will need to know and use, but they do include practically every pattern of English spelling and speaking.

The important rules of spelling are taught when they are needed for writing the words being studied. The logic of the language is clearly revealed. It is a logic so basic that the teacher can instruct the entire class as one in written spelling.

Since spelling is more difficult than reading, teaching it must be as scientific as possible if those many students of all ages who find our written language difficult are to learn. Through my method, spelling is taught from the spoken word to the written form.

The Writing Lesson

Writing instruction begins in kindergarten and first grade by teaching children to use spelling words in oral sentences. Learning to construct good oral sentences prepares children for writing and reinforces the meaning of unfamiliar spelling words. After a sufficient number of high-frequency words are written in the spelling notebook, children use them to compose and write two or three sentences daily. They begin reading from their original sentences. Composing original sentences is the skill that most fully requires the mind to apply all previously learned skills. Soon students are taught to use the writing process to compose informative and narrative paragraphs and compositions.

The Reading Lesson

Literary appreciation and comprehension are taught from the first day of class as children listen and respond to stories read by the teacher. Children enjoy the stories and expand their understanding of people and the world. When sufficient high-frequency words have been studied in the written spelling lesson (about two months of instruction), beginning classes are ready to start reading from books. A Spalding class is able to begin reading *well-written* books because they have been taught phonics and understand how words and sentences are constructed. They are not dependent on controlled vocabulary readers. By listening to and then reading literature, children develop a love of reading and a taste for good writing from the beginning. A suggested list of books for different age groups is given in "Instructional Materials" (see pages 206–211).

Educational Philosophy

The philosophy is based on principles of learning and instruction applied throughout The Spalding Method. Motivation to learn and retention of content are enhanced if consideration is given to these principles during lesson planning and delivery of instruction. A brief overview of the philosophy will serve as a guide to the method and to my more general views about education.

Child Centered

The physical and mental well-being of students must always be considered. Before beginning any instruction, attention is given to children's posture so they sit, write, and learn comfortably, permitting them to concentrate fully on the task at hand. Providing all students with the opportunity to succeed every day, to be respected and appreciated, ensures that their emotional needs are being met. Children need and desire strong guidance, leadership, and reasoned discipline from their teachers.

High Expectations

Students of all ability levels should be challenged to produce quality work that fully develops their intellect. When teachers have high expectations, children are more likely to set high standards for their own work.

Purpose and Meaning

Activities should always be relevant to advancing children's learning. Attention is enhanced when children understand the purpose for each task and how they will be able to use their new skills.

Higher-Level Thinking

The formal education of children should be focused on developing the ability to reason, to think for themselves, and on inculcating the desire to learn. Helping students to reason, analyze, and apply their skills and knowledge develops habits of mind that serve them well throughout their education and their lives.

Direct, Sequential Instruction

Lesson content is delivered most effectively when teaching is explicit and follows a logical order. I learned from Dr. Orton to divide each task into its component parts, build them sequentially, and *talk about* each part. This principle has guided every step of my method. Direct instruction provides explicit teaching of lesson content. Sequential instruction is structured to proceed from the simple to the complex.

Multisensory Instruction

Multisensory instruction reduces the amount of practice required for mastery. Students see, hear, say, and write using all channels to the brain, the stronger channels reinforcing the weaker. Using all four sensory channels helps to prevent or overcome the common tendency to reverse or confuse letters. The success of The Spalding Method, even with children with severe language problems, is in large part due to the multisensory nature of the method.

Active Participation

Student participation is an essential component of effective instruction. The mental work involved in applying knowledge of reading, writing, and spelling requires constant use of mind, voice, and hands on the part of all students throughout the lesson.

Diagnostic Teaching

Careful observation of student progress, planning appropriate instruction, and adjusting instruction to meet student needs maximize learning. The teacher's immediate correction of mistakes prevents errors from becoming fixed in a child's mind.

Integrated Instruction

The relationship between speaking, writing, and reading is constantly taught. Learning is enhanced when students apply language arts skills in other subjects.

The Teacher's Role

This book is written for the professional teacher who is pleased to study in order to promote and enjoy much better writing and reading progress by all students. When children enter school, regardless of home training or lack of it, they expect the teacher to teach them and to command their attention. They already speak a few thousand words, and they find it exciting to learn to write the letters that represent on paper the sounds they use in speaking. When they are taught to write down the sounds they speak, the whole world of letters becomes understandable and logical to them and learning to read and write becomes a pleasure. That pleasure is their reward for the effort they put forth; they need no other. Similarly, teachers experience great satisfaction when their competent teaching leads to students' success.

Dr. Orton said that the art of teaching is knowing what students need and being able to provide it. Among other skills, teachers must know when to adjust instruction, dropping interim steps as they become unnecessary. Teachers also must be aware that extra practice time is essential for some students.

The Spalding Method progresses at a much faster pace than do most programs. It is important that teachers not slow down the progress of their classes or that of the more able students in the class. It is a mistake to place any brake upon the advance of any student in the field of reading.

At its best, teaching is a creative activity, and creative people are open to constructive criticism, always striving to perfect their skills. Dr. Orton once told me to take my feelings off my shoulders and put them in my pocket so I could improve my teaching. Teachers must be able to look at the truth about their abilities and efforts and take upon themselves the responsibility to learn. Those who continue to grow professionally, who put forth the effort to expand their knowledge and to refine their technique, are able to help children learn and grow.

At all times, the teacher should be a model of precision, appropriate expression, and dignity. Oral and written communication is concise, descriptive, and coherent. When teachers consistently model these characteristics, students progress more rapidly.

It is important to know the method well before beginning instruction. The teacher must be familiar with this book, be able to follow its detailed teaching directions, and know where to find topics. The book is written without technical terms and is therefore valuable to parents, tutors, and clinicians for teaching any individual in need of improving reading and writing skills. It provides accurate and practical ways to teach by The Spalding Method.

The Reading Debate

Many schools now attempt to teach reading by the "eclectic" approach; that is, by a combination of methods, on the theory that some children learn best by one method and some by another. There are, in fact, but two methods, phonic analysis and the "look-say," whole-word, or whole-language, method. The latter has caused such a high percentage of reading failures among intelligent children that the Council for Basic Education has aptly called this a "hodge-podge of postponement and readiness, questionable interpretations of Gestalt psychology, word guessing and unorganized phonics." In actual practice, this comes down to the whole-word method with some phonics sporadically added over time. The phonics children may be taught is likely to be incomplete at best, since very few teachers have been taught the importance of teaching it directly. Even if a teacher does have the necessary training and the time to teach both methods to the class, children are likely to find the mixture confusing because they are based on opposing premises. (The whole-word method encourages children to guess, while the phonics method emphasizes attention to letters and the sounds they represent.)

Today numerous phonics approaches are presented to teachers, and they require a brief comment. Most are expensive. Many aim to take over part of the teacher's work, although at the expense of the child's progress. Most of the other phonics methods teach the phonograms from printed words, and the words, therefore, are taught in categories that illustrate the particular phonogram being learned, but this is not the way words occur in literate English sentences. Most overlook the prime importance of *saying* and *writing* the phonograms *before* combining them into written and spoken words and *before* starting to read books. The failings of most phonic methods may be summarized in that they neglect spelling and do not teach the saying and writing of the forty-five basic sounds of the language *before* children try to read.

Teaching instructions provided in *The Writing Road to Reading* are necessarily written for classes of beginners, whether in kindergarten or in first grade. Older students beginning with this method, regardless of their other training in lower grades, need this same teaching and practice as do children just entering school; but they are pretested to determine where to begin instruction, and they proceed at a faster pace.

Acknowledgments

I am deeply indebted to the late Dr. Samuel T. Orton, eminent neurologist and brain specialist, for his years of research and teaching in the field of spoken and written English. It was my privilege while a Bronxville, New York, public school teacher to successfully teach, under the meticulous supervision of Dr. Orton, an intelligent boy who had a severe writing disability. This thorough training enabled me then to tutor other similar, though older, children with his guidance, and soon to teach still others by the same techniques without his supervision. He invited me to attend a course that he gave to the class of pediatricians then graduating from the Columbia College of Medicine. His theory of the functioning of the brain in speaking, writing, and reading and his practical means to prevent or overcome confusions were clear, logical, and highly effective in practice. The value of Dr. Orton's pioneer work in this field cannot be overestimated.

My contribution has been chiefly to develop Dr. Orton's training into a method for classroom teaching. In 1968, the Massachusetts state director of special education stated that awareness of the great need of many able children for such help was the fruit of Dr. Orton's pioneer work.

Editor's Note

Thirty years later, Drs. Jack Fletcher and Reid Lyon found the need was even greater:

> The magnitude of the reading problem is significant. From NICHD (National Institute of Child Health and Human Development) and non-NICHD research, we know that at least 10 million school-age children in the United States are poor readers. . . . The number of children who are identified as disabled or who do not meet basic levels of proficiency on reading assessments such as the National Assessment of Reading Proficiency (more than 40 percent in 1994) should be cause for alarm. (Fletcher and Lyon, 1998, 52–53)

Chapter 1

THE SPELLING LESSON
CHAPTER OVERVIEW

Preparation for Reading and Writing

HISTORICALLY, every phonetic language has developed from speech, to letters that represent speech sounds, and then to words and sentences. A successful reading method follows this pattern. Preschool children love to listen to rhymes and participate in word play. Four-year-olds can learn to say the sounds correctly, and five-year-olds can learn to say and write the sounds. This section provides some suggestions for parents who wish to start literacy instruction before formal schooling.

Language Development
Reading to children and discussing with them what is read expands their oral vocabulary, background knowledge, and communication skills. Introducing them to the alphabet by using the alphabet song, blocks, or magnetic letters is an appropriate preparation activity.

Phonemic Awareness
Beginners, and older students who are having difficulty, need to understand that spoken words and syllables consist of sequences of speech sounds (phonemes). This understanding is essential for learning to read an alphabetic language because alphabet letters and letter combinations represent basic speech sounds. Young children love to play with words. Through informal activities such as listening and responding to rhymes, children develop awareness that words consist of individual sounds. Additionally, the teacher or parent can say a word like *me*, hold up two fingers and say /m/ /ē/ while pointing to each finger, and have students say the sounds. (Use the high-frequency words that children will later write in their spelling/vocabulary notebook.) Teachers need to make sure each child hears the individual sounds in each word.

Phonograms

A phonogram is a single letter, or a fixed combination of two, three, or four letters, that is the symbol for one sound in a given word. English has seventy common phonograms (twenty-six letters and forty-four fixed combinations of two, three, and four letters) that represent the forty-five basic sounds used in speaking. The fixed combinations absorb most of the silent letters (e.g., *igh* says /ī/).

Forty-seven phonograms have only one sound, making them easy to learn. Eleven phonograms have two sounds, ten have three sounds, one has four sounds, and one has six sounds. Phonograms are identified by their sound or sounds, whenever practical, and *not* by their letter names.

The seventy phonograms, which were carefully worked out many years ago, are still the best for teaching English. They have stood the test of more than four decades of use because they simplify English spelling by avoiding the teaching of nearly all silent letters, except the final *e*'s. The latter are easily taught in this method by showing reasons for most of them. The preschool teacher or parent uses cards that show the phonograms. The cards have words printed on the back that are only for the teacher's information. Do not teach the sounds by having children learn these words. Before teaching the sounds, it is advisable for teachers to check and correct their pronunciation of the phonograms. For example, the sound of /l/ is not *el*, the sound /k/ is not *kuh*, and the sound /b/ is not *buh*. We say *rob*, not *robuh*. Preschoolers learn only the sounds and when in kindergarten, will learn how to write them. Demonstrate to children that the words they say are made up of separate sounds by using Ayres words (see page 252). Segment the phonogram sounds in the words as a check on pronunciation.

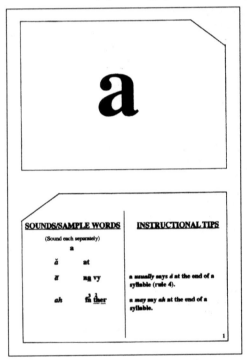

Young children learn to recognize and say the sounds of the single-letter phonograms in any order. The teacher shows the printed cards, says the sounds precisely, and then listens while students say all the sounds for each phonogram.

Prewriting

Many young children want to write. Appropriate prewriting activities include providing multiple opportunities to develop fine-motor control (stringing beads, cutting, gluing, coloring); teaching the positions on an analog clock (see page 17); and using a sand tray, carpet, velvet, or board to teach drawing circles starting at 2 on the clock. Use a star or other symbol at the top of the tray or material to indicate the "up" position.

Children also need to learn the concept of halfway (midpoint), which is essential for understanding the size relationship between tall and short letters. Demonstrate this concept by putting one block on top of another and pointing to the *midpoint* between the blocks. Have children practice by pointing to the midpoint between blocks. Demonstrate rolling clay to form a tall line, marking the midpoint, and then dividing it into two equal parts. Have children follow the same procedure. Next, demonstrate rolling clay to represent a tall and a short line. Finally, demonstrate this concept using vertical lines drawn on the board. Have children practice drawing tall and short lines on the board and at their desks.

The correct method of holding a pencil is vitally important to prevent fatigue and to develop correct letter formation. When children have developed correct directionality and some fine-motor control, teach them the pencil grip (see pages 13–15). On paper or individual chalk boards, have them form large circles beginning at 2 on the clock and going up and around (counterclockwise). When children are ready to practice spelling the phonograms by writing them on lined paper, follow the procedures described in the next section.

Teaching Handwriting with Phonograms

Teaching handwriting and written spelling should precede reading from books. This is fundamental. The title of this book, *The Writing Road to Reading,* means exactly that: Writing and the phonograms create a wide-open road to knowing and using the written language. *All* children want to do well in speech, writing (spelling), and reading. These skills are basic to our culture, and writing is the one that does most to unite and reinforce the others. Getting a child to understand and follow the mechanics of each of these processes is vital.

Five-year-old children learn with no self-consciousness. They do not know they can fail. Teachers prepare kindergartners for learning by using the activities previously described. In this way, children easily learn to read the phonograms and are then ready to write the phonograms and spell words in their notebooks as described in this chapter. For appropriate lesson planning, see chapter 5, page 170, and the language arts scope and sequence in "Instructional Materials" (beginning on page 442).

From the beginning, it is important to teach the techniques of easy, legible, and neat handwriting, using the phonograms for daily writing practice. The kinesthetic sense combines with hearing and then with seeing and reading the phonogram the child has just written. This is a basic principle that is used for teaching spelling through these four combined channels to the mind—hearing, saying, writing, and seeing. No other way of teaching the phonograms and written spelling of words is so effective.

For over fifty years, Mrs. Spalding worked with thousands of individual children who found handwriting and spelling difficult. Her lessons on handwriting, along with those on learning the phonograms, prevented many beginners from developing reading and language problems. She also rescued many older children from the frustrating failures to which these problems condemned them.

In The Spalding Method, children learn that the mind directs the hand to write accurately. The only parts of the body actively engaged are the *mind;* the *mouth,* which quietly says (aloud at first) the detailed steps necessary to write each letter; the *hand* holding the pencil to write; and the other *hand,* which holds and moves the paper. Small errors prevent children from learning to write easily, legibly, and neatly. Children require careful and *continued* teaching of all the handwriting techniques. From the beginning, they need to be taught to follow directions, articulate the purpose of the task, and describe the steps involved. Success in these writing skills gives children great pride and interest in learning each day's lesson. Mastery of each skill builds self-confidence.

First, check that chairs and desks or tables are the right height to ensure children's comfort. Children's feet should touch the floor and their arms should rest comfortably on the desks. Teach the following techniques to primary children, and, indeed, to higher grades, to prevent tensions that otherwise build. If teachers will learn and teach these techniques, all students will make rapid progress, because their focus can be on learning rather than being distracted by physical discomfort.

Position and Techniques for Both Left- and Right-Handed Children

- Clear the desk of books and materials not needed.
- Sit with *hips against the back* of the chair, *feet flat* on the floor, and *back straight,* with *head high.* The straight spinal column supports the head.
- Keep two inches between the body and the desk. Lean forward just enough to see the paper clearly, but *keep the head high.* Let the chair carry the weight of the body. Do not let the head fall forward, because its heavy weight would then be carried by the neck and back muscles.
- Place both *forearms on the desk* with the *elbows just off the edge* and *comfortably close* to the body.
- Use one hand for holding the pencil and writing. The *wrist* should be *straight,* and the whole hand and arm should be *below the base line* on which you write. (Never use the writing hand to hold the paper.)
- Place the hand that does not hold the pencil across the top edge of the paper to hold it steady or to move it back and forth and up and down as needed.
- Keep the *side edge* of the *paper* and the *arm* of the hand that holds the pencil *parallel* like the two rails of a railroad track.

The *left-handed* child needs special attention to be sure the paper is *parallel* to the *writing (left) arm.* A strip of tape placed near the top of the desk will show the correct slant for the top edge of the paper. This keeps the paper from being turned like that of right-handed students. Teach them from the start that writing English requires that the hand move *in the direction in which we write.* This training can save children from developing writing problems that are hard to correct. Have left-handed students sit on the side of the room to the teacher's right so they can easily face the teacher as they look up from their writing.

Correct writing position
for left-handed child.

A *six-sided,* common *wood pencil* is recommended for every age because it can be controlled more easily than a round one. The pencil weighs so little that minimal pressure from the hand is required to hold and move it. Have each child hold a pencil across the palm of his or her hand to demonstrate that it weighs next to nothing. Train children to consciously write with no real pressure in the arm or fingers. The arm and fingers should feel as light and soft as the leg and paw of a friendly kitten. Hold a child's elbow in one of your hands and the child's hand in the other to demonstrate that no weight is felt in the arm and hand.

Pencil Grip

- The *middle* finger and *thumb* form a vise for holding the pencil. The index, or *pointing,* finger rests between the middle finger and the thumb.

Correct writing position
for right-handed child.

- The *pointing* finger curves, and the end of the nail sits on the pencil where the paint ends, about an inch from the point. All *knuckles,* including the thumb, should be *bent* and the fingers and thumb *rounded* to the same degree (liken this to the way a cat's claws are rounded). Let a little light show through under the big knuckle of the little finger so that the writing hand can move easily.
- The *elbow* (hinge) on the writing arm should be *stationary.*
- Write with the *point* of the pencil. The pencil should rest forward of the main knuckle. The other hand moves the paper enough so that the pencil point remains in a small area just forward of the center of the body.

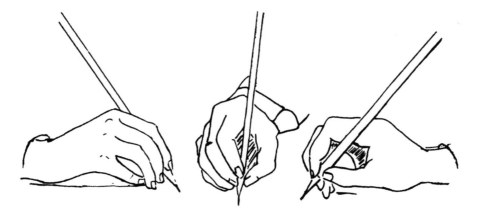

These sketches show how the pencil is held in the right hand.

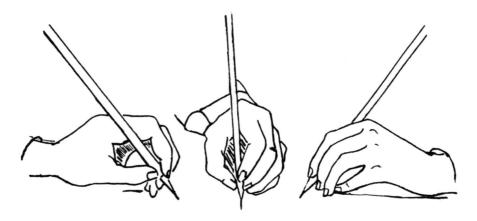

The pencil is held this way in the left hand.

Paper for Writing

For beginners through second grade, use paper with ⅝-inch (1.6 cm) spacing between lines. Wider spacing forces children to draw letters instead of writing. Paper with a dotted midline is not used because it is hard for children to touch the base line *and* the midline. Instead, teach the concept of halfway between lines and allow students time to visualize placement (see pages 10–11). For third grade and above, use paper with standard ⅜-inch (1.0 cm) spacing.

Position at the Board

Each child should stand comfortably close to the board and write no higher than the top of his or her head. It is helpful to use a wax pencil or a marker (for a dry-erase board) to draw lines about three inches (7.5 cm) apart. The top line should be no higher than the tallest child.

Chalk Grip

When using a chalkboard, hold the chalk with four fingers along its length. The thumb is on the opposite side. Write with the side of the point and not the point itself to eliminate squeaking and slipping.

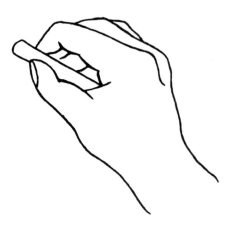

Erasing

When erasing, start where the writing began. Begin from the top and go down, moving up and down across the board in the direction we read and write.

Teacher Instruction at the Board or at a Desk

When pointing to anything on the board, stand to the left of what is to be read and place your index finger before the center of the first letter. Do this as well when pointing to words on paper or in a book. Slide your finger over what is read so that your index finger is always at the place where the reading is taking place. This is very helpful for those children who tend to confuse the proper direction of letters.

Overview for Teaching the Sounds and Formation of Letters

The function of letters and letter combinations (phonograms) in an alphabetic language is to represent spoken sounds. Manuscript writing is used at first, no matter the age of the child, because it makes the needed visible link between handwriting and all printed matter. Manuscript is also needed for lettering maps, diagrams, and drawings.

Many teachers and parents fail to realize the importance of teaching the correct formation of letters from the very start of teaching the written language. Teachers must demonstrate and explain precisely how each letter, number, and punctuation mark should be formed and placed. The strange, awkward ways in which nearly all children contrive to form some of their letters show how much they need all these techniques of handwriting. In writing, the brain directs the hand. This cannot be done correctly unless there is a thorough knowledge of how each letter and number is made. Unless children write correctly, they do not see the correct symbols for the sounds, and motor patterns once formed are difficult to correct. Children need much *patient* supervision at this beginning stage.

When spelling words, use phonogram sounds, not letter names, because the names of only five letters (the vowels *a, e, i, o,* and *u*) are sounds, and their names are not their most common sounds. Introduce handwriting by showing the class each of the printed phonogram cards (see Resources) in the order found on pages 213–221, saying the sound or sounds of each phonogram and having the whole class repeat them. The letters *a, g,* and *y* may have quite different forms in print from those in manuscript. Point out the differences between the print on these cards and the more simple manuscript letters. This familiarizes the class with both the printed form and the written manuscript form of these letters, thus eliminating confusion when they begin to read from books.

Teach all of the writing techniques in this chapter to beginning students of any age to help them acquire the correct motor patterns. Saying the sounds and writing the phonograms are basic means of preventing or overcoming the confusions and reversals in spelling and in reading from which so many children needlessly suffer.

When you talk to children about the act of writing, do *not* use the words *left* or *right.* Instead, consistently say from the start "the direction in which we write." Many children, both left-and right-handed, learn to make horizontal lines correctly, but before lifting the pencil, they retrace them backward. Make certain that children do not do this, for it reverses the habit that helps them learn to write and read accurately.

Teach first-grade children no fewer than four phonograms in the first lesson. In each subsequent daily lesson, review all previously introduced phonograms (see pages 39–42) and teach additional phonograms. Three weeks may be needed for teaching the sounds and the writing of the first forty-five phonograms up to and including *ea,* card 45 (see page 218). Students who begin this method in any grade higher than the first (regardless of their prior instruction) need to be taught using these techniques, although at a faster pace appropriate for their age. As many as fifty-four phonograms can be taught to older children in a few days, as fast as they can learn them.

Reference Points

Manuscript letters are made of a circle, or parts of it, and straight lines. Explain to children that the *clock face* is used as a reference point for forming the following features: a circle, all letters that begin at two on the clock, and parts of letters.

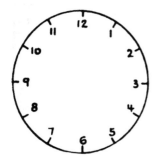

The Clock Face

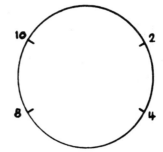

These are the four points used most often.

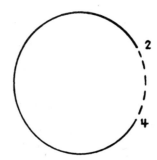

This shows how the clock is used to write *c* (from 2 to 4).

Introduce, or review, the term *midpoint* as the reference point for *halfway* (see pages 10–11). Using ⅝-inch (1.6 cm) lined paper, explain the terms *top line* and *base line*. Have children identify the top line and the base line and point to the midpoint. This practice prepares children for learning feature and letter formation.

General Handwriting Rules

Explain that general rules govern the formation of manuscript letters:

- All letters sit on a base line.
- For letters that begin at 2 on the clock, rounding conforms to the curve of the circle. Every round letter should fit on the same-sized clock.
- Lines begin at the top and are straight and parallel. All letters that go below the base line go the same distance below the base line as above it.
- Letters or parts of letters are of two sizes. They are either tall or short. Tall letters or tall parts approach but do not touch the line above. Short letters or short parts are half as high as tall letters. They begin at the *midpoint* between the height of a tall letter and the base line.
- Dots and crossbars are tiny, formed just above the *midpoint;* crossbars are formed in the direction in which we write.

Six Features Used to Form Twenty-six Alphabet Letters

Using the board, demonstrate and explain the formation of the following six features, which are used to form all alphabet letters:

1. A circle that begins just below the midpoint at 2 and goes up and around the clock to 2
2. A short line that begins at the midpoint and sits on the base line
3. A tall line that begins just below the line above and sits on the base line
4. A straight line that begins at the midpoint and extends the same distance below the base line
5. A line that begins at the midpoint and slants to the base line in the direction we write
6. A short horizontal line in the direction we write

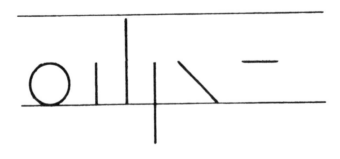

Have children practice identifying 2 on the clock and the hand and arm movement involved in making a circle beginning at 2 on the clock (see page 17). (A poster with the clock face and the four points may be helpful initially.) Then, have them practice forming the six features using ⅝-inch (1.6 cm) lined paper. Monitor while children practice making circles that begin just below the midpoint, at 2 on the clock; short lines that begin at the midpoint; and tall lines that begin just below the line above.

Manuscript Letters That Begin at 2 on the Clock

Clock letters start *just far enough* away from the previous letter to make a circle. They start at 2 and *go up and around* the clock. Show how the clock face is used as a reference to form the clock letters. See below.

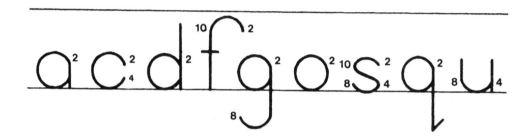

Show a phonogram card. Say each sound precisely (not run together) in a staccato manner. Have children repeat the sound precisely. Model writing each phonogram on the board and precisely explain how it is formed. Guide as children repeat the sound(s) and then the directions for writing each phonogram. To ensure precise pronunciation and correct letter formation from the beginning, monitor as children say the sounds softly and write the phonograms, helping students as needed.

Procedures for Introducing Phonograms 1–8 with Precise Dialogue

Show card 1 and say the three sounds: /ă/ /ā/ /ah/. Class repeats the sounds.

"I will show you how each letter is written. This is a short letter. Short letters fill the space between the *midpoint* and the base line. Form the letter without lifting the pencil. Start far enough in from the edge of your paper to make a clock face. *Start at 2; go up and around the clock, touching the base line and stopping at 2. Pull a straight line down to the base line.*"

Guide as children say the sounds and repeat the directions (italicized) softly as they write the letter on their papers.

continued

Show card 2 and say the two sounds: /k/ /s/. Class repeats the sounds.

"This is a short letter. It starts just far enough from *a* to make the clock face. *Start at 2; go up and around the clock, touching the base line and stopping at 4.*"

Guide as children say the sounds and repeat the directions (italicized) softly as they write the letter on their papers.

Show card 3 and say the sound: /d/. Class repeats the sound.

"This is a short letter with a tall part. Form the letter without lifting the pencil." Put your finger before the round part to show that the round part comes first. Draw attention to the feel of the upturned tongue where it touches the upper ridge behind the teeth as the letter *d* is sounded. Say, "*Start at 2; go up and around the clock, touching the base line and closing the circle at 2. Continue straight up toward the line above but do not touch it. Retrace the straight line down to the base line.*"

Guide as children say the sound and repeat the directions (italicized) softly as they write the letter on their papers. Make sure that the tall part is twice the height of the short part.

Show card 4 and say the sound: /f/. Class repeats the sound. (Demonstrate on a clock where this letter begins and that it conforms to the width of a clock. Emphasize that the crossbar is formed in the direction in which we write.)

"This is a tall letter. *Start at 2 just below the line above. Without touching the top line, go up and around to 10, and pull a straight line down to the base line. Make a tiny crossbar just above the midpoint and lift the pencil.*"

Guide as children say the sound and repeat the directions (italicized) softly as they write the letter on their papers. Monitor students to ensure that they begin at 2. Make sure each child writes the letter *f* *before* making the crossbar in the direction we write. Check that children do not retrace the crossbar backward.

Show card 5 and say the two sounds: /g/ /j/. Class repeats the sounds.

"This is a short letter. *Start at 2; go up and around the clock, touching the base line and stopping at 2. Pull a straight line down the same distance below the base line and round from 4 to 8.*"

Guide as children say the sounds and repeat the directions (italicized) softly as they write the letter on their papers. Make sure the width below the line matches the round part above and that a short letter could sit on the base line beneath *g* without touching *g*.

Show card 6 and say the three sounds: /ŏ/ /ō/ /ōō/. Class repeats the sounds.

"This is a short letter. *Start at 2; go up and around the clock, touching the base line and stopping at 2.*"

Guide as children say the sounds and repeat the directions (italicized) softly as they write the letter on their papers.

Show card 7 and say the two sounds: /s/ /z/. Class repeats the sounds.

"This is a short letter. *Start at 2; go up and around to 10; slide across to 4* (directly below 2). *Curve down, touching the base line and curving up to 8* (directly below 10)."

Guide as children say the sounds and repeat the directions (italicized) softly as they write the letter on their papers. Make sure each child begins at 2 and goes up, then finishes at 8 on the clock.

Show card 8 and say the sound: /kw/. Class repeats the sound.

"It takes two letters to say /kw/. Both are short letters. Each is formed without lifting the pencil. The tiny flag is formed in the direction in which we write. The second letter sits close. *Start the first one at 2, go up and around the clock, touching the base line and stopping at 2. Pull a straight line down the same distance below the base line, and make a tiny flag. Start at the midpoint with a short down line to 8, round from 8 to 4 touching the base line, continue up to the midpoint, and retrace the straight line down to the base line.*"

Guide as children say the sound and repeat the directions (italicized) softly as they write the letter on their papers.

After initial introduction, have children practice writing the phonograms across the page to develop ease of formation and correct spacing between the clock letters.

Their papers should look like this. Note that each phonogram is written once.

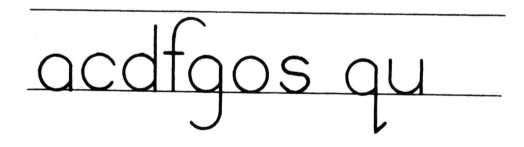

Manuscript Letters That Begin with Lines

Teach line letters as soon as children are adept at starting clock letters far enough from the preceding letter to make the circle and are able to begin each letter at 2 and *go up and around* the clock.

Model *forming* line letters close to the preceding letter. Do not lift the pencil off the paper to complete any of the lowercase letters except in making the second part of *k*, crossbars, and dots. Show how the numbers on the clock face are used to write line letters with clock parts. See illustration:

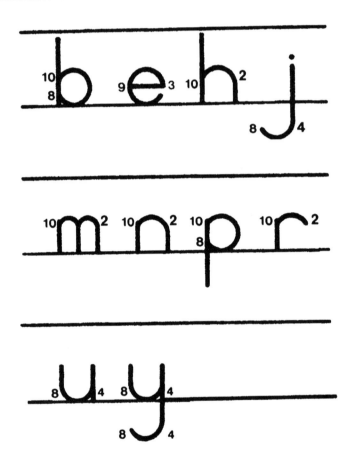

Procedures for Introducing Phonograms 9–26 with Precise Dialogue

Show card 9 and say the sound: /b/. Class repeats the sound. "This is a tall letter with a short part. The lips form a line when saying /b/. This helps you remember to start with a line when writing this phonogram. Form the letter without lifting the pencil. *Start at the top just below the line above; pull the pencil down to the base line. Retrace to 10; curve around the clock to 2, touching the base line and curving up to 8.*" Have all children feel the line their lips make when they say /b/. (The kinesthetic feel of the two letters *b* and *d* can keep children from reversing them. Do not teach them together, however.)

Guide as children say the sound and repeat the directions (italicized) softly as they write the letter on their papers.

Show card 10 and say the two sounds: /ĕ/ /ē/. Class repeats the sounds. (Put 9 and 3 on a clock face to show letter formation.)

"This letter is short. Form it without lifting the pencil. *Start midway between the height of a short letter and the base line. Make a straight line from 9 to 3 on a clock. Form a corner by continuing up and around the clock, touching the base line and stopping at 4.*"

Guide as children say the sounds and repeat the directions (italicized) softly as they write the letter on their papers. See the model line on page 22. Note that *e* is the *only* letter for which a *line* is made in reference to the clock face.

Show card 11 and say the sound: /h/. Class repeats the sound.

"This is a tall letter with a short part. Form it without lifting the pencil. *Start at the top just below the line above; pull a straight line down to the base line. Retrace to 10, round from 10 to 2, and pull a straight line to the base line.*"

Guide as children say the sound and repeat the directions (italicized) softly as they write the letter on their papers.

Show card 12 and say the two sounds: /ĭ/ /ī/. Class repeats the sounds.

"This is a short letter. *Start at the midpoint and pull a straight line to the base line. Make a small dot by pressing the pencil just above the letter and lifting it.*"

Guide as children say the sounds, and repeat the directions (italicized) softly as they write the letter on their papers.

continued

Show card 13 and say the sound: /j/. Class repeats the sound.

"This is a short letter that goes below the base line. *Start at the midpoint, pull a straight line down the same distance below the base line, and round from 4 to 8. Make a small dot by pressing the pencil just above the letter and lifting it.*"

Guide as children say the sound and repeat the directions (italicized) softly as they write the letter on their papers.

Show card 14 and say the sound /k/. Class repeats the sound.

"This is a tall letter with a short part. *Start at the top and pull a straight line to the base line. Start the short part at the midpoint, slant down and in to the tall line, and then slant down and out to the base line.*"

Guide as children say the sound and repeat the directions (italicized) softly as they write the letter on their papers. Make sure the second part starts at the midpoint slants down and in to the tall line, then slants down and out to the base line.

Show card 15 and say the sound: /l/. Class repeats the sound.

"This is a tall letter. *Start at the top and pull a straight line to the base line.*"

Guide as children say the sound, and repeat the directions (italicized) softly as they write the letter on their papers.

Show card 16 and say the sound: /m/. Class repeats the sound.

"This is a short letter. *Start at the midpoint and pull a straight line down to the base line, retrace to 10, round from 10 to 2 and pull a straight line to the base line. Retrace to 10, round from 10 to 2, and pull a straight line to the base line.*"

Guide as children say the sound and repeat the directions (italicized) softly as they write the letter on their papers.

Show card 17 and say the sound: /n/. Class repeats the sound.

"This is a short letter. *Start at the midpoint and pull a straight line down to the base line, retrace to 10, round from 10 to 2, and pull a straight line to the base line.*"

Guide as children say the sound and repeat the directions (italicized) softly as they write the letter on their papers.

Show card 18 and say the sound: /p/. Class repeats the sound.

"This is a short letter that goes below the base line. *Start at the midpoint, pull a straight line down the same distance below the base line, retrace to 10 and curve around the clock, touching the base line and curving up to 8.*"

Guide as children say the sound, and repeat the directions (italicized) softly as they write the letter on their papers.

Show card 19 and say the sound: /r/. Class repeats the sound.

"This is a short letter." Demonstrate that it conforms to the width of a clock face. "*Start at the midpoint, pull a straight line to the base line, retrace to 10, and round from 10 to 2.*"

Guide as children say the sound and repeat the directions (italicized) softly as they write the letter on their papers. Make sure that each child rounds the curved part over to 2 on the clock.

Show card 20 and say the sound: /t/. Class repeats the sound.

"This is a tall letter. Form the crossbar in the direction we write. *Start at the top, and pull a straight line to the base line. Draw a tiny crossbar just above the midpoint and lift the pencil.*"

Guide as children say the sound and repeat the directions (italicized) softly as they write the letter on their papers. Make sure each child writes the letter *t before* making the tiny crossbar in the direction we write. Check that children do not retrace the crossbar backward.

Show card 21 and say the three sounds: /ŭ/ /ū/ /o͝o/. Class repeats the sounds.

"This is a short letter. *Start at the midpoint with a short down line to 8, round from 8 to 4 touching the base line, continue up with a straight line to the midpoint, and retrace a straight line down to the base line.*"

Guide as children say the sounds and repeat the directions (italicized) softly as they write the letter on their papers.

Show card 22 and say the sound: /v/. Class repeats the sound.

"This is a short letter. Write it without lifting the pencil and slant lines in the direction in which we write. *Start at the midpoint, slant a straight line down to the base line in the direction in which we write. Slant a straight line up to the midpoint.*"

Guide as children say the sound and repeat the directions (italicized) softly as they write the letter on their papers.

continued

Show card 23 and say the sound: /w/. Class repeats the sound.

"This is a short letter. Write it without lifting the pencil and slant lines in the direction in which we write. *Start at the midpoint and slant a straight line down to the base line. Slant a straight line up to the midpoint, slant a straight line down to the base line, then slant a straight line up to the midpoint.*"

Guide as children say the sound and repeat the directions (italicized) softly as they write the letter on their papers.

Show card 24 and say the sound: /ks/. Class repeats the sound.

"This is a short letter. Slant the first line in the direction in which we write. *Start at the midpoint and slant a straight line down to the base line. Lift the pencil and starting at the midpoint, slant a straight crossbar through the middle of the letter down to the base line.*"

Guide as children say the sound and repeat the directions (italicized) softly as they write the letter on their papers. Check that children do not retrace.

Show card 25 and say the three sounds: /y/ /ĭ/ /ī/. Class repeats the sounds.

"This is a short letter that goes below the base line. Form it without lifting the pencil. *Start at the midpoint with a short down line to 8, round from 8 to 4 touching the base line, and continue up to the midpoint. Pull a straight line down the same distance below the base line, and round from 4 to 8.*"

Guide as children say the sounds and repeat the directions (italicized) softly as they write the letter on their papers. Make sure the width below the line matches the round part above.

Show card 26 and say the sound: /z/. Class repeats the sound.

"This is a short letter. Form the first horizontal line in the direction in which we write. Form the letter without lifting the pencil. *Start at the midpoint, pull a straight horizontal line. Slant a straight line to the base line below the starting point of the top line. Make a straight line in the direction in which we write.* The top and bottom lines should be parallel."

Guide as children say the sound and repeat the directions (italicized) softly as they write the letter on their papers. Make sure the top and bottom lines are parallel.

As with clock letters, have children practice writing line letters across the page to develop ease of formation and correct spacing between letters.

The papers should look like this:

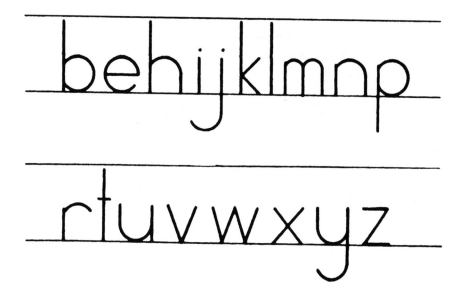

Those letters that begin at 2 on the clock have been taught and also those that begin with a line. Teach the spacing of both kinds of letters by dictating the alphabet, saying only each letter's sound or sounds. Have children say the sounds and write the letters across the page. The first letter written on a page should be written carefully, because every letter that follows should be of the same relative size.

The papers should look like this:

When students are learning to write the single phonograms, teach them to articulate the directions (italicized) as they write. After clearly demonstrating and precisely explaining the general rules and features of the phonograms, ask questions to check students' understanding. Questions such as "Where do all letters sit?" allow children to state general rules. Other questions, such as "How would I write the phonogram *a*?" give students the opportunity to verbalize the formation of letters. Observe students' writing and listen as they explain the concepts and procedures. Then provide further instruction or refinements to increase their understanding. When students practice single phonograms, have them write at least three different letters at a time (e.g., *a b c*), rather than a row of each letter. This requires them to use their minds while practicing letter formation.

Have small groups take turns writing at the board. Send one row of children at a time to the board to review each day's lesson. Make sure each child holds the chalk (or marker) properly, says the sounds and writes each letter correctly, and then erases correctly. Errors in writing can thus be readily caught and corrected. Clear and easy handwriting takes patient supervision and consistent feedback from the teacher, as well as personal evaluation from children to develop a sense of pride and accomplishment.

After teaching the sounds and writing of single manuscript letters, present all the other phonograms on the seventy cards in the same manner as the single letters were presented. Continue to emphasize correct formation and spacing while writing two, three, and four-letter phonograms. When a phonogram of more than one letter is written, the question "Where does the next letter start?" should bring one of two responses: "At 2 on the clock. Start just far enough away to make a clock" *or* "It begins with a *line* that *sits close* to the last letter. A line starts at the top."

When words are introduced, the spacing of letters within a word follows the above rules. A space the size of one round letter is left between words. (Show the children that pressing the space bar once on a computer leaves such a space.) Children's papers are more easily read if they leave the space of two letters between sentences.

Mrs. Spalding explained in detail what to say to children who are learning to write because it is necessary to be specific if handwriting is to become a correct and facile tool for learning. If letters are made incorrectly, they are mentally pictured incorrectly also. This is a serious cause of *reading* failure because beginners do not then recognize the letters when they appear in print.

Rehearse the phonograms and all their common sounds until the children see each in a printed word as standing out as a *sound,* not merely as a letter or letters. Phonograms are practiced two ways daily: The children read the sounds from the cards, which is called an oral phonogram review, and the teacher dictates the sounds of the phonograms for the children to write in a written review. Establish a consistent routine that makes daily oral and written phonogram reviews efficient. (See pages 39–42.)

Manuscript Capital Letters

Be sure the lower-case letters are well learned before introducing all the capital letters. Some capital letters are needed early, such as the first letters in each child's name. Children should be taught the rules for the use of capital letters and be required to give the reason each time they use a capital. When children learn that a capital is used *only* where the rules of English require it, they will not insert capitals indiscriminately.

All capital letters are *tall.* They are twice as high as short letters. They almost fill the space between the base line and line above. The rules for *round* lower-case letters also apply to the following capital letters. They each start at 2 on the clock and *go up.* Since these are tall letters, the round parts are somewhat elongated vertically. Give the sound(s) of each capital letter before showing how to write it, and have children repeat the sound(s) before they write each letter. The crossbar on the Q starts at the top and slants *in the direction in which we write,* ending *just below* the base line.

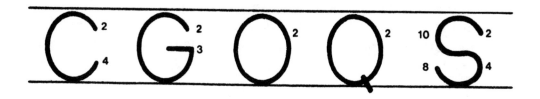

In writing capital letters beginning with lines, make the vertical line first, starting at the top. The horizontal lines of *A, E, F, H, I,* and *T* are made in the direction in which we write. Where there is more than one horizontal line, make the top one first (*E, F,* and *I*). The pencil is lifted before making the second lines of *A, B, D, E, F, H, I, K, M, N, P, R,* and *T,* and they also begin at the top. *Y* is the only capital that is finished below the base line.

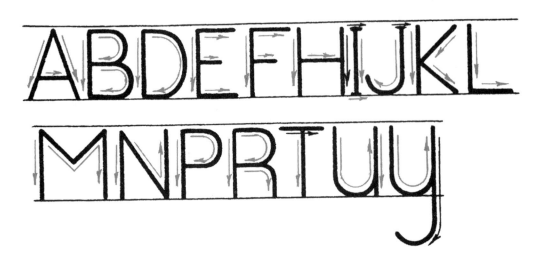

The capital letters *V, W,* and *X* are made just like their lower-case letters. First, start at the top and make the line that slants in the direction in which we write. *V* and *W* are made without lifting the pencil. The second line of *X* starts at the top. *Z* is formed the same as its lower-case letter. The top line is drawn in the direction in which we write, and it is finished without taking the pencil off the paper.

Numbers

All numbers should be made halfway between the size of a short and a tall letter so that the number 1 will not be confused with the letter *l* and the number 0 will not be confused with a capital O.

The numbers 8, 9, and 0 begin at 2 on the clock. Since they are taller than short letters, elongate them somewhat vertically. The rule for the spacing of numbers that begin at 2 on the clock is the same as for manuscript letters. Start just far enough away to begin a new number at 2 on the clock.

$$8^2 \quad 9^2 \quad 0^2$$

The numbers 1, 4, 5, 6, and 7 begin with a line, and all lines start at the top. The left-hand vertical line of 4 is written first. The horizontal line of the 5 is short and is drawn last *in the direction in which we write*. The bottom of 6 ends on the base line so it never looks like 0. The number 7 begins with a line drawn *in the direction in which we write*.

The numbers 1, 4, 5, and 6 sit very close to the preceding number.

$$1 \quad 4 \quad 5 \quad 6 \quad 7$$

Numbers 2 and 3 begin at 10 on the clock and sit very close to the preceding number. Note that no lower-case letter starts at 10, so these two numbers should be thoroughly understood by children who show confusion about direction. Before the children write 2 and 3, ask where these two numbers start until every child knows they begin at 10 on the clock. This is very important to prevent reversing.

$$2 \quad 3$$

Now have children write all the numbers on a line showing the proper spacing:

$$1 2 3 4 5 6 7 8 9 0$$

Punctuation Marks

- When introducing a *period* (full stop), say, "A period (full stop) is made by pressing the pencil on the line close to the letter it follows and lifting the pencil."
- A *comma* is a *tiny* half-clock. It starts on the base line close to the letter it follows and goes below the line, rounding from 12 to 6 on the clock. This explicit teaching keeps children from setting periods (full stops) and commas just anyplace and also provides a precise kinesthetic feel. It also helps them to notice commas and periods on the printed page.
- Parentheses, question marks, exclamation marks, quotation marks, and apostrophes are started at the same height as numbers.

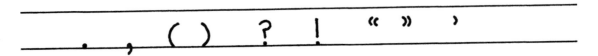

After children can easily form the letters and numbers correctly, they should learn to reduce the size of their handwriting to prepare themselves for cursive writing as described below. Students now begin using the ⅜-inch (1.0 cm) in place of the ⅝-inch (1.6 cm) lined paper.

Cursive Handwriting Rules

Cursive writing is learned from *correct* manuscript writing. Regardless of age, the letters of cursive writing should be taught only after manuscript writing has been mastered and no longer requires any special attention. This *may* be at the beginning of second semester in the *second* grade, but many schools teach cursive at the beginning of third grade. Children want to learn cursive writing. A promise to teach it as soon as they perfect basic manuscript writing is an incentive for real effort to improve.

General rules for cursive writing are as follows:

- All letters sit on the base line.
- All letters or parts of letters are of two sizes: tall or short. Short letters are half the size of tall letters.
- All letters within a word are connected.
- All upswings for lower-case letters are forward.
- All vertical (down) lines start at the top and are straight and parallel.
- Vertical lines may slant slightly forward for the right-handed child or slightly backward for the left-handed child. (Left-handed writers can write straight up and down.)
- All letters except *b, o, v,* and *w* end with a short upswing from the base line. The letters *b, o, v,* and *w* end with dips.

Connecting Lines between Letters

a short upswing from the base line

a tall upswing from the base line

a short upswing that curves over to 2 on the clock

a short dip kept at the height of a short letter across to the start of the next letter, or as a tiny ending on the letters *b*, *o*, *v*, and *w*

a short dip that curves over to 2 on the clock.

Cursive Writing

As with manuscript writing, model saying the sound(s) of the phonogram and then demonstrate the letter formation. Guide as students say the sound(s) and write the letter. This procedure helps children make the connection between the sounds of speech and the letters representing those sounds and will make the transition to cursive easier.

Begin by having children write the entire manuscript alphabet as shown below, saying all the sounds of the phonograms just before they write them.

abcdefghijklmnopqrstuvwxyz

Next, introduce the connecting lines, emphasizing directionality. Model writing the cursive letters with connecting lines over the manuscript letters on the board as shown below. Use colored chalk or marker to demonstrate the differences. The solid lines in the following illustration show to what extent the letters are alike. Most of the differences between manuscript and cursive writing are shown by the dotted lines.

abcdefghijklmnopqrstuvwxyz

At this point, discuss the similarities and differences between the two types of writing and emphasize that clear manuscript will facilitate the writing of cursive. Note that the letters *d* and *p* have no loops. Have students write cursive over their own alphabets while you again demonstrate and precisely describe the letter formation and connections. (Students may do this using a red checking pencil or other colored pencil.)

Demonstrate the following lower-case letter formations and provide time for practice and evaluation. Letters *b*, *e*, *f*, *k*, *r*, *s*, and *z* are the cursive letters that are most different from manuscript.

Procedures for Introducing Selected Cursive Letters with Precise Dialogue

"I will demonstrate and explain how each letter is written. Start *b* with a tall upswing; curve back sharply and pull *straight down* to the base line, curving around to 12 on the clock and finishing with a tiny dip."

Guide as students form the letter.

"Start *e* with a short upswing; curve back sharply and pull *straight down* to the base line, finishing with a short upswing."

Guide as students form the letter.

"Start *f* with a tall upswing; curve back sharply and pull *straight down* below the base line the distance of a short letter. Curve sharply forward to form a narrow loop, touching the down line at the *underside* of the base line and finishing with a short upswing."

Guide as students form the letter.

"Start *k* with a tall upswing; curve back sharply and pull *straight down* to the base line, then retrace up to the height of a short letter, curving around to touch the down line. Pull out and straight to the base line, finishing with a short upswing."

Guide as students form the letter.

"Start *r* with a short upswing, slant down slightly, and then pull *straight down* to the base line, finishing with a short upswing."

Guide as students form the letter.

"Start *s* with a short upswing, pull *straight down* to the base line, and then curve over to touch the upswing, finishing with a short upswing."

Guide as students form the letter.

"Start *z* at 10 on the clock, curve around to 2 continue down to 6, and then curve slightly into a *straight down* line. Curve back sharply to form a narrow loop, touching the down line at the underside of the base line and finishing with a short upswing."

Provide additional practice that focuses on letters having similar formations.

Tall Upswings

Letters *b*, *f*, *h*, *k*, and *l* start with an upswing that makes a sharp curve backward at the top to start the straight down line. Students' papers should look like this:

Short Upswings

Letters *i, p, u, v, w,* and *y* begin with a short upswing. The points on cursive *v* and *w* are rounded, and they curve into 12 on the clock before ending with a tiny dip.

i p u v w y

Narrow Loops below the Base Line

For letters *g, j, y,* and *z,* pull a straight line down the same distance below the base line, and curve sharply *backward* forming a narrow loop that crosses at the *underside* of the base line.

g j y z

For letters *f* and *q,* pull a straight line down to the midpoint below the base line, and curve sharply *forward* forming a narrow loop that crosses at the *underside* of the base line.

f q

Difficult Endings

Letters *b, v,* and *w* curve into 12 and then end with a tiny dip. Letter *o* ends at 2 with a tiny dip. These letters do not return to the base line.

b v w o

Initial Letters in Words

When letters *a, c, d, g, o,* and *q* are written alone or are the first letters of words, they begin at 2.

_a c d g o q_

When letters *m, n, x,* and *z* are written alone or at the beginning of a word, they begin *without* an initial upswing. Round into the down lines for *m* and *n*. The first down line is the same as the *first down line of the manuscript letter.* Round into the slanted down line of the *x.* This is the *same letter as the manuscript form,* and the crossbar is still made from the height of a short letter through the center of the letter. Begin at 10 and round to 2 for *z.*

_m n x z_

After the single phonograms have been practiced to the point of accuracy and proficiency, practice all the two-, three-, and four-letter phonograms.

Difficult Connections

Give special attention to *oa, oe, oo, ou, ow, oi, oy, wh, wor,* and *wr.* When a letter ends at the *midpoint,* use a dip to connect it to the next letter. Have students repeat the directions. Monitor that they do not return to the base line when connecting such letters. Their papers should look like this:

oa oe oo ou ow oi oy wh wor wr

In each week's list of spelling words, identify difficult connections and then practice all the possible connections. It is helpful to have children write them on a separate sheet of paper as a handwriting practice before entering them in their notebooks.

The connections between letters *be, bo, bu, by, ol, op, ot, ve, we,* and *wi* need to be explained and demonstrated before words are dictated for the children's notebooks.

be bo bu by ol op ot ve we wi

When *b, o,* and *w* are followed by *r* or *s,* the dip replaces the upswing. Notice that the *s* curves over to 8 on the clock and does not touch the dip.

br bs   or os   wr ws

Have students practice cursive daily during the written phonogram review. Each day, provide multiple opportunities for students to practice at the board followed by specific, immediate feedback on their performance. (See pages 40–41.)

Closely monitor students' cursive connections to ensure they maintain correct directionality. For example, when they are practicing an upswing over to 2 or a dip over to 2, teach them to stop at 2 and then go back up and around the clock. When writing words with *b, o, v,* and *w,* make sure they do not return to the base line. These common connecting errors can be prevented if practice is supervised.

As with manuscript writing, precise modeling by the teacher followed by daily practices with immediate feedback clarifies students' thinking about writing. Students are given the opportunity to evaluate their cursive writing and measure their progress. They feel successful as they develop ease with writing.

In many other methods, cursive is introduced by showing children a few letter formations per week, prolonging the process for weeks or months. In Spalding, students are immersed in cursive by first writing phonograms, words, and then short sentences. When students understand how closely cursive formation resembles manuscript and are directly taught how certain letters differ, their transition is accomplished more quickly and the quality of writing is remarkably good after about three weeks of instruction. Students are very proud of their accomplishment and immediately feel "older." Mastery of cursive writing also enables students to complete daily content area work in cursive and use manuscript only for lettering charts, maps, and the like.

Cursive Capital Letters

In cursive writing, capital letters *D, F, O, P, Q, V,* and *W* do not connect to the next letter. The forms of capital letters *D, E, F, T, G, I, J,* and *L* are different from their lower-case letters and manuscript letters.

- *B, D, P, R,* and *U* start with a straight down line and are completed without lifting the pencil.
- *A, C, E, L, O,* and *Q* begin at 2 on the clock.
- *G* and *S* start alike with an upswing from the base line.
- *I* and *J* are the only letters that begin at the base line with a backward upswing and curve forward at the top. *I* and *J* should be carefully taught together. As lower-case letters, they are the only ones that are dotted. As capitals, they are the only ones that begin with a backward upswing.
- *F* and *T* begin with a dip at the top.
- *Z* begins at 10 on the clock.

The Capital Letters in Cursive Writing

Mrs. Spalding gave a great deal of study to the techniques of teaching good and easy handwriting, not only for its own sake, but also for the facility of self-expression and the clarification of one's ideas that result from a command of easy, readable writing. The prime reason is that it is the simplest, most direct means of learning the sounds of English as they are represented in our written language. Few, if any, books on handwriting connect the *sounds* of the letters with their forms. Yet, what meaning can the form of a letter have unless it conveys its sound as the child learns to write it? This is one of the reasons why *writing* is the logical road to *reading*.

Oral Phonogram Review

Saying the phonogram sounds automatically is the skill needed for reading words fluently and for sounding out unfamiliar words. Require children to explain these two purposes for learning phonograms to make certain they understand their importance.

Introduce the first four phonograms and practice those for two to three minutes several times during the day. Each day, introduce four new phonograms and then practice all previously introduced phonograms for a few minutes. After practicing them for several days, sort into two piles: (1) those that students can say accurately and automatically (without hesitation) and (2) those that they mispronounce or don't know. Every day, add new phonograms and continue to review the ones that are not automatic. Periodically review all phonograms to maintain them in long-term memory.

Once students are familiar with the routine, oral review of twenty to thirty phonograms should be accomplished in five to eight minutes. This practice initially occurs in two steps: (1) Students read the phonograms while the teacher listens for accuracy and automaticity. (2) Students read the phonograms again, and the teacher asks questions to help students determine how phonogram placement affects pronunciation and spelling.

Oral Phonogram Review Procedures

Step 1 *Accurate and Automatic Pronunciation*

TEACHER: Show students the phonogram card.

STUDENTS: Say (read) sound(s) in unison.

TEACHER: Immediately correct mispronunciations as needed.

Step 2 *Pronunciation and Spelling Alternatives*

TEACHER: Show students phonograms that have different pronunciations (e.g., *a, c*) or spellings depending on their placement (e.g., *ay, ai*).

STUDENTS: Say (read) sounds in unison.

TEACHER: Ask questions that clarify which pronunciation or which phonogram to use in different locations within a word. Examples: "What would you expect this phonogram (show *a*) to say at the end of a syllable?" "May I use this phonogram (show *ai*) at the end of a word? Why? Why not?" (See rule 18, page 224.) Immediately clarify misunderstandings.

STUDENTS: Respond and explain.

Written Phonogram Review

Writing the phonograms automatically is the skill needed for spelling words. It is a more difficult skill because students must hear the phonogram sounds and think of the symbols that represent those sounds. The goal is to train students to think before writing. Knowledge of phonograms is tested by having the teacher dictate the sound or sounds of each phonogram (without showing the phonogram card) and having the children write the phonogram.

While the first twenty-six phonograms are being reviewed, children write them across the page to practice correct spacing of phonograms in words. Review *b* and *d* separately until children know them well. Teach students to think about the position of lips or tongue before writing these letters.

As soon as the two-letter phonograms have been introduced, students should write them in columns down the page rather than across the page. When efficient routines are taught and established from the beginning, a written phonogram review should be accomplished in five to ten minutes, depending on the number reviewed (no more than thirty). Teach children the following routine:

1. Fold the paper to form two columns.
2. Say and write each phonogram.
3. Draw a short horizontal line in place of an unknown phonogram.
4. Look at the teacher after writing each one.
5. Move to the second column when directed.
6. Use the crease to line up the second column.

Handwriting principles are also practiced during written phonogram reviews. Combining these tasks provides multisensory practice, which helps students remember the phonograms more quickly.

For initial written phonogram reviews, emphasize only one handwriting rule. First, have children focus on beginning at 2 on the clock, *going up,* and conforming the letter to the shape of a circle. When the class becomes quite good at this, have them focus on writing all letters on the base line. Finally, focus their attention on the relative size of tall and short letters. For example, a clock letter may be nicely formed, yet it may be slightly larger or smaller than the midpoint. Directionality (beginning at two on the clock and going up) and conforming to the curve of a circle are easier tasks than maintaining the relative size of tall and short letters. Continue to teach and reinforce correct spacing between letters. Daily practice will bring mastery of handwriting rules if students understand the features and can explain letter formation.

After written review, require children to explain letter formation. Clarifying questions such as "Which features are used to form the letter *d?*" should bring the response "A circle and a tall line." Next, demonstrate how to analyze and evaluate letter formations. Help children evaluate their own handwriting by evaluating your handwriting. For example, say something like this: "When I wrote my phonograms on the board, I put a star beside /ă/ /ā/ /ah/ because it starts at 2, sits on the base line, and is rounded nicely."

Then, have students analyze their own papers and put stars beside their best letters.

Require them to explain why they picked the ones they did. When children analyze and evaluate their own handwriting, they are not only reinforcing correct letter formation but also developing a sense of pride in their work. After they are comfortable with explaining their own choices, have them analyze a classmate's paper.

The phonograms must be thoroughly learned with the accurate sounds, and they must be correctly written (not copied). To achieve these goals, teach the following procedures. After dictating *new* phonograms, provide immediate feedback. When students become *accurate* on *familiar* phonograms, provide delayed feedback.

Written Phonogram Review Procedures

Step 1   *While Phonograms 1–26 Are Being Practiced*

TEACHER: Say sound(s) of the phonogram on the card.

STUDENTS: Say sound(s) in unison. Then say sound(s) softly just before writing the phonogram.

Immediate feedback (new phonograms only):

TEACHER: Show the card immediately after students have written each new phonogram. Have students cross out the incorrect phonogram. Write the correct phonogram either beside the incorrect one or beside the line designating a missed phonogram. Repeat this process until all phonograms have been dictated.

Delayed feedback (when students can accurately say and write phonograms):

STUDENTS: In unison, dictate to the teacher the sound(s) for each phonogram written.

TEACHER: Say sound(s) of each phonogram. Then say again softly just before writing on the board.

STUDENTS: Proofread their work and correct errors as needed.

Step 2   *While Phonograms 27–70 Are Being Practiced*

TEACHER: Say sound(s) of the phonogram on the card.

STUDENTS: Say sound(s) in unison.

TEACHER: Clarify which phonogram when needed. Example: For *ay* say, "Two-letter /ā/ used at the end of a word."

STUDENTS: Say sound(s) softly just before writing the phonogram.

Immediate feedback (new phonograms only):

TEACHER: Show each card.

STUDENTS: Proof for accuracy and correct any errors.

continued

Delayed feedback (when students can accurately say and write phonograms):

STUDENTS: In unison dictate the sound(s) for each phonogram they have written and clarify when needed.

TEACHER: Say sound(s) and write the phonogram on the board. (Note: Before writing phonograms with more than one spelling for a single sound, wait for students to provide clarifying information and then write the phonogram.)

STUDENTS: Proofread their work and correct errors as needed.

Children who have difficulty learning need extra practice. Seat them nearby during class instruction, and during the day, make time to provide the *extra* practice. For those with severe motor or memory problems, preteach difficult concepts of the next day's lesson in a small group before presenting it to the whole class. This provides these children the opportunity to learn as a member of the class, thus preventing failure. Teach their parents from *the start* so that they can help at home. If parents cannot help, make extra time in school so that these children do not fall behind the rest of the class. The children who need help should be given the specific directions in this chapter over and over until they can direct their hands in writing and no longer make errors in direction or orientation. This is where extra practice is an essential part of teaching if all children are to learn. *The teacher cannot be said to have taught unless and until the student learns.*

Teaching Spelling Using Phonograms and Rules

The spelling of English words is the major obstacle to easy writing and accurate reading. English spelling may seem inconsistent; in fact, it follows certain patterns and rules (with few exceptions). Learning to spell words by applying phonograms and rules unites the spoken sounds of English words with their written forms. Spelling should be taught from the spoken word. Most spelling books are not suitable because they do not include all the sounds found in words. Children who merely copy words do not make progress because they rely on visual recall alone without the added assistance of sound.

Overview
In the first few years of life, children learn to use or understand *at least* 3,000 words. In The Spalding Method, the connection between speech and print is taught by writing high-frequency words in a spelling/vocabulary notebook. In this process, children analyze the *written* spelling of words that will be most useful to them. Of the 1,000 words we use most often, the first 700 are in the spoken vocabulary of most five- and six-year-old children.

Learning to spell words by writing them from dictation connects the spoken sounds to their written symbols. *All* children can learn using this method because every avenue to the mind is used. They *hear* the teacher say the word. Then they *say* each sound *just before* they *write* it. They *see* what they have written as they then *read* it. No other method can fix sooner or more securely in their memories the words they can write and read at a glance, thus building their sight vocabularies. Common words soon are recognized as representing ideas, without the need to separate their component phonograms for reading.

New words are always learned by studying the phonetic sounds of the spoken word. This distinguishes The Spalding Method from most other phonetic methods. Twenty-nine rules explain how pronunciation, spelling, and syllable division are determined (see page 222). Rules are taught as facts about the language just before they are needed to spell a word. Thus, they are learned from examples rather than as isolated facts.

Precise pronunciation of each syllable written in the spelling lesson is required of both teacher and students. It clarifies the sounds for children as nothing else can. It facilitates clear speech and can thus counteract the tendency toward slurring the sounds of our language. *Pronounce* the vowel sounds in nonaccented syllables as they are written. For example, the word *silent* should be taught as *si lent,* not *si lunt,* and the word *travel* as *trav el,* not *trav ul.* Unless we pronounce *e* in each of these words, neither spelling nor speech is apt to be precise. Spelling has remained relatively constant over the years, while pronunciations have varied among geographical regions and countries. By reading the dictated words two ways, for spelling and for reading, children quickly learn both the spelling and the pronunciation of these words without using the schwa (ə).

Extended Ayres Word List

The spelling words listed in this edition of *The Writing Road to Reading* include most frequently used words compiled by Dr. Leonard P. Ayres and additional high-frequency words. The Ayres list was compiled by examining 368,000 words in newspapers, letters, and literature. A recent computer comparison of the Ayres list with other high-frequency lists and the *Collins COBUILD English Dictionary* (1995) has shown that the Ayres list is remarkably up to date. The *COBUILD* dictionary draws from the "Bank of English," 200 million words covering a vast range of current British and American English. Words are ranked in five frequency bands, with five being the highest frequency. Words ranked two or higher are considered part of the essential core vocabulary of the language. In this edition of *The Writing Road to Reading,* words are either in the core vocabulary or provide practice of phonograms or spelling rules. The Extended Ayres Word List is included in "Instructional Materials" (see pages 252–397).

Primary Spelling/Vocabulary Notebook

Children in kindergarten through grade two write the words in a *sewn,* stiff-cover composition book, 8½ by 6¾ inches (21.6 cm × 17.1 cm), with thirty-four leaves, each having twelve lines with ⅝-inch (1.6 cm) spacing. (A thicker book raises a primary child's arm too high to write comfortably.)

Construction of the notebook teaches children to analyze the *written* spelling of words so they can spell, write, and read words encountered in books. Writing the Extended Ayres Word List is begun on page 1 of the primary notebook after children have learned the first forty-five phonograms. The more words children analyze and read from their notebooks, the more familiar they become with language and spelling rules. This notebook becomes their prized spelling book to which they constantly refer. (See pages 228–234, in "Instructional Materials.")

Intermediate Spelling/Vocabulary Notebook

Students in grades three and above write words in a sewn, hardcover composition book. The intermediate notebook is 9¾ by 7½ inches (24.8 × 19.0 cm), with fifty leaves, each having twenty-three lines with ⅜-inch (1.0 cm) spacing.

The intermediate notebook has two parts: rule pages and the Extended Ayres Word List. The pages designated as *rule pages* include phonograms and example words for the first sixteen rules. Lists of multiletter phonograms and additional, less common phonograms are included for your convenience. (See pages 237–251, in "Instructional Materials.") The Extended Ayres Word List is begun in the middle of the notebook, where the stitching makes it open easily. Older students begin writing the Extended Ayres Word List after they have learned to say and write all seventy phonograms in manuscript and cursive writing, have written all numbers, and have written rule pages 1 and 7 in cursive.

Construction of either the primary or the intermediate notebook is the heart of The Spalding Method. It not only provides multisensory instruction of high-frequency spelling words, but also integrates vocabulary instruction with rules of the language. The notebook is the foundation for language arts instruction; therefore, construction of the notebook is the critical activity for student achievement in this method.

Twenty-Nine Rules

Rules that govern spelling, capitalization, pronunciation, and grammar usage are directly taught in The Spalding Method. These spelling and language rules are listed along with instructional tips in the "Instructional Materials" (see pages 222–225). Rules are not rotely memorized. Rather, each rule is taught prior to dictation of the word to which it applies. It should be made clear to students that although no rule is absolute, rules hold true often enough to be very helpful. Rule numbers are marked in the notebook after rules are introduced. Students continue to mark rule numbers in their notebooks until they can explain and consistently apply them while reading and writing. They should also be alerted to recognize words that do not conform to the rules, a task they usually take pleasure in doing. Sometimes, they "discover" words to which the rules do not apply and learn why they do not if an explanation is known. Recognizing these exceptions makes a lasting impression.

Words that illustrate the first sixteen rules are written on the rule pages of the intermediate notebook. Specific directions for teaching the rule pages are found on pages 53–70.

Spalding Marking System

The marking system helps students of any age connect speech sounds to the written symbols representing those sounds. The goal is automatic word recognition. Phonograms of two, three, or four letters are *underlined in the direction we write* to unite these letters as the symbol for a single sound in a given word. Sounds other than the first sound are *numbered*. For example, in the word *do*, a small number 3 above the *o* reminds students that the third sound of *o* is used (see page 213). Some words are bracketed to show relationships. Use of underlines, numbers, and brackets requires children to think and helps them analyze the spelling and pronunciation of words. The following conventions explain the simple markings used to teach students how the rules and phonograms actually work:

- A vowel is underlined at the end of a syllable when it says /ā/, /ē/, /ī/, /ō/, or /ū/.

  m<u>e</u>   <u>o</u> pen   Ju l<u>y</u>

- Phonograms of two or more letters are underlined to indicate one sound.

  <u>th</u>in   bri<u>dge</u>   <u>eigh</u>t

- Silent letters are underlined twice: ha<u>l</u>f (We say "*haf*" but write *half*.) If the sound of a phonogram is not given on the phonogram card, the phonogram is underlined twice: fr<u>ie</u>nd (/ĕ/ is not a common sound of *ie*.) The silent *e* at the end of a base word is one of five different kinds of silent *e*'s (see pages 56–57) and each is marked as shown below. All except the first have a small number beside the double underline to show which kind it is.

  t<u>ime</u>
  ha<u>ve</u>₂   bl<u>ue</u>₂
  <u>ch</u>an<u>ce</u>₃   <u>ch</u>ar<u>ge</u>₃
  lit tl<u>e</u>₄
  <u>are</u>₅

- Numbers are placed above a phonogram when its sound is not the first sound.

  d$\overset{3}{o}$ l$\overset{2}{o}$w
  w$\overset{3}{a}\overset{2}{s}$ y$\overset{3}{ou}$
  p$\overset{3}{u}$t   c$\overset{4}{ou}$n try
  <u>th$\overset{5}{ou}$</u>ght
  dr<u>$\overset{6}{ou}$</u>ght

- Some words are bracketed together to compare (1) a derived word with a base word (*coming/come*), (2) words with the same spelling pattern (*catch, catcher, kitchen*), (3) words that sound the same but use different phonograms to denote meaning (*meet/meat*), or (4) two words that might easily be confused (*form/from*). Bracketing words connects spelling and language and alerts the teacher to relationships that need to be taught in the integrated spelling and writing lesson.

For underlines, numbers, and brackets to serve as visual signals, children must be taught to underline, number, and form brackets carefully and accurately as explained in the next section.

Preparation for Dictation in the Spelling/Vocabulary Notebook

On the first day of school, point out that there are only forty-five sounds of English and seventy ways to spell those sounds. Begin at once to teach the class to say the sounds and to write the phonograms. Teach parents so they can enjoy helping their children at home, especially those students who need extra help.

After clock letters have been introduced, model the formation of words on the board, using the phonograms that begin at two on the clock, such as *dad, fad, fog, sad,* and *sag.* Demonstrate how to sound each phonogram, blend them together, and then read the word. Repeat by having children sound, blend, and then read the words with you.

After line letters have been introduced, write a few words on chart paper or the board (e.g., *bag, bed, had, has*). These models provide a visual picture of letter formation and spacing, as well as an opportunity to teach general dictation procedures. Have students sound, blend, and then read these words. Most handwriting practice is done with phonograms. It is also appropriate to have kindergartners and first graders practice writing some words on ⅝-inch (1.6 cm) lined paper, getting them ready for writing words in their spelling/vocabulary notebooks.

While students of any age are mastering the first forty-five phonograms, write Ayres words in sections A–G (see pages 254–262) on chart paper or the board to teach the following terms, concepts, and rules needed to begin spelling dictation.

Syllable

Teach children that a syllable is a single word or that part of a word that is pronounced by a single impulse of the voice. (This is the basic phonological unit of speech in all languages.) Tap the palm to demonstrate the meaning of impulse or beat (e.g., *me, do, lit tle*).

Vowel

Teach children that *a, e, i, o,* and *u* are a special set of alphabet letters called vowels and that every syllable must have at least one vowel. The letter *y* is considered a vowel when it says /ĭ/ /ī/.

Using Ayres words written on chart paper or the board (e.g., *me, do, and, go, at*), demonstrate that there is a vowel in every word. Next, have students identify the vowels in each word.

Some children will have difficulty hearing the differences between vowel sounds (e.g., /ĕ/ and /ĭ/). Demonstrate that your mouth remains *open* as you say each vowel sound, *but* the *shape* of the mouth changes. Have these children practice saying the sounds until they hear and feel the difference. (It is helpful to understand that a vowel is a speech sound made when the air leaving the lungs is vibrated in the voice box [larynx or Adam's apple] and released. Different vowel sounds occur depending on how the mouth is shaped as the air passes through.)

Consonant

Teach children that alphabet letters that are not vowels are consonants. Using previously written Ayres words, identify the consonants. Then have students identify the consonants in each word.

When students have difficulty hearing or saying consonant sounds (e.g., /b/ versus /p/), explain the position of the mouth, lips, and tongue. (A consonant is a speech sound that occurs when the airflow is obstructed [blocked] in some way. For example, the consonant sound /b/ is made by letting air build behind the lips before the sound is released from the mouth [voiced]. The consonant sound /p/ is also made by letting air build behind the lips, but only air is released from the mouth [unvoiced]. See the explanations accompanying the phonograms listed on pages 213–221.)

Underlines

Teach children that an underline is drawn *just under the base line* but far enough below the base line to clearly distinguish it. There should be a small white space between the base line and the underline.

Using the word *me*, demonstrate underlining the exact width of the *e*. Using the word *she*, demonstrate underlining the exact width of the /sh/ by starting at the beginning of the phonogram, going to the end of the phonogram, and *lifting the pencil*. The underline signals that those two letters represent one sound. Have children use a separate piece of lined paper to practice writing words and underlining phonograms.

Numbering

Teach children that a small number is placed just above (not touching) the middle of the letter in a single-letter phonogram that has more than one sound. For a multiletter phonogram, the number is written just above and between the letters to indicate the sound. When no number is written above, it signifies that the first sound is the one used in the word. Silent final *e*'s are also numbered as shown on page 45.

Using the word *do*, demonstrate that the number 3 is written neatly just above the *o* to say /o͞o/. Using the word *the,* demonstrate that the number 2 is written neatly between the *t* and the *h* to say /th/. Have children use a separate piece of lined paper to practice writing words and numbering phonograms.

Brackets and Braces

Teach children that these markings are used to show relationships between and among words. Brackets are used for manuscript and braces for cursive writing.

Using the two words *your* and *you,* demonstrate that a bracket begins with a tiny horizontal line halfway between the top and the base line, continues with a straight vertical line down to just below the base line under the last word of the set, and ends with a tiny horizontal line in the direction we write. The bracket must be clearly separate from the first letter of each word so the word is easy to read. Have children use a separate piece of paper to practice writing these words and forming brackets. (When older children are ready for cursive writing, demonstrate forming braces and provide practice. A brace begins with a curve into a straight vertical line down to the midpoint, forms a slight point, continues the straight line down to just below the base line under the last word of the set, and ends with a curve in the direction we write.)

Rules

Rules are taught when needed to spell a word. The first Ayres word, *me*, illustrates rule 4: "Vowels *a*, *e*, *o*, and *u* usually say /ā/, /ē/, /ō/, and /ū/ at the end of a syllable." The whole rule is not *directly* taught (or memorized). Rather, the part of the rule that explains the spelling of individual words is taught. Students soon learn that rule 4 applies to vowels *a*, *e*, *o*, and *u*.

For the word *me*, hold up two fingers of one hand, and with the other hand, point to the finger representing the sound /m/, then the finger representing the sound /ē/. Make certain the orientation is in the direction students read. Explain that the *e* says /ē/ at the end of *me*. Tell students that the *e* is underlined to remind them that *e* says /ē/ at the end of a syllable (see page 254). Explain the term *abbreviation*. Demonstrate writing *r.* as the abbreviation for *rule* and the number 4 one inch (2.5 cm) from the word *me*. Using the words *go*, *a*, *she*, *so*, and *no*, demonstrate that rule 4 also helps us know how to pronounce the vowels *a* and *o* at the end of a syllable. Next, have children explain why the vowel is underlined in these words. Their response should sound something like this: "The *o* says /ō/ in *go* (or *no*) because it is at the end of a syllable (or one-syllable word)."

Spacing between Syllables

Teach students to leave the space of one clock letter between syllables in the notebook (*lit tle*, *a go*). Have them practice on a separate piece of paper.

Show students the primary (or intermediate) notebook and explain that the purpose for writing the spelling/vocabulary notebook is to understand how the English language works. Many classes of high school students and many people of college age and older need this information and have written notebooks.

Dictation in the Spelling/Vocabulary Notebook

The purpose of spelling dictation is to develop independent thinkers who understand the structure of the language and, therefore, apply the phonograms and rules to spelling and reading words automatically.

Dictate the words in the order presented in the Extended Ayres Word List. If the derived word is paired with its base word, *dictate* the base word *first* to show how to form the derived word.

Teaching students the procedures listed below makes the lessons more efficient and effective. At first, demonstrate (model) every step of the process. As students attempt the task, guide or prompt, and finally provide support only when needed, allowing students to do the thinking and responding. For detailed explanation of this progression from modeling by the teacher to student independence, see "Principles of Instruction," in chapter 4.

While students are learning the procedures, the process takes a little longer; as soon as the procedures become routine, spelling dictation should average about one word per minute.

Spelling Dictation Procedures

TEACHER: Say the *whole* word as spoken in *normal conversation* (not by syllables).

K–1
Give a short sentence that demonstrates the meaning of the word and good sentence construction.

Grade 2 and Above
Give sentences whenever needed to clarify meaning.

All Beginners
Use fingers to provide a visual clue of individual sounds, or use arms to denote syllables (see Rules, pages 223–225). To catch errors quickly, listen while students say sounds or syllables. As needed, model precise pronunciation of phonograms or syllables. Have students repeat sounds precisely.

STUDENTS: *One-Syllable Words*
In unison, say each phonogram. Say each again softly just before writing it. Mark word if needed. Look at teacher.

Multisyllable Words
In unison, say each syllable. Say each again softly just before writing it. Mark word if needed. Look at teacher.

TEACHER: Monitor students' writing, then give a signal for them to dictate the word in unison (e.g., chalk to board).

STUDENTS: *One-Syllable Words*
Dictate only sounds (/m/ /ē/). As teacher finishes writing the word, dictate only the sound of phonogram to be underlined (/ē/). Read word.

Multisyllable Words
Dictate syllables (*o ver*). As teacher finishes writing the word, dictate markings (/ō/ /er/) and then read word. Note rule and number if applicable (r. 4).

TEACHER: As students dictate, write sounds or syllables and add markings. (If needed, clarify students' pronunciation or markings.)

STUDENTS: Read whole word as in normal conversation.
Check own words and markings against words and markings on board for accuracy. Read all words for spelling (by sound or syllable). Read all words for reading (as whole words).

The following is a sample class dialogue for a kindergarten or first grade. Although this dialogue is presented for beginners, the basic procedures are the same for students of any age. The primary focus of the *first* dictation lesson is learning the procedures. The class has been pretaught rule 4 and the terms *syllable, underline,* and *number.* If not already taught, teach students the capitals *A* and *G* for the heading to sections A–G. Students have practiced underlining and numbering. The teacher does most of the talking because he or she is demonstrating the procedures.

Spelling Dictation—Example Dialogue (see page 229)

TEACHER:	"Class, you have been eager to write spelling words in your notebooks. You are doing well with underlining and numbering. Today we begin the notebook. Center the heading *A–G* on the first line of column 1." (Demonstrate.)
STUDENTS:	(Write the title *A–G* in capitals on the top line as teacher monitors.)
TEACHER:	"This is the procedure we will follow: I will say the word in normal speech and use it in a sentence. Then you will say each sound precisely as I use my fingers to represent the sounds. Next, you will say sounds again softly just before you write them. Last, look up at me to show that you are ready for the next step. Listen carefully as I say the word. '*me*. Give the book to *me*.' Say the sounds with me."
STUDENTS:	In unison, say, "/m/ /ē/."
TEACHER:	"Now say each sound softly just before you write it in your notebook."
STUDENTS:	(Say sounds softly. Write in notebook. Look up at teacher.)
TEACHER:	"We have talked about the rule that tells us that the phonogram *e* usually says /ē/ when it comes at the end of a syllable. I will think out loud as I decide how to mark this word. The word *me* is one syllable. To show that *e* says /ē/, I will underline it and then write 'r. 4' *one inch* away from the word to remind me that *e usually* says /ē/ at the end of a syllable." (Demonstrate.) "Now underline the /ē/ and write 'r. 4' one inch away from the word."
STUDENTS:	(Underline the *e* and write "r. 4" one inch from the word as teacher monitors.)
TEACHER:	"Now you be the teacher and dictate the sounds as soon as you see I'm ready to write on the board. Then say *only* the sound I should underline and tell me which rule to write."
STUDENTS:	In unison, dictate, "/m/, /ē/, /ē/, me, rule 4."
TEACHER:	"Now read the word in normal speech."
STUDENTS:	"*me*."
TEACHER:	"*do. Do* your work carefully.' Say each sound."
STUDENTS:	In unison, say, "/d/ /o͞o/."

TEACHER:	"We use the phonogram that says /ŏ/ /ō/ /o͞o/. Say each sound just before you write it."
STUDENTS:	In unison, say, "/d/ /o͞o/."
TEACHER:	"Write a tiny three above the /o͞o/ to show that it says its third sound. Then dictate the sounds to me as soon as you see I'm ready to write on the board. Then say the sound and the number to mark."
STUDENTS:	In unison, dictate, "/d/ /o͞o/. /o͞o/, three."
TEACHER:	"Read the whole word."
STUDENTS:	*"do."*

Whenever there could be confusion about which phonogram to use, identify the correct phonogram to prevent failure. After a few days of modeling each step of these procedures, require students to tell you simple markings (such as underlining the *e* in a rule 4 word) without prompting. When students can say the sounds and markings independently, have them do so. The more students do the thinking and responding, the more quickly they can apply the rules when reading and writing.

Important Points to Remember

- Students in kindergarten through second grade begin the Extended Ayres Word List on the first page of the primary notebook. Third-grade and older students begin writing Ayres words in the middle of the intermediate notebook, where the stitching makes it open easily. Pages are folded, forming a crease, so two columns can be written.

- Number the primary and intermediate notebook pages for quick reference. Students' notebooks will be alike and can be used for reading words two ways: for spelling and for reading.

- Include difficult phonograms in the daily oral and written phonogram reviews just prior to the dictation lesson in which they will be used. When students know phonograms automatically, it helps them say and write words more quickly.

- Children do *not* repeat the word the teacher says. They know the word from hearing it said. Their job is to immediately give the first sound or first syllable. Children must learn to say the sounds sequentially when they write words and later sentences.

- Sentences should be short and should be models of good English. They need not be dull or unimaginative. Rather, they can restate useful facts such as how the children should sit, hold the pencil, or form letters, facts about how the language works, and so on. Tell the class how good they are at reasoning, studying, and playing. Insert philosophical ideas about learning. Sentences should serve as standards for the type of sentences children will construct when it is their turn to use a word in a sentence (at first orally). Vocabulary development or detailed rule explanations are taught in the integrated spelling and writing lesson rather than during dictation (see chapter 2).

- The *names* of the letters are *not* said unless the sound and the name are the same. This permits each child to write about as fast as he or she can speak distinctly, and it unites writing (spelling) with speech and reading. It is one of the most valuable parts of all the techniques. Avoid using the terms *name* of a letter, the *long* or *short* vowel. Instead, use the sound itself, because the other words are only names for sounds and are thus less direct.

- Never discuss other phonograms that *might* have the same sound in a given word *(ee, ea)*. Teach the exact phonogram shown in the dictionary, which is the standard for spelling. Students should say only the sound of the phonogram used in the word (never all possible sounds for the phonogram).

- When students pronounce each syllable before they write it, have them *stress* the vowel sound to agree with the spelling wherever possible (*cŏme*, not *cum*). The dictionary states that a monosyllable such as the word *do*, when pronounced alone, always stresses the vowel. Stressing vowel sounds makes spelling more phonetic and easy to learn. Dictionaries explain the variations in pronouncing words in different contexts and uses.

- When you get to the word *little*, explain that you will now begin dictating two-syllable words by syllable. Holding up three fingers of your right hand, say *lit* and have students write it. Then hold up three fingers of your left hand and say *tle* and have students write it. This procedure teaches children to spell by breaking multisyllabic words into syllables. Even young children can learn to spell large words when they understand this principle.

- In multisyllabic words, use the right hand to demonstrate the first syllable and the left hand to represent the second syllable, then cross the right arm over the left to represent succeeding syllables. For students having difficulty writing words in syllables, help them establish correct directionality. Have them stand before the word written in syllables on the board and place one hand on the first syllable and the other hand on the second one. (Do not confuse by calling the hands left and right.) This kinesthetic effect has proved helpful to many regardless of age.

- When multisyllabic words are encountered in the Extended Ayres Word List, help children apply knowledge of six common syllable structures. These structures are explained under "Syllable Division," in "Instructional Materials" (see page 226).

- Do not use nonsense syllables (*pif, rif*). Everything written and read should be sensible so that pupils come to expect the words they write and read to make sense.

- When reading two ways (for spelling and reading), have students read the words across two rows as well as down the columns so as to change the order. This practice is needed until words are read easily enough to require no attention when they occur in stories. Emphasize that *saying* the sounds of a phonogram or syllable precedes writing it so that *the mind can direct the hand* in forming the correct phonogram or phonograms. In reading, the eyes must *first see* the phonograms in proper sequence so the *mind* can direct the pronunciation of the word. The eyes must be on what is being read.

- When students can explain and consistently apply a rule while reading and spelling, stop marking it in the notebook.
- Each day after the initial spelling dictation lesson, start with a written quiz, dictating the previous day's new words in a changed sequence.

Teaching Language Rule Application

Rule application is taught in two ways: by applying rules to words in the Extended Ayres Word List and by writing words that illustrate rules on intermediate notebook rule pages. All teachers need to be fully conversant with the concepts taught on every rule page in order to teach and explain correctly any word that occurs in speech, writing, and reading. The rules taught on rule pages 1 through 4 are so basic, they are taught to all children even though primary children do not write the rule pages in their notebooks. Do not rush through the explanation of concepts on each rule page. Rule application helps children develop analytical thinking skills.

A parent or teacher who is under the impression that young children lack the ability to learn, understand, and apply such rules will be surprised and delighted to see how quickly they do so, and how eager they are to demonstrate this ability to use reasoning in their work.

Students in third grade and above should write the rule pages in their notebooks each year. *On each rule page, use the spelling dictation procedure as described on page 49, including rereading the words for spelling and reading.* Students use red pencils to underline and number phonograms that illustrate the rule being taught. The rule pages are the only place where the red pencil is used. Have students number the rule pages as shown in "Instructional Materials" (see pages 237–251) *before* dictating any words. These pages become their reference for the phonograms and the rules of spelling and pronunciation.

Reproductions of the rule pages are on pages 237–251. Spelling rules, explanatory notes, miniature reproductions, and rule page instructions for the teacher are given below. Follow the rule page procedures carefully because completion of these pages helps develop students' analytical thinking skills. Ensure that students explain how the rule applies to the pronunciation or spelling of words on each rule page.

Rule Page 1 (Rules 1–7)

Rule page 1 includes one two-letter (*qu*) and twenty single-letter consonants, the six single-letter vowels (and words to show the common sounds of each vowel), and the five kinds of silent final *e*'s. The first seven rules (see page 223) are applied on rule page 1.

After primary children have learned the first forty-five phonograms (see pages 213–218), systematically introduce and write each section of rule page 1 on chart paper or the board. Teach and practice the rules and concepts in each section. Third-grade and older students should write rule page 1 in cursive writing in the black-and-white notebook after they have mastered the first forty-five phonograms and practiced writing all seventy phonograms in manuscript and cursive writing.

For third and fourth graders or for older students just beginning The Spalding Method, divide the page into separate lessons. Older students who have previously had Spalding instruction may write rule page 1 in one sitting.

Rule Page 1 Procedures with Precise Dialogue

Day 1

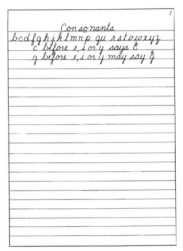

1. Explain that the first section of rule page 1 includes the consonants and rules 1, 2, and 3.
2. Dictate the word *consonants* in normal speech. Explain that the title is capitalized and written in syllables. Demonstrate by centering the title on the first line. Have students say the first syllable *Con* and then say it again softly to themselves as they write it in the middle of the first line. Next, have them say the syllable *so* and repeat it softly as they write it close to, but not touching, the first syllable. Finally, have students say the last syllable by sounds /n/ /ă/ /n/ /t/ /s/ so they will write it correctly. Have students underline the *o* in black.
3. Say, "On the next line, we will write the single consonants and the two-letter consonant *qu* (/kw/). Say the sound for the first consonant /b/, then write it."
4. With the class, say the sound(s) for each consonant in unison just before writing each. Have them leave the space of a round letter before and after the two-letter consonant *qu* (/kw/).
5. Say, "On the third line, write, '*c* before *e*, *i*, or *y* says $\overset{2}{c}$.'" (This is the only time *c* is written with a two above it. Rule 2 explains which sound to use.)
6. Say, "On the fourth line, write, '*g* before *e*, *i*, or *y* may say $\overset{2}{g}$.'" (This is the only time where *g* is written with a two above it. Rule 3 explains which sound to use.)
7. Explain that each consonant, except *c*, *g*, and *s*, has but a single sound. Only *s* when it says /z/ needs a two placed above it.

Model Thinking

Use rules 1, 2, and 3 (see page 223) to explain the pronunciation of words that include phonograms *c*, *g*, and *qu*. Say, "As I look at the word *queen*, I remember that /kw/ is a two-letter consonant sound, so I pronounce the word /kw/ /ē/ /n/. In the word *cat*, *c* says /k/ because it is not followed by an *e*, *i*, or *y*."

✔ *Check for Understanding*

Ask students to explain why given words are pronounced as they are. Their replies should sound something like this: "In the word *cent*, the *c* says /s/ because it is followed by an *e*." "In the word *gem*, the *g* says /j/ because it is followed by an *e*."

☆ *Provide Practice*

Have students categorize example words from a textbook paragraph to show that *c* followed by *e, i,* or *y* says /s/ and *g* followed by *e, i,* or *y* may say /j/. This exercise demonstrates that rule 2 is much more frequently used than rule 3.

Day 2

1. Explain that the second section of rule page 1 includes the vowels, words that illustrate the vowel sounds, and rules 4, 5, and 6.

2. Have students skip one space to separate the consonant and vowel sections. Explain that they will center and capitalize the title *Vowels*. Demonstrate in the same manner as on day 1.

3. Have students say and write the title *Vowels* in syllables. Have them underline and number in black.

4. Dictate vowel *a* and have students write it about a half inch from the stitching. Dictate the rest of the vowels to form a column as shown in the illustration.

5. Have students draw a vertical line to form a column separating the vowels from the example words as shown in the illustration.

6. Dictate and have students say and write the example words for vowel *a* in three columns. Have them underline and number in black. Proceed to dictate each set in order.

7. Have students brace the words *big* and *gym*, which illustrate the sound /ĭ/.

8. Have students use a *red* pencil to underline the vowels saying their second sounds and to number the third sounds for vowels *a, o,* and *u* as shown in the illustration.

9. After all words in the vowel section have been written, marked, and checked for accuracy, have students read the words for spelling and reading.

💡 *Model Thinking*

Use rules 4, 5, and 6 (see page 223) to explain how to read words that have vowels *a, e, i, o,* and *u* at the end of a syllable. For example, say, "*Navy* must have two syllables because it has two vowels, *a* and *y*. I know that *a usually* says /ā/ at the end of a syllable. I know that *y usually* says /ĭ/ at the end of a syllable. I will read the word, *na vy.*"

continued

✓ *Check for Understanding*

Have students explain the pronunciation of other words such as *my*. Their response should sound like this: "In the word *my*, I read /m/ /ī/ because *y* may say /ī/. To spell *my*, I use the phonogram *y* because English words do not end with *i*."

☆ *Provide Practice*

On a separate piece of paper, have students write a few words that illustrate the different vowel sounds. Use words in sections A–G.

Day 3

1. Explain that the last section of rule page 1 includes words that illustrate the five kinds of silent final *e*'s (rule 7).

2. Have students skip one space to separate the sections. Then dictate the word *time*. Explain that the silent *e* lets the vowel *i* say /ī/ in *time*. Explain that single vowels before any single consonant can say /ā/ /ē/ /ī/ /ō/ /ū/ if a silent *e* ends the base word. Have students say the sounds softly as they write this word.

3. Dictate the word *have*. Explain that English words do not end with *v*. A silent *e* is added. Have students say the sounds softly as they write *have*. Dictate the word *blue*. Explain that English words do not end with the single vowel *u*. A silent *e* is added. Have students say the sounds softly as they write *blue* on the same line as *have*.

4. Dictate the word *chance*. Explain that the silent *e* lets the *c* say /s/. Rule 2 explains this. Have students say the sounds softly as they write the word and then underline the phonogram /ch/ in *chance* in black. Dictate the word *charge*. Explain that the silent *e* lets the *g* say /j/. Rule 3 explains this. Have students softly say the sounds as they write the word on the same line as *chance* and then underline the /ch/ and /ar/ phonograms in black.

5. On the next line, dictate the word *little*. Remind students to say and write *little* in syllables. Explain that every syllable must have at least one vowel. (Words in which the second syllable is *ble*, *cle*, *dle*, *fle*, *gle*, *kle*, *ple*, *sle*, *tle*, and *zle* have a silent *e* added so each can be a separate syllable. All other syllables in English have a vowel sound.)

6. On the next line, dictate the word *are*. Have students say the sounds softly as they write the word and then underline the phonogram /ar/ in black. The *e* has no job. After the word *are*, have students write *no job e* in parenthesis.

7. Have students use a red pencil to underline and number as follows:

In *time,* underline the *i, m,* and *e.* The first job of *e* is not numbered just as the first phonogram sound is not numbered. Underlining the vowel, consonant, and silent final *e* provides a visual signal that the *e* lets the vowel say its second sound. (Job 1.)

In *have* and *blue,* have students underline the *v* and *u* once and the *e* twice and write small twos beside the double underlining to signal that English words do not end in *v* or *u.* (Job 2.)

In *chance* and *charge,* underline the *c* and *g* once and the *e* twice and write small threes beside each double underlining to signal that the *e* lets the *c* and *g* say their second sounds. (Job 3.)

In *little,* underline the *e* twice and write a small four beside the double underlining to signal that every syllable must have a vowel. (Job 4.)

In *are,* underline the *e* twice and write a tiny five beside the double underlining to signal that this *e* is retained from Old English. (Job 5—no job *e.*)

8. Have students use a black pencil to draw a brace in front of the set of silent final *e* words. Have them write the title *Silent final e's* before the brace as shown.

9. After all words have been written, marked, and checked for accuracy, have students read all the words for spelling and reading.

💡 Model Thinking

Use rule 7 (see page 223) to read and write final silent *e* words. Demonstrate on the board and say, "When I see a silent final *e* word like *line,* I will read *līne* because I know the *e* lets the *i* say /ī/. When I want to spell the word *give,* I know I write a silent *e* because English words don't end in *v.*"

✓ Check for Understanding

Provide example words and have students mark and explain the jobs of *e.*

☆ Provide Practice

Provide a list of silent final *e* words and have students categorize them under one of the five jobs and explain their reasoning.

✐ Check Application

In the writing lesson, dictate sentences that include silent final *e* words from the spelling lesson. Have students proofread these sentences written on the board or at their desks. Finally, check their application of the rule when they write words independently in sentences and compositions.

On a *daily* basis, review words that use the first seven rules taught on rule page 1 and shown in "Instructional Materials," on page 223. Explain to students that these are facts about the language that will help them write and read words. Making constant reference to the facts either on the rule page 1 chart in the primary classroom or rule page 1 in the intermediate notebook gives students understanding and security in speaking, writing, and reading.

Rule Page 2 (Rule 8)

Rule page 2 includes words that illustrate the five spellings for the sound /er/. Rule 8, "The phonogram *or* may say /er/ when it follows *w* (*work*)," is also illustrated on this page.

Before primary children write the word *over* in sections A–G, write the nonsense sentence *Her first nurse works early* on chart paper or the board. Under each word, list the Ayres words that illustrate that spelling as it occurs in spelling dictation and words encountered in their reading lessons.

Have students in third grade and above write rule page 2 just before you dictate the first Ayres word that uses one of the five spellings of the sound /er/.

Children of all ages should memorize the sentence that lists the *er*'s to enhance retention. Explain that the spelling *er* is used most often.

Rule Page 2 Procedures with Precise Dialogue

Day 1

1. Have students measure side 1 of the page to divide into three equal columns. Have them draw lines between the columns as shown and fold side 2 of rule page 2 in half, providing a total of five columns.

2. Dictate the nonsense sentence *Her first nurse works early*. Demonstrate how to center each word in a separate column on the

Her	first	nurse	works	early
serve	sir	turn	worm	learn
herd	bird	hurt	word	heard
dinner	third	burn	world	search
perfect	girl	church	worth	earn
nerve	fir	fur	worthy	earth
berth	birth	purpose	worse	earnest
western	skirt	surprise	worst	pearl
merge	circle	hurdle	worry	rehearse
grocery	firm	Thursday	worship	
perch	thirst	Saturday		
sterling	squirt	further		
verse	squirm	disturb		
clerk	chirp	curtain		
certain	confirm	curve		

top line and write the word *early* in syllables. Have students write the sentence and underline and number the silent *e* in *nurse* in black. Then have them underline the five spellings of *er* in red. They do *not* underline the *w* in the word *works*.

3. Have students skip a space. Then dictate the next five words across the columns on the third line. Have students underline and number the *v* and *e* in black. (For third-grade students, writing three rows may be sufficient for day 1.) Have them underline the *er*'s in red to focus attention on the five spellings of *er*.

4. After the words have been written, marked, and checked for accuracy, have students read the words in each column for spelling and reading.

✓ *Check for Understanding*

Ask questions about words using these spellings. For example, "Which /er/ is in *church*?" The answer is, "The /er/ of *nurse*."

☆ *Provide Practice*

Cover the words on the board. Dictate a word using one of the five spellings for *er*. Have students write it on the board or at their desks.

✎ *Check Application*

In the writing lesson, dictate sentences that include these words. Have students proofread their sentences. Finally, check their application of the rule when they write words independently in sentences and compositions.

Day 2

1. Finish dictating words across columns, having students underline in black. Then underline the *er*'s in red.
2. After the words have been written, marked, and checked for accuracy, have students read the words down each column for spelling and reading. Reading each column of words helps students remember which phonogram is used in each word.

✓ *Check for Understanding*

Ask students to clarify which /er/ is used in any word on this page.

☆ *Provide Practice*

Provide multiple opportunities to read for spelling and reading. Cover the words on the board. Dictate a word and have students write it on the board or at their desks.

✎ *Check Application*

In the writing lesson, dictate sentences using these words. Have students proofread their sentences. Finally, check their application of the rule when they write words independently in sentences and compositions.

Rule Page 3 (Rule 9 and 10)

This rule page includes words that illustrate how to form derived words by adding to base words suffixes that begin with a vowel. Students in all grades receive instruction and practice in these rules because they are basic to English spelling. Reasoning is required to spell words that follow these rules.

Teach primary children rule 9 just before writing the first derived word in the notebook (*setting* in section K of the Extended Ayres Word List). "For *one*-syllable words that have *one* vowel, and end in *one* consonant (*hop*), write another final consonant (*hop + ped*) before adding endings that begin with a vowel." Rule 9 can be called the *one-one-one* rule. On the left side of chart paper or the board, write base words. On the bottom right, add most common endings (e.g., *ing, er, ed*). Explain how to use the rule to spell derived words. See the explanation below.

Have students in grades three and above write the words on rule page 3 in the intermediate notebook just before you dictate the first Ayres word that illustrates rule 9.

Rule Page 3 Procedures with Precise Dialogue

Side 1—Rule 9

1. Side 1 of rule page 3 is already folded in half.
2. Dictate the heading *hop*. Have students center it on the first line in column 1.
3. Have students skip a space. Dictate all base words in column 1. Have students underline and number in black as appropriate.
4. Have students skip three spaces, and then dictate the title *Endings which begin with a vowel*. Demonstrate how to center the title on three lines in column 1.
5. Have students skip one space below the last base word in column 1 and move to column 2. Dictate the endings. Have students write the endings one below the other, underlining, numbering, and bracing pairs in black. Have them use a black pencil to draw a brace in front of the set of endings that begin with a vowel.

Model Thinking

Say, "I want to add the ending *ing* to *hop*. This ending begins with a vowel. *Hop* is *one syllable*, ending in *one consonant*, *p*, with *one vowel*, *o*, before it, so I must write another *p* before adding the ending *ing*." Think aloud as you explain that the added consonant preserves the vowel sound in *hop*.

6. Dictate the heading *hopping*. Have students write it in syllables on the first line of the second column and underline *ng* in black. Then have them underline the added *p* twice in red to indicate that the consonant is needed to preserve the vowel sound but is silent when read.
7. Have students skip a space. Dictate each derived word. Have students explain and then apply the rule to each word as they write it in column 2 opposite the base word

in column 1 (see "Check for Understanding"). Students underline and number in black as appropriate. Explain that the word *writ* is the archaic past tense of *write*. The word *writ* is still used as a noun in some documents. Writing the base word helps children understand why we write *writ ten*. After dictating *ship*, explain that *shipped* is one syllable because the base word does not end in the sound /d/ or /t/ (see rule 28, page 225).

8. Have students underline the added consonant in each word twice in red to indicate that the consonant is added for spelling but is silent when read.

9. After all words have been written, marked, and checked for accuracy, have students read derived words for spelling and reading.

✔ Check for Understanding

Ask, "How do we add *ing* to *set*?" The student replies, "We write a second /t/, since *set* has one syllable, one consonant at the end, one vowel before the last consonant, and the ending begins with a vowel." Ask, "How do you add the ending *ment* to *ship*?" The answer should be, "We do not add another /p/ to *ship* because *ment* begins with a consonant, not a vowel." Ask, "How do we add the past tense ending (*ed*) to *talk*?" The reply should be, "We do not write a second /k/, since this base word ends in two consonants, not just one."

☆ Provide Practice

The Spalding Word Builder Cards (see Resources) provide opportunities for guided and independent practice adding endings to base words. Use Word Builders in whole or small groups. Have students explain that the purpose of adding a consonant to a base word before adding an ending that begins with a vowel is to preserve the vowel sounds. Also have students explain how the meaning of the ending changes the meaning of the base word. (For example, the ending *er* changes the verb *run* to a noun meaning "one who runs.")

✐ Check Application

In the writing lesson, dictate sentences. Have students write them on the board or at their desks and proofread the sentences. Finally, check their application of the rule when they write words independently in sentences and compositions.

Next, teach the concept of an accented syllable. Say the word with the accent on the correct and then the incorrect syllable. If children have difficulty, use the word in a sentence, alternating the correct and incorrect accents. After students can identify which syllable has the accent, teach rule page 3, side 2 (rule 10), "Words of two syllables (*be gin*) in which the second syllable (*gin*) is *accented* and ends in *one* consonant, with *one* vowel before it, need another final consonant (*be gin + ning*) before adding an ending that begins with a vowel."

Side 2—Rule 10

1. Fold side 2 in half. Explain that on side 2, we will write words that add endings that begin with vowels to two-syllable words.
2. Dictate the heading *begin*. Have students write it in syllables centered on the first line of column 1 of side 2 and then underline *e* in black. They use their red pencils to place the accent on the second syllable.
3. Have students skip one space. Dictate all the base words in column 1.
4. After students write all words in syllables and appropriately underline phonograms in black, have them use a red pencil to mark the accented syllables.

Model Thinking

Say, "I want to add the ending *ing* to the verb *begin*. The ending *ing* begins with a vowel. The accent is on the second syllable *gin*, and *gin* ends with one consonant, *n*, with one vowel, *i*, before it, so I must add another consonant, *n*, before adding the ending *ing*."

5. Dictate the heading *beginning*. Have students write it in syllables centered on the first line of column 2. Students underline *e* and *ng* in black, then underline the added *n* twice in red to show that it is silent when read.
6. Have students skip a space. Dictate each derived word. Have students explain and apply the rule to each word as they write it in column 2 opposite the base word in column 1, underlining in black (see "Check for Understanding").
7. Have students underline the added consonants in each word twice in red to indicate that the consonant is added for spelling but is silent when read.
8. Have students skip three spaces to separate the sections. Dictate the base words that do not have the accent on the second syllable. Students underline appropriately and mark the accented syllables in black.
9. Dictate the derived words that do not add another consonant. Students underline and number appropriately in black.
10. After all words have been written, marked, and checked for accuracy, have students read the words down and across two columns for spelling and reading.

✓ *Check for Understanding*

Ask, "How do you add the ending *ence* to *occur*?" The students' answer should be, "The ending *ence* begins with a vowel. We add another /r/ to *cur* because the accent is on *cur*, which has one vowel, *u*, followed by one consonant, *r*." Ask, "How do we add the past tense ending (*ed*) to *enter*?" The reply should be, "We do not write a second /r/, since the accent is on the first syllable, *en*."

Provide Practice

Use Word Builder Cards in whole or small groups. Have students add endings to multisyllabic base words that meet the criteria of rule 10 and those that do not until students can easily apply this rule when they are independently writing.

✍ *Check Application*

In the writing lesson, dictate sentences. Have students write these sentences on the board or at their desks. Have students proofread sentences. Finally, check their application of the rule when they write words independently in sentences and compositions.

Rule Page 4 (Rule 11)

Rule page 4 includes words that illustrate how to form derived words by adding suffixes that begin with a vowel to base words that end in a final silent *e*. "Words ending with a silent final *e* (*come*) are written without the *e* when adding an ending that begins with a vowel."

Teach primary children rule 11 just before they write *coming* from section K of the Extended Ayres Word List (see page 287). On the left side of chart paper or the board, write base words. On the bottom right, add most common endings (e.g., *ing, er, ed*). Explain how to use the rule to spell derived words. See the explanation below. Have third-grade and older students write the words on rule page 4 in the intermediate notebook after they complete rule page 3 and just before you dictate the first Ayres word that illustrates rule 11.

Rule Page 4 Procedures with Precise Dialogue

Side 1—Rule 11

1. Explain that rule page 4 is single-sided. On this page, we will add endings that begin with vowels to words that end in silent final *e*.

2. Dictate the heading *hope*. Have students center it on the first line in the first column. Have them underline the *o, p,* and *e* in red.

3. Have students skip a space. Dictate and have students write the base words in the first column, underlining and numbering in black as appropriate. After all words are written, have students use a red pencil to underline and number the silent final *e*'s.

continued

4. Have students skip three spaces. Dictate the title *Endings beginning with a vowel.* Demonstrate how to center the title on three lines in column 1.

5. Have students skip one space below the last base word in column 1 and move to column 2.

6. Dictate the endings. Have students write them in column 2 one below the other, underlining, numbering, and bracing pairs in black (see page 242). Have them use a black pencil to draw a brace in front of the set of endings beginning with a vowel.

🔆 Model Thinking

Say, "I want to add the ending *ing* to *hope.* This ending begins with a vowel. In column 2, I'll write *hope* without the *e* and add the ending to form *hoping.*" (Demonstrate.)

7. Dictate the heading *hoping.* Have students write the word in syllables on the first line of column 2 and underline *ng* in black.

8. Have students skip a space. Dictate each derived word. Have students explain and apply the rule to each word as they write it in column 2 opposite the base word in column 1 (see "Check for Understanding"). Students underline and number each word appropriately in black.

9. After all words have been written, marked, and checked for accuracy, have students read the words down the columns and across two rows for reading and spelling.

✓ Check for Understanding

Ask, "How do you add the ending *ing* to *come*?" The answer should be, "The ending *ing* begins with a vowel. Write *come* without the *e* before adding the ending *ing.*" Have students explain adding endings to words ending with silent final *e.*

☆ Provide Practice

Use Word Builder Cards in whole or small groups. Have students practice thinking aloud as they add endings to base words that end in silent final *e.* Their responses should sound like this: "I write the base word *desire* without the *e* before adding the ending *able* because *able* begins with a vowel." *Frequently have students identify base words in derived words.*

✎ Check Application

In the writing lesson, dictate sentences. Students proofread these sentences written on the board or at their desks. Finally, check their application of the rule when they write words independently in sentences and compositions.

Students must be well taught to see that these endings are added to base words. They must recognize each base word even when the ending forms a separate syllable and the single vowel in the preceding syllable is not marked (*hop ing*).

Rule Page 5 (Rule 12)

This rule page includes words that illustrate rule 12 (see page 224). It is necessary when teaching this rule page to say the names of the letters *ie* and *ei*. Rule 12 tells which phonogram to use: "After *c* we use *ei* (*receive*). If we say /ā/, we use *ei* (*vein*). In the list of exceptions, we use *ei*. In all other words, the phonogram *ie* is used."

This spelling rule is taught to *primary* students as needed to spell Ayres words. For grade two, write the column headings *ie, cei,* and *ei says "ā"* on chart paper or on the board. Add words containing these spellings as needed, beginning with *field* in section L of the Extended Ayres Word List. Have students in *third grade or above* write the words on rule page 5 just before you dictate the first Ayres word that includes one of these two phonograms.

Rule Page 5 Procedures with Precise Dialogue

Day 1

1. Have students fold both sides of rule page 5 in half to form four columns.

2. Using the names of the letters, have students center *ie* in column 1, *cei* in column 2, and *ei says "ā"* in column 3. Students underline each phonogram in red.

ie	*cei*	*ei says "ā"*	Exceptions
believe	receive	their	Neither
belief	perceive	veil	foreign
fierce	ceiling	heir	sovereign
brief	receipt	rein	seized (the)
niece	conceit	reign	counterfeit (and)
priest		vein	forfeited
field		surveillance	leisure
chief		skein	
siege			either
achieve			weird
piece			protein
pie			heifer
lie			
prairie			
mischief			
friend			

3. Have students skip a space. Dictate words going across columns 1, 2, and 3 (not down the page) to help students learn when to use *ie* or *ei*. Students underline, number, and brace appropriately in black. For students beginning third grade, five rows may be sufficient for day 1. After these words have been written, have students use a red pencil to underline the *ie* or *ei*.

4. After all words have been written, marked, and checked for accuracy, have students read the words across and down two columns for reading and spelling.

✔ *Check for Understanding*
Ask, "Which spelling is used in *receive*?" The student should say, "I use *ei* because it comes after a *c*"; or if the word is *brief,* "I use *ie* because it comes after *r* and not after *c,* and the sound is not /ā/."

continued

☆ *Provide Practice*

Cover the words on the board. Dictate a word. Have students write it on the board or at their desks.

Day 2

1. Finish dictating columns 1, 2, and 3. Students underline, number, and brace appropriately in black. Note that *the ie* says /ĕ/ in *friend*. Have students underline it twice to indicate it is an uncommon sound for *ie*. After all words are written, have them underline *ie*'s and *ei*'s in red.

2. In column 4, dictate the title *Exceptions*. Have students write the word in syllables and begin with a capital. Have them underline and number in black.

3. Have students skip a space. Dictate the nonsense sentence *Neither foreign sovereign seized (the) counterfeit (and) forfeited leisure.* Demonstrate how to write it in column 4. Have students write it, underlining and numbering in black.

4. Have students skip a space. Dictate the extra words in column 4. Students write the words, underlining and numbering in black. After all words have been written, have students underline and number the *ei*'s in red.

5. After all words have been written, marked, and checked for accuracy, have students read the words across and down two columns for reading and spelling.

✓ *Check for Understanding*

Cover the words on the board. Ask which spelling, *ie* or *ei*, is used in the listed words. For example, "Which phonogram do we use in the word *vein*?" The student should say something like this: "I use *ei* because I hear the sound /ā/."

☆ *Provide Practice*

Dictate words for students to write at the board or at their desks. Have students explain the spelling. Have students memorize the nonsense sentence in column 4 to help them remember the exceptions.

✍ *Check Application*

In the writing lesson, dictate sentences. Students proofread sentences written on the board or at their desks. Finally, check their application of the rule when they write words independently in sentences and compositions.

Note that the phonogram *eigh* is not considered on this page because this phonogram says /ā/. It is not *ei* alone. In the word *foreign*, the *ei* says /ĭ/ and the *gn* says /n/. They are not one sound, as is *eigh*.

Rule Page 6 (Rules 13–16)

This page contains the usual spellings for the sound /sh/ at the beginning of any syllable after the first one (see page 224). These spelling rules are taught to primary students as needed to spell Ayres words. Write *ti*, *si*, and *ci* on chart paper. Add words containing these spellings as they are met, beginning with the word *question* in section N of the Extended Ayres Word List (see page 308). Have students in third grade or above write the words on rule page 6 just before you dictate the first Ayres word that illustrates one of these rules.

Rule Page 6 Procedures with Precise Dialogue

Side 1

1. Explain rule 13: "The phonogram /sh/ is used at the beginning or end of a base word (*she*, *dish*), at the end of a syllable (*fin ish*), but never at the beginning of a syllable after the first one except for the ending *ship* (*wor ship*, *friend ship*)."

2. Explain rule 14: "The phonograms *ti*, *si*, and *ci* are the spellings most frequently used to say /sh/ at the beginning of a second or subsequent syllable in a base word (*na tion*, *ses sion*, *fa cial*)."

3. Rule page 6, side 1, is already folded in half. Dictate the headings *ti* and *si*. Have students center the phonograms on the first line of columns 1 and 2. Have them use a red pencil to underline each phonogram.

4. Have students skip the next space. Dictate and have them write the words in column 1, underlining and numbering appropriately in black. After all words are written, have students use their red pencils to underline the *ti* phonogram saying /sh/.

5. Explain Rule 15: "The phonogram *si* is used to say /sh/ when the syllable before it ends in an *s* (*ses sion*) or when the base word has an *s* where the base word changes (*tense*, *ten sion*)."

ti	si
na tion	ses sion
col lec tion	com pres sion
po ten tial	dis cus sion
pa tient	de pres sion
am bi tion	ad mis sion
sub stan tial	or
in fec tion	(tense) ten sion
in flu en tial	(manse) man sion
con fi den tial	
im par tial	
su per sti tious	si
tor ren tial	
po la tial	vi sion
	di vi sion
	oc ca sion
	ex plo sion

 Model Thinking

Say, "I want to write *session*. Since the first syllable, *ses*, ends in *s*, I will use *si* to write *session*."

6. Dictate and have students write the first five words in column 2, underlining and numbering appropriately in black.

7. On the next line, have students center the word *or*.

continued

Model Thinking

Say, "I want to write *tension*. Since the base word, *tense*, ends in the sound /s/, I will use *si* to write *tension*."

8. Dictate and have students write the word *tense*. Have students put parentheses around *tense* to remind them there is an *s* where the base word will be changed. Dictate and have students write the word *tension* beside *tense*.

9. Repeat the procedure in step 8 to write the words *manse* and *mansion*.

10. Explain rule 16: "The phonogram *si* may also say /zh/ as in *vi sion*."

11. Skip two spaces. Have students write *si* and center a small two above and between the *s* and the *i*. Have them underline the phonogram in red.

12. Skip a space. Dictate and have students write the next four words, underlining in black as appropriate.

13. After all words in column 2 have been written, have students underline *si* in red. Have them write a small two above and between the *s* and the *i* in words that use *si* to say /zh/.

✔ *Check for Understanding*

Ask questions like, "Which phonogram is used in the word *discussion*?" The student's answer should be, "The phonogram that says /sh/ /zh/ because the syllable before it ends in *s*."

★ *Provide Practice*

Provide multiple opportunities to read for spelling and reading. Have students identify the phonogram in words given orally. Explain the spelling of words on this page. Continue to give words to students to write independently.

✔ *Check Application*

In the writing lesson, dictate sentences. Have students proofread sentences written on the board or at their desks. Finally, check their application of the rule when they write words independently in sentences and compositions.

Side 2

1. Have students fold side 2 in half, and then dictate the
   heading *ci*. Have students center the phonogram on the
   first line of column 1 of side 2. Have them use a red
   pencil to underline the phonogram.

💡 *Model Thinking*

Say, "I want to write *facial*. Since the base word, *face*,
has a *c* where the base word changes, I will use *ci* to
write *facial*."

ci
(face) *facial*
(space) *spacious*
(finance) *financial*
(music) *musician*
(electric) *electrician*
(physic) *physician*
social
special
especially
ancient
crucial
efficient
suspicious

2. Skip a space. Dictate and have students write the base
   word *face*. Have students put parentheses around *face*
   to remind them there is a *c* where the base word will be
   changed. Dictate and have students write the word *facial* beside *face*. Have students
   underline in black.

3. Dictate and have students write the next two sets of base and derived words, underlining and numbering in black as appropriate.

4. Skip a space. Dictate the base word *music*. Have students put parentheses around
   music to remind them there is a *c* where the base word will be changed. Dictate and
   have students write *musician* beside *music*, underlining and numbering in black.

5. Dictate and have students write the next two sets of base and derived words, underlining and numbering in black.

6. Skip a space. Dictate and have students write the next seven words, underlining and
   numbering in black.

7. After all words are written, have students underline *ci* in red.

8. Explain that in some words, no rule governs the choice of *ti, si,* or *ci* for the sound /sh/.
   The spelling must be memorized, as in *influential*.

9. After all words are written, have students read the words down and across the columns
   for spelling and for reading.

✔ *Check for Understanding*

Ask questions like, "Which phonogram is used in the word *spacious*?" The answer
should be, "The /sh/ that begins with a short letter because the base word ends in *c*."

⭐ *Provide Practice*

Provide multiple opportunities to read for spelling and reading. Have students identify
the phonogram in words given orally. Explain the spelling of words from rule page 6.
Continue to give words to students to write independently.

continued

✍ *Check Application*

In the writing lesson, dictate sentences. Have students proofread sentences written on the board or at their desks. Finally, check their application of the rule when they write words independently in sentences and compositions.

For spelling and precise speech, it is important that the vowel sounds in each of the last syllables of the words on rule page 6 be said accurately. Unless the phonograms are sounded aloud, many rules of spelling do not make sense. It is the failure to combine the sounds with the spelling of English that makes it seem so difficult to learn and makes so many common words seem to be exceptions to the general rules of spelling. This is another good reason why it is important always to teach any new word by writing from its spoken sounds. The use of the sounds of the phonograms enables students to see clearly the relationship between the spoken word, the writing of the word, and the reading of it. If students, in this way, explain and apply these rules often enough, they will apply them when they write. It is the ongoing problem of teaching children to think before they write or speak. This helps them develop the vital habit of using their minds in what they do and say.

Multiletter Phonograms (Notebook Page 7)

For primary children, write multiletter phonograms on chart paper, an easel, or the board when introduced. Have students occasionally read the phonograms from the chart as an alternative form of practice. Have children participate in practice activities as described below.

Have beginning third-grade and older students write the phonograms on page 7 of their notebooks (see pages 248–249). Older students who have previously had Spalding instruction may write this page in one sitting. All seventy phonograms are now either on chart paper or the board (primary) or in the notebook (third grade and above).

Notebook Page 7 Procedures

1. Side 1 is already folded in half. Have students fold side 2 in half to form four columns.

2. Dictate and have students write the title *Multiletter Phonograms,* centering it on the first line of side 1.

3. Dictate the multiletter phonograms down each of four columns as shown. For phonograms having more than one sound, dictate the number first and then the sounds.

Multiletter Phonograms [handwritten chart with phonograms arranged in four columns]

4. Have students say and write the phonograms, bracing phonograms as shown.

5. Have students participate in practice activities that develop higher-level thinking and enhance retention. Examples follow:

   - Have students read phonograms down each column and explain distinguishing characteristics about each phonogram. (e.g., "The phonogram *sh* may only be used at the beginning or end of a base word, or at the end of a syllable; the phonogram double *e* is memorized.)

   - Have students use a separate piece of paper to categorize phonograms that have similar characteristics, for example, rule-governed placement (*ay/ai, oy/oi*), same sound (*aw/au*).

   - Have students read or write phonograms that have single sounds (e.g., *sh, ee, ar*) and then read or write those that have two, then three sounds.

   - Have students explain the use of braces in each set of phonograms.

   - Have students explain how phonograms *ow* and *ou* are alike and different.

   (Both phonograms have the same first two sounds, but *ou* is the only phonogram with four sounds.)

Additional Phonograms (Notebook Page 8)

Students in grades three and above write additional phonograms on page 8 of their notebooks (see pages 250–251). These phonograms occur often enough to be useful for older students. Teach these additional phonograms as needed to spell words in the Extended Ayres Word List. Use the following page(s) to write additional words that have these phonograms.

Notebook Page 8 Procedures

1. Side 1 is already folded in half. Have students fold side 2 in half to form four columns.
2. Dictate and have students write the title *Additional Phonograms*, centering it on the first line of side 1.
3. Skip a space. Dictate each phonogram in column 1 as it is needed to spell an Ayres word using that phonogram.

Additional Phonograms			
tch	catch	cu	biscuit
eo	people	aigh	straight
eau	beauty	sc	scene
augh	daughter / laughter	ge	pigeon
ce	ocean	rh	rhyme
gh	ghost	eu	Europe
gi	region	sci	conscientious
our	journey	pn	pneumonia
di	soldier		

4. In column 2, dictate and have students write the first Ayres word that illustrates the phonogram sound, underlining and numbering in black.
5. Dictate the remainder of the additional phonograms in column 3 and the word that illustrates each phonogram in column 4.
6. Have students participate in practice activities that develop higher-level thinking and enhance retention. Examples follow:

- Have students read phonograms down each column.
- Have students use a separate piece of paper to categorize phonograms that have similar characteristics; for example, same sound (*di/gi/ge, rh/r/wr, pn/kn/gn, gh/gu*).

The teacher or parent who meticulously follows all the procedures and details of teaching required for the students' construction of this notebook will be well rewarded. This textbook is entitled *The Writing Road to Reading* because writing the notebook develops students' understanding of the way the language works. Thus, the mastery of the notebook is key to students' success. Progress of all students will henceforth make the work of teaching much lighter and a source of pleasure. This is where competent teaching really counts.

Chapter Summary

In this chapter, we described in detail the Spalding spelling lesson. We introduced procedures for preparing children for reading and writing, teaching handwriting with phonograms, teaching spelling using phonograms and rules, and teaching language rule application.

Chapter 2 | # THE WRITING LESSON
CHAPTER OVERVIEW

Teaching Sentence Construction with Spelling and Language Rules
From speaking to writing

Teaching Composition
Using the writing process to compose three basic types of writing

TO BECOME PROFICIENT writers of the English language, children must learn a great deal. Speech, tone of voice, inflection, facial expressions, and gestures help to communicate what we intend. Writing, however, is a solitary, not a social, activity. We must rely upon clear thinking, precise selection, and correct ordering of words to convey our meaning.

Anyone who has ever attempted to put thoughts on paper in a coherent manner, or to describe or persuade in print, has already begun to develop what teachers call "literary appreciation." That is, they will have some insight into the complexities of writing and an inkling of the elements that make up good writing.

Emphasizing quality literature in the reading lesson provides children with good models for developing quality writing. However, good models alone will not bring success. Children need explicit, sequential, and cumulative teaching of the structure of language (grammar) and daily opportunities to practice what they learned by writing sentences and compositions.

Precise pronunciation and word accuracy are stressed in chapter 1. In chapter 2, the emphasis is on precision in the selection and use of words. Fine writers have an excellent command of the English language. They vary simple, compound, and complex sentences, using precise language in artful, descriptive phrases to achieve the exact effect they want.

Literate writing, according to Jacques Barzun, "depends on tone, rhythm, sentence structure, selection and organization. The *com-position* of all the elements of writing is what occasions the reader's pleasure while ensuring his comprehension" (Barzun, 1975, 6–7).

The Spalding Method includes instruction in composition as defined by Barzun. Its diligent application will provide students of all ages with control over the elements of writing. We cannot teach students to weave words into compelling tapestries like a Dickens or a Churchill, but we can teach them to write with clarity and precision and to combine words so that they follow the conventions of English and thus help the reader find his or her way. Good writing, when properly taught, is within the grasp of all students.

Spalding writing lessons are divided into two main strands: sentence construction and composition. Both strands are taught throughout the grades. With students of any age, the writing lesson begins with sentence construction. Each day, children *work* with the high-frequency spelling words that were introduced during spelling dictation. Beginners initially compose oral sentences that demonstrate meaning and correct use of the spelling words. After approximately 100 words are in their notebooks, they *write,* and read, their own sentences. These daily integrated spelling and writing lessons reinforce word recognition and meaning, rule application, and sentence structure, including parts of speech. Children apply language rules more quickly because teachers explain the purpose for each rule and provide integrated, meaningful practice. Knowledge of sentence structure expands as children are introduced to increasingly more difficult concepts throughout the grades.

For primary children, composition instruction begins after the attributes of written sentences are learned. Within a few weeks, primary teachers model composing two or three sentences about a single topic and explain the concept of related thoughts. While students are still practicing related sentences, teachers explain and demonstrate how to use the writing process to compose different types of writing. For older children, sentence construction and composition instruction may begin simultaneously. During preparation for writing (prewriting), children learn to gather information and plan their writing for different audiences and purposes. After committing their thoughts to paper (composing), they learn to revise for precise language, sentence order, clarity, and meaning. Once they have revised content, they learn to edit their work for capitalization, punctuation, grammar, and spelling. Finally, children publish different types of writing that communicate effectively and reflect their knowledge of standard English structure and conventions.

Teaching Sentence Construction with Spelling and Language Rules

Many language texts have a chapter on sentence construction and separate chapters on each part of speech. Because each is taught in isolation, students often have a hard time seeing the relationship between the parts of speech. In The Spalding Method, instruction in word meanings, usage, and order (syntax) are integrated from the beginning. In the spelling lesson, children pronounce, spell, write, and read high-frequency words. In the writing lesson, the meanings and appropriate use of these common words are reinforced. Children learn the attributes of sentences by listening to and discussing the teacher's model sentences. Then they write and read their own sentences. Explaining the use of words using simple terms and short sample sentences helps children understand how the language works. According to Farnham-Diggory (1990), this concept of integrated language instruction can be traced to the Greeks and Romans. In the Roman system, children first listened as the teacher spoke or read aloud, the children spoke in response, then wrote, and finally read aloud what they had written. The Romans explained that sight, sound, and sense were to be constantly interrelated.

Daily practice using words from sections A–G in oral sentences enables primary children to smoothly transition to writing simple sentences, followed by easy compound and complex sentences. After learning how words are used when constructing quality sentences, children learn the names of the parts of speech. Upper-grade teachers use simple diagnostic techniques to determine where to begin language instruction for older students.

Integrating listening, speaking, reading, and writing in every lesson not only facilitates all children's understanding, but also enhances their retention of complex language concepts. Teachers use a simple plan of instruction. They explain and demonstrate each new language concept. All children are included in class discussions that enable teachers to check their understanding. Children immediately practice each new language concept by applying it in written sentences. In successive lessons, teachers continue to provide opportunities for students to apply new concepts. They are actively engaged in learning how to express their thoughts, making these lessons exciting and enjoyable for teachers and children.

Oral Sentences—Sections A–G of the Extended Ayres Word List

Children must have an adequate speaking vocabulary to achieve quality writing at any grade level. The Extended Ayres Word List is used to teach word usage and the meaning of words that may not be in children's spoken vocabulary. The first 1,000 words in the Extended Ayres list account for 85 percent of words used in writing and reading. Words in sections A–G include the ten most-used English words and a majority of the words most used in reading and writing. Thus, after only three weeks of spelling dictation, primary children have a valuable word bank for composing written sentences.

The focus of the first part of the writing lesson is on meaning and use of each Ayres word. However, initially in sections A–G, more time is spent on correct usage because the majority of these words are in the spoken vocabulary of most kindergarten and first-grade children. For example, the first ten Ayres words include the pronouns *me, it,* and *she;* verbs *do* and *go;* the linking/helping verb *is;* the conjunction *and;* prepositions *at* and *on;* and the adjective (article) *a.* Often, children who have had good sentence construction modeled are able to use these words appropriately. However, many children need direct instruction. With each succeeding lesson, teachers reinforce correct word usage. *Labels for the parts of speech need not be given initially, but their use is explained.*

The following procedures are helpful for teaching correct word use to children of any age:

Procedure for Teaching Word Usage

1. Provide one or more simple oral sentences to demonstrate correct use of each word.
2. Explain the use of the Ayres word in each sentence.

Model Thinking
Think out loud as you explain the use of the Ayres word in each sentence.

✓ Check for Understanding
Ask questions that enable children to explain word usage.

☆ Provide Practice
In whole group, have children demonstrate correct use of each word in oral sentences and explain their reasoning.

Check Application
Have children independently use Ayres words when speaking and later in writing.

The Spalding Method is *not* a scripted program. However, sample dialogues are provided to help teachers make sure that all instructional steps are included. Although the following sample dialogue is presented for beginners, the basic language concepts and the procedure for instruction are the same for students of any age.

The focus of *initial* lessons is on teaching children to *listen* carefully to how each Ayres word is used in sample sentences. Children use Ayres words correctly in oral and later in written sentences and explain their uses. The following dialogue is provided for the first nine Ayres words. Each step in the above procedure is identified only in the first sample dialogue.

Word Usage in Sections A–G—Example Dialogue

Word 1—Usage

TEACHER:	"Class, when I dictated words earlier this morning, I used each word in a sentence. Let's talk about those words now. First, I will compose a sentence using a spelling word. I will explain how the spelling word is used. Then I will ask you to answer questions to show you understand how the word is used. Last, I will ask you to use the spelling word in oral sentences.
me	"The first word in your notebook is *me*. Listen carefully as I compose a sentence using the word *me*.
(Provide a sentence.)	" 'Give the book to *me*.'

(Explain use.)	"*Me* is a little word that takes the place of the speaker's name.
(Model thinking.)	"I could have said, 'Give the book to (my name),' but I would get tired of saying my name over and over. I use the little word *me* to take the place of my name. It takes the place of the speaker's name.
(Check for understanding.)	"What job does *me* do?"
STUDENTS:	"The word *me* takes the place of your name."
TEACHER:	"Is it only *my* name?"
STUDENTS:	"No, it is whoever is talking."
TEACHER:	"Yes. You have done a good job of explaining that the word *me* takes the place of my name if I am talking and your name when you are talking.
(Provide practice.)	"Now say this sample sentence: "'Give the _____ to *me*.'" (Have children give objects to you and each other as they say the sample sentence.)
STUDENTS:	"Give the pencil to *me*." "Give the picture to *me*."
TEACHER:	"Those are good sentences using the word *me*."
(Check application.)	(Make certain children continue to use *me* correctly in successive lessons. Have children independently use *me* when speaking and later in writing.)

Word 2—Usage

TEACHER:	*do*	"Listen to my sentence for the next spelling word, *do*. "'Bill, *do* your lesson.' "When Bill does his lesson, he is not completely still. He shows action or movement. During spelling, Bill says and writes his phonograms. We say that *do* is an *action* word because it shows that something is happening. Now listen to this sentence. "'Bill, *do* the dishes.' "Is Bill completely still or moving?"
STUDENTS:		"Moving."
TEACHER:		"Yes. As Bill washes dishes, he shows *action*. Now give me sentences using the spelling word *do*."
STUDENTS:		"*Do* your math." "*Do* your homework."
TEACHER:		"Your sentences show that you understand that the spelling word *do* shows action or movement."

continued

(Follow procedures.)		(Make certain children continue to use *do* correctly in successive lessons. Have children independently use *do* when speaking and later in writing.)

Word 3—Usage

TEACHER:	*and*	"The next spelling word is *and*." (Have two girls come forward and join hands.) "Listen to this sentence: " 'Ann *and* Susie are girls.' "The little word *and* connects (joins) the names of two people in that sentence. Now listen to this sentence: " 'Bill *and* Bob are boys.' "What job does *and* have in this sentence?"
STUDENTS:		"The word *and* connects Bill and Bob."
TEACHER:		"Yes. The word *and* connects two people. Now use *and* to connect two people in sentences."
STUDENTS:		"Bill *and* Jim are boys." "Sally *and* Susie play at school."
TEACHER:		"You composed fine sentences to show that *and* may be used to connect the names of two people." (Next explain that *and* can also connect two things, as in "I have a pencil *and* a pen," and two places, as in, "We go to the cafeteria *and* the library." Demonstrate using objects and places children know. Make certain children continue to use *and* correctly in successive lessons. Have children independently use *and* when speaking and later in writing.)

Word 4—Usage

TEACHER:	*go*	"The next word is *go*. Listen to this sentence: " 'John, *go* to my desk.' " (Have a child go to go your desk.) "Notice when John goes to my desk, he moves. *Go* is another *action* word because it tells what is happening. Listen to this sentence: " 'Diane, *go* to the pencil sharpener.'

		"Tell me whether Diane is moving or still. Also tell me what kind of word *go* is."
STUDENTS:		"Diane is moving. *Go* is an action word."
TEACHER:		"Yes. It tells what is happening. Now give me sentences using *go*."
		(Make certain children continue to use *go* correctly in successive lessons. Have children independently use *go* when speaking and later in writing.)

Word 5—Usage

TEACHER:	*at*	"The next word is *at*. Listen carefully to this sentence: " 'The children are *at* school.' "*At* shows a relationship between the word that follows it and another word in the sentence. In this sentence, *at* shows a relationship between *school* and *children*. The words *at school* tell where the children are. Listen to this sentence: " 'The children are *at* home.' "Tell me where the children are in this sentence."
STUDENTS:		"At home."
TEACHER:		(Make certain children continue to use *at* correctly in successive lessons. Initially, keep all words in the sentences the same except the noun following *at* so children can focus on the new word *at*. Have children independently use *at* when speaking and later in writing.)

Word 6—Usage

TEACHER:	*on*	"Now we will talk about the word *on*. Listen: " 'The books are *on* the table.' "*On* is another little word that shows a relationship between words, *table* and *books*. The words *on the table* tell where the books are. Listen to this sentence. " 'The books are *on* the desk.' "Tell me where the books are."
STUDENTS:		"The books are *on* the desk."

continued

TEACHER:		"Yes. The little word *on* shows a relationship between *books* and *desk*." (Make certain children continue to use *on* correctly in successive lessons. Initially, keep all words in the sentences the same except the noun following *on* so children can focus on the new word *on*. Have children independently use *on* when speaking and later in writing.)

Word 7—Usage

TEACHER:	*a*	"The next Ayres word is the single letter *a*. It tells us that a person, place, or thing is coming. The word *a* may only be used before a word that begins with a consonant. Listen to this sentence: " 'Give me *a* ball.' "The word *a* comes before a *thing* that begins with the consonant *b*. Listen to this sentence: " 'Give me *a* pencil.' "Does *a* come before a person, place, or thing and does pencil *begin* with a consonant?"
STUDENTS:		"Yes, pencil is a thing. It begins with the consonant *p*."
TEACHER:		"Good job. You identified pencil as a thing and you knew that *pencil* begins with a consonant." (Make certain children continue to use *a* correctly in successive lessons. Be sure each word begins with a consonant. Have children independently use *a* when speaking and later in writing. When the other articles *an* and *the* occur in sections A–G, explain that *an* is used with words that begin with vowels, and that *the* is used to mean a *specific one*. Continue checking for understanding, providing practice, and checking application.)

Word 8—Usage

TEACHER:	*it*	"The next word, *it*, takes the place of a *place* or a *thing*. Listen to these sentences: " 'This is my pencil. *It* is red.'

"The word *it* takes the place of the word *pencil,* which is a thing. I could have repeated the words: '*My pencil* is red.'

"Listen to these sentences:

" 'The table is big. *It* is white.'

"Which word does *it* take the place of? Is it a person, place, or thing?"

STUDENTS: "*It* takes the place of *table,* which is a *thing.*"

TEACHER: "You did a good job of explaining that *it* takes the place of a thing."

(Have children practice using *it.* Make certain children continue to use *it* correctly in successive lessons. Have children independently use *it* when speaking and later in writing.)

Word 9—Usage

TEACHER: *is* "Listen to this sentence using the spelling word *is:*

" 'Bob *is* a boy.'

"The word *is* links Bob with boy. It tells *who* Bob is. Listen to this sentence, then tell me what two words are linked by the word *is:*

" 'Jane *is* my friend.' "

STUDENTS: "The word *is* links *Jane* and *friend.*"

TEACHER: 'Good thinking. The word *friend* tells *who* Jane is. Now listen to this sentence:

" 'Bob *is* happy.'

"The word *is* links *Bob* with *happy.* It tells *how* Bob feels.

"Listen to this sentence:

" 'The girl *is* sad.'

"Think first, then tell me which two words are linked by *is* and whether we know who the girl is or how she feels."

STUDENTS: "The words *girl* and *sad* are linked by *is.* We know how she feels."

TEACHER: "Good thinking. The word *sad* tells how the girl feels."

(Make certain children continue to use *is* correctly in successive lessons. Have children independently use *is* when speaking and later in writing.)

Since words in sections A–G are in the speaking vocabulary of most kindergarten and first-grade children, few words will need explanation of meaning. However, as children progress through the Ayres list, more words need explanations. The following procedures are useful for explicitly teaching meanings of unfamiliar words, including compounds, homonyms (*sea/see*), and homographs (*read/read*).

Procedure for Teaching Word Meaning (Vocabulary Development)

1. Provide one or more simple oral sentences that demonstrate the meaning of unfamiliar Ayres words.

   Model Thinking
   Think out loud as you use context clues to demonstrate the meaning of unfamiliar Ayres words.

2. Explain each new type of word (compound, homonym, homograph) before children write the example word in their notebooks. Reinforce the word type each time a new example is encountered.
   Compound words (*into* and *today*—sections A–G)
   Explain that each word has a meaning of its own, but when joined the meaning is changed.
   Homonyms (*sea* and *see*—sections A–G)
   Explain that these words sound alike but have different meanings and often different phonograms. Reinforce this concept each time a new set of homonyms is written. *Labels need not be introduced initially.*
   Homographs (*read/read* and *wind/wind*—section J)
   Explain that these words are spelled alike, but the pronunciation and meaning are different. Reinforce this concept each time a new set of homographs is written. *Labels need not be introduced initially.*

   ✓ *Check for Understanding*
   Ask questions that enable children to demonstrate understanding of word meanings.

   ☆ *Provide Practice*
   In whole group, have children demonstrate correct meaning of unfamiliar Ayres words by composing oral sentences.

   ✍ *Check application*
   Have children independently use Ayres words correctly when speaking and then later when writing.

Although the following sample dialogue is presented for beginners, the basic language concepts and the procedure for instruction are the same for students of any age. This dialogue demonstrates teaching meanings of unfamiliar Ayres words. It may be modified as needed to teach compounds, homonyms, or homographs.

Sections A–G Words—Example Dialogue

Word 1—Meaning

TEACHER:	"Class, we have been talking for several days about how Ayres words are *used* in sentences. Today, you wrote the word *tan,* which may not be familiar to you. We are going to talk about this word so you will be able to use it correctly in sentences. First, I will compose a sentence that includes words that help you figure out the meaning of *tan.* Next, I will talk about how I decided which words to choose. Then I will ask you to answer questions to show you understand the meaning of *tan.* Last, I will ask you to use *tan* in sentences that show me you understand the meaning. Listen to this sentence:
(Provide a sentence.)	" 'Our desks are *tan,* or light brown.'
(Model thinking.)	"When I composed my sentence, I used the words *or light brown* to help you understand the meaning of *tan. Tan* means light brown.
(Check understanding.)	"Could an orange be called *tan?*"
STUDENTS:	"No, because an orange is not light brown."
TEACHER:	"That is a good explanation of why we would not select the word *tan* to describe an orange.
(Provide practice.)	"Now complete this sentence. " 'The _____ is *tan,* or light brown.' "
STUDENTS:	"The door is *tan,* or light brown." "My shoes are *tan,* or light brown."
TEACHER:	"Good. Your sentences show me you understand the word *tan.*"
(Follow procedures.)	(Make certain children continue to use *tan* correctly in successive lessons. Have children independently use *tan* correctly when speaking and later in writing.)

Having all students compose *oral* sentences from the beginning of sections A–G provides *integrated, multisensory* practice, which facilitates the transition to *written* sentences.

Spelling and Language Rules—Sections A–G and Above

A common frustration voiced by teachers is that children may spell words correctly on weekly tests, but they spell the same words incorrectly when writing stories or other assignments. Incorrect spelling when writing compositions indicates that children are relying solely on visual memory rather than applying spelling and language rules. In The Spalding Method, the Ayres words are used to reinforce correct spelling of words in context.

During dictation of words in sections A–N, primary children write words that illustrate all twenty-nine spelling and language rules. They note each rule in their notebooks until they apply it automatically when reading and writing. (See pages 229–234).

In *The Writing Road to Reading, all* rules are noted throughout the Extended Ayres Word List to provide teachers with a reference for planning integrated writing lessons (see pages 254–397).

To speed spelling dictation, rules are introduced, practiced, and applied in the writing lesson. Rule application practice begins while students are working on *oral* sentences and continues after they begin *written* sentences. The following procedure is used in the writing lesson to help children develop automatic application of spelling and language rules:

Procedure for Teaching Rule Application in Kindergarten through Grade Two

1. For rules 1–16 (taught from rule pages 1–6), follow procedures in chapter 1, pages 53–70.
2. Teach rules 17–29 before the first word that illustrates each rule is dictated in the *spelling* lesson.
3. Review rules as needed to achieve mastery (see pages 223–225).

💡 *Model Thinking*

Think out loud as you apply *new* rules to words included in daily dictation.

✓ *Check for Understanding*

Have children explain application of the rule(s) *to the new spelling word(s)* rather than recite the rule(s) in isolation. For example, when asked to explain the *pronunciation* of the word *me,* students should reply, "In *me,* the *e* says /ē/ because it is at the end of a syllable." When asked to explain the *spelling* of the word *will,* students reply something like this: "We write another *l* because *will* is one syllable and the *l* follows a single vowel saying /ĭ/."

☆ *Provide Practice*

Have children write, mark and explain pronunciation or spelling of appropriate words on the board. For example, in sections A–G, daily practice in the writing lesson will focus on rules 4, 5, 6, 17, 18, and 19. In whole group, discuss and revise as needed. Then have children independently write and mark one or two words at their desks.

Continue to have children explain the application of previously introduced rules until they can apply the rules automatically.

✍ Check Application

Have children apply the rules to other words in sections A–G. After children have been introduced to written sentences, have them apply pronunciation and spelling rules when writing and reading sentences. *Markings and rule notations are never used with words dictated for a spelling test or incorporated in sentences.*

Pretest students in second grade and above to determine in which section of the Extended Ayres Word List to begin dictation (see chapter 5, page 188). After students in third grade or above have been introduced to the seventy phonograms, have practiced manuscript and cursive writing, and have written rule page 1, begin spelling dictation in the appropriate section(s). Use the following procedure for efficient practice of rule application:

Procedure for Teaching Rule Application in Grade 3 and Above

1. Review rules 1–7 introduced on rule page 1 and rules introduced in the daily dictation lesson.
2. Prior to writing the first word that illustrates a rule or rules taught on rule pages 2–6 (rules 8–16), teach the rule page, following procedures in Chapter 1, pages 58–70.
3. Teach the rule prior to writing the first Ayres word that illustrates one of the additional spelling and language rules (rules 17–29).
4. Review rules included in each daily dictation lesson.

💡 Model Thinking

Think out loud as you apply new rules to words included in daily dictation.

✔ Check for Understanding

Have students explain application of the rule(s) to the new spelling word(s) rather than write the rule(s) in isolation (see sample explanations above).

☆ Provide Practice

Have children write, mark, and explain pronunciation or spelling of appropriate words on the board. In whole group, discuss and revise as needed. Then have children independently write and mark one or two words at their desks. Words in earlier sections may be used for additional practice. Continue to have children explain the application of previously introduced rules until they can apply the rules automatically.

continued

✎ Check Application

Have children apply the rule(s) to other words in the dictated section of the Extended Ayres Word List. After children have been introduced to written sentences, have them apply pronunciation and spelling rules when writing and reading. *Markings and rule notations are never used with words dictated for a spelling test or incorporated in sentences.*

Written Sentences—Section H and Above

Prepare children for *writing* sentences by first writing *simple* sentences on the board. Use Ayres words from sections A–G so all children are able to read the sentences with you. Use the following procedures with beginners of any age. *Labels for the parts of speech need not be taught initially.*

Procedure for Teaching Attributes of Simple Sentences

1. Write a short, simple sentence on the board using Ayres words children can already spell and read fluently: "The boy plays."

2. Explain and demonstrate the following attributes of simple sentences:

   One Thought—Subject and Verb

   A simple sentence contains *one* thought about a person, place, or thing. The person, place, or thing is *who* or *what* the sentence is about (subject). The action word (verb) describes what is happening. (Later, teach linking and then helping verbs as described on pages 99–101).

   Beginning Capitalization and Ending Punctuation

   The first word is capitalized to signal where the author's thought begins.

   A period (full stop) signals where the thoughts ends. (Explain use of question marks when the word *may* occurs in the Extended Ayres Word List, page 258.)

   Logical Order

   Words and phrases are arranged in a logical order to convey meaning (syntax). After introducing questions, explain and demonstrate that the subject and verb are reversed in questions: "*May* the boy play?" "I *may* go." "*May* I go?"

   Precise Language

   Precise language is used to describe the subject ("The *big* boy plays") or action ("The boy plays *now*").

    Model Thinking

   Think out loud as you explain capitalization, punctuation, spelling, word use, and your choice of precise language to strengthen and clarify your sentence.

✔ *Check for Understanding*

Have children explain each attribute of simple sentences. Have them identify missing attributes in sentences written on the board.

☆ *Provide Practice*

Have children use spelling words in sections A–G to write simple sentences on the board. Edit in whole group. Then have them independently write one or two sentences using selected spelling words. Students who have language disabilities or difficulty with fine-motor control should continue composing oral sentences even after written sentences are introduced. These children will hear explicit instruction in whole group, participate in the dialogue, and *initially* compose one or two oral sentences, identifying the attributes they would add (capital and period) if written.

✐ *Check Application*

Have children demonstrate mastery of simple sentences by independently composing two or three simple sentences daily.

Although the following dialogue is presented for beginners, the basic language concepts and the procedures for instruction are the same for students of any age.

Teaching Attributes of Simple Sentences—Example Dialogue

Steps 1 and 2

TEACHER:	"Class, you have been using spelling words in oral sentences for a few weeks. Next week when you begin section H, you will compose *written* sentences using those spelling words.
(Write a sentence.)	"Today, I will write a sentence on the board to show you what to include in your sentences.
(Explain/demonstrate.)	"A simple sentence has one thought about a person, place, or thing. Look at this sentence: " 'The big man runs.' "The words *the man* tell *who* the sentence is about. This sentence is about a person. The word *big* tells *which* man runs. We call *big* a *describing* word (adjective). We call *runs* an *action* word because it shows what is happening. "A *written* sentence must start with a capital letter to show where the author's thought begins. This sentence does begin with a capital. The period (full stop) shows where the thought ends.

continued

"A sentence must have words in the right order to make sense. If I said, 'Runs big the man,' it would not make sense."

Step 3

TEACHER: "Now I will think out loud as I compose another sentence using spelling words we already know.

(Model thinking.) "One of our spelling words last week was *boy*. My sentence will be about a *boy*. I must choose an *action* word to tell what the boy is doing. I will choose *play* from our spelling words. I will use a capital with the first word, *the*. I must put an *s* on *play* because I am talking *about* the *boy*. I must put a period (full stop) at the end. Now I will read my sentence.

" 'The boy plays.'

"I forgot to tell which boy, so I will add the word *little* to describe the boy.

" 'The little boy plays.'

"Now I will proofread my sentence to see if I included all the attributes. I started with a capital and ended with a period (full stop). I told which boy and I used the ending *s* on *plays*. My sentence makes sense because the words are in the correct order."

Step 4

(Checking for understanding.) "One word in our dictation today is *hat*. Yesterday, you wrote *mother*. Look at this sentence:

" 'Mother sees a hat.'

"Who is this sentence about and what is the *action* word?"

STUDENTS: "It is about Mother. The action word is *sees*."

TEACHER: "Good job of identifying who the sentence is about and what is happening. Think about whether the sentence is about a person, a place, or a thing. Then tell me which one and how you decided."

STUDENTS: "It is about a person because Mother is a person."

TEACHER: "Good job. You identified a person and explained how you knew. Now, tell me why I began with a capital?"

STUDENTS: "You began with a capital to show where the author's thought begins."

TEACHER:	"Yes, a capital signals the beginning of a thought. Why did I use a period (full stop) at the end?"
STUDENTS:	"The period (full stop) shows the end of the sentence."
TEACHER:	"Yes. A period (full stop) tells where the thought ends. How do I know that the word order is correct?"
STUDENTS:	"The word order is correct because it makes sense."
TEACHER:	"Could I improve my sentence by adding a word that tells which hat? If so, suggest some words."
STUDENTS:	"Yes. 'Red.' 'Big.' 'Little.' 'Pretty.' "
TEACHER:	"Those are good words to tell which hat Mother sees."

Step 5

| TEACHER:
(Provide practice.) | (Have children use preselected Ayres words to compose two or three simple sentences that include all the attributes.) |

Step 6

| TEACHER:
(Check application.) | (Each day have children independently compose two or three simple sentences that include all the attributes.) |

When children compose oral sentences, they often use words that they cannot spell. When they begin writing sentences, have them use their spelling notebooks as a source of words. Teaching attributes of written sentences with Ayres words helps children be successful. (Their ability to sound out words they have not been taught increases as they learn additional phonograms.) The interactive dialogue and the written sentences make the learning multisensory and help you check students' understanding.

After children are familiar with the attributes of simple sentences, begin explicit instruction in identifying (labeling) types of sentences. Primary children may begin with declarative and interrogative sentences, then they learn exclamatory and imperative sentences. Use simple terms and examples with the following procedure:

Procedure for Teaching Four Types of Simple Sentences

1. In separate lessons, explain the following sentence types after children can accurately write simple sentences that include all the attributes:

   Statement
   A declarative sentence provides information about a person, place, or thing (subject) and includes all attributes of simple sentences: "Ann is tall."

continued

Question

An interrogative sentence asks for information about the subject. It begins with a capital letter, reverses the order of the subject and the action or linking word (verb), and ends with a question mark: "Is Ann tall?"

Exclamation

An exclamatory sentence shows strong feeling, begins with a capital letter, maintains subject-verb order, and ends with an exclamation point: "Ann is tall!"

Command

An imperative sentence gives an order, begins with a capital, usually omits the subject *you*, and ends with a period or an exclamation point: "Sit down."

2. After introducing each type of sentence, write examples on the board and explain how the attributes of simple sentences are included.

✓ *Check for Understanding*

As each type of sentence is introduced, have children orally define that type of sentence. For example, when asked to explain a statement, students should say something like, "A statement gives information about a person, place, or thing. The first word must begin with a capital, and the sentence ends with a period (full stop)." After two or more types have been introduced, ask students to explain the differences. For example, students might say, "A question asks for information instead of giving information." "The action or linking verb comes first." "It ends with a question mark instead of a period (full stop)."

☆ *Provide Practice*

After each sentence type has been introduced in whole group, have children use spelling words to compose oral sentences of that type. Write examples on the board and have students explain the attributes. Next, pair students to compose sentences that are then discussed and edited in whole group. Last, have students independently write one or two sentences of that type. After all sentence types have been introduced, have students categorize sentences by type and explain their reasoning.

✒ *Check Application*

After each sentence type has been practiced, have children independently write one or two sentences of that type. Have them use four types of sentences appropriately when they write paragraphs.

Primary children were introduced to the term *compound* when they wrote Ayres words *into* and *today* in sections A–G. After children of any age accurately write the four types of simple sentences, use the following procedure for introducing compound sentences:

Procedure for Teaching Attributes of Compound Sentences

1. Review the concept of compound by discussing compound words.
2. Explain and demonstrate the following concepts on the board:

   Compound Sentence

   A *compound sentence* is two independent sentences related to the same thought and joined with a *connecting* word (conjunction). A comma is used before the *connecting word* to show that each sentence could stand alone (independent). Other attributes of simple sentences apply (see pages 86–87).

   Coordinating Conjunctions

   The word *and* is used to join two related thoughts.

   The word *but* is used to join two contrasting thoughts.

   The word *or* is used to join two thoughts that involve choice.

Model Thinking

Think out loud as you decide whether two sentences may be combined, so children have a clear understanding of the concept of relatedness. Model thinking out loud as you decide which connecting word to use.

✓ Check for Understanding

Have children explain the attributes of compound sentences. Have them explain which connecting word (*and, but, or*) to use when combining simple sentences.

☆ Provide Practice

In whole group, have children explain which simple sentences may be combined and have them state their reasoning. Next, have children categorize sentences into simple or compound and have them explain how they differ. Then, in separate lessons on the board, have them write compound sentences using *and, or,* and *but*. Proofread in whole group. Last, have children independently write one or two compound sentences using *and, or,* and *but* appropriately.

✍ Check Application

After children have been introduced to paragraphs (see page 108), have them use compound sentences that use a comma with *and, but,* and *or.*

Although the following sample dialogue is presented for beginners, the basic language concepts and the procedure for instruction are the same for students of any age. Each step in this procedure is identified in the following sample dialogue:

Teaching Compound Sentences—Example Dialogue

Steps 1, 2, and 3

TEACHER:	"Class, you already know what to include in simple sentences. Today, I will teach you a new kind of sentence.
(Review.)	Think back to when you wrote the words *into* and *today* in your notebooks. You learned that these words are called *compound* words. Today, you will learn to compose *compound sentences*.
(Explain/demonstrate.)	"A compound sentence is two sentences related to the same thought and joined with connecting words. Look at these sentences while I demonstrate how to connect two sentences about the same thought:
	" 'Ann plays tag. Ann plays baseball.'
(Model Thinking.)	"These sentences are related because they are about games Ann plays. I may combine them by changing the period (full stop) after the first sentence to a comma and then adding the connecting word *and* before writing the second sentence. Read the new sentence with me:
	" 'Ann plays tag, and Ann plays baseball.' "

Step 4

TEACHER:	"Explain a compound sentence. Then tell me which
(Check for understanding.)	connecting word and what punctuation may be used."
STUDENTS:	"A compound sentence has two separate, related sentences connected by a comma before *and*."
TEACHER:	"What does the comma before *and* mean?"
STUDENTS:	"The comma before the word *and* means that two separate, related sentences are combined."
TEACHER:	"That is a good explanation."

Step 5

TEACHER:	"Look at these sentences. First, tell me if they can be
(Provide practice.)	combined, then tell me your reasoning.
	" 'The dog is small. He is white.' "
STUDENTS:	"These sentences may be combined because they both describe how the dog looks."
TEACHER:	"Good reasoning. You understand that the words *small* and *white* both describe the dog. Tell me what to do to write a compound sentence."

STUDENTS:	"Put a comma after the first sentence; add the connecting word *and*. Do not write *he* with a capital."
TEACHER:	(Provide additional simple sentences that may be combined and some that may not. Have children independently write compound sentences that use a comma before *and*.)

Step 6

TEACHER: (Check application.)	(Make certain children use compound sentences appropriately when they write paragraphs later.)

After children have practiced using a comma before the connecting word *and*, use the same procedure to introduce compound sentences using the connecting word *but*: "Ann plays tag, but Ann does not play baseball." Then extend their knowledge by introducing compound sentences using the connecting word *or*: "Each day we play tag, or we play baseball."

Although primary children may not have been introduced to the term *conjunction*, they have learned to use the *connecting* words *and, but,* and *or.* Beginning with the conjunction *if* in section H, primary children learn the attributes of easy complex sentences using the following procedure:

Procedure for Teaching Attributes of Complex Sentences

1. Review the attributes of compound sentences: Each sentence in a compound sentence can stand alone; the sentences are connected by the words *and, but,* and *or* (older students may also use *for, nor,* and *yet*); and they are punctuated with a comma.

2. Before the word *if* is written in section H, explain and demonstrate the following concepts. *Labels need not be introduced initially.*

   Complex Sentences

   A *complex sentence* is made up of an independent group of words (clause) and a dependent group of words (clause). An independent clause has a noun and a verb and can stand alone. A dependent clause has a noun and a verb, but it cannot stand alone. Other attributes of simple sentences apply (see pages 86–87).

   Subordinating Conjunctions

   The word *if* is used to introduce a dependent clause. When a dependent clause is written at the end of a complex sentence, no punctuation is needed: "We will go outside *if it does not rain.*" A comma is required when the dependent clause is written at the beginning of a complex sentence: "If it does not rain, we will go outside."

   continued

3. Introduce each conjunction used with dependent clauses just before it is written in the notebook (*if* and *as* in section H; *after* in section I; *when* in section J; *unless, because,* and *however* in section L; and *while* in section M). Older children write additional conjunctions included in sections P–Z.

✓ *Check for Understanding*

Have children explain the attributes of complex sentences. Using sentences written on the board, have children identify the group of words that can stand alone (independent clause) and the group of words that cannot stand alone (dependent clause). Have them identify the connecting word.

☆ *Provide Practice*

Write compound and complex sentences on the board and have children categorize them and explain how they differ. Next, have them write easy complex sentences on the board using commas appropriately.

✐ *Check Application*

After children have been introduced to paragraphs (see page 108), have them use subordinating conjunctions in complex sentences and include a comma where appropriate. Older students may use other conjunctions appropriate to grade level.

Parts of Speech—Section L and Above

The focus of writing lessons in sections H–K is on teaching beginners of any age the attributes of simple, compound, and easy complex sentences. Children develop mastery of these basic tools of composition by daily practice composing different types of sentences orally and then by independently writing sentences of each type.

Another tool for preparing children to write compositions is to teach them to think about and discuss the structure of language. Teach children to categorize different kinds of *words* according to the jobs they perform. Being able to name, define, and explain characteristics of a category requires higher-level thinking. It enables children to understand why words behave differently from each other and why position in a sentence affects meaning and sometimes punctuation. Children are familiar with, and enjoy, categorizing different kinds of animals, colors, and objects. They extend that ability in the integrated writing lesson. Interactive dialogue in whole group improves retention because children learn to explain the purpose for each part of speech and participate in meaningful language practice.

Some kindergartners who have been taught The Spalding Method learn the names for some parts of speech by the end of the year. Use words in sections A–G for beginners of any age because children can spell and read these words, and they include seven of the eight parts of speech. With beginners of any age, *initial lessons are done orally in whole group.* The order of instruction of the parts of speech is optional. However, starting with nouns followed by action verbs is recommended because they form the foundation for writing simple sentences.

Following daily practice composing sentences using words in sections A–K, children can easily learn the names of the parts of speech. Use the following procedure to simplify teaching the name of each part of speech to children in first grade and those upper-grade children who have not mastered these concepts:

Procedure for Teaching Parts of Speech

1. In separate lessons, use familiar Ayres words to name, define, and explain characteristics of the following parts of speech:

   Noun

   A *noun* names a person, place, or thing. Nouns also name a concept (*chance, charge, time, today*) or a quality (*love*). Only nouns can be plural. Nouns may be the subject of the sentence: "*Bill* hit the ball." Nouns may be the object of verbs or prepositions: "The ball hit *Bill*." "The ball was hit to *Bill*."

   Verb

   A *verb* expresses action, being, or state of being. An *action* verb expresses the *doing* of something or what is *happening*. The action may be physical (*run*) or mental (*think*). A *linking* verb expresses the relationship between the subject noun and the noun, adjective, or adverb following the linking verb: "Mrs. Brown *is* a teacher." "Mrs. Brown *is* happy." "Mrs. Brown *is* here." Common linking verbs are all forms of *be* (*am, are, is, was, were*), *become, seem, appear, remain, grow,* and verbs pertaining to the senses (*look, feel, smell, sound, taste*). An auxiliary (helping) verb helps to form other verbs: "I *can* go." "I *am* going." Common helping verbs are all forms of the following: *be, can, will, may, have, shall,* and *do.*

   Pronoun

   A *pronoun* takes the place of a noun. The pronouns *I, you, he, she, it, we, you,* and *they* take the place of a noun used as a subject: "Bill is tall." "*He* is tall." The pronouns *me, you, him, her, it, us, you,* and *them* take the place of nouns used as objects: "Give the book to (speaker's name)." "Give the book to *me.*"

   Adjective

   An *adjective* describes or limits a noun or pronoun. Articles *a, an,* and *the* signal that a noun follows. Adjectives may describe which one (*big, little, tan*) or how many (*one, two*).

   Adverb

   An *adverb* describes or limits verbs, adjectives, or other adverbs. Adverbs may describe when, where, or how the action happened (*now, here, well*) or explain to what extent (*very* happy).

continued

Conjunction

A *conjunction* is a word that connects words, phrases, or clauses. The conjunctions *and, but, or, nor,* and *for* connect words, phrases, or clauses of equal rank: "Ann *and* Jane are friends." The conjunctions *if, as, after, than, when, unless, because,* and *however* connect dependent clauses with independent clauses.

Preposition

A *preposition* is placed before a noun or pronoun to show its relation to some other word in the sentence (e.g., *at, on, in, up, of, out, into, by, over*).

The preposition with the noun or pronoun is called a prepositional phrase. The noun or pronoun is the object of the preposition. Prepositional phrases may describe the noun (adjective phrase) or the verb (adverb phrase).

2. Using short sample sentences, explain and demonstrate how to identify each part of speech.

 Model Thinking

Think out loud as you identify the part of speech based on what it does.

✓ *Check for Understanding*

As each new part of speech is introduced, have children define that part of speech and explain how it is used in simple sentences.

☆ *Provide Practice*

In daily integrated writing lessons, have children categorize new spelling words by what they do (parts of speech). In whole group, have them use the part of speech in oral sentences. Then select a few Ayres words for children to use in written sentences.

✐ *Check Application*

Have children independently compose sentences that use different parts of speech appropriately. Have them explain the use of each word they use.

Although the following sample dialogue is presented for beginners, the basic language concepts and the procedures for instruction are the same for students of any age. This sample dialogue introduces the term *noun*. Each step in this procedure is identified only in the first sample dialogue.

Teaching Nouns—Example Dialogue

Steps 1 and 2

TEACHER:

"Class, you have composed oral sentences that show you know the meaning of unfamiliar spelling words and how to use them. You already have learned to *group* (categorize) objects by color, size, and shape. Today, I'm going to teach you to group *words*.

(Name and define.)

"You learned that a sentence tells about persons, places, or things. *Nouns* are words that name persons, places, or things.

(Explain/demonstrate.)

"I will write *Nouns* as a big heading on the board. Then I will make three columns under *Nouns* labeled *Persons, Places,* and *Things.* Together we will read words in sections A–G for *reading.* I will stop you when we get to the first word that is a noun. Next, I will list Ayres words on the board under those headings (categories)."

(Have students read words in sections A–G words for *reading* in unison. Stop them when they read *man.*)

Step 3

TEACHER:
(Model thinking.)

"I will think out loud as I decide whether *man* names a person, place, or thing. I know *man* names a person because I can talk with a man. So I will write *man* under the heading *Persons.* Read on."

(Have students continue reading words in sections A–G. Stop them when they read *bed.*)

"I will think out loud as I decide whether *bed* names a person, place, or thing. I know *bed* is a thing because I can touch a bed, but it can't talk. I will write it under the category *Things.*"

(Have students read words in sections A–G for *reading* in unison. Stop them when they read *street.* If anyone identified *today,* say you will explain *today* in the next lesson.)

"I know *street* is a place I can walk to, but it is also a thing I can touch, so I will write street under *Places* and *Things.*"

Step 4

TEACHER:
(Check for Understanding.)

"What is a noun?"

STUDENTS:

"A noun names a person, place, or thing."

continued

TEACHER:	"Good definition. How do you decide whether a word is a person, place, or thing?"
STUDENTS:	"You can talk to a person, touch a thing, and go to a place."
TEACHER:	"Good explaining how to decide."

Step 5

TEACHER: (Provide practice.)	"Now it is your turn to identify words that are nouns. Read on until I tell you to stop. Then tell me whether the word is a person, place, or thing and how you decided." (Have students continue reading words in sections A–G. Stop students when they read *hand*.)
STUDENTS:	"Hand is a thing. You can touch it, but it can't talk."
TEACHER:	"Good thinking. You know that a thing can be touched, but it cannot talk." (In whole group, have students identify nouns in the new spelling words and categorize them as persons, places, or things. Have students use nouns in oral and written sentences in successive lessons.)

Step 6

| TEACHER: (Check application.) | (Have children use nouns appropriately in sentences they compose independently. Have them explain how the noun is used [subject, object].) |

Daily checks for understanding questions and oral practice help children rapidly identify nouns. After students are able to categorize and label persons, places, and things, teach them that some nouns are *concepts*. A *concept* can be described but cannot be touched. Add a new category beside *Persons, Places,* and *Things* on the board, and list each concept as encountered in the Extended Ayres Word List this far (*chance, charge, time,* and *today* in sections A–G, and *day* in section H). Older students learn that nouns that are concepts, attributes, or qualities are called *abstract* nouns. Children's knowledge of nouns continues to grow as they proceed through the grades. Refer to chapter 5 and the writing scope and sequence beginning on page 445 for teaching additional grade-appropriate noun objectives such as forming plurals, using nouns as subjects or objects, forming possessives, and categorizing nouns as concrete or abstract.

A sentence is not complete without a verb. The *use* of action, linking, and helping verbs was introduced on pages 77–79. In the following sample dialogues, the focus is on introducing the names for these high-frequency words. Although the sample dialogue is presented for beginners, the basic language concepts and the procedures for instruction are the same for students of any age (see page 76). Follow the same six-step procedure for teaching parts of speech. Each step in the following dialogue for verbs is the same as for nouns. The dialogue on pages 77–79 introduced the *function* of action verbs *do* and *go*. The following dialogue introduces the term *action verb* and defines it.

Teaching Action Verbs—Example Dialogue

TEACHER: "Class, you have had a great deal of practice categorizing (grouping) nouns as persons, places, and things. Today, we are going to name a new category of words. Words that show action are called *action verbs.* Turn to page 1 of your notebook. The second word is *do.* When we talked about this word, I gave you this sentence:

"'*Do* your work.'

"The word *do* shows *action.* I will list *do* under the heading *Action Verbs* because *do* tells what is happening. Tell me about the word *go* and explain your reasoning."

STUDENTS: "*Go* also shows action because you move when you go somewhere. List it under action."

TEACHER: "Yes. The word *go* shows action. Look at this sentence:

"'I see the dog.'

"Which word shows action?"

STUDENTS: "It is hard to tell because you are not moving when you *see.*"

TEACHER: "*See* is an action word because your eyes are moving."
(Have children continue to identify action words correctly in succeeding lessons. Make certain children continue to use action verbs appropriately in sentences.)

During initial introduction, use forms of the verb *be* (*am, is, are, was, were*) alone as linking verbs. The following sample dialogue introduces linking verbs and then compares action and linking verbs:

Teaching Linking Verbs—Example Dialogue

TEACHER: "You already know how to decide if a word is an action verb. Today, I will teach you to name a new kind of verb. A *linking verb* is used alone to connect two nouns. Look at this sentence:

"'Bob is a boy.'

"The word *is* links the nouns, *Bob* and *boy.* I will list it under the heading *Linking Verbs.* The sentence is about Bob. The noun that follows *is* identifies Bob. Look at this sentence:

continued

" 'I am your teacher.'

"I know the word *am* is also a *linking verb* because it links the speaker, *I*, with the noun *teacher*. The words *am* and *is* are called *linking verbs* because they connect two nouns. They do not show action. Look at this sentence:

" 'Mr. Brown is a teacher.'

"Why do we call the word *is* a linking verb instead of an action verb?"

STUDENTS: "Linking verbs connect two nouns. Action verbs show motion."

TEACHER: "Those are good explanations. The word *is* does not tell what Mr. Brown is doing. It tells us he is a teacher. The word *is* links *Mr. Brown* and *teacher*." (Have children categorize verbs in sections A–G as action or linking. Then have them write sentences on the board that use linking verbs *am, is,* and *are* with nouns. Discuss and revise as needed. Make certain children continue to use linking verbs appropriately in sentences.)

After students can accurately use the verbs *am, is,* and *are* as linking verbs to connect nouns, use the same procedure to identify linking verbs that connect nouns with adjectives ("Bob *is* tall").

Introduce the use of helping (auxiliary) verbs when words *can, will,* and *may* are written in the Ayres list. During those lessons, explain that all forms of the verb *be* are also helping verbs. (See dialogue below.) This sample dialogue introduces the term *helping verb* and extends children's learning to categorizing verbs as action, linking, or helping. The same six steps apply (see pages 95–96.)

Teaching Helping Verbs—Example Dialogue

TEACHER: "Class, we have been categorizing action and linking verbs. Today, I have listed a third heading, *Helping* (auxiliary) *Verbs.* Some verbs help other verbs. When I dictated the word *can* in sections A–G, I gave this sentence:

" 'I can sing.'

"We talked about the meaning of *can.* When used with *sing,* it means *able to sing.* I could have used a different action verb. I could have said,

" 'I can walk.'

"I know that *sing* and *walk* are action verbs. The word *can* adds more information. It tells that *I* am *able to* sing or walk.

"Tell me what a helping verb does."

STUDENTS: "A helping verb helps an action verb."

TEACHER: "Good explanation of a helping verb. Now, look at this:

" 'Jose can talk.'

"Tell me under which headings I should place *can* and *talk* and then tell me why."

STUDENTS:	"Place *can* under *Helping Verbs* because *can* means you are able to talk."
	"Write *talk* under *Action Verbs* because it shows action."
TEACHER:	"Yes. The word *can* helps the action verb *talk*."
	(Make certain children use *can* as a helping verb meaning *able to* in succeeding lessons. Have children continue to use helping verbs appropriately in sentences.)

In subsequent lessons, teach the helping verbs *will, am,* and *may*. Explain that the helping verb *may* means the subject has permission: "I *may* sing." The helping verb *will* means the action will occur in the future. The helping verb *am* means the action is happening now: "I *am* singing." Explain and demonstrate that all forms of the verb *be* (*am, is, are, was, were*) can be linking or helping verbs.

Although most verbs show action, linking and auxiliary (helping) verbs are important because they are frequently used in writing and reading. These verbs will be practiced again after children are introduced to pronouns. (See dialogue on page 103.)

Use the six steps of the procedures on pages 97 and 98 and the words in sections A–G to teach the names for each part of speech. Remind children of the use for each part of speech as you now name it. In whole group, have children categorize these words. For example, in one lesson, have them identify each verb; in another lesson, have them identify pronouns. For convenient reference, a list of all parts of speech in the order of introduction in the Extended Ayres Word List is in "Instructional Materials" (see pages 413–441). *Do not have children write the parts of speech in their notebooks. When the notebooks become cluttered, it is difficult for children to read what is written.*

The concept of *person* and *tense* can be explained using simple terms and whole group activities. These activities train the ear to hear correct use and the mind to use correct form when speaking and when writing compositions.

Practicing Subject Pronouns with Present Tense Action Verbs— Example Dialogue

TEACHER:	(Before class begins, write the sentence pattern below on the board.)
	"Today, we are going to practice using subject pronouns with action verbs. Listen as I read this pattern. Then I will teach you how to decide which pronoun to use." (Read singular, then plural sentences.)

Singular	*Plural*
I see.	We see.
You see.	You see.
He sees. She sees. It sees.	They see.

continued

"Now read the pattern with me. This time point to yourself when you say, '*I* see,' because *I* refers to the speaker (first person). Point to one other person when you say, '*You* see,' because you are *talking to* one person (second person). Point to a boy when you say, '*He* sees,' because you are *talking about* a male (third person). Point to a girl when you say, '*She* sees,' because you are talking about a female (third person). Point to an imaginary animal when you say, '*It* sees,' because you are talking about an animal (third person). Point to all of us when you say, '*We* see,' because you are talking about all of us seeing (first person plural). Point to the whole class when you say, '*You* see,' because you are *talking to* the whole class. Point to children on the other side of the room when you say, '*They* see,' because you are *talking about* a group of children."
(Have children read the pattern again.)

TEACHER: "Why did you point to yourself when you said, 'I see'?"

STUDENTS: "I pointed to myself to show that I was speaking."

TEACHER: "Good explanation. Why did we point to a boy when we said, 'He sees'?"

STUDENTS: "We pointed to one boy because we were *talking about* one boy."

TEACHER: "Why did we point to all of us when we said, "We see'?"

STUDENTS: "We pointed to all of us because all of us were doing the seeing."

TEACHER: "Good explanation. Now tell me when to use the pronoun *I*."

STUDENTS: "When I am the speaker, I use the pronoun *I*."

TEACHER: "Yes. Tell me when to use the pronoun *he, she,* or *it*."

STUDENTS: "Use the pronoun *he* when *talking about* one male, *she* when *talking about* one female, and *it* when *talking about* one animal (or thing)."

TEACHER: "Good explanation. Tell me when to use the pronoun *we*."

STUDENTS: "Use the pronoun *we* when including others."

TEACHER: "Yes. Use the pronoun *we* when you are part of a group. Now, tell me which pronoun to use when *talking about* another group of people."

STUDENTS: "Use the pronoun *they*."

TEACHER: "Class, you really understand how to use the subject pronouns."
(Make certain children use subject pronouns correctly in succeeding lessons. Have children use subject pronouns with present tense action verbs in sentences.)

Choral reading of these patterns with other action verbs provides multisensory practice that trains the ear to hear correct responses. This improves retention. When children have learned these patterns well, model adding direct object nouns to expand the sentence: "I *see* the dog." "She/He *sees* the dog." "I *run* the race." "She/He *runs* the race."

After children have practiced subject pronouns with present tense verbs (*I see, you see,* and so on) and direct objects ("I *see* the boy"), extend the practice to subject pronoun/past tense verb patterns. Begin with regular verbs (*look/looked, like/liked, live/lived, land/landed, play/played*) because you can add the past tense ending *ed*. Then use the pattern to practice the past tense of irregular verbs (*do/did, see/saw, run/ran, make/made*).

Subject pronoun/verb patterns help children visualize abstract concepts of *person* (first, second, third) and *tense* (changes in the form of verbs to indicate the time of the action). Constantly check students' understanding of the meaning of first- and third-person pronouns because they are needed for writing first- and third-person compositions (see page 108). *Terms for first-, second-, and third-person need not be introduced initially, but the concept is taught.*

When students can accurately use subject pronouns with common regular and irregular action verbs in sections A–G, use the pattern to practice subject pronouns with linking and helping verbs.

Practicing Subject Pronouns with Linking and Helping Verbs— Example Dialogue

TEACHER: (Before class begins, write the sentence pattern below on the board.) "Now let's use subject pronouns to review what we learned about linking and helping verbs. Remember that the verbs *am*, *is*, and *are* may be both linking and helping verbs. Let's read the sentences listed under *Linking Verbs* together." (Students join teacher in reading first column.)

Linking Verbs	*Helping Verbs*
I am happy.	I am singing.
You are happy.	You are singing.
He is happy.	He is singing.
She is happy.	She is singing.
It (bird) is happy.	It (bird) is singing.
We are happy.	We are singing.
You are happy.	You are singing.

TEACHER: "Why are the verbs *am*, *are*, and *is* in these sentences called linking verbs?"

STUDENTS: "They are called linking verbs because they tell *how* the person or animal feels."

TEACHER: "Good. Now read the sentences under *Helping Verbs* in unison." (Students read.) "Why are the verbs *am*, *are*, and *is* in these sentences called helping verbs?"

STUDENTS: "They are called helping verbs because they help the action verb *singing*."

TEACHER: "What do the helping verbs *am*, *is*, and *are* tell us about the *time* of the singing?"

STUDENTS: "They tell us the singing is happening *now*."

(Have students continue comparing linking and helping verbs in successive lessons. Be certain children use linking and helping verbs appropriately in sentences.)

Correct use of action, linking, and helping verbs is fundamental for competent writing. Primary children can learn these concepts when simple terms are used and multisensory practice is provided.

Teaching Sentence Construction with Spelling and Language Rules—Summary

Students' compositions are only as good as the individual sentences that comprise their paragraphs. Knowledge of the parts of speech provides a vocabulary for discussing how to improve children's writing. Categorizing parts of speech and writing sample sentences in whole group help children use words appropriately when independently writing simple, compound, and complex sentences. During integrated writing lessons children are introduced to and practice increasingly more difficult language concepts (e.g., prefixes and suffixes). Therefore, practice of sentence construction continues all year long in every grade (see "Recommended Language Arts Scope and Sequence" pages 442–453).

Important Points to Remember

- Explain and demonstrate each new language concept orally in whole group so that all children benefit. Use concrete, familiar examples and interactive dialogue to make the learning multisensory.
- Use higher-level-thinking questions to check children's understanding of each new concept before providing practice.
- Provide multisensory practice of each new concept first on the board in whole group, then have children explain or apply the concept individually.
- Preteach, then reteach, difficult concepts and provide additional practice in small groups for children who have difficulty learning.
- Check children's ability to apply each new language concept by having them compose sentences that incorporate these concepts throughout the year.

Integrated writing lessons provide a unique way of learning how the English language works. James D. Koerner pointed out that

such matters as the forms of verbs, the cases of pronouns, the plurals and possessives of nouns, for example, are not optional matters. . . . Students must learn to use the appropriate standard forms automatically, not merely by memorizing tables or charts, but by constructing large numbers of sentences involving the desired forms. (Koerner, 1959, 97)

Education has been defined as the patient process of mastering details. This is especially true of writing. The ability to understand and express ideas requires knowledge of standard English, a sense of good usage and style, and precision of expression. The writer must be able to assess thoughts, feelings, information, and experience in order to determine what is relevant to the task at hand. In short, writing calls upon all the student's resources. It invokes mental discipline and involves a combination of intellectual processes as well as many specific skills.

Teaching Composition

To write quality compositions, children need to draw on prior knowledge of vocabulary and many spelling and language rules and concepts. These prerequisites are introduced and practiced in the integrated spelling/writing lessons so children can apply them automatically when composing different types of writing. Becoming an accomplished writer takes years of practice as children grow in their knowledge and command of the English language.

Composition instruction begins with teaching children to write sentences that relate to a single topic. After they can independently compose simple sentences, introduce related sentences. This should occur before midyear of first grade.

Related Sentences

The following procedure helps children compose related sentences. Children first learned the concept of related thoughts during class discussions of compound sentences. Children who understand the concept of related thoughts avoid the common tendency to wander from one topic to another.

Procedure for Teaching Related Sentences

1. Review the terms *subject of a sentence, first- and third-person subject pronouns,* and *related sentences.*
2. Explain the term *topic* as the subject of two or more sentences and demonstrate identifying related sentences and those that are not related.

Model Thinking
Think out loud as you decide whether two or more sentences are related.

✔ *Check for Understanding*
Have children answer questions that demonstrate understanding of the terms *subject of a sentence, first-* and *third-person subject pronouns, related sentences,* and *topic.*

☆ *Provide Practice*
Have children categorize sentences written on the board as *related* or *not related.* Next, have them write related sentences on the board and explain why they are related. In whole group, edit for capitalization, punctuation, spelling, and grammar (English conventions).

continued

> ☆ *Check Application*
>
> In successive lessons, have children use Ayres words to independently compose related sentences. Hold them accountable for editing for English conventions.

Although the following sample dialogue is presented for beginners, the basic language concepts and the procedures for instruction are the same for students of any age. Each step in the above procedure is identified in the following dialogue.

Teaching Related Sentences—Example Dialogue

Steps 1 and 2

TEACHER: (Review terms.)	"Class, you can identify the *subject of a sentence* written on the board. Daily you use nouns and pronouns as subjects of good sentences. You have learned that the pronouns *I* and *we* are called *first-person* pronouns because they take the place of the speaker. You have also learned that we use the pronoun *he, she,* or *it* when we are talking about a male, a female, or a thing. Today, I will show you how to use these skills to write related sentences about a single subject.
(Explain/demonstrate.)	"Read the definition on the board with me. " 'A *topic* is the subject of two or more sentences.' "When two or more sentences are about one subject, we say those sentences are related to one topic. Look at these sentences: " 'I have a pet dog. His name is Sandy.'
(Model thinking.)	"I know that these sentences are related because they both talk about one topic, my pet dog. Read these sentences with me: " 'I have a pet dog.' " 'I had eggs today.' "I know these sentences are not related because one sentence is about my pet, and the second sentence is about what I ate for breakfast.
(Check for understanding.)	"Explain in your own words why these sentences are not related. Use the new word you just learned."
STUDENTS:	"The two sentences are not about one topic. One is about a pet and the other is about eggs."

TEACHER:	"Good. You explained that a topic is the subject of two or more sentences. Related sentences are about one topic.
(Provide practice.)	"Our topic today is pets. I will call on several children to give two sentences about a real or an *imaginary* pet. Use the pronoun *I* to show that you are the speaker. In the first sentence, say, " 'I have a pet _____.' "In the second sentence, say, " 'His (or her) name is _____.' "
STUDENTS:	"I have a pet cat. Her name is Boots." "I have a pet fish. His name is Spot."
TEACHER:	"Good. You composed sentences about the topic pets." (Have students continue to compose related sentences about real or imaginary pets until you are certain they understand the concept.)
(Check application.)	(In successive lessons, have children use Ayres words to compose related sentences. Hold them accountable for editing for English conventions.)

While students are still practicing related sentences, introduce the writing process.

The Writing Process in Three Basic Types of Compositions

In the reading lesson, beginners are introduced to three basic types of writing: narrative, informative (expository), and a combination of the two, which we call informative-narrative. In the writing lesson, children draw upon their knowledge of vocabulary, spelling, sentence construction, and related thoughts to compose each type of writing. Putting all this together requires higher-level thinking. Just as explicit, sequential instruction is required for learning how the language works, so children need to be taught the *writing process*. Although the process is presented as a series of stages (see page 108), writers frequently move from one stage to another. For example, during the revising stage, the writer may see the need to return to the prewriting stage to collect more information. Daily practice of the writing process helps children become analytical thinkers and good communicators. By the end of first grade, students should independently compose one or two paragraphs about a topic of their choice.

The order in which the types of compositions are introduced is optional. However, we have found that children easily progress from writing two or three statements about familiar topics, such as pets or toys, to writing a short (four to six sentences) first-person informative-narrative paragraph about the topic. The initial paragraph is a simple progression from related sentences.

Procedure for Using the Writing Process in Three Basic Types of Compositions

1. After students can consistently write two or three sentences related to one topic, teach the basic attributes of paragraphs.

   • A paragraph contains two or more sentences about a topic.
   • Sentences present a logical and orderly arrangement of ideas.
   • Appropriate indentations and margins are used.

2. Choose a topic that lends itself to informative-narrative writing, is familiar to all children, and is broad enough to use for the teacher's model, class paragraphs, and independent compositions.

3. Read a short (one or two paragraphs) informative-narrative composition. (Later, read informative, then narrative, paragraphs).

4. Review the terms, distinguishing characteristics, and elements of the type of writing you are teaching (see chapter 3, "The Reading Lesson").

5. Explain and demonstrate (model) only one stage of the writing process at a time:

   Prewriting

   Prewriting is preparation for writing. During the *prewriting* stage, writers consider their audience and purpose, choose a type of writing, and select a topic and/or main idea. They decide whether to write in first or third person and collect information.

   Composing

   Composing is committing thoughts to paper. During the *composing* stage, writers incorporate the elements of the type of writing they have chosen. For example, if they are writing a narrative, they describe the characters, setting, and the series of events (plot). If they are writing an informative paragraph, they compose a topic sentence and sentences that support the topic.

   Revising

   Revising is refining the composition. During the *revising* stage, writers switch attention from being the author to being the reader. They revise for preciseness, order, meaning, and purpose. They ensure that their vocabulary is direct, concrete, specific, or vivid. They also check that words and sentences are in a logical sequence. Finally, they ensure their meaning is communicated and their purpose is accomplished.

   Editing

   Editing is reviewing for English conventions. During the *editing* stage, writers review capitalization, punctuation, grammar, spelling, variations in sentence construction, and indentations and margins.

   Publishing

   Publishing is presenting to audiences in a variety of ways. These include reading the finished composition aloud, posting it on the class bulletin board, displaying in the library, and printing in the school paper.

💡 *Model Thinking*

Think out loud as you demonstrate each stage. The more explicit you are in describing your thinking, the easier it will be for your students to write.

✔ *Check for Understanding*

For each type of writing, have children answer questions that demonstrate their understanding of the stages of the writing process, including the decisions made during each stage.

☆ *Provide Practice*

In whole group, have children practice using each stage of the writing process to compose one or more paragraphs for each type of writing.

✔ *Check Application*

In successive lessons, have children use each stage of the writing process to independently compose each type of writing. Hold them accountable for editing for English conventions.

The following sample dialogue takes place after children have been taught the basic attributes of paragraphs. For beginners, we recommend that prewriting and composing take at least one lesson. Revising, editing, and publishing may take another lesson or two. This dialogue demonstrates writing a short informative-narrative in first person and does not include all the elements of a narrative. Each step in the procedure is identified only in the first example dialogue.

Teaching First-Person Informative-Narrative Writing—Example Dialogue

Prewriting

	(Before class begins, display an organizer as shown on page 110.)
TEACHER: (Review terms/elements.)	"Class, in the reading lesson today, I read a short first-person informative-narrative paragraph that had one or two characters, a setting, one event, and factual information. We knew it was first person because the author used first-person pronouns.
(Explain/demonstrate.)	"The first stage in the writing process is called *prewriting* because we plan what we want to write. During prewriting, I consider my audience and purpose for writing, my topic, and whether I will be a part of the paragraph. Today, I will model

continued

planning an informative-narrative paragraph. I will use this worksheet to help me organize my thoughts."

(Complete the organizer, as shown below, as you discuss each decision.)

(Model thinking.) "I will think out loud as I make these decisions. Beside the word *Audience*, I will write, 'My class,' because I am writing for you.

"Beside *Topic*, I will write, 'My pet dog,' because my class enjoys hearing about my dog.

"Beside *Author's Purpose*, I will write, 'To inform in an interesting way.'

"I will write, 'First person,' beside *Point of View*. This means I will participate in the story to make my paragraph more interesting. I may use the pronouns *I, me,* and *my*.

> **Informative-Narrative Initial Organizer**
> Audience
> Topic
> Author's Purpose
> Point of View
> Character
> Setting
> Event
> Facts

"Beside *Character*, I will write the pronoun *I*, because I am describing my dog.

"Because this is not just a narrative about my dog, I will decide which facts I want my students to know about my pet. When I was writing related sentences, I told them his name and color. Under *Facts*, I will write his name, Sandy, and his color, tan and white, and add *huge* to describe his size.

(Check for understanding.) "Class, what decisions did I make during the prewriting stage?"

STUDENTS: "Audience." "Topic." "Purpose." "Point of view."

TEACHER: "Great! Which elements did I choose?"

STUDENTS: "One character." "Facts."

TEACHER: "Yes. I am the only character because I wanted to emphasize facts about my pet."

Composing

TEACHER:
(Explain/demonstrate.) "Now that I have finished planning what I want to write, I will use my organizer to compose a paragraph. This is the second stage of the writing process, which is called *composing*. During this stage, I compose sentences that include the elements on my organizer.

(Model thinking.)	"I will think out loud as I write. I will begin with the related sentences I already wrote about my pet. " 'I have a pet dog. His name is Sandy.' "Now I will tell his color. I will write, " 'He is tan and white.' "To describe his size, I will add, " 'He is huge.' "Now that I have included everything from my organizer, I will put my paragraph away. Later, I will decide how to improve my paragraph.
(Check for understanding.)	"Explain what I did during the composing stage."
STUDENTS:	"You wrote sentences about your dog." "You included everything on the organizer."
TEACHER:	"You told me two very important points about *composing*. I wrote sentences that were *only* about my topic and checked my organizer to see that I didn't forget anything." (Continue the writing process in the next lesson.)

Revising

TEACHER: (Explain/demonstrate.)	"Now it is time to improve my paragraph. We call this the *revising* stage. I will read my paragraph to see if I used precise language to describe my topic. I will also check if all sentences are in a logical order to make my purpose clear. Last, I will ask if I have included enough information about my topic." (Use a different-colored chalk for revising.)
(Model thinking.)	"Now, I will think out loud as I check for these things: "The first sentence says, " 'I have a pet dog.' "I will add *sheep* to tell you what kind of dog. The second sentence tells his name and the third his color. To the sentence about his size, I will add to my description by writing, " 'Sandy is huge and he has a big, bushy tail.' "Now I must write a sentence to signal that my paragraph is finished. I will write, " 'I am glad Sandy is my pet'

continued

"I have added information and precise language. I reread my paragraph to see if my sentences are in a logical order. They clearly show that I am informing about my pet, not telling a story. I think I have enough facts about my topic because I have described my pet.

"Next, I will add a title. A phrase that signals what my paragraph is about helps the reader. I will write,
" 'My pet.'

(Check for understanding.)   "Tell me what I checked in the revising stage."

STUDENTS: "Precise language." "Information." "Order." "Clear purpose." "Title." "A sentence that signaled that you were finished."

TEACHER: "Yes. We improve our informative-narrative paragraph by revising for precise language and information, sentence order, clear purpose, and meaning."

Editing

TEACHER:

(Explain/demonstrate.)   "The next stage in the writing process is called *editing*. We *edit* for capitalization, punctuation, spelling, grammar, indentation, and margins."
(Use another color chalk for editing.)

(Model thinking.)   "I will think out loud as I check for capitals. I must capitalize *pet* in the title because every important word in a title must be written with a capital. Next, I check punctuation. I forgot to put a comma between the parts of the compound sentence. I forgot a period (full stop) at the end of the last sentence. I spelled all words correctly. I must indent the first word to show that these are related sentences.

(Check for understanding.)   "Class, tell me what I checked in the *editing* stage."

STUDENTS: "Capitals." "Commas." "Periods (full stops)." "Spelling." "Indents."

Publishing

TEACHER: "The final stage of the writing process is *publishing*. Now I share my finished paragraph with others. I could share my

final copy by posting it on the class bulletin board, in the library, or in the office. Today, I will read my paragraph aloud and then put it on our class bulletin board."
(Read to class):

My Pet

I have a pet sheep dog. His name is Sandy. He is tan and white. Sandy is huge, and he has a big, bushy tail. I am glad Sandy is my pet.

(Follow procedures.)

(In whole group, guide as children use the writing process to compose one or more informative-narrative paragraphs. Write these on the board. As children compose each new class paragraph, review the decisions made in each stage until the writing process becomes automatic. In successive lessons, have children independently use the writing process to write short informative-narrative paragraphs. Hold them accountable for editing for English conventions.)

For beginners, the informative part of the paragraph is limited to two or three declarative sentences. The narrative part is limited to one or two characters. As students progress through the grades, require them to include more narrative elements and more specific facts. For example, if your class is studying early settlers in fourth-grade social studies, assign students a first-person informative-narrative on that topic in which they pretend to be a settler. Have students use the facts they have learned in social studies in their compositions. This integration reinforces students' comprehension of important social studies facts and enables you to assess their knowledge of both social studies and informative-narrative writing. Although kindergartners may only write class paragraphs, they learn that writing is a process, and that will make them better writers in first grade.

Follow the same procedures to write third-person informative-narrative paragraphs. Remind students that the writer does not participate in the paragraph when writing in third person. For the initial example, we recommend using the same topic to emphasize the difference between writing in first and third person. For example, the third-person informative-narrative paragraph would look like this.

Jane's Pet

Jane has a pet sheep dog. His name is Sandy. He is tan and white. Sandy is huge, and he has a big, bushy tail. Jane is glad Sandy is her pet.

Teachers should model and have students write third-person informative-narrative paragraphs on other topics as well. After beginners have independently composed first- and third-person informative-narrative paragraphs, it is easy to teach them informative writing. The following dialogue introduces a simple informative paragraph on a topic of interest to first-grade children:

Teaching Informative Writing—Example Dialogue

Prewriting

(Before class begins, display an organizer as shown below.)

TEACHER: "Class, in the reading lesson today, I read a short informative paragraph about bears. You know that an informative paragraph explains facts about a topic. It is written in third person. It may have a topic sentence that signals the main idea of the paragraph. I have written the definition of a topic sentence on the board. Read it with me.

"'A topic sentence is one general sentence that states the most important point about the topic.'

"The writer uses a topic sentence to help the reader find the main idea of the paragraph. Read the definition of a concluding sentence.

"'A concluding sentence shows that the paragraph is finished. Sometimes this is done by restating the main idea.'

"In the prewriting stage, I use a worksheet to plan my informative paragraph. I have listed *Audience, Author's Purpose,* and the elements of informative writing." (Complete the worksheet as you discuss each decision.)

"Now I will think out loud. I have already decided that you are my audience, so I will write, 'My class,' beside *Audience.*

"Beside *Topic,* I will write, 'Bears,' because we have been reading about bears.

"Beside *Author's Purpose,* I will write, 'To inform about bears.'

"Beside *Point of View,* I will write, 'Third,' because I know informative paragraphs are written in third person.

"Under *Facts,* I will list facts we have learned about bears in phrases instead of sentences:

"'furry; eat in summer, sleep in winter; different colors; eat meat fish berries and other food.'

"Beside *Topic Sentence Ideas,* I will write, 'interesting animals.'"

(Ask children to name the elements of informative writing, describe the decisions required in prewriting, and state the purpose for writing topic and concluding sentences.)

Informative
Initial Organizer

Audience _____
Topic _____
Author's Purpose _____
Point of View_____
Facts _____
_____
_____
_____

Topic Sentence Ideas _____

Composing

TEACHER: "The next stage is *composing*. During this stage, I will write a topic sentence that states the most important point I want you to know about bears. Then I will write sentences that state facts about bears. Last, I will write a sentence that shows the paragraph is finished. I will think out loud as I compose. The most important point I want you to know is:

" 'Bears are interesting animals.'

"Now I must state facts about bears. I will begin,

" 'All bears are furry.'

"Next I will tell what they eat and when they sleep.

(Leave out the commas when writing the next sentence.)

" 'They eat meat fish berries and other food. Most bears sleep all winter.'

"Next, I want to show that bears can be different sizes and colors.

(Leave out the commas when writing the second sentence.)

" 'Bears may be large or small. Bears are black brown or white.'

"They live in different places, so I will write,

" 'Some bears live in the forest but others live where there are few trees and much ice and snow.'

"I have composed a topic sentence and stated facts about bears. Later, I will improve my paragraph."

(Ask leading questions to help children identify the elements of informative writing included in the composing stage.)

(In the next lesson(s), revise, edit, and publish the informative paragraph.)

Revising

TEACHER: "The next stage is *revising*. In this stage, I reread my paragraph to improve it. I like my topic sentence because it clearly states the most important point about my topic. The next three sentences are okay. I will combine the next two sentences to be more precise.

(Leave out the commas.)

" 'Bears may be large or small and their fur may be black brown or white.'

"I will also combine and revise the next two sentences. I will write, 'Some bears live in the forest but others live where there are few trees and much ice and snow.'

"Now I must finish my paragraph. I will write,

continued

" 'People can see bears in zoos.'
"I need a title that signals my topic. I will write the phrase,
" 'All about Bears.' "
(Ask leading questions to help children identify decisions made in the revising stage.)

Editing

TEACHER: "The next stage is *editing* for capitalization, punctuation, spelling, grammar, and indentations. I started all sentences with a capital, but I forgot to use commas between nouns, adjectives, and compound sentences. I will add commas between *meat, fish, berries, and other food.* I will add a comma between *small* and *and.* I will add commas between *black, brown, or white.* I will also add a comma between *forest* and *but.*" (Ask leading questions to help children identify what to check for in the editing stage.)

Publishing

TEACHER: "The last stage is publishing. I will think out loud as I decide how to share my informative paragraph. I think I will read my paragraph to my class and then post my final copy on our bulletin board. I must remember to indent." (Read to class):

All about Bears

Bears are interesting animals. All bears are furry. They eat meat, fish, berries, and other food. Most bears sleep all winter. Bears may be large or small, and their fur may be black, brown, or white. Some bears live in the forest, but others live where there are few trees and much ice and snow. People can see bears in zoos. (Ask leading questions to help children identify ways to publish their paragraphs. In whole group, guide as children use the writing process to compose one or more informative paragraphs. Write these on the board. As children compose each class paragraph, review the decisions made in each stage until children automatically use the writing process. In successive lessons, have children independently use the writing process to write short, informative paragraphs. Hold them accountable for editing for English conventions.)

After first-grade children have independently composed informative paragraphs, follow the same procedures to teach them to compose narrative paragraphs. In the reading lesson, children learn that narratives may be written in first or third person. This dialogue introduces a simple narrative paragraph written in third person. It does not include dialogue because appropriate punctuation has not yet been introduced.

Teaching Narrative Writing—Example Dialogue

Prewriting

(Before class begins, display an organizer as shown below.)

TEACHER: "Class, you know the stages of the writing process very well. You used the writing process to write informative-narrative and informative paragraphs.

"Today, I will use the writing process to compose a narrative paragraph. You learned in your reading lesson that narratives relate an event or tell a story. A narrative does not have a topic sentence, but it does have a main idea (theme) that the author wants you to understand. In today's reading lesson, I read a short narrative about a helpful little girl. The main idea the author wanted us to understand in that paragraph is that being helpful takes practice.

"Now I will think out loud as I use a narrative organizer.

"Beside *Audience,* I will write, 'my class.'

"Under *Main Idea,* I will write, 'helpfulness.'

"My *Purpose* for writing is to increase understanding of helpfulness.

"I did not participate in the event, so I will write, 'Third,' under *Point of View.*

"Under *Characters,* I will write, 'Lori, Pat, and Mrs. Lopez.'

"Under *Setting (Place/Time),* I will write, 'Playground at recess.'

"Under *Event,* I will write, 'Lori fell off the slide. Pat and Mrs. Lopez helped Lori.'

"Under *Main Idea,* I will write, 'being helpful.' "

Narrative Organizer		
Audience		
Purpose	Characters	Setting
Point of View		Place/Time
Main Idea	Event(s) (Plot)	

Composing

TEACHER: "Now that I have finished prewriting, I will compose. I will begin by introducing two of my characters and the setting. I will write,

continued

" 'Lori and Pat went to the school playground at recess. They planned to take turns going down the slide.'

"Now I must introduce an event. I will write,

" 'Lori went to the top of the slide. She looked down and fell to the ground.'

"Next, I must tell what her friend Pat did to help. I will write,

" 'Pat ran as fast as she could to get Mrs. Lopez, the school nurse. Mrs. Lopez ran to Lori and checked her. Then she carried Lori to her office. After a short rest, Lori felt better.'

"Now I must conclude my narrative. I will write,

" 'She was grateful to Pat and Mrs. Lopez for helping her.'

"Identify each element I included in my narrative."

STUDENTS: "The characters are Lori, Pat, and Mrs. Lopez." "The setting is the playground at recess." "The event is Lori's accident and Pat and Mrs. Lopez helping Lori."

TEACHER: "You have correctly identified the characters, setting, and event. Did I include the main idea that I want you to understand?"

STUDENTS: "Pat and Mrs. Lopez were helpful."

TEACHER: "Yes. They were helpful. I want to explain more about what happened, so I must revise. I will put my narrative aside until later, when I will improve it. (Continue the writing process in another lesson.)

Revising

TEACHER: "I will begin *revising* my paragraph by reading every sentence for precise descriptions."

(Use a different-colored chalk for revising.)

"In the first sentence, I will insert *morning* before recess to tell when the event happened. In the second sentence, I will insert the word *big* before *slide* to show it was a tall slide. The next sentence is okay. To explain how the event happened, I will add *When Lori leaned over to*. I will delete *she*, the past tense ending on *looked*, and the word *and*. I also will add *she* before *fell*. The next sentence is okay. The sentence after that does not tell why Mrs. Lopez checked Lori, so I will insert *for broken bones*. The next sentence is okay. Now I must make my main idea clear, so I will change the last two sentences and write, *After a short rest, Lori felt better because Pat and Mrs. Lopez helped her. Lori was grateful.*

"What did I look for as I revised my paragraph?"

STUDENTS:	"You looked for precise language." "You checked to see that your meaning was clear."
TEACHER:	"Yes. It is important to check for precise language and a clear main idea when you *revise* a paragraph."

Editing

TEACHER:	"Now I must *edit* my paragraph. "I have capital letters for the names in the first sentence, and periods in the first two sentences. When I combine two sentences, I need a comma to separate the part that cannot stand alone from the part that can stand alone. "Explain what we check for when we *edit* a paragraph."
STUDENTS:	"We check capitalization, punctuation, spelling, grammar, and indentation."
TEACHER:	"Yes. Those are the important points to check whenever you *edit*."

Publishing

TEACHER:	"Now I will publish my paragraph by reading it to you and posting it on our class bulletin board." (Read to class):

Helpful Friends

Lori and Pat went to the school playground at morning recess. They planned to take turns going down the big slide. Lori went to the top of the slide. When Lori leaned over to look down, she fell to the ground. Pat ran as fast as she could to get Mrs. Lopez, the school nurse. Mrs. Lopez ran to Lori and checked her for broken bones. Then she carried Lori to her office. After a short rest, Lori felt better because Pat and Mrs. Lopez helped her. Lori was grateful.

Teaching Composition—Summary

First-grade children learn to use the writing process to compose three basic types of writing. These form the foundation for a multitude of writing tasks needed by students of all ages. Specific instructional practices for teaching these and other skills are explained and demonstrated in Spalding courses.

Having a command of vocabulary and spelling, and language skills enables children to concentrate on expressing their thoughts and ideas.

Professor Richard Mitchell explained:

The literate person is in control of those techniques special to writing. . . . He can formulate sentences that make sense. He can choose the right word from an array of similar words. He can devise the structures that show how things and statements about things are related to one another. He can generate strings of sentences that develop logically related thoughts, and arrange them in such a way as to make that logic clear to others. . . . Because he can do these things, he can, in reading, determine whether or not someone else can do these things. (Mitchell, 1979, 170–171)

Chapter Summary

Learning to be a proficient writer continues throughout a student's school career and beyond. However, every journey begins with a single step, and it is a teacher's task to see that the journey is well planned—proceeding from well-chosen words correctly placed to related sentences to artfully written paragraphs and compositions.

Spalding teachers also show the way by providing a map of three basic types of writing for students to follow. The Spalding Method is designed to ensure that students have the directions they need for a successful journey.

THE READING LESSON

THE ABILITY, along with the desire, to read well-written books is one, if not the major, goal of language teaching. Fine books fill children's minds with a wealth of knowledge of character and philosophy, of history and science, of humor and wit. They lead children into a wider world of wonder, beauty, delight, and adventure. Books that have won literary awards, or are of that quality, should be used for reading lessons beginning in grade one.

Good books are magical things. They inform the mind and touch the heart. They provide pulse-racing adventures and teach us the beauty of well-chosen words. They supply a storehouse of practical wisdom with which to confront difficulties still unmet. They help us understand ourselves. Rebecca Lukens noted that "a classic is a book that, despite changes in society, finds new readers in each generation and gives repeated pleasure and understanding upon rereading" (Lukens, 1976, 28). She summarizes, "A classic is a book that lasts, not because it is continually enshrined on lists, but because it continues to be read" (Lukens, 1995, 57).

The storyteller has been with us for as long as the human race has memories. Stories can be told in prose or in poetry. Through the miracle of print, the most durable of these can be shared with future generations. As children listen to and later read literature, they derive pleasure and gain understanding of people and the world. Finally, skillfully written language is stored, consciously or unconsciously, in the reader's mind and affects the quality of his or her own thought and expression.

However, reading, like writing, is a complex process, composed of many subskills. Children who have not mastered the subskills do not find pleasure in reading, and they suffer academically and emotionally. In The Spalding Method, children develop the *ability* to read in the spelling lesson. Thus, from the beginning, the reading lesson is focused on the thoughts expressed by the author. To foster a *desire* to read, books chosen for reading lessons should stir the imagination and paint pictures for the mind's eye to see. The list of books in "Instructional Materials" (see pages 206–211) is suggested for use in the reading lessons. Recreational reading should also be encouraged. Each child should have a library book to read whenever time permits. A list of suggested books may be provided to children and parents to aid their selection.

Spalding reading instruction is divided into three strands: literary appreciation, text structure, and comprehension. These strands are taught throughout the grades using increasingly more challenging materials.

The reading lesson for students of every age begins with *literary appreciation*. Initially, the teacher reads expressively. Children learn that fluent and expressive reading enhances their pleasure and understanding. Time is taken to appreciate the well-turned phrase, to admire or censure a happening, to read again a part that is especially worthy. As the teacher demonstrates and explains the attributes of exemplary writing, children develop taste. As they discuss the author's skillful use of the elements of narrative writing, they better understand how to use those elements in their own writing.

Through reading aloud, children also learn to speak and to write well. Although modern technology has produced many fine innovations, these are not substitutes for children being read to or for children reading aloud from good books—a process which, in addition to its other values, unifies the class by providing common experiences.

During the second strand, *text structure*, children are taught that authors organize their writing differently depending on their purpose for writing. Spalding provides explicit instruction in the elements of three basic types of writing: narrative, informative (expository), and a combination of the two, which we call informative-narrative. Knowing the elements of the three types of writing enhances children's comprehension by enabling them to immediately focus attention on the pertinent elements. *McCall-Harby Test Lessons in Primary Reading* and *McCall-Crabbs Standard Test Lessons in Reading* are used to teach and test children's understanding of text structure (see Resources).

The third strand of reading instruction is *listening comprehension* and *reading comprehension*. Unlike skills used in sports, music, and spelling, comprehension is invisible. Teachers make it visible by thinking aloud while reading as they use each of five mental actions. *McCall-Harby Test Lessons in Primary Reading* and *McCall-Crabbs Standard Test Lessons in Reading* are *initially* used because the short passages keep the process simple. Identifying and explaining the use of each mental action increases children's comprehension. Children soon learn to *consciously* use these actions to comprehend all subjects. See the reading scope and sequence for teaching mental actions on page 453.

Teaching Literary Appreciation

Good literature deals with the whole fabric of human experience, deepening understanding and stimulating imagination and reflection. Children are introduced to people they have never met and places they have never been. We want to introduce them, through literature, to the best our civilization has to offer. In literary appreciation lessons, children are made aware of the way in which literature connects with, and sometimes reflects, personal feelings and experiences. They experience the power and beauty of words elegantly expressed. For example, read a descriptive paragraph or poem and discuss the wonderful pictures it evokes. A little time spent talking about descriptive language can add to the enchantment. In short, good books need to be savored for the experiences they share and the characters they portray, as well as for the beauty of the language. Teachers should ask thought-provoking questions that call for more than factual recall. Allusions can be made throughout the day to characters, phrases, and sentences encountered in books read or being read.

In literary appreciation lessons, children learn to identify and label five attributes of fine writing to help them determine literary merit. They also discuss the elements of narrative writing, deepening their appreciation of fine writing. Finally, through daily reading, children learn to read fluently and expressively, providing pleasure and enhancing comprehension.

Attributes of Quality Literature

In The Spalding Method, we identify and label five attributes that are commonly found in fine literature. The following procedure helps teach these in an orderly manner:

Procedure for Teaching Attributes of Quality Literature

1. In separate lessons, name and define the following attributes. The Spalding poster "Attributes of Quality Literature" provides a visual reference (see Comprehension/Writing Poster Set, in Resources).

   Precise Language
   Language is direct, concrete, specific, and vivid.
   Emotional Appeal
   Language and situations evoke sentiments (e.g., happiness, sadness, compassion).
   Content
   Information (e.g., science, history, geography) is embedded.
   Insight into People and Life
   Dialogue and situations enable readers to discern motives, desires, and rewards or consequences of different kinds of behavior.
   Universality
   Common traits or experiences are enjoyed by readers across time and cultures.

2. Explain and demonstrate how to identify each attribute of literature in selections previously read for enjoyment but not analyzed.

 Model Thinking

Think out loud as you identify each attribute in preselected paragraphs from previous reading.

✔ *Check for Understanding*

As each attribute is introduced in whole group, have children name and define the attribute and explain how it enhances their enjoyment or understanding.

continued

☆ *Provide Practice*

After daily oral reading, have children identify the attributes of literature and explain how each enhanced their enjoyment and/or understanding.

✐ *Check Application*

Have children identify the attributes of literature in library books. Have them explain how the authors' use of the attributes enhanced their enjoyment and/or understanding.

Although the following sample dialogue is presented for beginners, the basic attributes and the procedure of instruction are the same for students of any age. Each step in the procedure is identified. This dialogue introduces the first two attributes: precise language and emotional appeal. For young children, these attributes are introduced on separate days.

Teaching Attributes of Quality Literature—Example Dialogue

Precise Language

TEACHER: (Name and define.)	"You have enjoyed listening to the stories we have read each day. Today, I will teach you how authors use precise language to increase your enjoyment and understanding. Precise language means that authors *clearly describe* the people or animals, places, and events.
(Explain/demonstrate.)	"First, I will read a sentence or two from a story, Next, I will talk about the language that helps me enjoy and understand the story. We have read *The Ugly Duckling* by Hans Christian Andersen and talked about how much we enjoyed it. You told me your favorite parts. Today, I will pick out some sentences that use *precise language*.
(Model thinking.)	"Listen as I read and think out loud. "'After a while one shell cracked, then another, and another, and from each egg came a fluffy little yellow creature that lifted its head and cried, "Peep! peep!"' "When I read that, I could picture and almost hear the baby ducks. Andersen could just have said, 'The ducks hatched,' but that would not have given us a picture. I enjoy the story more when I can picture the people or animals, places, and events.
(Check for understanding.)	"What do we mean when we say an author uses *precise language*?"
STUDENTS:	"The author *clearly describes*."

TEACHER:	"Yes. The author uses words that help us picture the people or animals, places, and events. What words did Hans Christian Andersen use to describe the baby ducks?"
STUDENTS:	"Fluffy." "Little." "Yellow."
TEACHER:	"Yes. Those words clearly describe the baby ducks. Listen to this sentence and tell me which words help you picture what is happening and why:"
	" 'Then they climbed the slippery bank of the river and waddled after their mother.' "
STUDENTS:	"*Slippery bank* because I can picture the muddy edge of the water." "*Waddled* because I can picture the baby ducks swinging from side to side."
TEACHER:	"Good. You identified examples of *precise language*.
(Provide practice.)	Now listen to these sentences, and then tell me words that clearly describe:
	" 'He was no longer a dark, gray bird, ugly to look at.'
	"Which words did Andersen use to clearly describe the ugly duckling?"
STUDENTS:	"Dark." "Gray." "Ugly to look at."
TEACHER:	"Yes. Andersen describes the ugly duckling as dark and gray
(Provide practice.)	in contrast to his description of the fluffy little yellow ducks. Fine writers use *precise language* to clearly describe people or animals, places, and events." (For older beginners or remedial readers studying this or any other story, use sentences that provide more complex descriptions. Continue to have children identify precise language in successive reading lessons.)
(Check application.)	(Have children identify the attributes of literature in library books. Have them explain how the authors' use of the attributes enhances their enjoyment and/or understanding.)

Emotional Appeal

TEACHER:	"We have talked about precise language. Today, I want to teach you that fine authors also describe situations or events that cause us to feel in certain ways. We call how we feel *emotions*. When authors clearly describe how people or animals feel, we often remember feeling the same way. Today, I will read more sentences from *The Ugly Duckling*. I will think out loud as I explain how the sentences make me feel.

continued

	" 'An old duck who saw the new brood coming stared at them and said, "Do look; here is another brood, as if there were not enough of us already; and what a queer-looking fellow one of them is; we do not want him here," and then she flew at him and bit him in the neck.'
	"I have been picked on before, so I can imagine how sad the ugly duckling must be when the old duck is mean to him. The emotion the ugly duckling was feeling was sadness. Now listen to these sentences:
	" 'Then they threw bread and cake into the water for the new bird, and they said, "This is the finest of all, he is so young and graceful." The poor swan was so happy he did not know what to do, but he was not at all proud. He had been hated for being ugly, and now he heard them say that he was the most beautiful of all the birds. He rustled his feathers and curved his slender neck, and said, "Now, when people see me they will not be angry, they will be glad. I never dreamed of such happiness when I was an ugly duckling." '
	"How would you feel if you had been the ugly duckling and now you are a beautiful swan?"
STUDENTS:	"Happy."
TEACHER:	"Yes, the emotion you would feel is happiness."
(Follow procedures.)	(Have children identify other examples in successive lessons. Make certain that children can identify examples of emotional appeals in library books they read.)

The Ugly Duckling by Hans Christian Andersen can be used in different lessons to teach insight and universality. For example, children learn that making fun of another is hurtful (insight). Children all over the world can relate to feeling ugly or different (universality). Originally written in Danish, *The Ugly Duckling* has been translated into every language in the world.

Learning to recognize the attributes of quality literature increases children's enjoyment and their awareness of the writer's skill. Because *literary appreciation* is usually taught using narratives, the elements of narratives are the second area of focus.

Elements of Narratives

In text-structure lessons, children are taught to identify and name the *basic* elements of three types of writing using short, simple paragraphs. By coordinating lessons in text structure with literary appreciation, this basic knowledge is expanded. For example, children learn to distinguish between *main* and *supporting characters*, to differentiate between *set-*

tings that are important to the story and those that are not, and to discern the sequence of events called *plot*. Knowing the terms provides children with a common vocabulary to use in class discussions. This process develops students' critical discernment and facilitates their own writing. The following procedure provides an orderly sequence:

Procedure for Expanding Understanding of Narrative Elements

1. Beginning on the first day of school, read narratives to children. Start with the title, the author's name, and any interesting facts you might know about the author.
2. After reading each story, have children respond to *general* questions such as, "Who is this story about? Where did it happen? What was your favorite part?"
3. Coordinate text-structure lessons (see pages 133–134) with literary appreciation lessons. In text-structure lessons, teach author's purpose and point of view and *basic* elements of narratives using the short paragraphs in *McCall-Harby Test Lessons in Primary Reading*. After children can readily define and identify characters, simple settings, and events in text-structure lessons using *McCall-Harby Test Lessons in Primary Reading* and *McCall-Crabbs Standard Test Lessons in Reading*, explain and demonstrate use of the following terms and concepts using quality literature:

Character

A character is a person or a personified animal or object in a story. *Main* characters are fully described—their appearance, speech, actions, thoughts—through what others in the story or the author says about them. *Supporting* characters are important to the narrative but are not described in great detail.

Setting

A narrative is set in a time and place. Artful description of time and place prepares the scene for the events that will take place. An *integral* setting is one that is essential to the narrative. A *backdrop* setting is relatively unimportant to the narrative.

Plot

Plot is the sequence of events that show characters in action. A well-constructed plot puts events in a logical order the reader can follow, but it also produces action and conflict that hold the reader's interest. In a *chronological* plot, events are described in the order in which they occur (beginning, middle, end). The chronological plot is most common in young children's literature. When a normal time sequence is disrupted to recount episodes from the character's past, it is referred to as a *flashback*. The flashback is more suitable for intermediate grades.

Point of View

The author sees the story from a specific point of view. In a *first-person* (I, we) narrative, the author participates in the story. In a *third-person* (he, she, they) narrative, the author does not participate in the story but describes actions, thoughts, and feelings.

continued

Theme
The author conveys an underlying main idea about people, society, or the human condition. An *explicit* theme is stated clearly in the narrative. An *implicit* theme is implied but not directly stated.

Tone (intermediate grades)
Tone is the author's attitude toward the subject and the reader. This may be personal or impersonal, warm and friendly, or distant and cold.

Style (intermediate grades)
Style refers to the author's choice of words that create the tone readers perceive (mode of expression, the way the writer uses language to express ideas).

Model Thinking

In separate lessons using paragraphs from previously read narratives, think out loud as you identify main and supporting characters, important (integral) or unimportant (backdrop) settings, and the sequence of events (plot).

✓ Check for Understanding

In separate whole-group lessons, have children define each literary term and explain its use in narratives previously read for enjoyment but not analyzed.

☆ Provide Practice

In successive lessons, have children distinguish between main and supporting characters and important and unimportant settings. Have them recount the sequence of events within narratives they have listened to or read.

Check Application

Have children identify author's name, purpose for writing, main and supporting characters, important and unimportant settings, and the sequence of events in library books. (Older children identify all literary elements defined above.)

Although the following sample dialogue is presented for beginners, the basic attributes and the procedure of instruction are the same for students of any age. Each step in the procedure is identified. This *literary appreciation* sample dialogue introduces main and supporting characters *after* children have learned *basic* narrative elements in *text-structure* lessons (see pages 133–134).

Expanding Understanding of Narrative Elements—Example Dialogue

TEACHER: (Review terms.)	"In lessons on text structure you have learned that stories are also called narratives. We call the parts of narratives *elements*. Every narrative has at least one *character;* a time and place, which we call the *setting;* and one or more *events,* which may involve a *problem* and a *solution.* You learned that a *character* in a narrative may be a person, or an animal who behaves like a person.
(Name and define.)	"Today, we will learn about two kinds of *characters.* The *main* character is clearly described. We get to know the character by what he does, what he says, and by what is said about him. Usually there are other characters who *support* the main character. They are necessary to the story, but they are not described as fully.
(Explain and demonstrate.)	"In our literary appreciation lesson I read *Peter Rabbit,* and we talked about the author, Beatrix Potter. First, I will read some sentences from *Peter Rabbit.* Next, I will explain how I know who the *main* and *supporting* characters are.
(Model thinking.)	"Listen as I read and then think out loud. " 'Once upon a time there were four little Rabbits, and their names were—Flopsy, Mopsy, Cotton-tail, and Peter. They lived with their Mother in a sand-bank, underneath the root of a very big fir-tree.' "Beatrix Potter introduced five characters in the first sentence: Flopsy, Mopsy, Cotton-tail, Peter, and Mrs. Rabbit. Now listen to this sentence: " ' "Now, my dears," said old Mrs. Rabbit one morning, "you may go into the fields or down the lane, but don't go into Mr. McGregor's garden: your Father had an accident there; he was put in a pie by Mrs. McGregor." ' "I remember from reading the story earlier that Mr. McGregor chased Peter, so I know Mr. McGregor is also a character. Now I will read carefully to decide who this story is mainly about. " ' "Now run along, and don't get into mischief. I am going out . . ." Flopsy, Mopsy, and Cotton-tail, who were good little bunnies, went down the lane to gather blackberries. But Peter, who was very naughty, ran straight away to Mr. McGregor's garden, and squeezed under the gate! First he ate some lettuces and some French beans; and then he ate some radishes.'

continued

"I think Peter is the *main* character because I have learned so much about him. I learned that he was naughty, and that he immediately did what he was told not to do. I even know what he ate. I think that Flopsy, Mopsy, and Cotton-tail are *supporting* characters because I know very little about them, except that they were good little bunnies who did what they were told. I'll read on to be sure."

(Continue reading the rest of the story.)

"Now I know that Peter is the main character because I learned so much about him. Flopsy, Mopsy, and Cotton-tail, Mrs. Rabbit, and Mr. McGregor are *supporting* characters. They are necessary to the action, but they are not described in detail.

(Check for understanding.)	"What do we mean by the term *main character*?"
STUDENTS:	"A *main character* is the person or animal who is described the most."
TEACHER:	"Good explanation. What words did the author use to describe Peter more fully?"
STUDENTS:	"Peter was very naughty." "He ran straight to Mr. McGregor's garden." "He ate lettuces, beans, and radishes."
TEACHER:	"Yes. The author told us Peter was naughty and described where he went, what he ate, and the trouble he got into. Tell me what we call the other characters."
STUDENTS:	"Supporting characters."
TEACHER:	"Yes. Why are they called *supporting* characters?"
STUDENTS:	"They are not described as much."
TEACHER:	"That is true. They are necessary to the action, but the author does not describe them as clearly."
(Provide practice.)	(In successive whole-group lessons, have children identify main and supporting characters in different narratives. Have them refer to sentences in the narratives to defend their choices.)
(Check application.)	(Have children independently identify main and supporting characters in library books. Have them refer to sentences in the narratives to defend their choices.)

These basic literary terms introduced in first grade form the foundation for analysis of increasingly more difficult narratives as children progress through the grades. Specific instructional practices for teaching these and other literary analysis skills are explained and demonstrated in Spalding training courses.

Fluent and Expressive Reading

The final focus in a literary appreciation lesson is on developing fluent and expressive reading. Children must be able to read words fluently so they can concentrate on deriving meaning from text. As children listen to the teacher reading fluently and expressively, they learn that such reading not only provides pleasure but also enhances comprehension. When children read orally, the teacher identifies those children who have difficulty decoding and those who need instruction reading expressively. (If spelling words have been taught a year ahead as provided in spelling lessons, there will be few words that interrupt fluency and comprehension.)

During oral reading, children also learn that punctuation marks are signals that tell them which words go together, when to pause, and when to lower or raise their voices. The following procedure helps develop fluent, expressive reading:

Procedure for Teaching Fluent, Expressive Reading

1. Early in the year, read children's narratives fluently and expressively in daily literary appreciation lessons.

2. In daily spelling lessons, have children read words for spelling and for reading. Reading for spelling develops the ability to sound out unfamiliar words. Reading for reading develops automatic word recognition. Both are prerequisite skills for fluent reading with comprehension.

3. Explain that the goal of oral reading is to clearly convey the *author's* thoughts and feelings. Explain that authors select the words they use with great care to convey just the shade of meaning they intend.

4. Using appropriate paragraphs from narratives, explain and demonstrate the following attributes:

   Accuracy

   Reading is identifying exactly the words that are there (not guessing or substituting). Authors carefully select the exact words they want to convey their meaning; therefore, we do not insert, delete, or substitute words for what the author wrote.

   Fluency

   Reading smoothly without hesitation is necessary for comprehension. In oral reading, like speaking, we read words consecutively. We do not pause for each word.

   Phrasing

   Reading words together that go together conveys the author's intended meaning and enhances comprehension. A period (full stop) indicates the end of a complete thought. Therefore, the word at the end of a sentence is never read with the word beginning the next sentence. A comma indicates that the words separated by a comma are not read together. The comma is needed to make the meaning of the sentence clear.

continued

Intonation

Appropriately raising or lowering the pitch of the voice when reading aloud enhances listeners' comprehension and enjoyment. The pitch is lowered at the end of statements and raised at the end of questions. The pitch is raised or lowered depending on the character's emotional state (anger, sadness).

Enunciation

Articulating speech sounds distinctly when reading aloud enhances listeners' pleasure and comprehension. (Reading spelling words for reading in the spelling lesson trains children to speak distinctly.)

 Model Thinking

In separate lessons, think out loud as you explain and demonstrate how each of these attributes influences enjoyment and comprehension.

✓ *Check for Understanding*

As each new attribute is introduced in whole group, have children define that attribute and explain how each enhances their enjoyment and comprehension. Have children identify where the author's thought begins and ends. Have them explain how a comma influences their oral reading.

☆ *Provide Practice*

In daily oral reading, have children begin each new story by reading the title and the author's name. Make sure each child has the opportunity to read aloud at least once a day. If necessary, read more than one story. Without prior teaching of new words, have children softly sound out unfamiliar words. This develops the technique they will follow when reading independently. When a child needs help, say only the sound or syllable that is causing the problem. (No other child should help unless asked to do so by the teacher. The teacher should *teach* when help is required.) For children having difficulty, select easy passages to have them preread and then reread with the class. This builds confidence as well as providing needed practice. Take extra time for those students to read from their spelling notebooks and to read with you so they are prepared to read with the group.

✐ *Check Application*

During oral reading of content area subjects, have children read fluently and expressively using distinct enunciation and appropriate intonation.

Reading good literature aloud motivates children to practice their reading; in fact, the children don't realize they are practicing fluency. They are just enjoying the stories because they can read and understand them. Through reading aloud, children learn to speak and write well also. Finally, oral reading reveals what each child is doing in silent reading. If students are having difficulty with oral reading, silent reading is premature. Reading silently before they are able to sound out words inclines children to guess or continue reading even when the text does not make sense to them. *Children must be proficient at sounding out words before sustained silent reading can help them develop fluency.*

Teaching Literary Appreciation—a Summary

Literary appreciation lessons help children learn the attributes that distinguish fine writing. Thus, they begin developing critical discernment about what they read. They also expand their understanding of the elements of narratives, which helps them appreciate the author's skill. Knowing the attributes of fine writing and narrative elements enables children to incorporate them in their own writing. Finally, by reading quality literature aloud, children develop fluency in an enjoyable way. Another prerequisite skill for comprehension is discerning the type of text being read.

Teaching Text Structure

During *text-structure* lessons, children are taught that authors organize their writing differently depending on their purpose for writing. Knowledge of text organization helps children focus attention on what's most important in each type of text. Even beginners can learn the distinguishing characteristics of three *basic* types of writing: narrative, informative (expository), and a combination we call informative-narrative. *McCall-Harby Test Lessons in Primary Reading* and *McCall-Crabbs Standard Test Lessons in Reading* are used to teach and test children's understanding of text structure because they have short, interesting narrative, informative, and informative-narrative passages. These lessons do not have to be introduced in numerical order because the difficulty levels vary throughout the books.

Although the order of text-structure introduction is optional, we have found that narrative writing is the easiest for children to understand because parents and kindergarten teachers usually read aloud from nursery rhymes, fairy tales, and stories. The following procedure is recommended for teaching text structure:

Procedure for Teaching Text Structure

In separate whole-group lessons, read short *McCall-Harby* and *McCall-Crabbs* paragraphs to name, define, and explain characteristics of the three *basic* types of writing. Use *McCall-Harby* and *McCall-Crabbs User's Guides* to select paragraphs that are good examples for teaching the elements of each type of writing. Spalding Comprehension/Writing Posters provide a visual reference. (See Resources.)

continued

Narrative Writing (fiction)

A narrative relates an event or tells a story. Narrative elements include characters, setting, plot, point of view, theme, tone, and style (see pages 127–128). The author's purpose is to entertain and to develop understanding about people and the world. The author may write from a first- or third-person point of view.

Informative (Expository) Writing (nonfiction)

Expository writing sets forth a series of facts, propositions, or arguments in a logical sequence. This type of writing is organized around a topic (subject). Each paragraph has a stated or an implied main idea and essential information necessary to the main idea. If the paragraph's main idea is stated, it is called the topic sentence. (A thesis statement summarizes the main idea of multiparagraph passages.) Authors usually provide additional information to introduce, give background, elaborate on a detail, or conclude. The author's purpose is to inform, explain, or instruct. The author writes from a third-person point of view.

Informative-Narrative Writing

Writing that combines narrative and informative elements is called informative-narrative. The author's purpose is to inform, explain, or instruct in an interesting or personal way. The author may write from a first- or third-person point of view. The following narrative and informative elements may occur in any combination and may vary in degree.

Narrative Elements	Informative Elements
Real/imaginary characters	Real individuals
Real/imaginary setting	Factual location(s)
Plot (sequence of events)	Prominent factual information
Theme (main idea)	Topic, stated/implied main idea, thesis

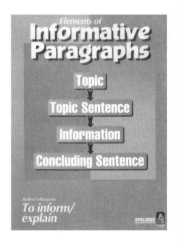

Primary-grade social studies texts frequently contain one or two characters to make factual information more interesting. Some authors write in first person to add a personal touch to factual information. Authors of historical novels may portray real events using fictional or real characters. They may also portray real characters in fictional events.

💡 Model Thinking

In separate whole-group lessons, think out loud as you identify the author's purpose and the elements of narrative and informative writing in short *McCall-Harby* and *McCall-Crabbs* passages. Next, read short *McCall-Harby/McCall-Crabbs* passages and think out loud as you complete narrative (see page 136), informative (see page 138), and informative-narrative organizers (see page 140) to make the abstract concepts concrete.

✔ Check for Understanding

As each new type of writing is introduced, have children identify the type of writing, the author's purpose, and the elements present.

☆ Provide Practice

In separate whole-group lessons, use short *McCall-Harby* and *McCall-Crabbs* passages to provide additional examples of three different types of writing. Have students use organizers to identify each type of writing, the author's purpose, and the elements. Next, have children defend their choices.

✍ Check Application

Have children independently identify the type of writing, the author's purpose, and the elements in short *McCall-Harby* and *McCall-Crabbs* passages. Have them defend their choices.

Primary children can readily identify the characteristics of narratives in *McCall-Harby Test Lessons in Primary Reading*. Although the following dialogue is presented for beginners, the basic elements and procedure of instruction are the same for students of any age. Each step in the procedure is identified. This sample dialogue uses lesson 1 in *McCall-Harby Test Lessons in Primary Reading*, a short narrative written in third person.

Teaching Narrative Structure—Example Dialogue

	(Before class begins, display an organizer as shown on page 136.)
TEACHER:	"Class, as I have read stories to you, we have talked about why authors write stories. You have learned that the author's purpose
(Name, define, explain.)	is to entertain and to help you understand people and the world. Today, I will teach you some new terms. Another word for a
(Refer to narrative poster.)	story is *narrative*. Narratives have several parts. We call the persons in a story *characters*. They can be real or imaginary. The term *setting* is used to describe where and when the story happened. The events that happened to the characters are called the *plot*. Sometimes these events cause a *problem* that has to be *solved*.

continued

(Model thinking.)	"Listen carefully as I read. I will think out loud as I decide if this paragraph is a narrative.
	" 'Harvey was not feeling well. He was sick. He told his mother he had a tummy ache. Harvey's father put him to bed and went to call the doctor.'
	"I *think* this is a narrative because there are three *characters*, Harvey, his mother, and his dad. The *setting* is Harvey's home. The *event,* or *problem,* is that Harvey is sick. I'll read on to see what happens next.
	" 'Then his mother said, "Harvey, did you eat something?"
	" ' "I ate breakfast," said Harvey.
	" ' "Did you eat anything since breakfast?"
	" ' "I ate a cookie."
	" ' "How many cookies, Harvey?"
	" ' "How many were in the cookie jar?" '
(Model thinking.)	"Now I *know* this is a story because it has three characters, a setting, and a problem. I'm sure the author's purpose was to entertain because it made me laugh. I think the author also wanted me to understand that if you eat too many cookies, you will get sick.
(Check for understanding.)	"Tell me another name for a story."
STUDENTS:	"Another name is narrative."
TEACHER:	"Yes. Tell me why authors write stories. What is their purpose or reason?"
STUDENTS:	"They want to entertain us." "They help us understand people."
TEACHER:	"Yes. What are the parts (elements) of stories we learned about today?"
STUDENTS:	"Characters." "Setting." "Event (plot)."
TEACHER:	"Yes. To show you the parts of a story, I will complete this narrative organizer.
	Under *Author's purpose,* I will write 'To entertain and develop understanding.'
	"Under *Characters,* I will write, 'Harvey, his mother, and his father.'
	"Under *Setting (Place/Time),* I will write, 'Harvey's home after breakfast.'
	"Under *Event (Plot),* I will write, 'Harvey got sick.' "

Narrative Initial Organizer

Purpose	Characters	Setting
		Place/Time

Event (Plot)

| (Provide practice.) | (In whole group, have students use graphic organizers to identify the author's purpose, the characters, the setting, and the events in other *McCall-Harby/McCall-Crabbs* passages.) |
| (Check application.) | (In *literary appreciation* lessons, have children independently identify the author's purpose and the elements of narratives.) |

Completing a narrative organizer makes abstract concepts concrete and provides multi-sensory experiences. After children can consistently identify the author's purpose and the elements of narratives, they are ready to learn the characteristics of informative paragraphs.

The following sample dialogue uses *McCall-Crabbs Standard Test Lessons in Reading, Book A-3* to introduce author's purpose and two elements of informative writing, topic and information:

Teaching Informative Structure—Example Dialogue

	(Before class begins, display an organizer as shown on page 138.)
TEACHER:	"Class, you can identify the characteristics of narratives very well. Today, I will introduce a different type of writing. In your daily integrated spelling/writing lessons, you have composed sentences that provide information. When the author's purpose is to provide information, we call it
(Name, define, explain.)	*informative* writing. Information that is true is called a *fact*. If I write, 'The sun comes up in the morning,' we know that is a fact. The *subject* of that sentence is *sun*. If I write more sentences about the sun, I would say that my *topic* is the *sun*.
(Refer to informative poster.)	"The *topic* is *what* the paragraph is about. *Facts* provide information about the topic. I will read a short paragraph and think out loud as I show you how I identify informative writing. Listen carefully.
(Read sentences:)	" 'Dandelions start to blossom very early in the spring. Some of the leaves stay green all winter. When warm weather comes, flowers peep from the center of the leaves.'

continued

(Model thinking.)	"I *think* this is an informative paragraph because the author told me *facts* about dandelions. There are no characters so far. I *think* the author's purpose is to teach me about dandelions, but I must read on to be sure." (Continue reading the rest of the paragraph.) "Now I *know* that the *topic* of this paragraph is dandelions and the author's purpose is to teach me *facts* about dandelions.
(Check for understanding.)	"Tell me the name of this type of writing."
STUDENTS:	"Informative."
TEACHER:	"Good. Now tell me what the author's purpose is."
STUDENTS:	"The author wants to teach us something."
TEACHER:	"Yes. Informative writing teaches us something. What is the topic?"
STUDENTS:	"Dandelions."
TEACHER:	"Yes. Now I will complete an informative initial organizer so you can see the parts of an informative paragraph. "Besides *Author's Purpose*, I will write 'To inform.' "Beside *Topic*, I will write 'Dandelions.' "Beside *Facts*, I will write, 'Dandelions bloom early in spring; some leaves stay green all winter; flowers peep from center when warm weather comes.' "
(Provide practice.)	(In whole group, have students identify the author's purpose, the topic, and the facts in other informative *McCall-Harby/McCall-Crabbs* passages as you fill out a graphic organizer.)
(Check application.)	(In different *McCall-Harby/McCall-Crabbs* paragraphs, have children independently identify the author's purpose and the elements of informative writing. Finally, have them identify the elements in science and social studies books.)

After children have learned to write topic sentences in *composition* lessons, have them identify topic sentences in *McCall-Crabbs* paragraphs. Do not discuss the content of the informative paragraphs when teaching the elements of informatives. The focus of these lessons is only on identifying the type of writing.

When children can easily distinguish between narrative and informative writing, they are ready to learn that authors sometimes combine the elements of both. The following sample dialogue uses *McCall-Crabbs Standard Test Lessons in Reading, Book A-2* to introduce author's purpose and a few elements of informative-narrative writing: characters, setting, and facts about baby robins.

Teaching Informative-Narrative Structure—Example Dialogue

	(Before class begins, display an organizer as shown on page 140.)
TEACHER:	"Class, you have learned to identify narratives and informatives. Today I will introduce another type of writing. Sometimes an author provides information
(Name, define, explain.)	in an interesting or more personal way. He may include one or two characters and a setting along with important factual information.
(Refer to informative-narrative poster.)	"We call that *informative-narrative* writing because it has elements of both kinds of writing. We say the author's purpose is to inform in an interesting way.
(Model thinking.)	"Listen carefully as I think out loud while reading a short informative-narrative paragraph.
	" ' "I am working very hard," said the robin. "I am looking for straw to build my nest. I shall use some mud, too. I shall line it with soft grass. This will make a nice home for my baby birds." So she made the nest in the old apple tree.'
	"I *think* this may be an *informative-narrative* paragraph because it has a character, a mother robin who talks, but it also has some facts about how nests are made. I must read on to see if there are more facts.
	" 'In a few days there were three little eggs in the nest. They were as blue as the sky. The mother bird sat on the eggs fourteen days. Soon there were three baby robins. They stretched their little necks and cried, "Peep, peep! Feed us." '

continued

"Now, I *know* this is an *informative-narrative* because there are more facts about how many and what color the eggs are and how long the mother robin sat on the nest. The author's purpose is to inform me about robins in such an interesting way that I will remember the facts more easily."

(Check for understanding.) "Tell me why we call this type of writing informative-narrative."

STUDENTS: "There are some narrative elements and some informative elements."

TEACHER: "That is correct. What elements of a narrative are present in this paragraph?"

STUDENTS: "Characters." "Setting." "Event (plot)."

TEACHER: "Good identification of narrative elements. What are the parts of informative writing?"

STUDENTS: "Facts."

TEACHER: "Yes. There are many facts about making a home for baby robins. Tell me the author's purpose."

STUDENTS: "The author's purpose is to teach us about robins in an interesting way."

TEACHER: "Yes. To help you see the parts, I will complete this informative-narrative organizer:

"First, beside *Characters,* I will write, 'mother robin and her babies.'

"Beside *Setting,* I will write, 'nest in apple tree.'

Besides *event,* I will write, 'birth of baby robins.'

"I will list some *facts* in phrases: 'nest built of straw, mud, grass; eggs blue as sky; fourteen days to hatch.' "

> **Informative-Narrative Initial Organizer**
>
> Author's Purpose _____
> Characters _____
> Setting _____
> Event _____
> Topic _____
> Facts _____
> _____
> _____

(Provide practice.) (In whole group, have students identify the author's purpose and the narrative and informative elements in other *McCall-Harby/McCall-Crabbs* passages as you complete a graphic organizer.)

(Check application.) (In different *McCall-Harby/McCall-Crabbs* paragraphs, have children independently identify the author's purpose and the elements of informative-narrative writing. Finally, have them identify the elements in other content-area books.)

Teaching Text Structure—a Summary

During lessons on text structure, children learn to identify three *basic* types of writing: narrative, informative, and a combination we call informative-narrative. These basic types of writing form the foundation for analysis of more advanced types of writing as children progress through the grades. Different types of writing require different levels of concentration. Rapid identification of text structure speeds comprehension by helping children focus on the important elements and adjust reading speed as needed. When children can easily distinguish between the three, basic types of writing they are ready to learn to consciously use the five mental actions necessary for comprehension.

Teaching Comprehension

It seems only common sense that before children are able to comprehend text, they must be able to read it. However, in many classrooms that simple principle does not guide instruction. That is why the most common reading problem, and the one most likely to inhibit comprehension, is inability to decode text. The Spalding Method is designed to prevent or overcome such common reading problems. Thus, daily spelling and writing lessons are devoted to decoding, expanding children's vocabulary, and teaching children to apply the rules of the English language in well-written sentences and compositions. With this Spalding knowledge base in place, children can focus on identifying the three basic types of writing in the reading lesson. Then they are ready to learn to consciously use mental actions to process information.

Explicit comprehension instruction begins in kindergarten as children listen to the teacher read *McCall-Harby* and *McCall-Crabbs* narrative, informative, and informative-narrative paragraphs. Children of any age learn to use the mental actions while listening, so they can apply them automatically when reading. Children are explicitly taught to be active listeners and readers by *monitoring their comprehension*. Skilled comprehenders are engaged—they know to ask questions or reread when something no longer makes sense—but poor comprehenders don't know how to check their understanding. They just limp along. To enrich their understanding, children are also taught to *make connections* between their prior knowledge and stated information. Using their knowledge about text structure, they can *predict* author's purpose, type of writing, topic and main idea. When they can *consciously* use the first three mental actions, children are taught to *reformat* (categorize) information into essential information needed to confirm or derive main ideas and additional or background information that introduces, elaborates, or concludes. Finally, they learn to use essential information to identify stated or implied topics and main ideas (*mentally summarize*).

The actions are not used in any order. Rather, each is used as needed—simultaneously or in parallel. Many children automatically engage in these mental actions while listening and reading. However, we now know that conscious use enhances all children's comprehension. The actions are specific strategies children can use to clarify meaning when comprehension breaks down. The following procedure makes instruction concrete and multisensory.

Procedure for Teaching Five Mental Actions

1. As soon as children can accurately identify the three basic types of writing (see page 134), name, define, and demonstrate use of the first three-mental actions in whole-group lessons. Spalding Mental Action Sentence Strips provide a visual representation (see Resources).

   Monitoring Comprehension

   Monitoring comprehension means checking understanding of words, phrases, and sentences to identify unfamiliar words or concepts (active listening/reading). Kindergarten and first-grade children may use the term *checking their understanding* instead of *monitoring comprehension.*

   Making Connections

   Making connections means linking stated information with information already learned, to draw conclusions (infer) and elaborate. (Initially, make connections only about meaning of unfamiliar words.)

   Making Predictions

   Making predictions means forecasting, supporting, and/or revising forecasts using stated information and information already learned. (At first, predict only type of writing.)

   💡 *Model Thinking*

   In a whole-group lesson, think out loud as you monitor comprehension and identify *only* one or two unfamiliar words, make connections to figure out an unfamiliar word(s), and predict *only* type of writing within the first few sentences. In a separate lesson, think out loud and name the mental action as you monitor comprehension, make connections, and predict type of writing.

   ✔ *Check for Understanding*

   In whole-group lessons, think out loud as you use the first three mental actions to comprehend a short *McCall-Harby* or *McCall-Crabbs* passage. Have children name and define the mental action you used. Have them explain how it enhanced comprehension.

   ☆ *Provide Practice*

   In whole-group lessons, have children describe their thinking and name the mental actions as you read different *McCall-Harby* and *McCall-Crabbs* passages.

   ✎ *Check Application*

   Have children use the first three mental actions while listening and later reading content-area texts.

2. When second-grade and older children can accurately name and explain how to monitor comprehension, make connections, and predict type of writing, name, define, and demonstrate the last two mental actions.

Reformatting

Reformatting means reorganizing and categorizing information into new forms (e.g., lists, outlines) to use for the immediate task or to file for later use.

Mentally Summarizing

Mentally summarizing means confirming or deriving the main idea using stated or inferred information and information already learned.

 Model Thinking

In whole-group lessons think out loud as you reformat information in short *McCall-Harby* and *McCall-Crabbs* passages to distinguish between essential and additional information. Then continue thinking out loud as you use the essential information to confirm or derive the main idea.

✔ Check for Understanding

In whole-group lessons, think out loud as you use the last two mental actions in a short *McCall-Harby* or *McCall-Crabbs* passage. Have children name and define the mental actions you used. Have them explain how they enhanced comprehension.

☆ Provide Practice

In whole-group lessons, have children describe their thinking and name and define the last two mental actions as you read different *McCall-Harby* and *McCall-Crabbs* passages.

✎ Check Application

Have children apply each of the five mental actions as they read any type of print.

Although the following sample dialogue is presented for beginners, the mental actions and the procedures of instruction are the same for students of any age and texts of any complexity. This sample dialogue occurs after kindergarten and first-grade children *consistently* identify the three *basic* types of writing. It introduces the first three mental actions using lesson 10 in *McCall-Harby Test Lessons in Primary Reading*.

Teaching the First Three Mental Actions—Example Dialogue

Modeling Three Mental Actions

TEACHER:	"Class, you are now so good at identifying narratives, informatives, and informative-narratives, that you are ready to learn how to improve your understanding of what you read. As I read the passage, I will stop and tell you what I am thinking.
	" 'Bess liked to play in the treetops with her brothers.'
(Model monitoring.)	"I understand every word.
(Model predicting.)	"I *think* this is a narrative because it has characters. I'll read on to find out if there is a setting.
	" 'Her mother said that Bess was a tomboy.'
(Model monitoring.)	"I understand every word, except *tomboy*. Maybe *tomboy* means a girl who likes to climb trees, like Bess did with her brothers. I'll read on.
	" 'One day Bess was up on the top of a very big tree. Her foot got stuck, and she couldn't get down out of the tree. She called, "Mother, Mother, my foot's stuck." '
(Model monitoring.)	"I understand every word.
(Model supporting prediction.)	"I'm quite sure this is a narrative because it has a setting and a problem. I'll read on to see if it has a solution.
	" 'Her mother saw Bess up in the tree and made the boys help her down. As soon as Bess was down from the tree, she said, "Mother, would you like to see me go up to the top of that tree again?" What do you think her mother said?'
(Model monitoring.)	"I understand every word.
(Model confirming prediction.)	"I know this is a narrative because it has characters, a setting, and an event.
	"Class, I used three mental actions to help me understand the paragraph."

Labeling Three Mental Actions

TEACHER:	(As you explain each mental action and name it, refer to Mental Action Sentence Strips.)
	"Now, class, I will teach you the names for the mental actions I used while thinking out loud.

("Monitoring Comprehension" strip.)	"The first mental action I used as I read was *monitoring comprehension*. This means I checked my understanding of each word, phrase, and sentence, and I identified a word I didn't understand.
("Making Connections" strip.)	"To figure out the unfamiliar word *tomboy*, I *made connections*. I used the first sentence to help me figure out the meaning of *tomboy*, so I made connections between sentences.
("Making Predictions" strip.)	"The third action is *making predictions*. Have you ever heard the daily weather report where they *forecast*, or *predict*, the weather? After the first sentence, I predicted that this is a narrative. That helped me focus on identifying characters, setting, and events as I continued to read the passage.
	"Now I will read the paragraph again. This time I will *describe* and *label* each of the three mental actions as I use them.
	" 'Bess liked to play in the treetops with her brothers.'
(Model/label monitoring.)	"I understand every word. I *checked my understanding*.
(Model/label predicting.)	"I *think* this is a narrative because it has characters. I *predicted* type of writing. I'll read on."
	" 'Her mother said that Bess was a tomboy.' "
(Model/label monitoring.)	"I understand every word, except *tomboy*. I *checked my understanding and identified an unfamiliar word*.
(Model/label making connections.)	"Maybe *tomboy* means a girl who likes to climb trees like a boy. I *made connections* with words in the first sentence to figure out the unfamiliar word. I'll read on.
	" 'One day Bess was up on the top of a very big tree. Her foot got stuck, and she couldn't get down out of the tree. She called, "Mother, Mother, my foot's stuck." '
(Model/name monitoring.)	"I understand every word. I *checked my understanding*."
	(Continue the dialogue thinking out loud as you complete the story.)
(Check for understanding.)	"Class, when I read sentences and say that I understand every word, which mental action am I using?"
STUDENTS:	"You are *checking your understanding* (monitoring comprehension)."

continued

TEACHER:	"Yes. When we read, we check our understanding of every word. Which mental action do we use when we don't understand a word?"
STUDENTS:	"We *make connections* with what we already know and what is in the story."
TEACHER:	"Good thinking. What mental action do we use when we forecast the type of writing?"
STUDENTS:	*"Predicting."*
TEACHER:	"You've done a good job of naming and defining three mental actions that help us understand what we read."
(Provide practice.)	(In whole-group lessons, have children define the first three mental actions, then describe their thinking and label the action used as you read different *McCall-Harby* and *McCall-Crabbs* passages.)
(Check application.)	(In whole-group lessons, have children use the first three mental actions as they listen to or read content-area books.)

When introducing the first three mental actions, do not discuss the content of the paragraphs. The focus of these lessons is only on using and naming the mental actions. Second-grade and older children learn to consciously use all five mental actions while listening to and later while reading all types of writing. Multisensory strategies and sample dialogues are provided in Spalding training courses, and abbreviated versions are included in *McCall-Harby* and *McCall-Crabbs User's Guides*.

Teaching Comprehension—A Summary

Children who are able to analyze their own thinking while listening and reading increase their comprehension and thereby significantly improve their performance in language arts and content-area subjects. During lessons on mental actions, kindergarten and first-grade children learn how to consciously check their understanding of words, phrases, and sentences, make connections between prior knowledge and the text; and predict the type of writing. Students in second grade and above expand their use of the first three mental actions and learn to consciously reformat and mentally summarize.

Chapter Summary

Even before children are able to read, they learn to recognize the attributes of quality literature. As their reading skills mature, so does their appreciation of well-written prose. Learning the elements of the three basic types of text structure enables students to channel their concentration appropriately. Finally, comprehension is enhanced when students are taught to apply the five mental actions.

The Spalding Method is a comprehensive language arts program that has successfully taught children to speak, write, and read well for almost five decades. In chapter 4, we will discuss its theoretical foundations and explain why The Spalding Method works.

WHY THE SPALDING METHOD WORKS
Theoretical Foundations

CHAPTER OVERVIEW

THE SPALDING METHOD has been grounded in sound principles of learning and instruction since its inception. Studying under eminent New York neurologist Dr. Samuel T. Orton, Dr. William McCall at Columbia Teachers College, and linguists of the day, Romalda Spalding gained extensive knowledge about essential components of reading instruction and why some children fail. Although much has been learned in the last sixty years, Dr. Orton "foresaw many principles of contemporary neuropsychology that awaited new technology for their verification" (Farnham-Diggory, 1992, 297). Drawing on that knowledge and over twenty-five years' experience working with children who had difficulty learning to read, Mrs. Spalding wrote *The Writing Road to Reading*. Farnham-Diggory observed that The Spalding Method works because it "capitalizes on a body of psychological principles that are dead right in contemporary theoretical terms" (see page xvi).

During the last three decades, reading research has focused on the complex process of reading, on how children *learn* to read, and on what causes some to fail. New technology, such as CAT scans and MRIs, have helped researchers identify principal subprocesses; where in the brain, and under what conditions, these subprocesses are activated; and how they interact.

Although it is not our purpose to summarize this vast body of research here, we selected six major research reports that provide both a historical perspective and a consensus on essential instructional components.

Review of Reading Research

Each of the following research summaries includes extensive bibliographies that are available for further study of the reading process and effective instructional practices. A crucial finding, basic to all these reports, is that reading is a *developmental* rather than a *single* process. Skilled reading is different from beginning reading (Chall, 1996a).

Becoming a Nation of Readers

In 1983, the National Academy of Education's Commission on Education and Public Policy, with the sponsorship of the National Institute of Education, established a commission to identify topics on which there was appreciable research and scholarship and to gather a panel of experts to survey, interpret, and synthesize research findings. *Becoming a Nation of Readers: The Report of the Commission on Reading* (Anderson et al.) was published in 1985 for a general audience. The commission reviewed studies of human cognition in the psychology of language, linguistics, child development, and behavioral science. Reviewing existing research, they reached consensus that "reading is a process of constructing meaning from written texts. It is a complex skill requiring the coordination of a number of interrelated sources of information" (Anderson et al., 1985, 7).

The commission confirmed that efficient word recognition and comprehension are companion skills from the time a child first learns to read and that the *purpose* of phonics instruction is to teach the relationship between letters and speech sounds (the alphabetic principle). They identified two basic approaches to phonics instruction:

> In explicit phonics instruction, the sounds associated with letters are identified in isolation and then "blended" together to form words. . . . In implicit phonics instruction, the sound associated with a letter is never supposed to be pronounced in isolation. (Anderson et al., 1985, 39)

They noted that a problem with implicit phonics is that it assumes an ability to identify separate speech sounds in spoken words, yet the evidence indicates that many young children are unable to extract an individual sound from hearing it within a word. Thus, they reported that the "research evidence tends to favor explicit phonics" (Anderson et al., 1985, 43). The commission asserted, "Readers must be able to decode words quickly and accurately so that this process can coordinate fluidly with the process of constructing meaning from text" (Anderson et al., 1985, 11). The commission issued seventeen specific recommendations for improving reading instruction that are still valid today. These recommendations encapsulate the information presented in the report about the conditions likely to produce skilled readers who derive joy from reading. Among these recommendations are the following:

- Parents should read to preschool children and informally teach them about reading and writing.

- Teachers of beginning reading should present well-designed phonics instruction.
- Teachers should devote more time to comprehension instruction.
- Children should spend more time writing.
- Teacher education programs should be lengthened and improved in quality.
- Schools should provide for the continuing professional development of teachers. (Anderson et al., 1985, 118--120)

Beginning to Read: Thinking and Learning about Print

Marilyn Jager Adams (1990), summarizing sixty years of reading research in *Beginning to Read: Thinking and Learning about Print,* confirmed that phonemic awareness (the understanding that spoken words and syllables consist of sequences of elementary speech sounds) is more highly related to learning to read than are general intelligence, reading readiness, and listening comprehension (Stanovich, 1986, 1993). Furthermore, lack of phonemic awareness is the most powerful predictor of reading failure because of its importance in learning how print represents spoken words (the alphabetic principle). If children cannot discriminate individual sounds within spoken words, they have an extremely difficult time learning symbols that represent speech sounds—the essence of decoding.

After examining the accumulated research, Adams reiterated the efficacy of explicit phonics: "Approaches in which systematic code instruction is included along with meaningful connected print result in superior reading achievement overall" (Adams, 1990, 12).

So, far from phonemic awareness interfering with the ability to draw meaning from print, she noted,

> research indicates that the most critical factor beneath fluent word reading is the ability to recognize letters, spelling patterns, and whole words, effortlessly, automatically, and visually. Moreover, the goal of all reading instruction—comprehension—depends critically on this ability. (Adams, 1990, 14)

Adams emphasized that this training should occur in an environment rich in literature and daily opportunities to write. By 1998, three major reports affirmed these findings and further expanded understanding of the reading process.

Reading: A Research-Based Approach

Over thirty years of reading research, funded by the National Institute of Child Health and Human Development (NICHD), is summarized by Drs. Jack Fletcher and Reid Lyon (1998) in the chapter, "Reading: A Research-Based Approach," in *What's Gone Wrong in America's Classrooms.* These studies, conducted in thirty-six sites in North America, support a prominent role for explicit instruction in phonics and phonological awareness skills for beginning reading instruction and for intervention with children having difficulty. NICHD studies also support a "major emphasis on reading and writing in environments that include good literature, reading for enjoyment, and other practices believed to facilitate the development of reading skills and literacy" (Fletcher and Lyon, 1998, 51).

NICHD studied the complex process of reading, how children learn to read, and what causes them to fail. Findings from research on how children learn to read were applied to the study of reading failure at five research sites: Bowman-Gray Medical School, Florida State University, the State University of New York at Albany, the University of Colorado, and the University of Texas–Houston Health Science Center.

Studies with both beginning and disabled readers demonstrated that problems in word recognition arise from inability to break apart words and syllables into individual phonemes (sounds). Fletcher and Lyons noted:

> This relationship is apparent in the majority of poor readers, including children, adolescents, and adults at all levels of IQ, and in children and adults from linguistically and culturally diverse backgrounds. (Fletcher and Lyon, 1998, 61)

These researchers also sought to determine whether disabled readers use the same or different processes as nondisabled readers when learning to read:

> The NICHD research has *not* found the processes underlying reading disability to be *qualitatively* different from those processes associated with early reading proficiency. Reading problems occur as part of a natural, unbroken continuum of ability. What causes good reading also leads to poor reading when the processes are deficient. (Fletcher and Lyon, 1998, 62)

The NICHD-funded studies found that while there are multiple causes for reading failure (e.g., neurological, familial, cultural), "most children's problems occur at the level of the single word" (Fletcher and Lyon, 1998, 62).

Preventing Reading Difficulties in Young Children

The importance of identifying the causes of reading failure led the U.S. Department of Education and the U.S. Department of Health and Human Services to ask the National Academy of Sciences to establish a committee to examine the *prevention* of reading difficulties. This 400-page report, *Preventing Reading Difficulties in Young Children* (Snow, Burns, and Griffin, 1998), reviewed research on normal reading development and instruction; on risk factors useful in identifying groups and individuals at risk of reading failure; and on prevention, intervention, and instructional approaches to ensure optimal reading outcomes.

As a result of this review, the committee identified three main stumbling blocks that throw children off course on their journey to skilled reading: (1) difficulty in understanding and using the alphabetic principle, (2) failure to acquire and use comprehension skills and strategies, and (3) loss of motivation.

The committee report points out that it is now possible to identify children at risk for reading difficulties even before they go to school and to provide interventions to support language and literacy development:

> There is converging research support for the proposition that getting started in reading depends critically on mapping the letters and the spelling of words onto the sounds and

speech units that they represent. Failure to master word recognition impedes text comprehension. (321)

Our analyses of the research literature in reading acquisition leads us to conclude that, in order to prevent reading difficulties, formal instruction in reading needs to focus on the development of two sorts of mastery: word recognition skills and comprehension skills. (322)

Although context and pictures can be used as a tool to monitor word recognition, children should not be taught to use them to substitute for information provided by the letters in the word. (323)

Finally, in the "Executive Summary," the committee concluded:

There is little evidence that children experiencing difficulties learning to read, even those with identifiable learning disabilities, need radically different sorts of supports than children at low risk, although they may need more intensive support. (Snow, Burns, and Griffin, 1998, 2)

Every Child Reading: An Action Plan of the Learning First Alliance

Early in 1998, twelve leading national education organizations issued a report entitled *Every Child Reading: An Action Plan of the Learning First Alliance*. The alliance sought to react quickly to new research but avoid falling victim to unsubstantiated fads. To meet this challenge, the alliance relied heavily on quantitative research to inform policy makers and educators of what must be done to improve students' reading skills. Drawing from such interdisciplinary fields as language, cognition, neurological science, and the psychology of reading, as well as longitudinal studies indicating correlations between teacher practices and reading success, the alliance reached consensus on these and other recommendations (*American Educator*, 1998):

- All children need explicit, systematic instruction in phonics *and* exposure to rich literature, both fiction and nonfiction.
- Comprehension instruction, language development, and writing instruction are essential from the beginning.
- Teacher preservice education should be improved and ongoing professional development provided.
- Education decisions should be based on evidence, not ideology.

Report of the National Reading Panel

In April 2000, NICHD issued the *Report of the National Reading Panel* in response to a congressional directive "to convene a national panel to assess the status of research-based knowledge, including the effectiveness of various approaches to teaching children to read" (National Reading Panel, 2000, 1). Building on the work of the National Research Council, the National Reading Panel (NRP) developed an objective research-review methodology. NRP staff identified more than 100,000 research studies on reading since 1966. From those, NRP identified the following essential instructional components:

Phonemic Awareness

Correlational studies have identified phonemic awareness as one of the best predictors of how well children will learn to read during the first two years of instruction. Results of recent experimental studies led the panel to conclude that "phonemic awareness training was the cause of improvement in students' phonemic awareness, reading and spelling following training" (NRP, 2000, 7). Furthermore, the effects of such instruction for children of varying abilities lasted well beyond the end of training.

Systematic Phonics

Among previous findings reaffirmed by the panel:

> Systematic phonics instruction produces significant benefits for students in kindergarten through sixth grade and for children having difficulty learning to read. Kindergartners who received systematic beginning phonics instruction demonstrated enhanced ability to read and spell words. First graders who were taught phonics systematically were better able to decode and spell, and they showed significant improvement in their ability to comprehend text. Older children receiving phonics instruction were better able to decode and spell words and to read text orally, but their comprehension of text was not significantly improved. (NRP, 2000, 9)

The panel concluded that phonics skills are necessary to learn to read, but they are not sufficient. They must be integrated with the development of phonemic awareness, fluency, and text reading comprehension skills.

Fluency

The panel found that "fluent readers are able to read orally with speed, accuracy, and proper expression" (NRP, 2000, 11). Fluency, therefore, is a prerequisite for reading comprehension, but it is often neglected in the classroom. Recent research has called attention to its importance and to the need for improved instructional practices that ensure fluency.

Vocabulary Comprehension

The panel pointed out the importance of teacher preparation for teaching vocabulary development and reached consensus on these recommendations: (1) Read to children daily, (2) begin direct instruction in kindergarten and continue throughout the grades, (3) use direct instruction but also encourage independent reading, which facilitates incidental vocabulary learning, (4) provide repeated and multiple exposures to new vocabulary, and (5) use both definitions and context clues. They emphasized that dependence on a single vocabulary instruction method will not result in optimal learning.

Text Comprehension

NRP summarized three prominent research findings:

Comprehension is a complex skill that depends on vocabulary development; it is an active process that requires intentional and thoughtful interaction between text and reader; and teacher preparation is intimately linked to students' achievement in comprehension. The panel recommended that teachers use a multiple-strategy method that includes comprehension monitoring, use of graphic and semantic organizers, posing questions, use of story structure, and summarization.

Review of Reading Research—Summary

Although knowledge continues to expand, we now have enough information to help almost all children learn to read, write, speak, and spell accurately and fluently.

Dr. Benita Blachman (1996), in "Preventing Early Reading Failure," a chapter in *Learning Disability: Lifelong Issues,* explains the current situation well:

The good news is that there have been scientific breakthroughs in our knowledge about the development of literacy. We know a great deal about how to address reading problems even before they begin. The tragedy is that we are not exploiting what is known about reducing the incidence of reading failure. Specifically, the instruction currently being provided to our children does not reflect what we know from research. Direct, systematic instruction about the alphabetic code is not routinely provided in kindergarten and first grade, despite the fact that, given what we know at the moment, this might be the most powerful weapon in the fight against illiteracy. (Blachman, 1996, 66–67)

To remedy this deficiency, these findings need to be part of teacher preparation. To be successful, reading teachers need to know what to teach (instructional components of reading); they need an appropriate sequence for teaching the components (principles of reading development); they need to understand how skills are acquired (principles of skill learning); and, finally, they need to understand and be able to deliver effective instruction (principles of instruction).

As indicated by Blachman, reading researchers have reached a general consensus on the components of successful reading instruction. In this edition of *The Writing Road to Reading,* we will explain how The Spalding Method implements current research findings in each category.

Instructional Components of Reading

The previous review of research has established that the act of reading is a complex process, involving many subprocesses occurring simultaneously or in parallel. Although readers use these subprocesses unconsciously to some degree, research supports systematic and explicit instruction to help all students use them more efficiently. We will explain each subprocess and how and where it is addressed in The Spalding Method.

Phonemic Awareness

The understanding that spoken words and syllables consist of sequences of elementary speech sounds is a powerful predictor of success in learning to read (Adams, 1990). Research findings demonstrate that phonemic awareness is more highly related to learning to read than are general intelligence, reading readiness, and listening comprehension (Stanovich, 1986, 1993). Furthermore, it is the most important core and causal factor separating normal and disabled readers (Share and Stanovich, 1995); and it is equally important in learning to spell (Ehri and Wilce, 1987; Treiman, 1985, 1993). Phonemic-awareness instruction is strongest when the sounds are presented with the symbols (Ball and Blachman, 1991; Byrne and Fielding-Barnsley, 1993, 1995; Hatcher, Hulme, and Ellis, 1994).

Chapter 1 provides strategies for explicitly teaching children to break (segment) spoken words or syllables into individual sounds (phonemes) and blend individual sounds into spoken words. In The Spalding Method, phonemic awareness is reinforced in daily oral and written phonogram reviews and spelling dictation.

Feature Recognition

Feature recognition is the ability to distinguish curves and vertical, diagonal, and horizontal lines. Research tells us the parts of the brain specialized for distinguishing curves and lines are activated by looking at print, although the reader may not be conscious of the fact (Farnham-Diggory, 1992). Thus, shapes of letters are not remembered as holistic patterns. Rather, the visual system analyzes each letter into these elementary features. Therefore, to be fluent at recognizing letters, students need to be familiar with the distinctive features of each letter (Adams, 1990).

The six features used to write the twenty-six manuscript letters are taught and practiced in The Spalding Method. These are illustrated and strategies for teaching them are found in chapter 1, page 18.

Letter Recognition

Letter recognition is the ability to group features into patterns, automatically recognizing letters as wholes. Previously, poor readers' errors with letter orientation were often considered signs of neurological dysfunction or immaturity. Yet, Adams noted:

> Letter reversals seem to be merely a symptom of low print knowledge, rather than a cause of reading problems. Moreover, training children to attend to the relevant contrasts between letters has been shown to hasten their ability to recognize and distinguish between them. (Adams, 1990, 65)

Because the ability to recognize lower-case letters is important for reading text, Adams suggested, "If working with first graders with little letter knowledge, it may be wiser to give priority to the lower case letters" (66).

In The Spalding Method, explicit handwriting instruction in combining features into manuscript letters is followed by practice forming lower-case letters in daily written phonogram reviews. To assist recall, students explain which features are used to form each manu-script letter. Strategies are taught in chapter 1, beginning on page 18.

Sound-Symbol Relationships (Decoding)

Research findings demonstrate that "the critical component of reading that must be taught is the relationship of print to speech" (Fletcher and Lyon, 1998, 57). Early and systematic emphasis on decoding leads to better achievement than late or more haphazard approaches (Adams, 1990; Beck and Juel, 1995; Chall, 1996a). University of Michigan professor Dr. Keith Stanovich asserted: "That direct instruction in alphabetic coding facilitates early read-ing instruction is one of the most well established conclusions in all of behavioral science" (Stanovich, 1994, 285).

In The Spalding Method, instructions for teaching students to simultaneously say and write seventy common sound-symbol relationships (phonograms) are provided in chapter 1, pages 19–26.

Spatial Placement

The spatial placement process enables the reader to recognize or anticipate where particular letters are likely to be located (Farnham-Diggory, 1992). This knowledge enhances students' ability to spell and read. For example, children learn that the letter *y* most frequently occurs at the ends of words.

Spalding students are taught to expect certain letters and letter combinations to occur in specific places and to differentiate the *"legal"* from *"illegal"* position of letters in print. For example, *ai, au, oi,* and *ui* do not occur at the end of English words. (See chapter 1, page 39.)

Vocabulary (Lexical Process)

Beginning in infancy, the brain stores the meanings of words and word parts (prefixes, base words, and suffixes). The lexical process, which includes both understanding of vocabulary and the morphology of language, enables the listener or reader to access those meanings (Farnham-Diggory, 1992). Research from as early as the 1920s has identified vocabulary knowledge as a significant factor in the development of reading skills.

In The Spalding Method, the Extended Ayres Word List is the foundation for vocabu-lary instruction. Children learn the meanings of high-frequency words as well as word parts (see chapter 2, pages 82–83). Vocabulary is extended through use of quality literature in the reading lessons; and extensive independent reading is encouraged.

Sentence Structure (Syntactic Process)

Language acquisition studies show that even very young children acquire knowledge of speech production, word meaning, classes of words (nouns, verbs), conversational formats, rhymes, and grammar. (A detailed summary may be found in *Cognitive Processes in Educa-tion,* Farnham-Diggory, 1992.) However, when children arrive at school, they need direct instruction in the written structure of the English language, including parts of speech, word order, and rules of capitalization, punctuation, and grammar. In a valuable reference work for teachers, *Speech to Print,* Dr. Louisa Cook Moats, former director, Washington, D.C. NICHD Early Intervention Project, stated:

> The teacher who understands language and how children are using it can give clear, accurate, and organized information about sounds, words, and sentences. The teacher who knows language will understand why students say and write the puzzling things that they do and will be able to judge what a particular student knows and needs to know about the printed word. (Moats, 2000, 1)

In The Spalding Method, teachers introduce students to twenty-nine language rules in the spelling lesson and expand students' knowledge of language structure and conventions in the writing lesson. (See chapters 1 and 2.)

Text Comprehension (Semantic Process)

The NRP report (2000) states that text comprehension is enhanced when readers (1) actively connect ideas in print to their prior knowledge and experiences, (2) construct mental representations, (3) use cognitive strategies, and (4) use reason strategically when their comprehension breaks down. They note it is helpful for teachers to demonstrate such strategies until the students are able to carry them out independently.

Spalding students are explicitly taught to consciously monitor comprehension and identify unfamiliar words, phrases, or sentences; make connections both within the text and with prior knowledge; make predictions; and reformat and summarize information. They practice these cognitive strategies (mental actions) on all types of print. (See chapter 3, page 141.)

Instructional Components of Reading—Summary

Knowing the principal processes that are active during skilled reading and how they interact helps teachers diagnose problems when students have difficulty reading. It is important to understand that vocabulary development, knowledge of sentence structure, and listening comprehension all begin in early childhood and are common to speech that all people develop naturally. However, phonemic awareness, feature and letter recognition, spatial placement, and sound-symbol relationships are common only to societies that have a written language. Research has confirmed that these are not learned naturally, they must be taught (Adams, 1990; Adams and Bruck, 1995; Liberman and Liberman, 1992). Furthermore, even those processes that begin in early childhood (vocabulary development, knowledge of sentence structure, and listening comprehension) are enhanced by direct, systematic instruction in school. Neuroscientist Steven Pinker expressed the consensus among scientists:

> Language is a human instinct, but written language is not. Language is found in all societies, present and past. . . . Compare all this with writing. Writing systems have been

invented a small number of times in history. . . . Until recently, most children never learned to read or write; even with today's universal education, many children struggle and fail. A group of children is no more likely to invent an alphabet than it is to invent the internal combustion engine. Children are wired for sound, but print is an optional accessory that must be painstakingly bolted on. This basic fact about human nature should be the starting point for any discussion of how to teach our children to read and write. (Pinker, 1999, ix–x)

In The Spalding Method, all children receive explicit, systematic instruction in each of these instructional components. Children who have dyslexia or related language disabilities are taught diagnostically until proficiency is reached. To prevent reading failure, classroom instruction must incorporate what we know about how children learn to read and why children fail to learn to read. To determine the scope and sequence of instruction, teachers need to understand how students progress from learning to read to reading to learn.

Principles of Reading Development

The late Dr. Jeanne Chall developed a framework for organizing an instructional sequence for reading while she served as the director of the Reading Laboratory at Harvard University. Chall (1983a) noticed that the facts of beginning reading fit a developmental rather than a single process. This suggests that readers are doing *different* things in relation to printed matter at each successive stage. Analysis of school results, laboratory experiments, and clinical findings indicate that the first task in learning to read is learning the relation between sounds and letters—decoding.

Teachers who know the developmental stages of reading are able to plan lessons that meet students' instructional needs at each stage. As we identify the first four stages, including the instructional components that should be emphasized from preschool through eighth grade, we will explain how The Spalding Method provides such instruction. (For more detailed descriptions of all six stages, see *Stages of Reading Development*, Chall, 1996b.) Chall noted that the ages or grade levels associated with each stage are *approximations* to identify where the instructional emphasis *typically* takes place. In many schools, Stage 1 begins in kindergarten.

Stage 0–Prereading (Birth–Age 6)
From birth to kindergarten, children develop three types of knowledge. First, they learn a basic vocabulary (e.g., labels for persons, places, things, events, and procedures in their environment). They develop a range of knowledge (facts and concepts) about letters, words, books, and the world around them. During these years, children also develop communication skills. The foundation for all communication is the ability to describe the people and events in their lives and the facts and concepts they have learned. Students who have traveled, have been read to extensively, or have watched educational television have an advantage. They have an extended vocabulary and quite a range of knowledge upon which to

draw. The research has shown that the abilities, knowledge, and skills acquired during the prereading stage are substantially related to success with reading at Stage 1.

Stage 1–Decoding (Grades 1–2, Ages 6–7)

The essential aspect of Stage 1 is learning the relationship between spoken sounds in words and the written symbols representing those sounds. Children learn to identify letters that represent speech sounds, to recognize differences between similar words (*bun/bug*), and to know when they have made a mistake. Experimental research has indicated that children go through phases in making oral reading errors (Biemiller, 1970).

In the first phase, children make word substitutions that are semantically and syntactically correct. Next, their errors have a graphic resemblance to the printed word. In the final phase, readers rely mostly on graphic exactness and somewhat on word meaning. Less skilled readers remain in the first phase, relying on word substitutions associated with meaning or a part of speech. Good readers pass through these stages quickly. They do not skip words or rely on context to decode words. Rather, eye movement studies show they see all the letters and read virtually every word (Foorman et al., 1997; Rieben and Perfetti, 1991; Vellutino and Scanlon, 1991; Vellutino, Scanlon, and Tanzman, 1994).

In The Spalding Method, children are directly taught to read and write seventy common phonograms and to blend these phonograms into high-frequency words. Daily oral and written phonogram reviews develop sound-symbol mastery. Reading the Extended Ayres Word List two ways (for spelling and for reading) helps children automatically decode these and other similar words when reading books.

Although the first 700 words in the Ayres list should be in the spoken vocabulary of kindergarten and first-grade children, The Spalding Method provides procedures for teaching the usage and meaning of any unfamiliar words (see pages 76–83). Beginning on the first day of school, appropriate oral sentence structure is taught, followed by the conventions of written sentences (see pages 86–87). By reading children's literature aloud and discussing what is read, kindergarten and first-grade children expand their vocabulary, their knowledge of facts and concepts, and their communication skills (see chapters 2 and 3). In this way, children who may not have had these advantages in their preschool environment or who have great difficulty learning language are helped to catch up.

Even though decoding is the *primary* emphasis in this stage, children are also introduced to the attributes and elements of quality writing, the structure of different types of writing, and the use of comprehension mental actions while listening to stories read aloud. Listening comprehension skills transfer quickly to reading.

Stage 2—Confirmation and Fluency (Grades 2–3, Ages 7–8)

Chall described Stage 2 as a consolidation of what is learned through reading familiar print and what is already known to the reader. By reading familiar stories, children can concentrate on the print because the content is known to them. This enables them to move beyond accuracy to fluency (automaticity). During Stages 1 and 2, most new information is still learned through listening and observing and through the muscular (kinesthetic) sense because the instructional emphasis is on *learning* to read. *Emphasis* means that extra time is allotted to the skills that need to be mastered at that stage. However, it does not mean other skills are ignored.

In The Spalding Method, children are pretested so teachers know where to begin instruction (see pages 187–189). Daily oral and written phonogram reviews and spelling dictation procedures, including reading words two ways, develop instant word recognition and fluent reading. Although the primary emphasis is still on mastery of decoding, instant word recognition, and fluency, instructional time is also spent on literary appreciation and listening comprehension. It is important to remember that decoding must be automatic before the instructional emphasis can shift to reading comprehension. The reader cannot pay attention to more than one thing at a time. Children cannot focus on meaning while struggling to decode words.

Stage 3—Reading for Information (Grades 4–8, Ages 9–13)

In Stages 1 and 2, children learn to connect print to speech. In Stage 3, they learn to connect print to ideas. Thus, the emphasis shifts from *learning to read* to *reading to learn*. At this stage, children read for information. Chall pointed out that the importance of prior knowledge becomes apparent at this stage. What a student already knows is the most important element in what he or she is able to learn. In addition, children also need to learn a process for finding information in a paragraph, chapter, or book. Chall noted that in the past, fourth grade was when content-area subjects (history, geography, and natural sciences) were *introduced* because children by then had presumably mastered literacy skills and could deal with learning about times, places, and ideas removed from their direct experience.

At the beginning of this stage, learning by reading is still less efficient than learning by listening and observing. But by eighth grade, the efficiency of reading should equal and begin to surpass the other means of gaining information.

In The Spalding Method, second-grade and older children are pretested at the beginning of each grade to determine where to begin instruction. Chapter 3 provides strategies for explicitly teaching text structure and listening and reading comprehension. In Stage 3, the *primary* instructional emphasis shifts from listening to reading comprehension. Children are explicitly taught to use five mental actions to comprehend text. They also learn basic research skills: identifying essential information in a paragraph, chapter, or book to determine the main idea(s); note-taking; and summarizing.

Principles of Reading Development—Summary

Chall's stages of reading development provide a useful framework for teachers to use in lesson planning. The instructional emphasis in kindergarten and first grade is on Stage 1 skills and reinforcing Stage 0 skills. Pretesting second-grade and older children reveals students' stage of reading development and tells teachers where to begin instruction. Research findings have clearly established that Stage 1 and 2 skills must be at the automatic level before children are able to comprehend easily and efficiently. The Spalding Method provides explicit instruction for Stages 0–3. It also provides procedures for pretesting children and guidance for lesson planning (see chapter 5).

Principles of Skill Learning

Over the past hundred years, a wealth of helpful information has been reported in the experimental literature on *skill learning*. The literature includes laboratory studies of every type of skill and studies of skill development in everyday life—from athletes to business entrepreneurs. Farnham-Diggory noted:

> Skill-acquisition in any field appears to include learning phases of three fundamental types: analysis, practice to the point of automaticity, and attention-management. When you learn a skill, you go in and out of these phases repeatedly. . . . You cannot be in more than one of these learning phases at the same time. . . . Each phase of skill learning has its own logical requirements, and they are not interchangeable. (Farnham-Diggory, 1992, 89)

We will discuss the requirements of each phase, then explain how they are incorporated in The Spalding Method.

The Analytical Phase (Task Analysis)

Dr. Orton taught Mrs. Spalding to divide every task into its parts, sequence the parts, and then directly teach each part. Spalding students are also taught to analyze each task. For example, during spelling lessons, students analyze the features of the alphabet letters, the sounds of spoken words, the phonogram to use when there are several possibilities, and the pronunciation of words when more than one pronunciation is possible.

During integrated spelling/writing lessons, children analyze the parts of speech and language rules and concepts. In composition lessons, they analyze their purpose for writing, their choice of a particular type of writing, and their use of the conventions of writing.

During reading lessons, children analyze the attributes of fine literature; the elements of narrative, informative, and informative-narrative writing; and their use of comprehension mental actions. With each of these analyses, children are required to explain their reasoning.

Practice to the Point of Automaticity

Farnham-Diggory noted in the Foreword (see page xi) that basic, or first-order, subskills must be automatic so that there is enough working memory available to focus on second- or third-order subskills. For this to occur, practice must be "well beyond the point where the action feels smooth and efficient" (Farnham-Diggory, 1992, 92). Psychologists call this *overlearning*. It is actually programming a part of the brain called the *cerebellum* to carry out an action automatically.

Learning a routine to the point of automaticity involves perceptual information, motor actions, and knowledge. One example is the routine of signing your name. When first learning to write, you try to remember letters and the rules for making them—jobs handled by other parts of the brain. As name-writing is practiced, features of individual letters are noticed first (feature recognition). With practice, the features are grouped and whole letters are *perceived* (letter recognition). With sufficient practice, a group of letters is perceived as a whole (your first name).

In the beginning, working and kinesthetic memory tell your pencil to move up and around, back and forth. Each *motor action* receives a separate command. With practice, all these *motor actions* for writing your name are activated with a single command.

Working memory also retrieves the particular letters in your first name (knowledge). At first, working memory retrieves one letter of your name at a time (maybe not even in the right order), but with practice, a single command retrieves all the letters of your name as a package.

The process of automating an activity is the process of shifting control from other parts of the brain (the cortex) to the cerebellum. When name-writing is automated, you can sign your name while talking to a friend; you begin and end at a fixed point; you finish once you start; it's difficult to start in the middle or recover if interrupted; and it's extremely difficult to change your signature once learned.

When a routine becomes automated, grouping of perceptual information, motor actions and knowledge has occurred. In this way, a symbol (your name) has come to control a large amount of information in a small amount of workspace.

At the beginning of learning a new task, practice is short but frequent to achieve accurate performance of the skill. Practice must be *distributed* over time to achieve automatically (overlearning). A few examples of how The Spalding Method provides practice to automaticity follow:

In spelling lessons, students review new phonograms daily until they can say and write them automatically. They read Ayres words two ways until they can read them fluently and spell them accurately (see chapter 1).

In integrated spelling/writing lessons, students compose oral (then written) sentences that demonstrate understanding of *unfamiliar* words. They compose sentences that demonstrate knowledge of the attributes of simple (later compound, complex) sentences. In composition lessons, students write related sentences, then informative-narrative (then informative, finally narrative) paragraphs that include the elements of each type of writing and that demonstrate the attributes of paragraphs (see chapter 2).

In reading lessons, students read aloud daily to develop fluency, identify attributes of quality literature, identify elements of narratives (then informatives, finally informative-narratives), and use and label three (then five) mental actions while listening to or reading *McCall-Harby* and *McCall-Crabbs* paragraphs. In Spalding spelling, writing, and reading lessons, students have extensive practice of perceptual, motor, and knowledge routines.

Attention Management

When routines become automated, space becomes available in working memory to choose among them. How you make those choices is an important part of learning any skill. Farnham-Diggory explained:

In general, attention-management involves the construction of higher-order timesharing programs. . . . The attention-management program says, in effect, "When this-and-this happens, switch your attention here. When that-and-that happens, switch your attention there." Learning to construct these higher-order timesharing programs is essential to skill development. (Farnham-Diggory, 1992, 94)

Since attention *can* be focused on only one task at a time, students develop attention control by actively participating in each part of the lesson. A few examples of how The Spalding Method requires active participation follow:

In spelling lessons, students respond in unison during oral and written phonogram reviews and spelling dictation, and all students write phonograms and spelling words.

In integrated spelling/writing lessons, students participate in group discussions about parts of speech and compose oral (then written) sentences. In composition lessons, students participate in group discussions of related sentences and the writing process. They compose group, then individual, informative-narrative, informative, and narrative paragraphs.

In reading lessons, students participate in group discussions of the attributes and elements of literature, read in unison and independently, answer questions, and use mental actions while listening or reading.

Part of attention management is teaching students to switch attention (focus) from one task to another. For example, in spelling lessons, students focus on reading individual sounds or syllables when reading for spelling, then focus on recognizing whole words when reading for reading.

In integrated spelling/writing lessons, students focus on demonstrating the meaning of an unfamiliar word, then switch attention to checking their use of English conventions (e.g., capitalization, punctuation). In composition lessons, they switch attention from composing, to revising for content, and, finally, to editing.

In reading lessons, students switch attention to decoding when they encounter an unfamiliar word, then reread the entire sentence to focus again on comprehension.

Further description of these phases of skill learning is provided in *Cognitive Processes in Education* (Farnham-Diggory, 1992).

Principles of Skill Learning—Summary

We know that to be effective, successful instruction must adhere to the principles of skill learning. Children acquire the requisite language skills most easily when teachers analyze each skill and present its component parts in a logical order, providing appropriate practice until automaticity is reached and the mind is able to focus on more sophisticated tasks. Farnham-Diggory noted:

Spalding's method fully incorporated the three critical skill learning principles. . . . There is extensive training in *analyzing* print, in *analyzing* the nature of the sound stream of the spoken language, and in *analyzing* the writing process. There are enormous amounts of *practice*. Students cycle back, over and over again, through materials they have learned earlier. And *attention management* strategies are explicitly taught. There are specific routines for directing your mind through spelling and reading activities. (Farnham-Diggory, 1987, 13)

But providing instruction at the appropriate level of difficulty, sufficient practice, and training in attention management is still not enough. There is one more set of principles teachers need to teach effectively.

Principles of Instruction

A successful model of instruction takes into consideration the nature of learning, how curricula should be organized, how classrooms should be managed, and what constitutes achievement. A model of cognitive apprenticeship was described by Dr. Allan Collins and his colleagues (1989) at the Center for the Study of Reading at the University of Illinois. This model is an instructional delivery system that is easily applied to any subject; it involves students in every lesson; it makes lessons more meaningful; and it develops students' critical thinking skills. We will define terms used in the Collins model and explain how this model of instruction is incorporated in The Spalding Method. Collins lists six principles of instruction: modeling, coaching, scaffolding and fading, articulation, reflection, and exploration.

Modeling

Collins noted that when *modeling,* an expert carries out a task "so that students can observe and build a conceptual model of the processes that are required to accomplish the task" (Collins et al., 1989, 22). Although many tasks are concrete and observable, this is not the case in cognitive tasks such as reasoning, problem solving, knowledge retrieval, and decision making. Therefore, the teacher needs to make these tasks visible by thinking out loud while describing the reasoning process. Examples of modeling (demonstrating and explaining) in The Spalding Method follow:

During spelling lessons, teachers model precise formation of features and letters and precise pronunciation of each new phonogram and each word in spelling dictation (see chapter 1).

During integrated/spelling writing lessons, teachers model composing sentences that demonstrate correct meaning and usage of unfamiliar or difficult spelling words.

For composition lessons, teachers model thinking out loud while composing clear, logical informative-narrative (then informative, finally narrative) paragraphs (see chapter 2).

For literary appreciation lessons, teachers model thinking out loud while identifying and explaining each attribute of literature. For text-structure lessons, they model identifying elements of each type of writing while reading *McCall-Harby* and *McCall-Crabbs* paragraphs. For listening (then reading) comprehension lessons, they model use of five mental actions while reading *McCall-Harby* and *McCall-Crabbs* paragraphs (see chapter 3).

Coaching

When coaching, the teacher guides, prompts, and provides feedback as the student performs a task, or part of one. The goal is to bring the performance of the novice closer to that of the expert. During the coaching phase, the teacher prompts a component of the working memory system. The teacher is also helping guide and supervise practice to the point of automaticity.

To use a baseball analogy, the coach guides as the players practice holding and swinging the bat. As soon as the novice attempts the task, the transition from modeling to coaching begins. The coach gives specific feedback, such as telling the novice player to grip the bat in a different way.

Spalding coaching begins after the teacher has provided one or more clear, specific models of each new spelling, writing, and reading skill. All students need some type of assistance performing each new task. Help ranges from stating the information needed to complete the task (e.g., telling which phonogram to use when more than one is possible) to signaling to remind students of previous learning (e.g., using fingers during dictation). A few examples of effective coaching during Spalding lessons follow:

In spelling lessons, during oral phonogram reviews, teachers say the sounds correctly as soon as a phonogram is mispronounced. During written phonogram reviews, they initially show each phonogram immediately after students write it so errors can be corrected quickly. As students' accuracy improves, teachers use delayed feedback.

In integrated spelling/writing lessons, teachers prompt as students compose oral sentences by giving additional examples and by providing specific, immediate feedback when grammar or word sequence is incorrect. In composition lessons, they guide as students decide the audience, the purpose for writing, and the elements to include.

In reading lessons, teachers guide as students identify examples of descriptive language. They help students articulate their reasons for choosing a specific word and provide immediate feedback. In text-structure lessons, they coach as students determine whether a passage is informative-narrative or narrative. During lessons on conscious use of mental actions, they guide as students think out loud and name the mental action they used. (For additional examples, see chapters 1–3.)

Scaffolding and Fading

In instructional terms, a scaffold is a support system. When *scaffolding,* the teacher provides support because novice learners are not yet able to independently perform the tasks. The difference between coaching and scaffolding is in degree. During the coaching phase, the new skill is not yet in long-term memory so *most* students need help *most* of the time. When the majority of students can accurately perform all or part of a skill, teachers fade (withdraw support). Fading occurs when the majority of students know the content and can apply their knowledge independently. One familiar example is a parent steadying the bicycle as a child is learning to ride. As soon as the child can manage alone, the parent removes support. The amount of practice required to reach this point varies significantly. Examples of scaffolding and fading in The Spalding Method follow:

In spelling lessons, teachers can usually fade quickly on single-sound consonants and easy multiletter phonograms, but they scaffold on multisound consonants, vowels, and difficult multiletter phonograms until mastery is achieved; they fade on easy words and syllables but scaffold when words or syllables have difficult phonograms or when more than one spelling is possible.

In integrated spelling/writing lessons, teachers can usually fade quickly on the attributes of *simple sentences* but scaffold for compound and complex sentences.

In composition lessons, they fade on composing related sentences but scaffold on using the writing process to compose the three basic types of writing.

In reading lessons, teachers can fade as soon as first-grade students identify *descriptive* words in literary appreciation lessons accurately, but scaffold all year on difficult concepts (e.g., insight and universality). In text-structure lessons, they fade as soon as students can identify clear examples of narratives and informatives, but scaffold all year on more difficult informative-narrative passages. Teachers may fade quite quickly on the first three mental actions but continue to provide support identifying implied main ideas.

During this process of modeling, coaching, and scaffolding and fading, teachers require students to participate so they can become independent learners.

Articulation

The teacher requires *students* to verbalize the principles, rules, or situations underlying knowledge use. This process can take place through dialogues, critiques, or summaries. It is well known in learning theory that verbalization aids transfer to new situations. As students put their understanding into words, they learn to generalize more efficiently and to discover aspects of the principles they did not understand before. A few examples of student articulation in The Spalding Method follow:

In spelling lessons, students explain formation of individual letters and how language rules apply to spelling words. In integrated spelling/writing lessons, they explain the attributes of *simple* (then compound, complex) sentences. In composition lessons, students decide the type of writing and identify the elements to include. In reading lessons, they explain the attributes and elements of literature and the five mental actions.

Reflection

Reflection applies to performance of motor tasks, problem solving skills, and thinking processes. During the process of reflection, teachers have students compare their performance with expert performance to determine progress toward proficiency. In sports, a team may watch videos to determine where they perform well and where they need more practice. A few examples of how The Spalding Method teaches reflection follow:

In spelling lessons, students compare their letter formation today with that of yesterday, their handwriting in new notebook sections with that of previous sections, and reflect on how knowing the rules has improved their spelling and reading. In writing lessons, students reflect on their daily performance composing written sentences and then paragraphs. (Saving some of students' work in file folders enables them to compare their progress frequently.) In reading lessons, students reflect on books they have read and explain how knowledge of text structure and use of mental actions assist their comprehension.

Exploration

During exploration, students are encouraged to apply skills to new situations; they figure out how and when each skill is relevant, and they take complete responsibility for their performance. In The Spalding Method, students apply their decoding skills to reading independently. They apply their knowledge of phonograms, spelling rules, and the attributes of sentences to compose simple, compound, and complex sentences and later to compose informative-narrative, informative, and narrative paragraphs. They use their knowledge of the five mental actions to comprehend library books and content-area texts read independently.

Principles of Instruction—Summary

Interactive instruction provides teachers with a great deal of information. When teachers believe students are ready to apply a skill to a new situation, they require independent performance. On the other hand, if students are not ready, teachers may need to return to modeling, coaching, or scaffolding.

Farnham-Diggory stated:

Instructionally, a Spalding teacher has been trained to *model* her own analytical processes; she is trained to *coach* rather than didactically preach; and she is trained in techniques of *scaffolding*. The whole curriculum is, in effect, a giant scaffold. It provides a supporting structure for dealing with print. *Articulation* of principles is consistently demanded of students. They must always explain and justify their reasoning. *Reflection* is embodied in the marking system—the simple but effective system for annotating parts of words that exemplify rules. . . . *Exploration* is assured through the program's emphasis on literature. Both teacher and students plunge into new realms together, and many is the time I've heard *teachers* express surprise and relief to discover that the principles they've been teaching really do come to their rescue in literature that was never written with those principles in mind. (Farnham-Diggory, 1987, 13–14)

Chapter Summary

In this chapter, we reviewed recent research that provides new insights about how children learn to read and about factors that cause children to fail. This discussion shed light on what children must know and be able to do to be articulate speakers, fluent readers, accurate spellers, and accomplished writers. We also discussed four factors identified by research as important for successful reading instruction. A successful reading program must include explicit instruction in all the essential instructional components; it must provide these components in an appropriate sequence for the child's stage of reading development; it must incorporate principles common to all skill learning; and it must incorporate principles of effective instruction. Finally, we demonstrated how The Spalding Method includes all of these factors. In chapter 5, we will show how these principles are used to develop successful lesson plans.

PLANNING INTEGRATED LANGUAGE ARTS LESSONS

CHAPTER OVERVIEW

Plan an Environment Conducive to Learning
Setting the conditions for learning

Design the Lesson
Aligning curriculum and student achievement with instruction

Monitor Student Achievement and Adjust Instruction
Meeting individual student needs

THE SPALDING METHOD is a *diagnostic* teaching method. This means that teachers continuously observe and informally evaluate students' performance and behavior to plan the most effective instruction. They compare student achievement with the grade-level curricula, determine students' instructional level, and plan appropriate lessons with sufficient practice activities. Romalda Spalding believed that teaching is a constant stream of professional decisions made before, during, and after interaction with students. She wanted teachers to be *decision makers.*

Teaching decisions fall into three categories: what content will be taught, what teachers will do to facilitate acquisition of the content, and what students will do to learn and to demonstrate that learning has occurred. Student achievement is enhanced when teachers' professional decisions are based on a thorough understanding of the content, sound principles of learning and instruction, and sensitivity to the student and the situation. Empowered with this knowledge and philosophy, teachers can design lessons that meet the needs of the class in general, of gifted students who need extra challenge, and of students with dyslexia or related disabilities who need additional help.

In this chapter, we will discuss how to plan a total of two to three hours for integrated spelling, writing, and reading lessons. (These may be divided into thirty-minute segments.) Lessons are organized around this Spalding language arts circle. The time allotted to each lesson varies

SPELLING
• Phonemic Awareness
• Phonograms with Handwriting
• High Frequency Vocabulary
• English Rules and Concepts

PHILOSOPHY

READING
• Literary Appreciation
• Text Structures
• Comprehension Actions

WRITING
• Sentences
• Compositions

depending on the grade and skill level of students. *Initially,* in the primary grades, more time is devoted to the spelling lesson because seven subskills of reading are taught there: phonemic awareness, feature and letter recognition, spatial placement, sound-symbols, a basic vocabulary, and language rules. When students have automated their performance on oral and written phonogram reviews and spelling dictation procedures, more time is planned for the writing and reading lessons. At that point, each day's spelling lesson should average thirty minutes, with the remaining time divided between reading and writing lessons. Upper-grade time allotments are adjusted according to student needs and school schedules. See "Framework for Planning Integrated Language Arts Lessons" on page 454.

This integrated language arts lesson plan is also effective in special education resource rooms or tutorial settings. Assuming a one-hour resource or tutorial session, allow approximately thirty minutes for the spelling lesson because it is the foundation for reading and writing. Plan about fifteen minutes for vocabulary development and oral sentence construction to reinforce the skills learned in spelling. Plan the remaining time for literary appreciation. Read an enjoyable poem or short story aloud so students see that the goal is pleasurable experiences with books. As soon as students have automated oral and written phonogram reviews and spelling dictation procedures, devote more time to the writing and reading lessons.

In this chapter, we plan an environment conducive to learning and provide procedures for designing successful lessons and for monitoring student achievement. Finally, we provide procedures for adjusting instruction to meet individual needs.

Plan an Environment Conducive to Learning

Each student's physical and mental well-being is a primary concern of Spalding teachers.

Physical Well-Being
Physical well-being means that students can learn without experiencing discomfort.

Procedure for Providing Physical Well-Being

1. Plan a quiet, orderly classroom, free from clutter and distracting visual stimuli. Include a centralized, convenient location for classroom materials.
2. Seat all students facing the front for *direct* instruction in spelling, writing, and reading lessons. This seating arrangement focuses students' attention on the lesson content. (Provide alternative study areas conducive to small-group and individual learning activities.)
3. Plan a seating arrangement that considers individual needs (e.g., seat students who have difficulty up front, where you can monitor their progress and adjust seating so that left-handed writers have an unobstructed view of the board or easel).

Mental Well-Being

Mental well-being involves feeling accepted and successful. The goal is for all children to grow and achieve their potential in an atmosphere of mutual respect.

Procedure for Facilitating Mental Well-Being

1. Plan class rules, expectations, and consequences that require all students to be treated with respect. Expect students to respect their own and others' property, work areas, and individual differences.
2. Establish a predictable daily schedule, allowing for flexibility as appropriate. (Provide copies of the schedule for students as needed.)
3. Establish daily routines that provide a sense of order and stability (e.g., students get materials only at the beginning and return them at the end of the class).
4. Plan to use visual materials, such as graphic organizers (e.g., Spalding charts) or illustrations, to make abstract concepts more concrete.
5. For students having difficulty learning, plan to break tasks into smaller parts, explain each part, and provide more practice. Be prepared to repeat directions or steps. Do not expect these students to generalize easily.
6. Plan appropriate, meaningful, clearly defined assignments that consider individual differences (e.g., allow students having difficulty writing to give sentences orally; provide challenging extensions for able learners).
7. Plan to emphasize each child's progress and strengths, not weaknesses (e.g., record the number of *correct* responses rather than the *incorrect* number on assignments and quizzes).

Plan an Environment Conducive to Learning—Summary

Lesson planning that provides for students' physical and mental well-being sets the stage for learning. Matching instruction to individual differences maximizes students' interest and confidence.

Design the Lesson

To design successful lessons, teachers (1) select instructional objectives at the correct level of difficulty, (2) select instructional delivery levels for each objective, (3) align information, responses, and activities to each lesson objective, and (4) prepare the introduction and conclusion.

Select Instructional Objectives at the Correct Level of Difficulty

The first step in successful lesson planning is selecting objectives at the correct level of difficulty. Teaching at the correct level enhances learning because children are not bored with material they already know, or frustrated by tasks that are too difficult. Determining the correct level of difficulty involves (1) analyzing the grade-level curriculum and (2) analyzing student achievement.

Analyze the Curriculum

Comprehensive Spalding curricula and instructional procedures are described in detail in chapters 1, 2, and 3. Study them until you have committed the procedures to memory. The primary emphasis (the most instructional time) in kindergarten through second or third grade is on the spelling lesson where children learn to read. The primary emphasis shifts from spelling to reading and writing when students have automated the first-order subskills (see Foreword, page xi). For many Spalding children, this transition occurs in the second grade. The Spalding structured, sequential curricula are set forth as grade-level *instructional objectives*. (See "Recommended Scope and Sequence," pages 442–453.)

An *instructional objective* is a clear statement of what you want students to know and be able to do at the completion of a learning task. Spalding instructional objectives are of two types. *Grade-level* objectives state what each student should know (general content) and be able to do (observable, measurable behavior) by the end of the year. *Lesson* objectives state what each student should know (specific content) and be able to do at the conclusion of a lesson. Both grade-level and lesson objectives have these two parts: the *content* to be learned (knowledge) and the *observable* and *measurable* student behavior that demonstrates performance.

Phonograms with Handwriting Grade-Level Objectives—Examples

The student will . . .

- segment spoken words into sounds and syllables.
- blend spoken sounds into words.
- explain the purpose for learning phonograms.
- explain the purpose for precise handwriting.
- precisely read phonograms one through seventy.
- precisely say and write phonograms one through seventy.

In the initial grade-level objective listed above, children are to master *the sounds in spoken words* (content). The observable, measurable student behavior is the ability to *segment*. Students are to analyze spoken words into sounds or syllables. In the second objective, the content is the individual *sounds* that comprise *words*; the behavior is the ability to *blend*.

Grade-level objectives listed in the scope and sequence chart (see pages 443–453) are analyzed into *daily lesson objectives* by the teacher and sequenced from easiest to hardest and from most concrete to most abstract. To plan clear, specific lesson objectives focus on the *information* to be taught, the *questions* to ask to check for understanding, your *responses*, and the *practice activities* to provide. Although the following are *first-grade* lesson objectives, they may be adjusted for beginning students at other grade levels. The *observable, measurable behavior* part of each objective remains the same, but the *specific content* (difficulty and number of words) varies according to grade level.

First-Grade Day 1 Lesson Objectives—Examples

Phonograms with Handwriting

The student will . . .

- segment the spoken words *me, do, and, go,* and *at* into individual sounds.
- blend individual sounds into spoken words *me, do, and, go,* and *at.*
- explain the purpose for learning phonograms with precise handwriting.
- precisely say and write phonograms *a, c, d,* and *f.*
- explain formation of phonograms *a, c, d,* and *f.*
- precisely read phonograms (say sounds) *a, c, d,* and *f.*
- precisely say and write phonograms *a, c, d,* and *f.*

Literary Appreciation

The student will . . .

- name the author of a *read-aloud* book.
- identify who the story is mainly about.
- identify a favorite part of the story.

Each successive day's spelling lesson plan should include introduction of new phonograms and oral and written phonogram reviews of all previously introduced phonograms. Each day's literary appreciation lesson should include these three *basic* and other objectives using different read-aloud books.

While students are learning the first forty-five phonograms, follow the preparation for spelling dictation procedures in chapter 1, page 46. After forty-five phonograms have been introduced (seventy for third grade and above), and children have completed preparation for spelling dictation procedures, begin spelling dictation lesson objectives at the appropriate level of difficulty.

> ### First-Grade Day 15 Lesson Objectives—Examples
>
> **Spelling Dictation**
>
> The student will . . .
>
> - precisely say, write, and read spelling words *me* through *she*.
> - precisely read *me* through *she* two ways: for spelling and reading.
> - mark spelling words *me, go, a,* and *she* and explain pronunciation (rule 4). (Having students explain the marking and pronunciation ensures they understand the rule well enough to apply it to new words.)
>
> **Writing**
>
> The student will . . .
>
> - compose oral sentences that demonstrate the meaning of spelling words *me* through *she*.

After children have written sections A–G in their notebooks, add the objective for written sentences listed below.

> ### First-Grade Day 25 Lesson Objective—Example
>
> **Writing**
>
> The student will . . .
>
> - write simple sentences that demonstrate the meaning of *lot, law,* and *just* in section H.

The basic *observable, measurable* student behaviors, "compose oral and written sentences," remain the same all year. The *specific content* changes as students learn more difficult words.

Analyze Student Achievement

It is not enough to analyze and understand the curricula. Planning objectives at the correct level of difficulty also requires recognizing able learners who need challenge, students who are experiencing difficulties, and students with language disabilities. For example, some kindergartners come to school knowing how to read. After initial whole-group introduction of phonograms and oral and written reviews, provide simple books for these children to read. (See kindergarten reading grade-level objectives in "Recommended Scope and Sequence," page 452.)

Some children having difficulty may need only preteaching and/or reteaching. Others may require considerably more help. Children with language-based learning disabilities may have difficulty remembering words they hear; naming common objects, colors, and numerals; learning sound-symbol relationships; comprehending and forming sentences; seeing word relationships; and understanding figurative language.

Dyslexia, a *language-based* learning disability, is manifested by difficulties with reading, writing, and spelling. Children with dyslexia always have difficulty with learning sound-symbol relationships, single-word decoding, and spelling. Research has shown these difficulties are not the result of generalized developmental disability, or visual or auditory impairment. Rather, dyslexia "is a specific language-based disorder of constitutional origin characterized by difficulties in single word decoding, usually reflecting insufficient phonological processing" (Lyon, 1995, 9).

NICHD-funded studies have found that both poor readers and children with dyslexia benefit by phonological awareness training and phonics. The research suggests:

> For children at risk for reading failure or who are poor readers, phonics knowledge should be presented explicitly and in an orderly progression. Such instruction in the early grades may actually prevent reading failure, which is why we feel it should be part of regular classroom practices for all children. (Fletcher and Lyon, 1998, 76)

If you teach kindergarten or first grade, plan to begin with Stage 1 skills. Children *should* be ready to transition from Stage 0 (prereading) to Stage 1 (decoding). However, if children are not ready, the Spalding curricula described in chapters 1 through 3 provide explicit procedures for *reinforcing* skills that should have been mastered in the prereading stage and for *introducing* all Stage 1 skills.

If you teach older or special needs students, pretest to ensure that the objectives are at the correct level of difficulty (see pages 187–189). Older students who have not mastered Stage 1 skills should receive direct instruction in phonograms with handwriting; most are able to progress more quickly than younger beginners.

Summary

The work of creating *grade-level* objectives has been done for you. Your task is to use *grade-level* objectives to write *lesson* objectives that meet your students' needs. The next step is to determine the appropriate instructional delivery level. Use the "Recommended Scope and Sequence" and the "Framework for Planning Integrated Language Arts Lessons" as your guide (see pages 442–457).

Select Instructional Delivery Level(s) for Each Objective

After selecting spelling, writing, and reading objectives at the correct level of difficulty, consider whether to model, coach, or scaffold and fade (see chapter 4). If your objective involves *initial learning,* you will always *model.* This means you will plan to provide *all* the information and demonstrate *all* the procedures. On the other hand, if the objective is a review of previous learning, plan to coach or scaffold. Now, instead of providing all the information, only use prompts to guide students' performance. When they do the thinking and articulating, they develop proficiency more quickly. Fade (withdraw support) as soon as students are accurate.

During each lesson, listen carefully to students' performance on each task. Be prepared to change the level of instruction as needed. Each level requires careful planning.

Strong Models for Initial Instruction

The more precise your initial demonstrations and explanations are, the less reteaching you have to do. Before *initial* spelling, writing, and reading instruction at any grade, practice modeling the desired performance and explain the steps to follow.

Planning Strong Models—Examples

Spelling Lesson

- Practice modeling precise formation of features and precise formation and pronunciation of letters and letter combinations (phonograms).
- Practice precise pronunciation of each new word for spelling dictation. (See chapter 1.)

Writing Lesson

- For integrated spelling/writing lessons, compose sample sentences that demonstrate correct meaning and usage of unfamiliar or difficult spelling words.
- For composition lessons, prepare clear, logical examples of informative-narrative, then informative, and finally narrative paragraphs to use when demonstrating the writing process. (See chapter 2.)

Reading Lesson

- For literary appreciation lessons, select clear examples of descriptive language (then other attributes) to demonstrate and explain the attributes of literature.
- For text-structure lessons, select passages from the *McCall-Harby* and *McCall-Crabbs User's Guides* that will provide strong examples of the elements of each type of writing.
- For listening (then reading) comprehension lessons, select paragraphs from the *McCall-Harby* and *McCall-Crabbs User's Guides* to demonstrate the five mental actions. (See chapter 3.)

Prompts for Coaching Students

Coaching begins immediately after you have provided one or more models and have explained each new task. Examples of planning for coaching follow:

Planning Prompts for Coaching—Examples

Spelling Lesson

- Specific prompts for guiding students through letter formation are provided on pages 19–26, in chapter 1.
- For daily oral and written phonogram reviews, identify phonograms most frequently missed. *Phonograms that are difficult to say (oral review) are frequently different from those that are hard to spell (written review).* Select a set of phonograms for oral review and a set for written review every day. Each day, listen carefully to students and note most frequently made errors so you can revise the sets to be practiced.
- For spelling dictation, review the instructional tips column beside the Ayres words you plan to dictate. These tips provide help with prompts. They range from using fingers to indicate number of sounds to *telling* students which phonogram to use when two are possible. Each class's needs are different.

Writing Lesson

- For writing lessons, review daily student performance on oral sentences to identify most frequently made errors, then prepare specific prompts to help students be successful.
- Prepare prompts for assisting students in each stage of the writing process.
- Later, review students' written compositions to determine where they will need additional assistance.

Reading Lesson

- For literary appreciation lessons, preselect examples of *descriptive* language so you can guide students who need help.
- For text-structure lessons, preread selections to identify trouble spots and prepare appropriate prompts.
- For comprehension lessons, identify unfamiliar words and prepare prompts that help students identify context clues.

If you teach first-grade or older students who have previously been taught The Spalding Method, analyze their pretest results. For example, if students are accurate on a skill (e.g., saying and writing the seventy phonograms), you may be able to bypass modeling and only occasionally coach or scaffold.

Plan to Scaffold and Fade

A scaffold is a support system. The difference between coaching and scaffolding is one of degree. When the majority of students know the content and can apply their knowledge independently, fade (withdraw support). The amount of practice required to reach this point varies significantly. Therefore, use students' daily performance to guide decisions to provide or remove support.

Planning to Scaffold and Fade—Examples

Spelling Lesson

- Plan to fade within a few months during most first-grade oral and written phonogram reviews. Continue to review daily performance until students can automatically say and write all seventy phonograms. (This may be within weeks for older students.)
- Review the set of spelling words you plan to dictate. Determine which instructional tips, provided in the Ayres list, are needed. When those prompts (tips) are no longer needed, stop using them. On the other hand, if your students require prompts, provide them.
- Plan to circulate while students are saying words and writing them in their notebooks so you can support students having difficulty. For example, on a word like *January*, most students may be able to write the entire word without prompts. However, individual students may need support with writing and marking the third syllable. At the student's desk, show two fingers and quietly say the two sounds.

Writing Lesson

- Plan to support first-grade students on the attributes of written simple sentences until most students are accurate. Then fade on the attributes of simple sentences, but provide support for compound and then complex sentences.
- Plan to compose, revise, and edit group paragraphs with kindergarten and first-grade students. When first-grade students are able, let them write simple paragraphs first with a partner, then independently. Have the partners provide feedback for each other before your final check.

Reading Lesson

- In literary appreciation lessons, plan to fade as soon as first-grade students identify descriptive words accurately. Plan to support them all year long as they attempt to identify examples of insight and universality.
- In text comprehension lessons, plan to fade as soon as students can accurately identify the basic elements of each type of writing. Support with more difficult elements (e.g., point of view, theme).
- In comprehension lessons, plan to fade on the first three mental actions, but support on the last two all year.

The Spalding notebook is itself a scaffold. The rule pages provide a support system that students can continually refer to as they progress into more difficult language rules and concepts.

Practice of Articulation and Reflection

Spalding provides an abundance of explicit training in student articulation and reflection. But it takes planning. Prepare questions that require students to *articulate* (e.g., "How are the letters *a* and *d* different?") and to *reflect* on their performance in spelling, writing, and reading lessons. A few examples of preparing for these two instructional steps follow:

Preparing for Student Articulation and Reflection—Examples

Spelling Lesson

- Allow time for students to explain which features they use and describe how to form individual letters (articulation). Allow time to compare their letter formation today with previous performance (reflection).
- Plan practice articulating language rules using the Spalding Word Builder Cards. Then, have students reflect on their use of the rules in daily sentences and compositions.

Writing Lesson

- Plan to have students explain (articulate) the attributes of *simple* (then compound, complex) sentences and reflect on their daily performance composing written sentences. (Saving some of students' work in file folders enables them to compare their progress frequently.)
- Plan time for students to explain the decisions made during each stage of the writing process, then have them reflect on how that thoughtful process improved their compositions.

Reading Lesson

- Plan questions that require students to explain the attributes and elements of literature, use of text structure, and use of mental actions to assist comprehension. Plan time for students to reflect on how their comprehension improved as a result of consciously using the mental actions.
- Plan to have students articulate why they enjoyed particular stories or books, then provide time for them to reflect on what they learned or what insights they derived from the books.

Additional sample check for understanding and reflection questions are found under each set of procedures in chapter 1–3.

Summary

A strength of interactive instruction is that it helps students become self-sufficient more quickly by having them work independently as soon as they are able. Be prepared to constantly adjust your instructional level. Before long, plan to model, coach, and support and fade—all in one lesson. *Continuing support when students no longer require it is as serious an error as failure to provide help when it is needed.*

Align Information, Questions, Responses, and Activities to Each Lesson Objective

After selecting an instructional objective and determining whether modeling, coaching, or scaffolding is required, prepare information, questions, responses to students, and practice activities aligned to your objective. That means that the content you present, the actions you select to facilitate student understanding, and the activities you plan are *focused* on the lesson objective.

Align Information to Each Objective

Information is the foundation for thinking and learning. It is impossible to comprehend, write, solve problems, or be creative without information. Since teachers have so much information to share, the following procedures help design aligned lesson content:

Procedures for Aligning Information to Each Objective

- Identify the information that is essential for achieving the objective (need to know).
- Organize the information so students will see the relationship of each part to other parts and to the whole.
- Plan simple and direct vocabulary that precisely describes distinguishing features, rules, or concepts to be taught.
- Prepare examples that are accurate and unambiguous, and highlight the distinguishing feature(s) or the essence of the concept or generalization to be taught. (Don't wait until you are in the midst of a lesson to think of an example.)

Aligning Information to Each Objective—Examples

Spelling Lesson

- If your objective is to "say and write phonograms *a, c, d,* and *f,*" the relevant information is the features and sounds of each phonogram. Chapter 1, pages 19–26, provides precise dialogue containing the relevant information for phonogram introduction. The sounds you say and the letters you write on the board are your clear examples. (Telling children what words they can form with those phonograms is *not* aligned to this objective. Save that information for the *writing* lesson.)

continued

- If your objective is to "precisely say, write, and read Ayres words *me* through *she*," the relevant information is the phonogram sounds and letter formation needed to correctly write those words. If children have practiced sounds and letter formation in written phonogram reviews, they can say and write the words without an example. (Explaining the meaning is not aligned to this objective. Save it for the *writing lesson*.)

Writing Lesson

- If your objective is to "write simple sentences," the relevant information is a capital letter to signal the beginning of the thought about a person, place, or thing; a verb to express the action; and a period (full stop) to signal the end of the thought. For this objective, one or more example sentences are needed to clearly demonstrate all the attributes of simple sentences.

Reading Lesson

- If your objective is to "identify descriptive language in a story read aloud," the relevant information is the characteristics of descriptive language (see chapter 3, pages 123–126). Preselect clear examples from the story to be read aloud.

Every class is different, and you have to tailor the amount of information needed and your examples from year to year to be at the correct level of difficulty. After planning carefully selected, clear examples, the next step is to plan questions that check students' understanding, and responses that reinforce students' learning. The adage "Half of knowing what something is, is knowing what it is not" is still true.

Align Questions and Responses to Each Objective
To maintain students' attention on the new learning, questions that check children's understanding of the information and your responses to their answers must also be aligned. The following procedures set direction for this important task:

Procedures for Preparing Aligned Questions and Responses

- Plan questions that require students to (1) make discriminations based on the presence or absence of the critical attributes that have been taught, (2) explain application of a rule, or (3) explain the essence of a concept.
- Plan responses to students' answers that (1) reinforce the correct information, (2) dignify their responses, then correct a wrong or incomplete answer, or (3) redirect attention to the objective.

Aligning Questions and Responses to Each Objective—Examples

- To check student understanding, ask, "What features do we use to form the letter *a*?"
- To reinforce correct responses, plan to reinforce critical attributes. For example, if a student answers, "The letter *a* is formed with a circle that begins at 2 on the clock and a short line," an aligned response is, "Yes, *a* has two features, a circle that begins at 2 on the clock and a short line."
- If a student's answer is incomplete, "The letter *a* is formed with a circle that begins at 2 on the clock," an aligned response is, "The letter *a* is formed with a circle that begins at 2 on the clock *and a short line.*"
- If students' questions or comments are not relevant to the objective, a standard response is, "That is a great question (or comment). We will discuss that in our writing (or reading, science, social studies) lesson." Then remember to do so. (See additional examples under each set of procedures in Chapters 1–3.)

Align Practice Activities to Each Lesson Objective

Well-planned lesson activities are aligned to the objective and incorporate the principles of skill learning: task analysis, practice, and attention management (see chapter 4). Each activity should provide opportunities for students to analyze the task, to practice it until mastery is achieved, and to manage their attention. Since attention can be focused on only one task at a time, having all students participate develops attention control.

Procedures for Preparing Aligned Practice Activities

Task Analysis

Plan practice activities that

- require students to articulate distinguishing features and attributes.
- require students to analyze and explain steps of a procedure or process.
- require students to analyze and explain application of a rule or the essence of a concept.

Practice

- For *new* learning, plan *short* and *frequent* practice.
- After students accurately perform a skill, explain application of a rule or explain a concept; plan to *distribute* practice over time to develop and maintain automaticity.

continued

Attention Management

- Plan to have all students *actively participate* to maintain attention on the task.
- Plan to monitor student participation daily (e.g., move about the room to ensure that students are on task, assisting as needed).
- For *check for understanding* and *reflection* questions, plan *think time* and some type of *visible* student responses that ensures active participation.
- Plan signals for students to switch attention to a higher or lower skill as needed to accomplish the task.

Planning Analytical Practice Activities—Examples

Spelling Lesson—Task Analysis

- If the objective is to "say and write phonograms *a, c, d,* and *f,*" plan to have students articulate the distinguishing features of each letter.
- If the objective is to "say, write, and read *me* through *she,*" plan to have students analyze (segment) the sounds in *me,* say and write the phonograms that represent those sounds, and then read the word. A word of caution: When analyzing sounds in a particular word (e.g., *me*), do not talk about the other sound of phonogram *e.* That diverts attention from the objective, to "say, write, and read the word *me.*"

Writing Lesson—Task Analysis

- If the objective is to "identify attributes of a simple sentence," plan time for students to identify the word to capitalize, the subject noun or pronoun, the action word, and the end punctuation of one or more example sentences.
- If the objective is to "compose an informative-narrative," plan time for students to analyze decisions to be made during each stage of the writing process.

Reading Lesson—Task Analysis

- If the objective is to "identify descriptive language," preselect words for students to analyze and explain why the author chose those words.

Mastery of an instructional objective also requires planning short, frequent (massed) practice for new learning and practice that is distributed over time to develop and maintain automaticity.

Planning Massed and Distributed Practice Activities—Examples

Spelling Lesson—Massed Practice and Distributed Practice

- After introducing the first four phonograms, plan two-minute oral phonogram reviews four times a day, rather than an eight-minute review once a day. As more phonograms are introduced and students become more proficient, plan to review twenty to thirty phonograms in five to eight minutes once a day prior to spelling dictation.
- Remove single-letter phonograms from the daily review pile as soon as students say and write them accurately. Review these once a week, then once a month. Include difficult phonograms each time they occur in the week's spelling dictation lessons until mastery is achieved.

Writing Lesson—Massed Practice and Distributed Practice

- After sections A–G have been written in the notebook, plan to have students write two to three *simple* sentences *daily* until most students consistently include all the attributes of *simple* sentences.
- Plan to reinforce the attributes of *simple* sentences throughout the year by having students write and edit the three basic types of compositions.

Reading Lesson—Massed Practice and Distributed Practice

- Plan time to have students identify descriptive language until they can accurately identify descriptive words in new stories.
- Plan to review narrative structure on a regular basis after introducing informatives.

Finally, aligned practice activities should also provide students with opportunities to manage their attention so new learning can be mastered quickly. Through daily practice, students learn to maintain and switch attention as needed to accomplish the task.

Planning Practice Activities That Develop Attention Management— Examples

Spelling Lesson—Maintaining Attention

- Plan choral rather than individual responses during oral and written phonogram reviews and spelling dictation.

Spelling Lesson—Switching Attention

- Provide time for reading Ayres words two ways: Reading for spelling practices processing sounds sequentially; reading the whole word develops fluency. Explain to students that daily practice switching attention prepares them for using this strategy when reading books.

Writing Lesson—Maintaining Attention

- Plan to have students individually mark the subject noun or pronoun in a sentence. Have them check with a partner before whole-group discussion.

Writing Lesson—Switching Attention

- Plan opportunities for students to revise sentences written on the board for word choice, then have them switch attention to editing for English conventions. Explain that this prepares them for the same process when writing compositions.

Reading Lesson—Maintaining Attention

- After stating *check for understanding* or *reflection* questions, ask *all* students to *think about* the questions and then to respond by writing responses on *think* pads or individual slates or by raising their hands. Then call on one or more individuals to respond.

Reading Lesson—Switching Attention

- When students stumble over an unfamiliar word, repeat the last word read correctly (signal), then coach as they decode the unfamiliar word. Have them reread the entire sentence to regain comprehension. Have students use the same process when reading silently.

Prepare the Introduction and Conclusion

After preparing aligned information, questions and responses, and activities, design an introduction and conclusion that are also aligned to the objective.

Introducing the Lesson

Students usually expend more effort and consequently increase their learning if they know *what* they will be learning and *why* it is important (purpose for learning). *Making connections* with prior (background) knowledge is the foundation for inferential thinking and mentally summarizing (see chapter 3). Active participation by all students is required to increase learning and to help students develop attention control, an essential principle of skill learning (see chapter 4).

Procedure for Designing Lesson Introductions

- Plan an introduction that focuses attention on the new lesson content and connects to students' prior learning.
- Plan active participation by *all* students.

Planning Lesson Introductions—Examples

Spelling Lesson

TEACHER: "Yesterday you practiced saying and writing four phonograms. Let's review those sounds."

STUDENTS: "/ă/ /ā/ /ah/ /k/ /s/ /d/ /f/"

TEACHER: "You remembered the sounds of the first four very well. Today you will learn to say and write four new phonograms: *g, o, qu,* and *s.*"

Writing Lesson

TEACHER: "You have been composing oral sentences using words in sections A–G. Tell me what you included in those sentences."

STUDENTS: "We included who the sentence was about and what was happening."

TEACHER: "Yes. A good *oral* sentence tells who the sentence is about and what is happening to a person or animal. Today, I will explain what else you must include when you *write* sentences."

Reading Lesson

TEACHER: "You have identified descriptive words in stories I have read aloud. Think about some of the descriptive words we've talked about, then tell me what descriptive words are and why authors select words carefully."

continued

| STUDENTS: | "Descriptive words paint a picture of the characters and the setting. This makes you feel like you know the characters. You can imagine where they are and what they are doing." |
| TEACHER: | "Yes. When the author clearly describes the characters, the setting, and the action, the story becomes real. Today, I will teach you that authors also *appeal to our emotions* by the words they choose." |

These sample introductions direct students' attention to the new objective, they connect with students' prior knowledge, and they require active participation.

Closing the Lesson

An effective closing of the lesson requires students to summarize their learning. It also includes a transition to the new objective that makes clear the interrelationship within and between language arts subjects. To enhance student learning, use the following procedures:

Procedures for Closing a Lesson

- Plan active participation by all students: Prepare questions that require students to *mentally summarize* what they learned about critical aspects of the lesson objective; provide wait time for each child to think, then ask individual children to share; and hold all children accountable by calling on different students (nonvolunteers) in successive lessons.
- Plan smooth transitions from one objective within a lesson to another and between spelling, writing, and reading lessons.

Planning Lesson Closings—Examples

Transitions within Lessons

TEACHER:	"We just finished reviewing two-letter phonograms that have different pronunciations or different spellings depending on their location within a word. Tell me how that helps you read and spell."
STUDENTS:	"Knowing that we use *ay* to say /ā/ at the end of English words helps to improve our spelling." "Knowing that letter *a* usually says /ā/ at the end of a syllable helps us read words more quickly."
TEACHER:	"Yes. You can read these phonograms automatically, so you will be able to read books fluently. Now we will practice writing them so you can spell accurately."

Transitions between Lessons

TEACHER: "In the reading lesson today, you read an informative-narrative passage. What were the narrative and the informative elements of the story?" (Guide as students identify the elements.)

"Yes. This informative-narrative had two characters, a simple setting, and lots of facts. Today, I will teach you to write an informative-narrative paragraph."

Transitions are made more efficient by developing daily routines in spelling, writing, and reading lessons. Well-developed routines free students' working memory for concentration on the new information to be presented (see chapter 4, pages 161–163).

Design the Lesson—Summary

It is often said that preparation is 90 percent of any task. Providing a suitable climate and preparing well-designed lessons ensure that most of your language arts lessons will be successful for most students. We have discussed planning an environment conducive to learning and designing lessons aligned to one objective at a time. However, there is one more important step in a diagnostic teaching approach.

Monitor Student Achievement and Adjust Instruction

In The Spalding Method, the term *assessment* includes *informally* observing and evaluating students' daily behavior and progress, as well as measuring their performance on tests and quizzes. Assessment of first-grade or older student achievement may begin before the first day of school (if the prior year's achievement records are available), and it continues all year. The *Spelling Assessment Manual* is aligned to instruction in The Spalding Method and includes phonogram and spelling assessment procedures and forms to make record keeping easy.

We recommend using both norm-referenced, standardized tests and performance assessments to measure student achievement. Standardized tests evaluate student performance relative to other students in the same categories and are used by many school administrations. Performance assessments reveal student performance by evaluating observable actions or accomplished tasks.

Analyze Student Achievement (First Grade and Above)

Analyze prior-year reading and language standardized achievement test scores (if available) to help determine initial instructional levels. For example, if incoming students scored below grade level on vocabulary and comprehension subtests, admister a phonogram pretest to determine if the problem is inability to decode the words. If students can decode, the problem may be poor vocabulary development. Simple pretests, administered during the first week of school, provide a quick indication of older students' ability to decode, their knowledge of the basic structure of language, and their listening (oral language) comprehension.

Procedures for Determining Initial Instructional Levels (First Grade and Above)

Spelling Pretests

- If students have had prior Spalding training, plan time to give oral and written phonogram pretests on the first day of school to determine which phonograms have been mastered.
- Plan time to pretest first-grade and older students using the forms in the *Spelling Assessment Manual* (see Resources). This determines where in the Extended Ayres Word List to begin spelling dictation. Scores on this pretest demonstrate how well students spell and what previous learning must be reviewed.

Writing Pretests

- Select a topic for a short (four to six sentences) informative paragraph. This simple *pretest* will demonstrate how many of your students have mastered simple sentence structure and language conventions. Save their work to compare with paragraphs they write at the end of the year.

Reading Pretests

- To pretest listening (oral language) comprehension, select a grade-level *McCall-Crabbs* passage to read aloud. Have paper available for students to write their answers to the questions.

The next step is to analyze the pretest information to design lessons at the correct level of difficulty.

Procedures for Analyzing Pretest Information

Spelling

- For students who have not had Spalding, plan to introduce handwriting with phonograms as presented in chapter 1, pages 12–30, but move more rapidly.
- Follow specific directions in the *Spelling Assessment Manual* to determine initial instructional levels for individual students and the class.

Writing

- Select a familiar topic and have students compose a four- to six-sentence informative paragraph. If a majority of students include fragments and run-on sentences, poor word choices, errors in capitalization, punctuation, spelling, and grammar, plan to teach the attributes of simple sentences as described in chapter 2, pages 86–87. If the majority demonstrate mastery of the attributes of simple sentences, teach compound, complex sentences and use the writing process to teach the types of writing.

Reading

- If the majority of students achieve a grade-level score on the *listening* comprehension pretest but fail the phonogram pretest, assume that low *reading* comprehension or low vocabulary scores on the standardized test are due to an inability to decode.

In addition to beginning instruction at the correct level of difficulty, it is also important to analyze student achievement on an *ongoing* basis. The following procedures help you maintain instruction at the correct level:

Procedures for Maintaining the Correct Level of Difficulty

Analyze Daily Student Achievement

- Each day, analyze students' performance on oral and written phonogram reviews (including handwriting) to select phonograms for continued daily practice.
- Plan time to check accuracy of students' notebooks every day after dictation. List phonograms, rules, and handwriting concepts that require reteaching. Note progress toward accuracy of spelling and markings to share with students. (Accuracy of students' notebooks is achieved quickly if the procedures described in the *Spelling Assessment Manual* are followed faithfully.)
- Analyze students' performance on daily writing assignments to share progress and to identify concepts/skills that need reteaching.
- Analyze students' participation in reading class discussion and in daily oral reading to determine where to place instructional emphasis.

Analyze Weekly Achievement

- Analyze students' performance on weekly written phonogram quizzes. Plan to include phonograms missed in daily reviews until automaticity is achieved. Plan to note hand-

continued

writing concepts that need reteaching. For example, feature recognition (tall lines are not twice the height of short lines), letter recognition (clock letters are not rounded), and spatial placement (*plai/play*).

- Plan weekly spelling tests. In addition, select a few Ayres words and have students write and explain the spelling and/or pronunciation. After the test, analyze spelling performance and note errors (words, rules, phonogram placement) to determine what needs to be retaught.

- After teaching text structure and comprehension mental actions, select two or three lessons from *McCall-Crabbs Standard Test Lessons in Reading* as weekly tests. Record raw scores on the *McCall-Crabbs Record Sheet*. (These raw scores may be used as part of a reading grade on report cards.) Note types of questions students missed (e.g., inferential versus recall) and reteach the concepts (e.g., finding a stated or implied main idea).

Analyze Monthly Achievement

- The *Spelling Assessment Manual* provides specific directions for evaluating students' progress each month. (Students should spell one year ahead of their grade placement to be able to decode unfamiliar words encountered in subject-area reading.)

- Analyze students' scores. If the majority of students show gains each month, they are making steady progress, and you know you are teaching at the correct level of difficulty. If most students stay at the same score for several months, it may be for one of the following reasons: (1) Students are not progressing through the Ayres sections quickly enough to learn new rules required for spelling more difficult words. (2) Students are not reading from the notebook daily. (3) Students are not articulating how rules apply to spelling words. (4) Students are not reviewing previously taught words.

- Evaluate students' responses. Note errors to determine instructional components that need reteaching (e.g., feature and letter recognition, spatial placement, phonograms, vocabulary, spelling rules).

When a lesson does not go well, or some students are not progressing as they should, it is important to adjust instruction. The following procedure helps you use the Spalding content and sound principles of learning and instruction to diagnosis problems:

Procedure for Adjusting Instruction

Components of Learning

Have I . . .

- correctly identified students' reading development stage (Chall)?
- taught all the prerequisite subskills needed to accomplish the objective?
- taught at the correct instructional level (model, coach, scaffold/fade [Collins])?
- provided enough opportunities for students to analyze the task, practice it to automaticity, and develop attention control (principles of skill learning)?

Adjusting Instruction—Examples

If students are having difficulty with . . .

Handwriting

- determine problem feature and letter formations and plan to model them correctly.
- allow time for students to articulate correct feature and letter formations, then reflect on their formations compared with the standard.
- plan to provide daily practice of difficult letter formations in written phonogram reviews until mastery is reached.

Phonograms

- identify frequently mispronounced phonograms and plan to model correct pronunciation and explain correct mouth and tongue positions.
- allow time for students to explain correct mouth and tongue positions and reflect on their performance.
- plan to include these phonograms in daily oral phonogram reviews until mastery is reached. For students having difficulty, provide a Spalding compact disk of correct phonogram pronunciations for individual practice.

Vocabulary

- compose additional oral and written sentences that clearly demonstrate meaning and usage of difficult or unfamiliar words.
- allow time for students to articulate distinguishing characteristics of similar words, e.g., *sea/see*: Explain and then have students explain that we use the phonogram that says /ē/ /ĕ/ /ā/ when we mean a body of water, but we use the double *ee* when we mean to *see* with our eyes. Compare the two *ee*'s with two eyes.

continued

- plan to have students use these words in oral and, later, written sentences until mastery is achieved.

Rules

- plan to reteach the rule, modeling the application with familiar words (e.g., rule 4 in words like *me, go, no,* and *so*) or modeling the use of capitalization (rule 26) or the use of word endings in sentences.
- allow time for students to articulate how the rule applies to words.
- allow time for *additional* practice applying spelling and language rules until mastered.

Writing

- identify the type of writing students find difficult (informative-narrative, narrative, or informative).
- select a topic broad enough (e.g., pets) to use for your model, one or more group paragraphs, and students' independent paragraphs.
- compose a new model emphasizing the stage of the writing process that caused the greatest difficulty.
- plan time for one or more group paragraphs and compose questions that guide students through the decisions made during the writing process.
- plan sufficient time for students to compose independent paragraphs.
- analyze new paragraphs and compose questions that require students to reflect on their improvement.

Reading

- identify the problem area (literary appreciation, text structure, or mental actions).
- select a paragraph that provides opportunity to reteach the problem concept (e.g., identifying insights).
- compose *check for understanding* questions.
- select additional paragraphs to analyze in whole group.
- allow time for students to reflect on their increased understanding following additional practice.

Monitor Student Achievement and Adjust Instruction—Summary

Romalda Spalding often referred to the ability to identify each student's *growth* points (instructional levels) as the *art* of teaching. Although monitoring student achievement and appropriately adjusting instruction may be the hardest part of teaching, it is also the most rewarding. When you have developed this ability, you will be rewarded with successful, eager learners who are motivated to learn. The *Spelling Assessment Manual* is designed to help you achieve that goal.

Chapter Summary

Successful practitioners of The Spalding Method must know the content to be taught, the most effective way to teach it (see chapters 1–3), and the principles of learning and instruction (See chapter 4). Chapter 5 *puts it all together.* Integrating content, principles, and procedures empowers teachers to be successful decisions makers, equipping them with the ability to help *all* children learn to read and write.

The Writing Road to Reading is a guide to teaching The Spalding Method. It can be used by anyone to teach spelling, writing, and reading. In chapter 6, we will discuss the mission and outreach of Spalding Education International (SEI), a nonprofit 501(c)(3) corporation. SEI provides parent and teacher training courses that elaborate on the information provided in this book.

ADVANCING LITERACY
CHAPTER OVERVIEW

Mission

Developing skilled readers, critical listeners, accomplished writers and spellers

SEI Services

Professional development, personnel certification, school accreditation, materials

Validating the Method

Data collection, pilot studies, quasi-experimental studies

ROMALDA SPALDING DEVOTED a lifetime to advancing literacy. The need today is as great as or greater than when she began her quest. Dr. Reid Lyon, chief of the Child Development and Behavior Branch at the National Institute of Child Health and Human Development (NICHD), stated in testimony before a congressional committee, January 22, 2001:

> The NICHD considers that teaching and learning in today's schools is not only a critical educational and social issue, but a significant public health issue as well. Our research has shown that if children do not learn to use language to communicate ideas and perspectives, read and write, calculate and reason mathematically, and be able to solve problems strategically, their opportunities for a fulfilling and rewarding life are seriously compromised. Specifically, in our NICHD longitudinal studies, we have learned that school failure has devastating consequences with respect to self-esteem, social development, and opportunities for advanced education. (Lyon, 2001, 1)

In the Foreword to this book, Dr. Sylvia Farnham-Diggory described how The Spalding Method spread through a field network centered in Maricopa County, Arizona. Administrators from six districts formed a consortium to fund the training of local teachers to become Spalding instructors. A pilot project, comparing Spalding with the program in use in one district, was initiated (see "Validating the Method," page 198). When the results of the experimental study demonstrated significant gains in student achievement, Mrs. Spalding was persuaded to form a nonprofit foundation (Spalding Education Foundation, now Spalding Education International [SEI]) to perpetuate her method and to maintain consistent instruction. SEI teachers and instructors meet rigorous Spalding certification requirements.

Mission

Spalding Education International, a nonprofit 501 (c)(3) corporation, is committed to developing skilled readers, critical listeners, and accomplished writers and spellers. SEI is governed by a volunteer board of directors dedicated to advancing literacy through courses and other services for teachers, administrators, and parents. In addition, SEI actively pursues outreach to the business sector, community leaders, literacy organizations, and other groups who share a commitment to literacy.

The text *The Writing Road to Reading* provides the knowledge and procedures needed to achieve rapid mastery of the basic elements of English. Adult disabled readers and those studying English as a second language enjoy success when taught by this method. Experience also demonstrates that general and special education students and those with limited English proficiency make great gains when teachers use *The Writing Road to Reading*.

Because the first years in school are the most important for rapidly acquiring the basic elements of English, this book introduces each new skill, with the accompanying procedures, from a kindergarten and first-grade perspective. Directions for initiating The Method with older students or adult disabled readers are also provided.

We have reason to hope that this book and the method it teaches will lead to increased literacy and a genuine upgrading of content and standards of scholarship. Spalding Education International is committed to maintaining excellence in its literacy mission.

SEI Services

Spalding Courses

Dr. Reid Lyon testified before a congressional committee that teachers feel unprepared to address students' individual learning needs and feel particularly unprepared to provide adequate reading instruction. He noted that a survey conducted by the National Center for Educational Statistics indicated that only 20 percent of teachers surveyed felt adequately prepared to teach their students. According to Lyon, the problem is insufficient information about reading development and inadequate reading instruction during undergraduate and even graduate studies, "with the average teacher completing only one or two reading courses" (Lyon, 2001, 3).

Recognizing this lack, SEI provides training for general and special education teachers, speech and language therapists, psychologists, administrators, interested citizens, and parents. To meet the needs of diverse populations requesting Spalding training, SEI contracts with various colleges and universities, departments of education, school districts, schools, civic organizations, social agencies, and corporations. The content of all courses, in-service workshops, and seminars reflects the original philosophy and precepts of Romalda Spalding's total language arts approach to literacy. To maintain the integrity and effectiveness of The Spalding Method, only SEI-certified personnel teach SEI-approved Spalding courses (see "Spalding Certification," below). All SEI-approved courses are scheduled by contacting the director of certification and instruction at Spalding Education International. Professional development seminars are held annually for Spalding Certified Teachers and Instructors. Recognizing the importance of the principal's role as instructional leader, annual conferences are also held for Spalding administrators.

SEI offers the following basic courses:

A Parent's Introduction to The Spalding Method

"A Parent's Introduction to The Spalding Method" provides an overview of the text *The Writing Road to Reading.* The instructional emphasis (greatest amount of course time) is on teaching spelling because this is where the subskills of reading are taught. This course is designed for parents who wish to home-school as well as for those who want to support Spalding instruction their children receive in school.

Integrated Language Arts 1

"Integrated Language Arts 1" provides instruction in The Spalding Method, a total language arts approach for teaching spelling (including phonemic awareness, handwriting, and phonics), grammar and composition, literary appreciation, and listening and reading comprehension. The spelling lesson receives the greatest emphasis because this is where the subskills of reading are taught. Participants practice basic procedures described in the text *The Writing Road to Reading.* This forty-five-hour course is designed for general and special education teachers, administrators, curriculum specialists, and speech and reading specialists and is recommended for instructional assistants and tutors. Home-schooling parents may also wish to enroll in this more comprehensive course. Each course participant receives materials needed to teach the basics of integrated language arts.

Integrated Language Arts 2 (Prerequisite: "Integrated Language Arts 1")

"Integrated Language Arts 2" emphasizes literary appreciation, composition, comprehension, principles of learning and instruction, and lesson planning, while continuing to reinforce the spelling concepts taught in Integrated Language Arts 1. Participants in this forty-five-hour course practice identifying and composing three basic types of writing, modeling comprehension strategies, and designing lessons for students of all ability levels. Participants receive additional materials aligned to the text *The Writing Road to Reading.* Completing "Integrated Language Arts 1 and 2" empowers participants to teach a comprehensive, integrated language arts curriculum in any educational setting.

Spalding Certification

Spalding certification assures that Romalda Spalding's concern for students' intellectual and physical well-being will be manifest by those carrying out her quest of "literacy for all." SEI certification at any level signifies professional competence because these individuals have not only completed the required courses, but have also been formally observed working with students. To ensure that practitioners of the method will have an appropriate level of training, SEI established the following certification levels.

Spalding Authorized Tutor (SAT)
Spalding Authorized Tutors implement The Spalding Method as tutors in schools, reading or literacy centers, or other educational settings. Some Spalding schools provide before- and after-school programs for students who need additional practice. Parents and others who become Spalding Authorized Tutors are invaluable for providing the help needed by some students.

Spalding Certified Teacher (SCT)
Spalding Certified Teachers implement The Spalding Method in schools, reading or literacy centers, or other educational settings. They are qualified to teach "A Parent's Introduction to The Spalding Method" and to demonstrate and explain The Spalding Method to parents and teachers. Many SCTs also provide individual tutoring.

Spalding Certified Teacher Instructors (SCTIs)
Spalding Certified Teacher Instructors are the backbone of the method. They bring Spalding training to locations as diverse as New York City, Indian reservations in Maine and the Southwestern United States, Australia, London, and Singapore. There are three levels of SCTIs. In addition to instructing children and parents, all levels are qualified to teach "Integrated Language Arts 1." Only Level III Instructors have the necessary training to teach "Integrated Language Arts 2."

Staff Development
SEI recognizes that information and methodology presented in a training course is best retained with follow-up instructional support. Therefore, SEI offers the School Professional Development Program, which supports teachers in effectively implementing Spalding content and methodology. Experienced Spalding Instructors go on-site to model correct instructional procedures and answer teacher questions. This program facilitates correct implementation and consistent exemplary student achievement across all grade levels.

School Accreditation
Just as certification ensures that instruction is provided by qualified instructors, so accreditation signifies that school administration and staff are committed to raising student achievement by consistent use of The Spalding Method throughout the grades. The designation Spalding Accredited School is evidence for parents and others that a school has voluntarily met demanding external standards for The Spalding Method.

Quarterly Publication
SEI publishes the *Spalding News,* a quarterly journal that provides current reading research, news from Spalding classrooms, information about in-service workshops, answers to readers' questions, and instructional tips.

Spalding Materials Distribution
SEI holds the copyright to *The Writing Road to Reading,* published by HarperCollins. In addition, SEI holds sole rights to all SEI-authorized educational materials. A list of author-

ized materials is found in the Resources, page 458. An instructional materials catalog is available from the SEI office (see Resources) or through the SEI Web site: *www.spalding.org.*

Validating the Method

From the beginning, Mrs. Spalding was interested in validating and improving her method. Over the years, she received a large volume of standardized test scores from public and private school administrators throughout the country. All median reading and spelling scores for the various Spalding student populations showed considerable gains above the U.S. norms in every grade.

Dr. Robert Aukerman, in his text *Approaches to Beginning Reading* (1984), validated Mrs. Spalding's finding. He investigated and described over 100 different approaches to beginning reading. Aukerman devoted ten pages to The Spalding Method, citing national test scores from many Spalding schools in twelve states. He stated:

> A rather significant and up-to-date body of data has been assembled showing the *indisputable* success that many schools are enjoying with The Spalding Method. . . . They cover scores on standardized achievement tests in reading, and are the results reported by the schools for children of a wide range of backgrounds and intelligence. Moreover, they are from a representative sampling of small and large schools, public, parochial, and private (Arizona, California, Hawaii, Idaho, Illinois, New Hampshire, Texas, and Virginia). It should be noted, also, that the class sizes range all the way from a small class of only eight students to the large classes of 50 or more. In all, 20 schools of varied types and localities are represented with more than 120 *different teachers.* (Aukerman, 1984, 541)

> The Spalding Method was observed in several Honolulu schools in 1967 and again in 1982. In January, for example, in a first-grade class the children were reading at an almost unbelievable level of comprehension, voice inflection, knowledge of word-attack. . . . Scores that are consistently far beyond the national norms and testimonials of gains made by illiterate adults, new arrivals from the rim of the Pacific, learning disabled children, and others who had not previously learned to read in regular classrooms using standard means should be proof enough of the effectiveness of *The Writing Road to Reading.* (Aukerman, 1984, 545–546)

The average grade-level score of the fourteen first grades in his sample was 2.8; of the sixteen second grades, 3.76; of the twelve third grades, 5.24.

SEI has expanded on this data collection, reporting Arizona Spalding student achievement scores on the IOWA Test of Basic Skills annually from 1986, when SEI was formed, until statewide testing ended in 1991. When the legislature resumed statewide standardized, norm-referenced testing in 1996 using the Stanford Achievement Test, SEI resumed reporting student scores. Under state guidelines, schools administer the tests in the spring of each year, and tests are scored by the publisher. Using the Arizona Department of Education published scores, SEI reports grade-level comparisons of reading and language scores for schools using Spalding with district and state scores. Standardized test scores from schools in other states in which Spalding is taught are also included. Schools are included in the annual Spalding *Special Report on Student Achievement* if the administration formally adopted Spalding as the basic language arts program and Spalding training and follow-up have been provided for the entire faculty. Spalding student reading percentile rank scores range from ten to forty-two points higher than district and state norms. The difference would be even greater if Spalding schools were not included in the district and state averages. (For copies of Spalding *Special Reports,* contact the SEI office.)

Previously published quasi-experimental studies that demonstrate exemplary student achievement in Spalding schools are included in this edition of *The Writing Road to Reading:*

In 1954, the first quasi-experimental study of The Spalding Method was conducted in twenty-four large schools in Hawaii (reported in detail in the first edition of *The Writing Road to Reading,* 1957). The experimental group contained 369 children; the control classes included 328 children. Mrs. Spalding trained all teachers in the experimental group; the control group used the existing program. All students were tested on the Metropolitan Achievement Test, a nationally standardized measure. Scores in the experimental group were significantly higher than those in the control group.

In the early 1980s, the Peoria (Arizona) Unified School District's standardized achievement test scores were at or below the 50th percentile rank. A pilot study was designed to compare the effectiveness of The Spalding Method with the district's adopted program. Kindergarten through third-grade classes were matched in five schools: one high socioeconomic school, two average socioeconomic schools, and two low socioeconomic schools. Mrs. Spalding trained the twenty pilot teachers. By the end of the 1985–86 pilot year, Peoria Spalding class percentile-rank scores for reading comprehension ranged from the upper 80s to the high 90s on the state-adopted IOWA Test of Basic Skills. Scores for the control classes remained at or below the 50th percentile rank. The Governing Board adopted Spalding for kindergarten through third grade in 1986. A decline in learning disability resource room populations was noted after classroom instruction incorporated The Spalding Method.

The pilot project was extended into grades four through eight as a spelling program in 1986. Matched classes compared Spalding with a commercial spelling program. Spelling scores, measured on the IOWA Test of Basic Skills in April of the 1987–88 pilot year, demonstrated that Spalding-trained students had a 5 percentile–rank advantage over non-Spalding-trained students. Statistical analysis was done by a researcher at Arizona State University. The Peoria Governing Board adopted Spalding for spelling in grades four through eight in 1988. Peoria's achievement test scores for the period 1986 to 1991 are available at the SEI office. Results of this and other pilot studies were reported in the *Annals of Dyslexia* (North, 1991), published by the Orton Dyslexia Society (now the International Dyslexia Association).

In the Foreword to this edition, Dr. Sylvia Farnham-Diggory explained why The Spalding Method works. In a text entitled *Cognitive Processes in Education* (1992), she described an experimental study conducted at the Reading Research Center:

We have also conducted evaluation studies of several types. When our program was first introduced, local schools routinely administered a standardized test called the Comprehensive Test of Basic Skills (CTBS) at the end of each year. Since only a few classrooms had begun to adopt our program, it was a simple matter to find a matching classroom that had not. . . . Except for the reading program, children from experimental and control classrooms received the same curriculum. At the end of the school year, we compared a first, second, and third grade to their respective control classrooms on the CTBS total reading scale. The percentile ranks for our Intensive Literacy (Spalding) first-, second-, and third-grade classrooms were 66th, 67th, and 67th, respectively, while the percentile ranks for the control classrooms were 43rd, 54th, and 47th, respectively. These differences were significant statistically and were also meaningful intuitively. The control classes were testing at or below average . . . , whereas the Intensive Literacy classes had moved well above average. (Farnham-Diggory, 1992, 307–308)

Spalding has also been shown to be effective with at-risk students. A quasi-experimental study, conducted by the Tasmanian Office of Education (Australia), in 1999 of at-risk students (including attention deficit disorder [ADD] and dyslexic) in grades one and two at the Youngtown Primary School showed significant progress on three assessments: In 8 teaching months, first-grade students made 12 months', 14 months', and 16 months' progress on the *Morrison-McCall Spelling Test, Wadding Bray Spelling Test,* and *South Australian Spelling Test,* respectively. Second-grade progress in 8 teaching months was 14, 10, and 19 on the above assessments.

Two longitudinal studies were reported in *Clinical Studies of Multisensory Structured Language Education for Students with Dyslexia and Related Disorders.* The effects of Spalding language arts instruction on special education students in a resource-room setting was studied by the El Paso Independent School District. The primary purpose of this longitudinal study was to quantify students' growth using The Spalding Method. During the third year, over 500 boys and girls in grades one through eight who met the Texas Education Agency eligibility criteria for a handicapping condition were studied. Students made statistically significant gains in reading, writing, and spelling as assessed by the *Brigance Diagnostic Comprehensive Inventory of Basic Skills,* a written composition, and the *Morrison-McCall Spelling Scale* (North, 1995).

The Spalding Method was used in a seven-year longitudinal study with the entire special education population at Middletown High School in Delaware to determine whether high school is too late to improve the literacy skills of low-performing students. Statistical analyses of pre- and post-achievement test scores for 111 students demonstrated significant improvements in word recognition, passage comprehension, and spelling. Convincing evidence was found that, with appropriate instruction, high school is not too late to improve the literacy skills of most high school special education students (Hoerl and Koons, 1995).

Spalding Education International looks forward to additional experimental studies of the method in the future.

Chapter Summary

Spalding Certified Teachers and Instructors represent a unique cadre of highly trained specialists dedicated to advancing literacy in their schools and communities. Spalding courses are now taught around the world. The efficacy of The Spalding Method has led to its popularity among home-schooling parents and among teachers and administrators searching for a better way to teach reading.

Spalding Accredited Schools demonstrate the exemplary student achievement possible when teachers receive the instruction they need.

SEI is dedicated to validating and improving The Spalding Method. We invite all who are interested in participating in this effort to contact:

Spalding Education International
2814 West Bell Road, Suite 1405
Phoenix, AZ 85053
Phone: (602) 866-7801
Fax: (602) 866-7488
Web site: *www.spalding.org*
E-mail: *staff@spalding.org.*

Part Two

INSTRUCTIONAL MATERIALS

Children's Literature Recommendations

Phonograms

Rules of Pronunciation, Spelling, and Language

Syllable Division

Primary and Intermediate Spelling/Vocabulary Notebooks—
  Sample Pages

Extended Ayres Word List: Order of Instruction

Extended Ayres Word List: Alphabetized

Extended Ayres Word List: Parts of Speech

Recommended Language Arts Scope and Sequence

Framework for Planning Integrated Language Arts Lessons

Resources

CHILDREN'S LITERATURE RECOMMENDATIONS

Becoming a Nation of Readers: The Report of the Commission on Reading recommends, "Parents should read to preschool children and informally teach them about reading and writing" (Anderson et al., 1985, 117). Children whose parents follow this advice enjoy a considerable advantage. Their vocabulary and knowledge of syntax are enlarged and they are better prepared for more formal classroom instruction.

Spalding kindergarten teachers foster a desire to read in literary appreciation classes. We recommend that teachers at all grade levels read good literature aloud to demonstrate fluent, expressive reading and to foster a love of reading. We also recommend that each class have its own classroom library, including collections of poetry. A list of trade book titles is provided as a resource so that listening comprehension and literary appreciation may be taught from the first day of class. It is not an exhaustive list, but we believe it represents some of the better children's books available. Nonetheless, to ascertain appropriateness for your classroom and circumstance, it is important to *read each book before reading it aloud or having students read it.*

Suggested grade-level designations are based upon phonograms taught, children's interests, and the level of language used. They are not an attempt to control what is read at each grade level. *Teachers should always be guided by students' progress and abilities.*

In the Foreword, Dr. Farnham-Diggory points out that children are never really "taught" to read in The Spalding Method. They just begin reading after writing and then reading words in their spelling notebooks. Although all children benefit greatly from listening to fine literature read aloud by their teachers, some *initially* require books selected for practice reading of the phonograms rather than for their literary merit. These are called decodable books. The following list is organized by level of difficulty as students learn the first sixty-two phonograms. The decodable books have been carefully selected to provide interesting text as well as practice of phonograms. We do not recommend prolonged use of these.

Decodable Readers

Author	Title	Publisher	Grade
Hillert, Margaret	The Three Little Pigs	Modern Curriculum Press	K
Hillert, Margaret	The Three Bears	Modern Curriculum Press	K
Hillert, Margaret	Not I, Not I	Modern Curriculum Press	K
Hillert, Margaret	The Three Goats	Modern Curriculum Press	K
Hillert, Margaret	The Yellow Boat	Modern Curriculum Press	K
Hillert, Margaret	What Am I?	Modern Curriculum Press	K
Hillert, Margaret	Little Red Riding Hood	Modern Curriculum Press	K
Krauss, Ruth	The Carrot Seed	Scholastic	K–1
Appleton-Smith, Laura	The Sunset Pond	Flyleaf	K–1
Appleton-Smith, Laura	Jen's Best Gift	Flyleaf	K–1
Dr. Seuss	Green Eggs and Ham	Random House	K–1
Appleton-Smith, Laura	Frank the Fish Gets His Wish	Flyleaf	K–1
Appleton-Smith, Laura	Meg and Jim's Sled Trip	Flyleaf	K–1
Appleton-Smith, Laura	It is Halloween!	Flyleaf	K–1
Appleton-Smith, Laura	Lin Lin and the Gulls	Flyleaf	K–1
Appleton-Smith, Laura	A Sled Dog Morning	Flyleaf	K–1
Appleton-Smith, Laura	Mr. Sanchez and the Kickball	Flyleaf	K–1
Le Sieg, Theodore	Ten Apples Up on Top	Random House	K–1
Eastman, P.D.	Go, Dog, Go	Random House	K–1
Lopshire, Robert	Put Me in the Zoo	Random House	K–1
Eastman, P.D.	Are You My Mother?	Random House	K–1

After section L, children are ready to read the following books. We recommend classroom sets of several titles at each grade level to be used for instruction.

Appleton-Smith, Laura	Shep: The Sheep of Caladeen	Flyleaf	K–1
Appleton-Smith, Laura	Bon-Bon the Downtown Cow	Flyleaf	K–1
Appleton-Smith, Laura	Pearl Learns a Lesson	Flyleaf	K–1
Appleton-Smith, Laura	Snail Hits the Trail	Flyleaf	K–1
Appleton-Smith, Laura	Oh My! It Must Be the Sky	Flyleaf	K–1

Children's Literature

After section M, children are ready to read the following books:

Author	Title	Publisher	Grade
De Regniers, Beatrice	*May I Bring a Friend?*	Atheneum	K–1
Flack, Marjorie	*Angus and the Ducks*	Doubleday	K–1
Flack, Marjorie	*The Story about Ping*	Viking	K–1
Galdone, Paul	*The Gingerbread Boy*	Houghton Mifflin	K–1
Galdone, Paul	*Three Billy Goats Gruff*	Houghton Mifflin	K–1
Galdone, Paul	*The Three Little Pigs*	Houghton Mifflin	K–1
Hoban, Lillian	*Arthur's Pen Pal*	HarperCollins	K–1
Hoban, Russell	*A Bargain for Frances*	HarperCollins	K–1
Hoff, Syd	*Danny and the Dinosaur*	HarperCollins	K–1
Hoff, Syd	*Sammy the Seal*	HarperCollins	K–1
Leaf, Mauro	*The Story of Ferdinand*	Viking	K–1
Ward, Lynd	*The Biggest Bear*	Houghton Mifflin	K–1

After section O, children are ready to read any of the following books:

Author	Title	Publisher	Grade
Appleton-Smith, Laura	*Marvin's Trip to Mars*	Flyleaf	1
Beskow, Elsa	*Pelle's New Suit*	Gryphon House	1
Bishop, Claire Hatchet	*Five Chinese Brothers*	Putnam	1
Calhoun, Mary	*Cross-Country Cat*	William Morrow	1
Dougherty, James	*Andy and the Lion*	Viking	1
Ets, Marie	*Just Me*	Viking	1
Gag, Wanda	*Millions of Cats*	Coward	1
Geisel, T. S.	*And to Think I Saw It on Mulberry Street*	Vanguard	1
Hader, B. and E.	*The Big Snow*	Macmillan	1
Keats, Ezra	*Whistle for Willie*	Viking	1
Lamorisse, Albert	*The Red Balloon*	Doubleday	1
Lionni, Leo	*Frederick*	Obolensky	1
Lionni, Leo	*Inch by Inch*	Obolensky	1
Lobel, Arnold	*Frog and Toad* (series)	HarperCollins	1
Minarik, Else	*Little Bear*	HarperCollins	1
Minarik, Else	*No Fighting, No Biting*	HarperCollins	1
Piper, Watty	*The Little Engine That Could*	Platt	1
Potter, Beatrix	*The Tale of Peter Rabbit* (series)	F. Warne	1
Rey, H. A., and Margaret	*Curious George* (series)	Houghton Mifflin	1
Sendak, Maurice	*Where the Wild Things Are*	HarperCollins	1
Slobodkina, Esphyr	*Caps for Sale*	HarperCollins	1

Second Grade

Author	Title	Publisher	Grade
Andersen, Hans C.	*The Emperor's New Clothes*	Harcourt Brace	2
Andersen, Hans C.	*The Steadfast Tin Soldier*	Scribner	2
Anglund, Joan	*Christmas Is a Time of Giving*	Harcourt Brace	2
Anglund, Joan	*In a Pumpkin Shell*	Harcourt Brace	2
Anglund, Joan	*Spring Is a New Beginning*	Harcourt Brace	2
Bemelmans, Ludwig	*Madeline* (series)	Viking	2
Coerr, Eleanor B.	*Sadako and the Thousand Paper Cranes*	Putnam	2
Dalgliesh, Alice	*The Bears on Hemlock Mountain*	Scribner	2
Grimm, Jacob	*The Wolf and the Seven Kids*	Harcourt Brace	2
Kessel, Joyce K.	*Squanto and the First Thanksgiving*	Lerner Publishing Group	2
Lindgren, Astrid	*Pippi Longstocking* (series)	Viking	2
McCloskey, Robert	*Blueberries for Sal*	Viking	2
McCloskey, Robert	*One Morning in Maine*	Viking	2
McCloskey, Robert	*Time of Wonder*	Viking	2
Merriam, Eve	*Blackberry Ink*	William Morrow	2
Parish, Peggy	*Amelia Bedelia* (series)	Greenwillow	2
Perrault, Charles	*Cinderella*	Scribner	2
Petersham, Maud	*The Rooster Crows*	Macmillan	2
Peterson, John	*The Littles* (series)	Scholastic Books	2
Politi, Leo	*Song of Swallows*	Scribner	2
Thurber, James	*Many Moons*	Harcourt Brace	2
Williams, Margery	*The Velveteen Rabbit*	Doubleday	2
Yolen, Jane	*Owl Moon*	Putnam	2

Third Grade

Author	Title	Publisher	Grade
Alexander, Beatrice	*Famous Myths of the Golden Age*	Random House	3
Atwater, Richard	*Mr. Popper's Penguins*	Little, Brown	3
Butterworth, Oliver	*The Enormous Egg*	Little, Brown	3
Carlson, Natalie	*The Family under the Bridge*	HarperCollins	3
Clark, Ann	*In My Mother's House (Pueblo)*	Viking	3
Cleary, Beverly	*Henry Huggins* (series)	William Morrow	3
Cleary, Beverly	*The Mouse on the Motorcycle*	William Morrow	3

Author	Title	Publisher	Grade
Cleary, Beverly	*Ramona the Pest* (series)	William Morrow	3
Dalgliesh, Alice	*The Courage of Sarah Noble*	Scribner	3
Dalgliesh, Alice	*The Fourth of July Story*	Scribner	3
Dalgliesh, Alice	*The Thanksgiving Story*	Scribner	3
D'Aulaire, I. and E.	*Abraham Lincoln*	Doubleday	3
D'Aulaire, I. and E.	*Benjamin Franklin*	Doubleday	3
D'Aulaire, I. and E.	*Columbus*	Doubleday	3
D'Aulaire, I. and E.	*George Washington*	Doubleday	3
D'Aulaire, I. and E.	*Leif the Lucky*	Doubleday	3
De Angeli, Marguerite	*Thee, Hannah!*	Doubleday	3
Gannett, Ruth	*My Father's Dragon* (series)	Random House	3
Grimm, J.	*Grimm's Fairy Tales*	Routledge & Kegan Paul	3
Holling, H. C.	*Paddle to the Sea*	Houghton Mifflin	3
Lawson, Peter	*Rabbit Hill*	Viking	3
Lawson, Robert	*Ben and Me*	Little, Brown	3
MacLachlan, Patricia	*Sarah Plain and Tall*	Harper & Row	3
Milne, A. A.	*The World of Christopher Robin*	Penguin Putnam	3
Milne, A. A.	*Winnie-the-Pooh*	Penguin Putnam	3
Simon, Seymour	*Jupiter*	William Morrow	3
Simon, Seymour	*Saturn*	William Morrow	3
Van Alsberg, Chris	*Polar Express*	Houghton Mifflin	3
White, E. B.	*Charlotte's Web*	HarperCollins	3
White, E. B.	*Stuart Little*	HarperCollins	3

Fourth Grade

Author	Title	Publisher	Grade
Aesop	*The Fables of Aesop*	Macmillan	4
Cleary, Beverly	*Dear Mr. Henshaw*	William Morrow	4
D'Aulaire, I. and E.	*Pocahontas*	Doubleday	4
DeJong, Meindert	*The House of Sixty Fathers*	HarperCollins	4
Dodge, Mary	*Hans Brinker, or the Silver Skates*	Scribner	4
Edmonds, Walter	*The Matchlock Gun*	Econo-Clad	4
Estes, Eleanor	*Ginger Pye*	Harcourt Brace	4
Forbes, Esther	*America's Paul Revere*	Houghton Mifflin	4
Grimm, J.	*Household Stories of the Brothers Grimm*	Dover	4
Kipling, Rudyard	*Just So Stories*	Doubleday	4
Krumgold, Joseph	*. . . and Now Miguel*	Harper Trophy	4

Author	Title	Publisher	Grade
Lewis, C. S.	*Chronicles of Narnia* (series)	HarperCollins	4
Seldon, George	*The Cricket in Times Square*	Bantam Doubleday Dell	4
Spyri, Joanna	*Heidi*	Kidsbooks, Inc.	4
Travers, P. L.	*Mary Poppins* (series)	Harcourt Brace	4
Van Allsburg, Chris	*The Garden of Abdul Gasozi*	Houghton Mifflin	4

Fifth Grade

Author	Title	Publisher	Grade
Burnford, Sheila	*The Incredible Journey*	Bantam	5
Carroll, Lewis	*Alice's Adventures in Wonderland*	Macmillan	5
Crisman, Arthur	*Shen of the Sea*	Dutton	5
Daugherty, James	*Landing of the Pilgrims*	Random House	5
De Angeli, Marguerite	*Door in the Wall*	Doubleday	5
DeJong, Meindert	*The Wheel on the School*	HarperCollins	5
DuBois, W. P.	*The Twenty-one Balloons*	Viking	5
Gates, Doris	*Blue Willow*	Viking	5
George, Jean	*My Side of the Mountain*	Dutton	5
Grahame, Kenneth	*Wind in the Willows*	Scribner	5
Kelly, Eric	*The Trumpeteer of Krakow*	Macmillan	5
Latham, Jean	*Carry On, Mr. Bowditch*	Houghton Mifflin	5
Lowery, Lois	*Number the Stars*	Houghton Mifflin	5
O'Dell, Scott	*Island of the Blue Dolphins*	Houghton Mifflin	5
Seredy, Kate	*The Good Master*	Penguin Putnam	5
Seredy, Kate	*The White Stag*	Penguin Putnam	5
Sperry, Armstrong	*Call It Courage*	Macmillan	5

Sixth Grade

Author	Title	Publisher	Grade
Alcott, Louisa May	*Little Men*	Dover	6
Alcott, Louisa May	*Little Women*	Penguin Putnam	6
Brink, Carol	*Caddie Woodlawn*	Macmillan	6
Byars, Betsy	*The Summer of the Swans*	Penguin Putnam	6
Colum, Padraic	*The Children's Homer*	Macmillan	6
Colum, Padraic	*The Golden Fleece and the Heroes Who Lived before Achilles*	Macmillan	6
D'Aulaire, I. and E.	*Book of Greek Myths*	Doubleday	6

Author	Title	Publisher	Grade
D'Aulaire, I. and E.	*Norse Gods and Giants*	Doubleday	6
Defoe, Daniel	*Robinson Crusoe*	Lippincott	6
Field, Rachel	*Hitty: Her First Hundred Years*	Macmillan	6
Gray, Elizabeth	*Adam of the Road*	Penguin Putnam	6
Krumgold, Joseph	*Onion John*	Crowell	6
Malory, Sir Thomas	*The Boy's King Arthur*	Scribner	6
McGraw, Eloise J.	*The Golden Goblet*	Coward-McCann	6
Quang Nhunog Nhuong	*The Land I Lost*	HarperCollins	6
Rawlings, Marjorie	*The Yearling*	Scribner	6
Sandburg, Carl	*Abe Lincoln Grows Up*	Harcourt Brace	6
Speare, Elizabeth	*The Bronze Bow*	Houghton Mifflin	6
Stevenson, Robert L.	*Treasure Island*	Macmillan	6
Sutcliff, Rosemary	*Light Beyond the Forest*	Penguin Putnam	6
Sutcliff, Rosemary	*Road to Camlaan*	Penguin Putnam	6
Sutcliff, Rosemary	*Sword and the Circle*	Penguin Putnam	6
Wyss, Johann David	*The Swiss Family Robinson*	Viking Penguin	6
Yates, Elizabeth	*Amos Fortune, Free Man*	Penguin Putnam	6
Zim, H. S., and Baker, H.	*Stars: A Guide to the Constellations, Sun, Moon, Planets and Other Features of the Heavens*	Western Publishing	6

PHONOGRAMS

THE SPALDING METHOD introduces seventy common phonograms to all novice readers whether they are first-grade children or adult disabled readers. To aid teachers, the phonograms, with their sounds, are listed on the following pages.

Column 1 of pages 213–221 lists the seventy phonograms in the order of *instruction*. Students of all ages first learn the sounds of the letters that begin at two on the clock; then they learn the sounds of those letters that begin with a line. The remainder of the phonograms are introduced in the order needed for writing Extended Ayres words in the spelling/vocabulary notebook. All seventy phonograms are introduced before students write words in section N.

Column 2 lists the symbols that represent phonogram sounds and sample words that illustrate correct pronunciation. The sample words are given as an aid to the teacher's pronunciation; they are not to be memorized by students as *key* words. When a phonogram represents more than one sound, the sounds are listed in the order of frequency of use.

Column 3 provides instructional tips: directions for pronouncing phonogram sounds correctly and information to help students pronounce and spell words. For example, children learn that phonogram *a* says /ă/ when it is followed by one or more consonants (*at, bath*), that it usually says /ā/ at the end of a syllable (nā vy), but that it *may* say /ah/ at the end of a syllable (*fa ther*). During phonogram reviews, children discuss and explain how phonograms work in words, but rules are never rotely memorized.

Phonograms (In order of instruction)	Sounds/Sample Words	Instructional Tips
a	Sound each separately. ă at ā n<u>a</u> vy ah fa³ <u>ther</u>²	**1** a *usually* says ā at the end of a syllable (rule 4). a *may* say *ah* at the end of a syllable.
c	Sound each separately. k **can** s **cent**	**2** c before e, i, or y says *s* but followed by any other letter says *k* (rule 2).
d	d **lid**	**3** Press tip of tongue against upper ridge behind teeth, then voice sound. Keep jaw still.
f	f **if**	**4** Gently bite on lower lip and blow (unvoiced).
g	Sound each separately. g **bag** j **gem**	**5** g before e, i, or y *may* say *j* and followed by any other letter says *g* (rule 3).
o	Sound each separately. ŏ **odd** ō **<u>o</u> pen** o͞o d<u>o</u>³	**6** o *usually* says ō at the end of a syllable (rule 4). o *may* say ō *(most)* when followed by two consonants (rule 19).
s	Sound each separately. s **us** z a<u>s</u>²	**7**

Phonograms (In order of instruction)	Sounds/Sample Words		Instructional Tips
qu	*kw*	<u>qu</u>it	8 Raise back of tongue to soft palate and release breath (unvoiced). q is always followed by u saying the consonant sound *w* (rule 1).
b	*b*	ri<u>b</u>	9 Close lips to form a line, then voice sound.
e	Sound each separately. *ĕ* **end** *ē* **m<u>e</u>**		10 e *usually* says *ē* at the end of a syllable (rule 4).
h	*h*	him	11 Open mouth and release breath (unvoiced).
i	Sound each separately. *ĭ* **big** *ī* **s<u>i</u> lent**		12 i usually says *ĭ* (rule 5). i may say *ī* at the end of a syllable (rule 5). i may say *ī (find)* when followed by two consonants (rule 19).
j	*j*	jam	13 Keep jaw still.
k	*k*	in<u>k</u>	14
l	*l*	lag	15 Broaden tip of tongue against ridge behind teeth and voice sound.

Phonograms (In order of instruction)	Sounds/Sample Words		Instructional Tips
m	*m*	ham	Close lips and voice sound. [16]
n	*n*	win	Press tongue against roof of mouth and voice sound. [17]
p	*p*	map	Close lips to form line, then release breath (unvoiced). [18]
r	*r*	rat	Move back of tongue upward and back at the same time forming contact with upper molars and back edges of tongue. Keep position and voice sound. (r is not pronounced *er*.) [19]
t	*t*	bat	Press tongue against roof of mouth and release breath (unvoiced). [20]
u	Sound each separately. $\breve{u}$ $\bar{u}$ $\breve{o}o$	up mu̱²sic pu̱³t	u *usually* says $\bar{u}$ at the end of a syllable (rule 4). [21]
v	*v*	viv id	Gently bite on lower lip and voice sound (feel vibration). Teach students to hear and feel the difference between *f* and *v*. [22]
w	*w*	wit	Round lips, then release breath while voicing sound. Keep jaw still. (w is not pronounced *wh*.) [23]

Phonograms (In order of instruction)	Sounds/Sample Words	Instructional Tips
x	*ks* box	24 x has two sounds blended.
y	Sound each separately. *y* yet *ĭ* gym *ī* my	25 The consonant sound *y* is used *only* at the beginning of a syllable, *usually* the first one. *y* usually says *ĭ*, but may say *ī* (*my*) at the end of a syllable (rule 5). y, not i, is used at the end of English words (rule 6).
z	*z* zest	26 Words beginning with the sound *z* are *always* spelled with a z, never an s (rule 27).
sh	*sh* di<u>sh</u>	27 *sh* is used at the beginning or end of a base word, at the end of a syllable, but not at the beginning of a syllable after the first one except for the ending *ship* (rule 13).
ee	*ē* s<u>ee</u>	28
th	Sound each separately. *th* <u>th</u>in *th* <u>t</u>his[2]	29 Place extreme tip of tongue barely between teeth and release breath (unvoiced). Place extreme tip of tongue barely between teeth and release breath with voice (feel vibration).
ow	Sound each separately. *ow* h<u>ow</u> *ō* l<u>ow</u>[2]	30

Phonograms (In order of instruction)	Sounds/Sample Words	Instructional Tips	
ou	Sound each separately. ow — round ō — soul [2] ōō — you [3] ŭ — coun try [4]	Pronounce as in *up*.	31
oo	Sound each separately. ōō — boot ŏŏ — foot [2]		32
ch	Sound each separately. ch — much k — school [2] sh — chef [3]		33
ar	ar — far		34
ay	ā — day		35
ai	ā — paint		36
oy	oy — boy	Say quickly with one impulse of voice.	37
oi	oi — point	Say quickly with one impulse of voice.	38
er	er — her		39
ir	ir — first		40
ur	ur — nurse [5]		41

Phonograms (In order of instruction)	Sounds/Sample Words		Instructional Tips
wor	*wor*	w<u>or</u>ks	42 *wor* has two phonograms. or may say *er* after w (rule 8).
ear	*er*	<u>ear</u> ly	43
ng	*ng*	ra<u>ng</u>	44 Raise back of tongue as if to say *k*. Keep position, and voice sound through nose (nasal). Do not pronounce g.
ea	Sound each separately. $\bar{e}$ $\breve{e}$ $\bar{a}$	<u>ea</u>t h<u>e</u>²<u>a</u>d br<u>e</u>³<u>a</u>k	45
aw	*aw*	l<u>aw</u>	46 Drop jaw and resonate from vocal cords.
au	*au*	<u>au</u> thor	47 Drop jaw and resonate from vocal cords.
or	*or*	f<u>or</u>	48
ck	*k*	ne<u>ck</u>	49
wh	*wh*	<u>wh</u>en	50 Blow softly on palm of hand. Air should be felt when saying *wh*. (wh is not pronounced *w*.)

Phonograms (In order of instruction)	Sounds/Sample Words Sound each separately.	Instructional Tips	
ed	ĕd grad **ed** d lov**ĕd**² t **wr**eck **ĕd**³	Keep jaw still. Keep jaw still.	51
ew	Sound each separately. ōō gr**ew** ū f**ĕw**²	Sound the same as *ui*.	52
ui	Sound each separately. ōō fr**ui**t ū s**ŭi**²t	Sound the same as *ew*.	53
oa	ō b**oa**t		54
gu	g **gu**ess		55
ph	f **ph**one	Gently bite on lower lip and blow (unvoiced).	56
ough	Sound each separately. ō th**ough**² ōō thr**ough**² ŭf r**ough**³ ŏf c**ough**⁴ aw th**ough**t⁵ ow dr**ough**t⁶		57
oe	ō t**oe**		58
ey	Sound each separately. ā th**ey**² ē k**ey**² ĭ val l**ey**³		59
igh	ī s**igh**		60

Phonograms (In order of instruction)	Sounds/Sample Words		Instructional Tips	
kn	n	k<u>n</u>ot	Press tongue against roof of mouth and voice sound.	61
gn	n	si<u>gn</u>	Press tongue against roof of mouth and voice sound.	62
wr	r	<u>wr</u>ap	Move back of tongue upward and back at the same time forming contact with upper molars and back edges of tongue. Keep position and voice sound. (r is not pronounced er.)	63
ie	Sound each separately. $\bar{e}$ $\bar{\imath}$ $\breve{\imath}$	f<u>ie</u>ld pi<u>e</u> lil <u>ie</u>s		64
dge	j	bri<u>dge</u>	Keep jaw still.	65
ei	Sound each separately. $\bar{e}$ $\bar{a}$ $\breve{\imath}$	con c<u>ei</u>t v<u>ei</u>l for f<u>ei</u>t		66
eigh	$\bar{a}$	w<u>eigh</u>		67
ti	sh	n<u>a</u> <u>ti</u>on		68

Phonograms	Sounds/Sample Words	Instructional Tips	
(In order of instruction)	Sound each separately.		69
si	*sh* ses _sion_		
	zh vi _sion_²		
ci	*sh* f_a_ _ci_al		70

RULES OF PRONUNCIATION, SPELLING, AND LANGUAGE

FOR CONVENIENT REFERENCE, all rules introduced in *The Writing Road to Reading* are listed on pages 223–225. The rule number is followed by the rule, explanations, instructional tips, and example words as needed.

Pronunciation rules are introduced in phonogram reviews, reinforced during spelling dictation, and applied during reading. Spelling rules are also taught in phonogram reviews and reinforced in spelling dictation, but are applied during writing. Language rules are taught during spelling dictation and applied during writing.

For kindergarten through second-grade students, the teacher demonstrates how the rules work in words. Children then write the words that illustrate each rule in their primary notebooks. Students in grade three and above write words that illustrate the first sixteen rules in the first six pages of the intermediate spelling/vocabulary notebook. All students learn to apply the rules by participating in practice activities described in chapter 1 (see pages 53–70). Students need daily practice applying the rules. Just memorizing a rule does not mean students understand or are able to apply it. Spalding Word Builder Cards (see Resources) are used to provide guided and independent practice of rules 9, 10, 11, 21, 22, and 24.

RULES   EXPLANATION AND INSTRUCTIONAL TIPS

Rule Page 1 (Rules 1–7)

1. The letter q is always followed by u and together they say *kw* (*queen*). The u is not considered a vowel here.

2. The letter c before e, i, or y says *s* (*cent, city, cycle*), but followed by any other letter says *k* (*cat, cot, cut*).

   The c is not numbered and the abbreviation for rule 2 is not written in student notebooks because the letter following c identifies the sound.

3. The letter g before e, i, or y may say *j* (*page, giant, gym*), but followed by any other letter says *g* (*gate, go, gust*). The letters e and i following g do not always make the g say *j* (*get, girl, give*).

   The g is not numbered and the abbreviation for rule 3 is not written in student notebooks.

4. Vowels a, e, o, and u usually say *ā, ē, ō,* and *ū* at the end of a syllable (*na vy, me, o pen, mu sic*).

   This rule helps students pronounce the vowel correctly in unfamiliar vowel-consonant-vowel (vcv) words (*re port*).

5. The letters *i* and *y* usually say *ĭ* (*big, gym*), but may say *ī* (*si lent, my, type*).

6. The letter y, not i, is used at the end of an English word (*my*).

7. There are five kinds of silent final e's. (In short words such as *me, she,* and *he,* the e says *ē,* but in longer words where a single e appears at the end, the e is silent. We retain the first four kinds of silent e's because we need them. [See chapter 1, pages 56–57.] The fifth is probably a relic from Old English.)

   The abbreviation for rule 7 is not written in student notebooks, but the job of the silent final e is marked for each word as encountered. During dictation, including reading of the Ayres words for spelling, the silent e's are sounded *(t ī m ē)*.

Rule Page 2 (Rule 8)

8. There are five spellings for the sound *er*. The phonogram *or* may say *er* when it follows w (*work*).

   During phonogram reviews and reading multisyllable Ayres words for spelling, students say the blended sound *wer*. When reading or writing one-syllable words (*work*) in the notebook, students say *wer k*. (They learn that the w influences the sound of *or*.) It is helpful for primary teachers to write a chart for the five spellings of *er*. Add each word that uses one of the five spellings when encountered in the Extended Ayres Word List.

Rule Page 3 (Rules 9–10)

9. For *one*-syllable words that have *one* vowel and end in *one* consonant (*hop*), write another final consonant (*hop + ped*) before adding endings that begin with a vowel. (Referring to rule 9 as the one-one-one rule helps students remember the criteria for

applying the rule. This rule does not apply to words ending in x because x has two sounds.)

10. Words of *two* syllables (*begin*) in which the second syllable (*gin*) is accented and ends in *one* consonant, with *one* vowel before it, need another final consonant (*be gin´ + ning*) before adding an ending that begins with a vowel. (Refer to rule 10 as the two-one-one rule. This rule is applied more consistently in American English than in British English.)

Rule Page 4 (Rule 11)

11. Words ending with a silent final e (*come*) are written without the e when adding an ending that begins with a vowel.

Rule Page 5 (Rule 12)

12. After c we use ei (*receive*). If we say *a*, we use ei (*vein*). In the list of exceptions, we use ei. In all other words, the phonogram ie is used.

Rule Page 6 (Rules 13–16)

13. The phonogram sh is used at the beginning or end of a base word (*she, dish*), at the end of a syllable (*fin ish*), but never at the beginning of a syllable after the first one except for the ending *ship* (*wor ship, friend ship*).

14. The phonograms ti, si, and ci are the spellings most frequently used to say *sh* at the beginning of a second or subsequent syllable in a base word (*na tion, ses sion, fa cial*).

15. The phonogram si is used to say *sh* when the syllable before it ends in an s (*ses sion*) or when the base word has an s where the base word changes (*tense, ten sion*).

16. The phonogram si may also say *zh* as in *vi sion*.

Additional Rules (Rules 17–29)

17. We often double l, f, and s following a single vowel at the end of a one-syllable word (*will, off, miss*). Rule 17 sometimes applies to two-syllable words like *recess*.

    While reading the word (e.g., *will*) for spelling, students say the extra consonant sound (e.g., *w i l l*).

18. We often use ay to say *ā* at end of a base word, never a alone.

    Students just say the sound *ā*.

19. Vowels i and o may say *ī* and *ō* if followed by two consonants (*find, old*).

20. The letter s never follows x. The phonogram x includes an *s* sound (*ks*).

21. *All*, written alone, has two l's, but when written with another syllable, only one l is written (*al so, al most*).

22. *Till* and *full*, written alone, have two l's, but when written with another syllable, only one l is written (*un til, beau ti ful*).

    Students also need practice explaining how the addition of these endings changes word meanings and usage.

23. The phonogram dge may be used *only* after a single vowel that says ă, ĕ, ĭ, ŏ, or ŭ (*badge, edge, bridge, lodge, budge*).

24. When adding an ending to a word that ends with a consonant and y, use i instead of y unless the ending is *ing*.

    Students also need practice explaining how the addition of these endings changes word meanings and usage (plurals of nouns: *baby/babies;* verb tense: *try/tried*).

25. The phonogram ck may be used only after a single vowel that says ă, ĕ, ĭ, ŏ, or ŭ (*back, neck, lick, rock, duck*).

26. Words that are the names or titles of people, places, books, days, or months are capitalized (*Mary, Honolulu, Amazon River, Bible, Monday, July*).

    Initially, students need to explain their use of capitals so they do not use them indiscriminately.

27. Words *beginning* with the sound z are always spelled with z, never s (*zoo*).

28. The phonogram ed has three sounds and is used to form the past tense of verbs. If the verb ends in the sound d or t, adding ed makes another syllable that says *ed* (*hand ed, land ed, paint ed, plant ed*). If the verb ends in an unvoiced consonant, the ending ed says t (*looked, liked, jumped, washed*). In all other verbs, the ending ed says d (*lived, killed, played, belonged*).

29. Words are usually divided between double consonants within a base word. For speaking and reading, only the consonant in the accented syllable is pronounced; the consonant in the unaccented syllable is silent (*lit´ le*).

    During dictation of words in sections A–H, focus only on having students pronounce both consonants to spell the words correctly. When reading words for spelling, students sound both consonants, but in speaking or reading, they say the consonant only in the accented syllable. When reading words for reading, be sure students read double-consonant words correctly (*lit´ le, a count´, o cur´, e fect´, a rive´, of´ i cer*).

SYLLABLE DIVISION

AS CHILDREN PROGRESS through the grades, they encounter thousands of words they have not been directly taught. To be independent readers, they must be able to quickly and accurately pronounce (decode) words so they can connect them with their spoken vocabulary or identify them as unfamiliar words. Knowing English syllable division patterns facilitates rapid pronunciation of unfamiliar multisyllable words.

Prior to beginning dictation, teachers preteach the meaning of syllable (see page 46) and demonstrate that each syllable has a vowel (see page 46). If adjacent vowels are not phonograms, they form separate syllables (tri al, pe ri od). The arrangement of vowels and consonants influences the vowel sound: syllables that end in a vowel are commonly called *open*, and the vowel *usually* says its second sound (commonly called *long* - me); syllables that end in one or more consonants are called *closed*, and the vowel usually says its first sound (*short* - and). After each multisyllable word is introduced in the spelling lesson, teach syllable division. Syllable patterns that help children decode unfamiliar words are listed in the order of introduction.

Patterns

1. In a consonant + le pattern (c + le), the word is divided before the consonant plus le.

   There are ten possible combinations: ble, cle, dle, fle, gle, kle, ple, sle, tle, zle.

   lit tle (A–G)   ap ple (H)   a ble (L)   gen tle (M)   un cle (O)
   Consonant + *le* always forms a *separate* syllable.

2. In a vowel-consonant-vowel (vcv) pattern, the word is divided after the first vowel.

   o ver (A–G)   be long (H)   ba by (H)   pa per (I)   ze ro (I)
   Vowels *a, e, o, u usually* say /ā/, /ē/, /ō/, /ū/ at the end of a syllable (rule 4). Vowels *i* and *y* usually say /ĭ/ (big, gym), but they may say /ī/ (*si lent, my* - rule 5).

3. In a consonant-vowel-consonant (cvc) or vowel-consonant (vc) pattern, the word is divided after the consonant that follows the vowel.

   riv er (I)   ver y (I)   sev en (J)   cov er (J)   an y (K)
   A vowel followed by a consonant (closed), *usually* says its first (short) sound.

4. Compound words (cw) are divided between the base words.

    in to (A–G)   to day (A–G)   Sun day (I)   in side (J)   af ter noon (K)

    If either base word has more than one syllable (afternoon), divide it as a single word.

5. Multiletter phonograms (digraphs/diphthongs/r-controlled vowels) are *not* divided regardless of other patterns, such as vcv or vccv.

    moth er (A–G)   oth er (H)   au thor (H)   broth er (K)   flow er (L)

    Demonstrate the *sound* of the word if the letters in a multiletter phonogram (phg) were divided. (mot her, ot her, aut hor, flo wer)

6. In a vowel-consonant-consonant-vowel (vccv) pattern the word is *usually* divided between the consonants.

    yel low (H)   win ter (I)   let ter (I)   din ner (I)   hap py (J)

    In a vowel-consonant-consonant-consonant-vowel (vcccv) pattern the word is *usually* divided after the first consonant in the series.

    coun try (L)   con tract (M)   dis trict (O)   ad dress (O)   en trance (P)

7. Prefixes (p) *always* include vowels, making them *separate* syllables.

    re port (J)   ex tra (M)   un a ble (M)   re cov er (M)   re turn (M)

    A prefix is a letter or group of letters added to the beginning of a base word or root to change the meaning completely (un a ble) or clarify by adding information (re cov er).

    Suffixes (s) *usually* include vowels, making them separate syllables.

    plant ed (I)   on ly (K)   set ting (K)   com ing (K)   eas y (K)

    A suffix is a letter or a group of letters added to the end of a base word or root. Suffixes may add information to the meaning of the word (help ful), or they may indicate number (boys), time (la ter), part of speech (catch/catch er), and tense (com ing). The suffix *ed only* forms a separate syllable when the base word ends in the sound /d/ or /t/ (ground ed, plant ed). The suffix y *often* combines with the preceding consonant to form a syllable (fun ny).

Tip: When more than one pattern explains the division, either is correct. Example: re port (vcv and/or p) Older or gifted primary students may recognize that *re* is a prefix (p).

PRIMARY AND INTERMEDIATE SPELLING/VOCABULARY NOTEBOOKS—SAMPLE PAGES

DURING CONSTRUCTION of the primary and intermediate spelling/ vocabulary notebooks, children learn to analyze the *written* spelling of high-frequency words, using their minds to apply the rules of the language, not rote memorization. Construction of the notebook, therefore, is the central activity for student achievement in this method because it is the foundation for other language arts instruction.

Primary Notebook

Children in kindergarten through grade two write the Extended Ayres words in a *sewn* purple-and-white, stiff-cover composition book containing thirty-four leaves, each having twelve lines with ⅝-inch (1.6 cm) spacing. Writing the words in manuscript begins on page 1 of the primary notebook after children have learned the first forty-five phonograms and developed fine-motor skills—usually about midyear for kindergarten children and after three or four weeks for first-grade children. While kindergartners are developing fine-motor skills, the teacher writes words in sections A–G on chart paper or the board, as illustrated on example pages 229–234. Students read the words for spelling and for reading. Many kindergartners write more than sections A–G in their notebooks. The more words children analyze and read from their notebooks, the quicker they become independent readers. Second-grade children are pretested to determine where to begin dictation in the Extended Ayres Word List.

1

A-G	
me r.4	can
do[3]	see
and	run
go r.4	the[2] r.4
at	in
on	so r.4
a r.4	no r.4
it	now
is[2]	man
she r.4	

2	
ten	an
tan	my r.5, 6
tin	up
ton	last
bed	not
top	us
he r.4	am
you[3]	good[2]
will r.17	
we r.4	

3

[time	red
have blue =₂ =₂	of
chance charge =₃ =₃	be r.4
lit tle =₄	but
[are (no job e) =₅	this
	all r.17
lit tle =₄	[your
a go r.4	[you
old r.19	out
bad	time

4	
m<u>ay</u> r.18	<u>by</u> r.5,6
in t³o	h<u>a</u>v<u>e</u> =2
him	<u>are</u> =5
t³o d<u>ay</u> r.18	had
l²<u>oo</u>k	<u>o</u> ver r.4
did	must
l<u>i</u>k<u>e</u>	m<u>a</u>k<u>e</u>
six	str<u>ee</u>t
<u>boy</u>	<u>say</u> r.18
b²<u>oo</u>k	<u>come</u> =5

5

hand	[big
ring	[bag
[live	[beg
[live =2	[bog
kill r.17	[bug
late	moth er
let	three
	land
	cold r.19
	hot

6	
h<u>o</u>t	<u>f</u>ur
<u>ch</u>ild r.19	<u>gr</u><u>ee</u>n
<u>i</u>ce	<u>oi</u>l
<u>pl</u><u>ay</u> r.18	<u>p</u><u>ai</u>nt
[s<u>ea</u>	p<u>oo</u>l
[s<u>ee</u>	[t<u>oo</u>th
<u>b</u>ird	[t<u>ee</u>th
c<u>oo</u>l	w<u>or</u>m r.8
<u>ea</u>rth	
<u>f</u><u>ee</u>d	

Intermediate Notebook

Students in grade three and above write words in a *sewn* black-and-white, hardcover composition book, containing fifty leaves, each having twenty-three lines with ⅜-inch (1.0 cm) spacing. The intermediate notebook has two parts: rule pages and the Extended Ayres Word List. Rule pages, including phonograms and example words for the first sixteen rules, multi-letter phonograms, and additional, less common phonograms are illustrated on pages 237–251. See chapter 1 for detailed procedures for teaching each rule page.

Older students begin writing Extended Ayres words after they have learned to say and write all seventy phonograms in manuscript and cursive writing, have written all numbers, and have written rule pages 1 and 7 in cursive. Pretest to determine in which section of the Extended Ayres Word List to begin dictation. Students begin writing the Extended Ayres words in the middle of the notebook, where the stitching makes it open easily. (See chapter 5, pages 187–189, for pretest procedures.)

1

Consonants

b c d f g h j k l m n p qu r s t v w x y z

c before e, i or y says c̆

g before e, i or y may say ğ

Vowels²

a	at	na̲vy	fȧ̲ther³
e	end	me̲	
i	big	si̲lent	
y	gym	my̲	
o	odd	o̲pen	do̊³
u	up	mu̲s̆ic²	pu̇t³

silent
final e's

- time
- have blue
- chance charge
- lit tle
- are (no̊ job e)

Her	first	nurse =5
serve =2	sir	turn
herd	bird	hurt
dinner	third	burn
perfect	girl	church
nerve =2	fir	fur
berth	birth	purpose =5
western	skirt	surprise
merge =3	circle =4	hurdle =4
grocery	firm	Thursday
perch	thirst	Saturday
sterling	squirt	further
verse =5	squirm	disturb
clerk	chirp	curtain
certain	confirm	curve =2

2

works   early.

worm   learn
word   heard
world   search
worth   earn
worthy   earth
worse   earnest
worst   pearl
worry   rehearse
worship

hop	hopping
set	setting
run	running
red	reddish
hot	hottest
mud	muddy
flat	flatten
writ	written
ship	shipped shipper
stop	stopped stopper

	ing	ice	ous
	er	ish	ist
Endings which	ed	age	ible
begin with a	est	{ ance	{ able
vowel	y	{ ant	{ ably
	al	{ ence	{ ancy
	en	{ ent	{ ency

3

be gin'	be gin ning
for got'	for got ten
con trol'	con trol la ble
oc cur'	oc cur rence
ex cel'	ex celled
ad mit'	ad mit tance
trans mit'	trans mit ter
ac quit'	ac quit tal
o mit'	o mit ted
en' ter	en ter ing
prof' it	prof it a ble
brid' get	brid get ed
ed' it	ed it ing

hope hoping

come coming
fierce fiercest
write writer
change changed
serve service
nerve nervous
desire desirable
settle settling
ease easy
rehearse rehearsal

Endings beginning with a vowel	ing	ice	ous
	er	ish	ist
	ed	age	ible
	est	ance	able
	y	ant	ably
	al	ence	ancy
	en	ent	ency
	or		

4

ie	cei
be lieve	re ceive
be lief	per ceive
fierce	ceil ing
brief	re ceipt
niece	con ceit
priest	
field	
chief	
siege	
a chieve	
piece	
pie	
lie	
prai rie	
mis chief	
friend	

5

ei says "ā"   Exceptions[2]

their   Nei ther
veil   for eign
heir   sov er eign
{ rein   seiz ed (the)
{ reign   coun ter feit (and)
vein   for feit ed
sur veil lance   lei sure.
skein

                         ei ther
                         weird
                         pro tein
                         heif er

ti	*si*
na tion	ses sion
col lec tion	com pres sion
po ten tial	dis cus sion
pa tient	de pres sion
am bi tion	ad mis sion
sub stan tial	or
in fec tion	(tense) ten sion
in flu en tial	(manse) man sion
con fi den tial	
im par tial	
su per sti tious	*si*
tor ren tial	
pá la tial	vi sion
	di vi sion
	oc ca sion
	ex plo sion

6

ci

(face) facial
(space) spacious
(finance) financial

(music) musician
(electric) electrician
(physic) physician

social
special
especially
ancient
crucial
efficient
suspicious

Multiletter Phonograms

sh	{ er
	ir
ee	ur
	wor
2 th	ear
{ 2 ow	ng
{ 4 ou	
	3 ea
2 oo	
	{ aw
3 ch	{ au
ar	or
{ ay	ck
{ ai	
	wh
{ oy	
{ oi	

7

3 ed	{ kn
	gn
{ 2 ew	
{ 2 ui	wr
oa	3 ie
	3 ei
qu	
	dge
ph	
	eigh
6 ough	
	{ ti
oe	{ 2 si
	{ ci
3 ey	
igh	

Additional Phonograms

tch	catch
eo	people =4
eau	beauty
augh	daughter
	laughter
ce	ocean
gh	ghost
gi	region
our	journey 3
di	soldier

8

cu	bis<u>cu</u>it
aigh	str<u>aigh</u>t
sc	<u>sc</u>ene
ge	pi<u>ge</u>ons[2]
rh	<u>rh</u>yme
eu	<u>Eu</u>rope
sci	con<u>sci</u>en<u>tio</u>us[4]
pn	<u>pneu</u>m<u>o</u>ni<u>a</u>[3]

EXTENDED AYRES WORD LIST: ORDER OF INSTRUCTION

THE EXTENDED AYRES (EA) Word List consists of over 2,300 high-frequency words that are listed (1) in the order of instruction, (2) alphabetically, and (3) as parts of speech. Chapter 1 describes in detail how EA words are used to teach spelling, reinforce handwriting, and develop fluent word recognition. Chapter 2 provides explicit procedures and example lessons for using these words to teach sentence construction and parts of speech. EA words are listed alphabetically to facilitate lesson planning.

The basic 1,000 high-frequency words were compiled by Dr. Leonard P. Ayres. In this edition, additional words (*extensions*) are either in the core vocabulary identified in the *Collins COBUILD English Dictionary* (1995) or provide practice of phonograms and rules. Dr. Ayres divided words by sections. Sections A through G are combined in *The Writing Road to Reading* because there are so few words in the first seven sections. Kindergartners, first graders, and older severely disabled readers begin with sections A–G. First-grade and older students are pretested to determine in which section to begin. (See chapter 5, pages 187–189.)

Column 1 of pages 254–397 lists the EA words in the order of instruction. The Ayres words are printed in boldface type; additional words are printed in italics. Some words are bracketed together to demonstrate relationships that need to be taught in integrated spelling/writing lessons.

Column 2 lists rules that apply to EA words. In this edition, all rules are listed throughout sections A–Z for convenient reference and for use in lesson planning. This enables upper-grade teachers to quickly find words (in earlier sections of the EA list) to use for additional rule practice.

Column 3 lists instructional tips that provide facts specific to particular words or information needed for students' success (e.g., the correct phonogram to use when several are possible). Most words in the Extended Ayres Word List have a single pronunciation. In this edition, alternative pronunciations and spellings are designated British English (B.E.) and marked accordingly as specified in the *Collins COBUILD English Dictionary*.

Instructional tips are based on the Collins model of instruction. Initially, teachers provide complete information to prevent student errors. Then, they guide as students attempt to independently say, write, mark, and read each word. Finally, support is provided only when needed, allowing students to do the thinking and responding. (For detailed explanation of this progression from teacher modeling to student independence, see chapter 4, pages 164–167). *When students no longer need a tip, it should no longer be used.*

To facilitate student independence, instructional tips are gradually phased out. If first-grade students complete writing section N, they are introduced to all twenty-nine rules; *specific* tips are provided for the majority of words. However, beginning in section O, *specific* tips are provided only to avoid common spelling or pronunciation errors such as writing the wrong vowel in unaccented syllables and choosing the wrong phonogram among possible alternatives. To avoid repetition *general tips* are provided only the *first* time they apply. There are four kinds of *general tips*.

1. General tip for rule 29 words: "Continue to require correct pronunciation for spelling and reading throughout the section."
2. General tip for words that have a final phonogram y saying ĭ: "Continue to require precise pronunciation of vowels in unaccented syllables throughout the section." (By section Z, this statement includes all vowels in the unaccented syllable.)
3. General tip for words that end in ct, pt, bt: "Continue to require precise pronunciation throughout the section."
4. General tip for base and derived words: "Continue to dictate the base word first throughout the section."

EXTENDED AYRES WORD LIST

Sections A–G
113 Words for Spelling, Writing, and Reading

Spelling Word	Rule(s)	Instructional Tips
m<u>e</u>	r. 4	In *me*, the e says ē at the end of a syllable. Remind students that a syllable is a word or part of a word that is said in one impulse (beat) of the voice.
do³		After children say the sounds for *do*, say, "Use the phonogram that says ŏ, ō, o͞o. Write a three above the o to show the third sound, o͞o."
and		
g<u>o</u>	r. 4	In *go*, the o says ō at the end of a syllable.
at		
on		
<u>a</u>	r. 4	In the word *a*, the a says ā at the end of a syllable. Say ā for spelling. When reading, the accent is almost never on the word *a* (*a man, a house*).
it		
is²		After children say the sounds for *is*, say, "Use the phonogram that says s, z. Write a two above the s to show the second sound, z."
<u>sh</u><u>e</u>	r. 4	Underline the two-letter phonogram that says *sh* at the beginning of a word (r. 13). In *she*, the e says ē at the end of a syllable.
can		

Spelling Word	Rule(s)	Instructional Tips
s<u>ee</u>		After children say the sounds for *see*, say, "Use the double *ee* to write *ē* in *see*."
run		
²<u>th</u>e	r. 4	After children say the sounds for *the*, say "Use the phonogram that says *th*, *th*. Write two above and between the letters t and h to show the second sound, *th*." For spelling, say *ē* distinctly. For reading, the e is not accented.
in		
s<u>o</u>	r. 4	In *so*, the o says *ō* at the end of a syllable.
n<u>o</u>	r. 4	In *no*, the o says *ō* at the end of a syllable.
n<u>ow</u>		After children say the sounds for *now*, say, "Use the phonogram that says *ow*, *ō*."
man		
[ten tan tin ton		In *ten*, use the phonogram that says *ĕ*, *ē*. In *tan*, use *ă*, *ā*, *ah*. In *tin*, use *ĭ*, *ī*. In *ton*, use *ŏ*, *ō*, *o͞o*. Have children say *ŏ* precisely. British English (B.E.): *Ton* is colloquial. In the writing lesson, explain the importance of using the right vowel to spell the intended word.
bed		
top		
h<u>e</u>	r. 4	In *he*, the e says *ē* at the end of a syllable.

Spelling Word	Rule(s)	Instructional Tips
yo͞u (with 3 above)		After children say the sounds for *you*, say, "Use the phonogram that says *ow*, *ō*, *o͞o*, *ŭ*. Write three above and between the o and u to show the third sound, *o͞o*." (*You* is one of the few words that end with ou.)
will	r. 17	After children say the sounds for *will*, say, "Write another l because the l is often doubled following a single vowel at the end of a one-syllable word." For spelling, say both *l*'s.
we̲	r. 4	In *we*, the e says *ē* at the end of a syllable.
an		
my̲	r. 5, 6	In *my*, the y may say *ī*. The letter y, not i, is used at the end of an English word.
u̲p		
last		B.E.: låst.
not		
us		
am		
go͝od (with 2 above)		After children say the sounds for *good*, say, "Use the phonogram that says *o͞o*, *o͝o*. Write two above and between the o's to show the second sound, *o͝o*."

Spelling Word	Rule(s)	Instructional Tips
time ha**ve**₂ bl**ue**₂ _chan**ce**₃_ charg**e**₌₃ lit tl**e**₄ **are**₅ (no job e)		Rule 7 explains silent final e's. The e lets the i say $\bar{\imath}$ (job 1). English words do not end in v or u (job 2). The e lets c say *s* and g say *j* (job 3). Every syllable must have a vowel (job 4). Remnant of Old English (job 5).
lit tl**e**₄		Use two hands to demonstrate two syllables (two impulses of the voice). Children say *lit* and write *lit,* then say *tle* and write *tle* (job 4). For spelling, be sure they say both *t*'s (rule 29).
a go	r. 4	Children say $\bar{a}$ and write it, then *go* and write it. Say $\bar{a}$ for spelling, but accent *go* when reading.
old	r. 19	In *old,* the o may say $\bar{o}$ because it is followed by two consonants. It is not necessary to write the two above o because rule 19 explains which sound is used.
bad		
red		
of		Say $\breve{o}f$ for spelling but $\breve{o}v$ for reading. Both must be learned. Underline the f twice to indicate an uncommon sound for *f*.
be	r. 4	In *be,* the e says $\bar{e}$ at the end of a syllable.
but		
this		Write two above and between the letters t and h to show the second sound, *th*.

Spelling Word	Rule(s)	Instructional Tips
åll	r. 17	After children say the sounds for *all*, say, "Use the phonogram that says ă, ā, ah." For spelling say both *l*'s. B.E.: The sound of a may be altered when followed by an l.
[your [you		Skip a space after the word *all*. Dictate the base word, *you*, first, then the derived word, *your*, on the line above.
out		After children say the sounds for *out*, say, "Use the phonogram that says ow, ō, ōō, ŭ."
time		In *time*, the e lets the i say ī (job 1 on primary notebook page 3 and intermediate notebook rule page 1).
may	r. 18	After children say the sounds for *may*, say, "Use the phonogram that says ā at the end of a base word."
in tŏ		After children say the syllable *to*, say, "Use the phonogram that says ŏ, ō, ōō. Write a three above the o to show the third sound, ōō."
him		
tŏ day	r. 18	After children say the syllable *day*, say, "Use the phonogram that says ā at the end of a base word."
loŏk		After children say the sounds for *look*, say, "Use the phonogram that says ōō ŏŏ."
did		

Spelling Word	Rule(s)	Instructional Tips
l**ike**		After children say the sounds for *like,* say, "Use *k.*" The silent e lets the i say *ī* (job 1 on primary notebook page 3 and intermediate notebook rule page 1).
six		The letter x has two sounds, *ks.*
b**oy**		After children say the sounds for *boy,* say, "Use the phonogram that says *oy* at the end of a word."
b**oͦo**k		After children say the sounds for *book,* say, "Use the phonogram that says *ōo, ŏo.*"
b**y**	r. 5, 6	In *by,* the y may say *ī.* The letter y, not i, is used at the end of an English word.
ha**ve**₂		English words do not end with a v (job 2). Refer to the five kinds of silent e on primary notebook page 3 or intermediate notebook rule page 1.
are₅		In *are,* the silent e has no job (job 5). Refer to primary notebook page 3 or intermediate notebook rule page 1.
had		
o v**er**	r. 4	Before dictating the word *over,* write, "Her first nurse₅ works early," on chart paper or the board (see page 58). After children say the syllable *ver,* say, "The *er* in *her* is the one we use most often."
must		
m**ake**		After children say the sounds for *make,* say, "Use *k.*" The e lets the a say *ā* (job 1).

Spelling Word	Rule(s)	Instructional Tips
str<u>ee</u>t		After children say the sounds for *street*, say, "Use the double *ee*." Say each phonogram separately.
s<u>ay</u>	r. 18	After children say the sounds for *say*, say, "Use the phonogram that says *ā* at the end of a base word."
com<u>e</u>₅		For spelling, say *ŏ*. In *come*, the silent e has no job (job 5). Refer to primary notebook page 3 or intermediate notebook rule page 1.
hand		
ri<u>ng</u>		Be sure students say *ĭ* and *ng* correctly.
[l<u>iv</u>e / *liv<u>e</u>₂*		In *live*, the e lets the i say *ī* (job 1) and keeps the word from ending in a v (job 2). Mark only the first job. The i says *ĭ*, but the silent e is needed because English words do not end with v (job 2).
kill	r. 17	After children say the sounds for *kill*, say, "Use *k*." For spelling, say both *l*'s.
l<u>ate</u>		In *late*, the e lets the a say *ā* (job 1).
let		
[big / *bag* / beg / *bog* / *bug*		Dictate the Ayres word *big*, then each word in order. In the writing lesson, review the importance of using the right vowel to spell the intended word.

Spelling Word	Rule(s)	Instructional Tips
mo<u>th</u> <u>er</u>		After children say the syllable *moth,* say, "Use the phonogram that says ŏ, ō, ōō." After the syllable *er,* say, "Use the *er* of *her.*"
<u>th</u>r<u>ee</u>		After children say the sounds for *three,* say, "Use the double *ee.*"
land		
cold	r. 19	In *cold,* the o says ō because it is followed by two consonants.
hot		
hat		
<u>ch</u>ild	r. 19	In *child,* the i says ī because it is followed by two consonants.
<u>i</u>c<u>e</u>		In *ice,* the e lets the i say ī (job 1) and lets the c say *s* (job 3). Mark only the first job.
pl<u>ay</u>	r. 18	Use the phonogram that says ā at the end of a base word.
⎡ s<u>ea</u> ⎣ s<u>ee</u>		After children say the sounds for *sea,* say, "Use the phonogram that says ē, ĕ, ā." The phonograms ee and ea (each saying ē) show that the words have different meanings.

The three usual ways for a vowel to say ā, ē, ī, ō, or ū have now been introduced.

1. By ending the syllable *(m<u>e</u>).*
2. By being followed by a consonant and a silent e *(t<u>i</u>m<u>e</u>).*
3. By having two consonants follow an i or an o *(old, child).*

When reading, teach children to try the first sound unless one of these conditions exists.

Spelling Word	Rule(s)	Instructional Tips
b<u>ir</u>d		After children say the sounds for *bird*, say, "Use the *er* of *first*."
c<u>oo</u>l		After children say the sounds for *cool*, say, "Use $\bar{oo}$, $\breve{oo}$."
<u>ear</u>th		After children say the sounds for *earth*, say, "Use the *er* of *early*."
f<u>ee</u>d		After children say the sounds for *feed*, say, "Use the double *ee*."
f<u>ur</u>		After children say the sounds for *fur*, say, "Use the *er* of *nurse*."
gr<u>ee</u>n		After children say the sounds for *green*, say, "Use the double *ee*."
<u>oi</u>l		After children say the sounds for *oil*, say, "Use *oi* that we don't use at the end of a word."
p<u>ai</u>nt		After children say the sounds for *paint*, say, "Use the two-letter *ā* not used at the end of a word."
p<u>oo</u>l		After children say the sounds for *pool*, say, "Use $\bar{oo}$, $\breve{oo}$."
[t<u>oo</u>th [t<u>ee</u>th		After children say the sounds for *tooth*, say, "Use $\bar{oo}$, $\breve{oo}$." After children say the sounds for *teeth*, say, "Use the double *ee*."
w<u>or</u>m	r. 8	

Section H
73 Words for Spelling, Writing, and Reading

Spelling Word	Rule(s)	Instructional Tips
d<u>ay</u>	r. 18	
<u>ea</u>t		After children say the sounds for *eat*, say, "Use $\bar{e}, \breve{e}, \bar{a}$."
[*sits* *sit*		Skip a space. Dictate the base word, *sit*, first.
lot		In the writing lesson, teach *lot* as a piece of property.
box		The letter x has two sounds, *ks*.
sc<u>hoo</u>l²		After children say the sounds for *school*, say, "Use the phonogram that says *ch, k, sh*. Use $\bar{oo}, \breve{oo}$. Write two just above and between the letters c and h to show the second sound *k*." Point out that it takes four phonograms to write *school*.
be lo<u>ng</u>	r. 4	
[d<u>oo</u>r fl<u>oo</u>r		After children say the sounds for *door*, say, "Use $\bar{oo}, \breve{oo}$." For spelling, say $\bar{oo}$. Underline the *oo* twice to indicate an uncommon sound. For reading, say *dor*.
yes		
l<u>ow</u>²		After children say the sounds for *low*, say, "Use *ow*, $\bar{o}$."
soft		

Spelling Word	Rule(s)	Instructional Tips
⌈ *stands*² ⌊ stand		Skip a space. Dictate the base word, *stand*, first. After children say the sounds for *stands*, say, "Use *s, z.*"
y<u>ar</u>d		
bri<u>ng</u>		Be sure children say *ĭ* and *ng* correctly.
tell	r. 17	For spelling, say both *l*'s.
f<u>i</u><u>ve</u>		In *five*, the e lets the i say *ī* (job 1) and keeps the word from ending in a v (job 2). Mark only the first job.
bȧ̊ll	r. 17	After children say the sounds for *ball*, say, "Use *ă, ā, ah.*" For spelling, say both *l*'s. B.E.: The sound of a may be altered when followed by an l.
l<u>aw</u>		After children say the sounds for *law*, say, "Use the phonogram that says *aw* at the end of English words."
ask		After children say the sounds for *ask*, say, "Use *k.*" B.E.: ȧ̊sk.
just		
w<u>ay</u>	r. 18	After children say the sounds for *way*, say, "Use the phonogram that says *ā* at the end of a base word."
get		
h<u>o</u><u>me</u>		The e lets the o say *ō* (job 1).
mu<u>ch</u>		

Spelling Word	Rule(s)	Instructional Tips
cäll	r. 17	After children say the sounds for *call*, say, "Use ă, ā, ah." For spelling, say both *l*'s. B.E.: The sound of a may be altered when followed by an l.
lo**ng**		
lo**ve**₂		For spelling, say ŏ. The e is needed, since English words do not end in v (job 2).
then		
h**ouse**₅		After children say the sounds for *house*, say, "Use ow, ō, ōō, ŭ." The e has no job (job 5).
y**ear**		After children say the sounds for *year*, say, "Use ē, ě, ā." *Year* has three phonograms.
tö		
I	r. 5	The pronoun *I* is always capitalized. Explain that early printers thought the lower-case *i* looked insignificant as a word.
aš		After children say the sounds in *as*, say, "Use s, z."
send		
[**a** lo**ne** *lo**ne*** **one**	r. 4	Skip two spaces after the word *send*. On the third line, write the base word, *one*. For spelling, say letter names o, n, e, because *one* is not phonetic. For reading, say *won*. On the second line, write *lone*. On the first line, write *alone*. B.E.: For reading, say *wun*.

Spelling Word	Rule(s)	Instructional Tips
ha͞s[2]		After children say the sounds for *has*, say, "Use *s, z*."
som͟e͟₅		For spelling, say ŏ. The e has no job (job 5).
if		
h<u>ow</u>		After children say the sounds for *how*, say, "Use *ow, ō*."
h<u>er</u>		After children say the sounds for *her*, say, "Use *er* of *her*."
<u>th</u>em[2]		
o<u>th</u> e̍r[2]		After children say the syllables, say, "In the first syllable, use ŏ, ō, o͞o. In the second syllable, use *er* of *her*."
b<u>a</u> by	r. 4, 6	For spelling, say *bā bĭ*. The accent is on the first syllable.
well	r. 17	For spelling, say both *l*'s.
<u>a</u> b<u>ou</u>t	r. 4	For spelling, say *ā bout*. For reading, the *ā* is not accented.
⎡men ⎣man		
f<u>or</u>		
⎡ran ⎣run		
w<u>a͞s</u>[3][2]		After children say the sounds for *was*, say, "Use the phonograms ă, ā, ah, and s, z." B.E.: The sound of *a* may be altered after *w*.

Spelling Word	Rule(s)	Instructional Tips
t̲hat²		
hi̲s²		After children say the sounds for *his*, say, "Use *s, z*."
led		
l̲a̲y	r. 18	
ap pl̲e̲₄		For spelling, say both *p*'s (rule 29). Every syllable must have a vowel (job 4).
a̲t̲e̲		In *ate*, the e lets the a say ā (job 1).
a̲u t̲h̲o̲r		After children say the syllables, say, "In the first syllable, use the phonogram that we do not use at the end of English words." For spelling, say *or*, not *er*."
br̲e̲ad²		After children say the sounds for *bread*, say, "Use ē, ĕ, ā."
br̲o̲wn		After children say the sounds for *brown*, say, "Use *ow*, ō."
dog		
e̲a̲ts²		After children say the sounds for *eats*, say, "Use ē, ĕ, ā."
f̲ast		B.E.: fȧst³.
f̲o̲o̲d		After children say the sounds for *food*, say, "Use ōō, ŏŏ."
jump		

sleep		After children say the sounds for *sleep*, say, "Use the double *ee*."
wȧsh		After children say the sounds for *wash*, say, "Use ă, ā, ah." B.E.: The sound of a may be altered after w.
yel lȯw		For spelling, say both *l*'s (rule 29). After children say the syllables, say, "In the last syllable, use *ow, ō*."

Section I
90 Words for Spelling, Writing, and Reading

Spelling Word	Rule(s)	Instructional Tips
nine		In *nine*, the e lets the i say ī (job 1).
face		After children say the sounds for *face*, say, "Use *k, s*." In *face*, the e lets the a say ā (job 1) and the c say s (job 3). Mark only the first job.
miss	r. 17	
⌈ *rides* ⌊ **ride**		Skip a space. Dictate the base word, *ride*, first. In *ride*, the e lets the i say ī (job 1) (see tips for *nine*, above).
tree		
sick	r. 25	After children say the sounds for *sick*, say, "Use the phonogram that says *k* after a single vowel that says ĭ."
got		
north		

Spelling Word	Rule(s)	Instructional Tips
wh<u>i</u>t<u>e</u>		The phonogram *wh* has no sound but air can be felt on the hand held before the lips. Have children blow air out and feel it on their hands as they say *white* (not *wite*). In *white*, the e lets the i say $\bar{i}$ (job 1).
spent		
[f$\overset{2}{\underline{oo}}$t **f<u>ee</u>t**		After children say the sounds for *foot*, say, "Use $\overline{oo}$, $\breve{oo}$."
[bl$\overset{2}{\underline{ow}}$$\overset{2}{s}$ **bl$\overset{2}{\underline{ow}}$**		Skip a space. Dictate the base word, *blow*, first. After children say the sounds for *blow*, say, "Use *ow*, $\bar{o}$." After children say the sounds for *blows*, say, "Use *s, z*."
blo<u>ck</u>	**r. 25**	After children say the sounds for *block*, say, "Use the phonogram that says *k* after a single vowel that says $\breve{o}$."
spri<u>ng</u>		Be sure children say $\breve{i}$ and *ng* correctly.
riv <u>er</u>		After children say the syllables, say, "In the last syllable, use *er* of *her*. This *er* is used most often at the end of words."
[plant <u>ed</u> **plant**	**r. 28**	Skip a space. Dictate the base word, *plant*, first (rule 28).
cut		

Spelling Word	Rule(s)	Instructional Tips
song sing sang sung		In the writing lesson, review the importance of using the right vowel to spell the intended word.
win ter		
stone		In *stone,* the e lets the o say $\bar{o}$ (job 1).
free		
lake lace		In *lake,* the e lets the a say $\bar{a}$ (job 1). After children say the sounds for *lace,* say, "Use *k, s.*" The e lets the a say $\bar{a}$ (job 1) and the c say *s* (job 3). Mark only the first job.
page		After children say the sounds for *page,* say, "Use *g, j.*" The e lets the a say $\bar{a}$ (job 1) and the g say *j* (job 3). Mark only the first job.
nice		After children say the sounds for *nice,* say, "Use *k, s.*" The e lets the i say $\bar{i}$ (job 1) and the c say *s* (job 3). Mark only the first job.
end		
fall	r. 17	After children say the sounds for *fall,* say, "Use $\breve{a}, \bar{a}, ah.$" B.E.: The sound of a may be altered when followed by an l.
went		

Spelling Word	Rule(s)	Instructional Tips
ba<u>ck</u>	r. 25	After children say the sounds for *back*, say, "Use the phonogram that says *k* after a single vowel that says *ă*."
<u>a</u> w<u>ay</u>	r. 4, 18	For spelling, say *ā way*. In reading, the a is not accented.
p<u>a</u> p<u>er</u>	r. 4	
pu̇t		After children say the sounds for *put*, say, "Use *ŭ, ū, o͝o*."
<u>ea</u>ch		After children say the sounds for *each*, say, "Use *ē, ĕ, ā*."
s<u>oo</u>n		After children say the sounds for *soon*, say, "Use *o͞o, o͝o*."
c<u>a</u>m<u>e</u>		In *came*, the e lets the a say *ā* (job 1).
Sun d<u>ay</u>	r. 26, 18	After children say *Sun day* in syllables, say, "Use a capital letter because *Sunday* is the name of one day. Like a person's name, it must be written with a capital letter." In the writing lesson, explain that *Sunday* was named for the sun.
sh<u>ȯ</u>w		After children say the sounds for *show*, say, "Use *ow, ō*."
Mon d<u>ay</u> *m<u>oo</u>n*	r. 26, 18	After children say *Mon day* in syllables, say, "Use a capital letter because *Monday* is the name of one day and must be written with a capital letter." In the writing lesson, explain that *Monday* was named for the moon. *Moon* is not capitalized because there are many moons.

Spelling Word	Rule(s)	Instructional Tips
yet		
find	r. 19	
gi̲v̲e₂		In *give*, the e is needed, since English words do not end in v (job 2).
ne̅w̲		After children say the sounds for *new*, say, "Use the phonogram that says $\overline{oo}$, $\bar{u}$ at the end of a word."
let te̲r	r. 29	For spelling say both *t*'s. For reading, say the t in the accented syllable *let*. Begin marking rule 29 in the notebook.
ta̲k̲e		In *take*, the e lets the a say $\bar{a}$ (job 1).
Mr. = M̲is te̲r	r. 26	Say, "I will write the word *Mister* in syllables. Now I will demonstrate how to write an abbreviation for *Mister*. I will use a capital *M* because this abbreviation is always written with a person's name. I will use the first and last letters and a period to show that it is an abbreviation." Have students follow your model on the board. B.E.: Full stop (period) is not used. *Mr* is the international alternative.
af te̲r		B.E.: ẚf te̲r
t̲h̲i̲ng̲		Be sure children say *ĭ* and *ng* correctly.
wh̃åt		Have children blow air as they say *what*, not *watt*. Use *ă*, *ā*, *ah*. B.E.: The sound of a may be altered after a *wh*.
t̊h̲an		

Spelling Word	Rule(s)	Instructional Tips
[its, hi$\overset{2}{s}$, h<u>er</u> it's = it (i)$\overset{2}{s}$		Demonstrate writing bracketed words *(its, his,* and *her)* on the first line to show they are possessive pronouns. (An apostrophe is not used with *its* because *its* is not a contraction.) Demonstrate writing *it's = it (i)$\overset{2}{s}$.* The apostrophe replaces the ĭ of *is.* In the writing lesson, explain the meaning of a contraction.
v$\overset{1}{e}$r y	r. 6	Have children say *vĕr ĭ.* Put a one above the ĕ to show it is not *er.*
<u>or</u>		B.E.: Pronounce *or* for spelling.
<u>th</u>ank		For spelling, say *th ă n k.*
d<u>ea</u>r		After children say the sounds for *dear,* say, "Use ē, ĕ, ā."
west		
sold	r. 19	
told	r. 19	
best		
f<u>or</u>m		B.E.: Pronounce *or* for spelling.
f<u>ar</u>		B.E.: Pronounce *ar* for spelling.
g<u>a</u><u>ve</u>		In *gave,* the e lets the a say ā (job 1) and keeps the word from ending in a v (job 2). Mark only the first job.
<u>a</u> l<u>i</u><u>ke</u>	r. 4	For spelling, say *ā like.* For reading, the a is not accented. The e lets the i say ī (job 1).

Spelling Word	Rule(s)	Instructional Tips
add		
brave		In *brave,* the e lets the a say *ā* (job 1) and keeps the word from ending in a v (job 2). Mark only the first job.
corn		
dance₃		In *dance,* the e lets the c say *s* (job 3).
din ner	r. 29	For spelling, say both *n*'s. For reading, say the *n* in the accented syllable *din.*
doll	r. 17	
egg		
fruit		After children say the sounds for *fruit,* say, "Use $\overline{oo}$, *ū,* that we do not use at the end of English words."
looks		After children say the sounds for *looks,* say, "Use $\overline{oo}$, *ŏŏ.*"
pick	r. 25	After children say the sounds for *pick,* say, "Use the phonogram that says *k* after a single vowel that says *ĭ.*"
rich		
[*zoo*	r. 27	Words beginning with the sound *z* are always spelled with a z, never an s.
zip	r. 27	
ze ro	r. 27, 4	

Section J
105 Words for Writing, Reading, and Spelling

Spelling Word	Rule(s)	Instructional Tips
sev en		Say ĕn, not ĭn.
f<u>or</u> get		
hap py	r. 29, 6	For spelling, say both *p*'s and ĭ. For reading, say the *p* in the accented syllable *hap*.
n<u>oo</u>n		After children say the sounds for *noon*, say, "Use ōō, ŏo."
<u>th</u>ink		Say ĭ precisely.
sis t<u>er</u>		
<u>c</u>ast		B.E: că̇st.
<u>c</u><u>ar</u>d		
s<u>outh</u>		After children say the sounds for *south*, say, "Use *ow*, ō, ōō, ŭ."
d<u>ee</u>p		
in s<u>ide</u>		Job 1.
bl<u>ue</u>₂		Job 2.
post	r. 19	
t<u>ow</u>n		After children say the sounds for *town*, say, "Use *ow*, ō."
st<u>ay</u>	r. 18	
grand		

Spelling Word	Rule(s)	Instructional Tips
<u>ou</u>t s<u>i</u>d<u>e</u>		Job 1.
d<u>ar</u>k		
band		
<u>ga</u>m<u>e</u>		Job 1.
b<u>oa</u>t		After children say the sounds for *boat*, say, "Use the ō of boat."
rest		
<u>e</u>ast		After children say the sounds for *east*, say, "Use ē, ĕ, ā."
son *sun*		For spelling, say ŏ.
help		
h<u>ar</u>d		
r<u>a</u><u>ce</u>		In *race*, the e lets the a say ā (job 1) and the c say *s* (job 3). Mark only the first job.
cov <u>er</u>		
f<u>i</u>r<u>e</u> w<u>i</u>r<u>e</u> t<u>i</u>r<u>e</u>		Say *fire* as one syllable. Children say *fire*, not *fi er* (job 1). Say *wire* as one syllable (job 1). Say *tire* as one syllable (job 1). B.E.: *Noun* spelling is t<u>yr</u>e.
<u>a</u><u>ge</u>		In *age*, the e lets the a say ā (job 1) and the g say *j* (job 2). Mark only the first job.

Spelling Word	Rule(s)	Instructional Tips
gold	r. 19	
r<u>ea</u>d (a book) **r<u>ĕ́a</u>d**² (a book) **red**		After the children say the sounds for *read*, say, "Use *ē, ĕ, ā*." Write *(a book)* after *read*. Write *(a book)* after *rĕ́ad*².
f<u>i</u>ne		Job 1.
can not		For spelling and reading, say both *n*'s. In the writing lesson, teach this as a compound word, not as double letters.
May **may**	r. 26, 18 r. 18	
l<u>i</u>ne		Job 1.
left		
<u>sh</u>ip		After children say the sounds for *ship*, say, "Use the two-letter phonogram that says *sh* at the beginning of a word" (r. 13).
tr<u>ai</u>n		After children say the sounds for *train*, say, "Use two-letter *ai* that we do not use at the end of a word."
s<u>aw</u>		
p<u>ay</u>	r. 18	
large		Job 3.
n<u>ea</u>r		After children say the sounds for *near*, say, "Use *ē, ĕ, ā*."

Spelling Word	Rule(s)	Instructional Tips
d**ow**n		After children say the sounds for *down*, say, "Use *ow, ō*."
why	r. 5, 6	Have children say *wh ī* (not *w ī*).
bi**ll**	r. 17	
wånt		B.E.: The sound of a may be altered after w.
girls² / g**ir**l		Skip a space. Dictate the base word, *girl*, first. After children say the sounds for *girl*, say, "Use *er* of *first*."
p**ar**t		
sti**ll**	r. 17	
pl**ace**		In *place*, the e lets the a say *ā* (job 1) and the c say *s* (job 3). Mark only the first job.
r**e** p**or**t	r. 4	
nev **er**		
f**ou**nd		After children say the sounds for *found*, say, "Use *ow, ō, ōō, ŭ*."
s**ide**		Job 1.
kind	r. 19	
l**ife**		Job 1.
h**ere**		Job 1.
c**ar**		

Spelling Word	Rule(s)	Instructional Tips
w<u>or</u>d	r. 8	
ev <u>er</u> y	r. 6	For spelling, say *ĭ*.
un d<u>er</u>		
most	r. 19	
m<u>a</u>d<u>e</u>		Job 1.
s<u>ai</u>d say$\overset{2}{s}$ s<u>ay</u>	r. 18	After *made,* skip two spaces. Write the base word, *say.* On the second line, write *says.* For spelling, say *say$\overset{2}{s}$.* For reading, say *se$\overset{2}{s}$.* On the first line, write *said.* For spelling, say *s<u>ai</u>d.* For reading, say *sĕ<u>d</u>.*
w<u>or</u>k	r. 8	
<u>ou</u>r		After children say the sounds for *our,* say, "Use *ow, ō, ōō, ŭ.*"
m<u>o</u>r<u>e</u>		Job 1. Use of job 1 reinforces correct spelling.
<u>wh</u>en		Have children blow as they say *wh* (not *w*).
from f<u>or</u>m		*From* has four phonograms. *Form* has three phonograms.
wind w$\overset{2}{i}$nd (a toy)	r. 19	(An i does not have to say *ī* when followed by two consonants.) Write the two over i to distinguish *w$\overset{2}{i}$nd* from *wind.* Write *(a toy)* after *w$\overset{2}{i}$nd,* then *r. 19.*
print		

Spelling Word	Rule(s)	Instructional Tips
a̲ir		After children say the sounds for *air,* say, "Use the two-letter *ai* that is not used at the end of a word."
fill	r. 17	
a̲ lo̲ng	r. 4	For spelling, say *ā long.* For reading, the a is not accented.
lost		
n̲a̲m̲e		Job 1.
r̲o̲o̲m		After children say the sounds for *room,* say, "Use o̅o̅, ŏŏ."
h̲o̲p̲e		Job 1.
s̲a̲m̲e		Job 1.
glad		
wit̲h²		
m̲i̲n̲e		Job 1.
cha̲ir		After children say the sounds for *chair,* say, "Use the two-letter *ai* that is not used at the end of a word."
fo̲r got		
g̲uess	r. 17	After children say the sounds for *guess,* say, "Use two-letter *g.*"
han̲g		Make sure children say ă and *ng* correctly.
me̲a̲t		After children say the sounds for *meat,* say, "Use ē, ĕ, ā."

Spelling Word	Rule(s)	Instructional Tips
m**ouse**₅		After children say the sounds for *mouse*, say, "Use *ow, ō, ōō, ŭ*" (job 5).
phone		After children say the sounds for *phone*, say, "Use two-letter *f*" (job 1).
st**ore**		Job 1. Use of job 1 reinforces correct spelling.
sup p**er**	r. 29	For spelling, say both *p*'s. For reading, say the *p* in the accented syllable *sup*.
thr**o͞u̯gh**		After children say the sounds for *through*, say, "Use *ō, ōō, ŭf, ŏf, aw, ow.*"
t**oe**		After children say the sounds for *toe*, say, "Use *ō* of *toe*."

Section K
120 Words for Spelling, Writing, and Reading

Spelling Word	Rule(s)	Instructional Tips
b**e** c**ame**	r. 4	
bro**t̶h̲** **er**		For spelling, say *ŏ*.
r**ai**n		
k**ee**p		
st**ar**t		
m**ai**l m**ale** f**e** m**ale**	 r. 4	

Spelling Word	Rule(s)	Instructional Tips
[eye l̤	r. 26, 5	*Eye* is not phonetic. Say the names of the letters *e y e*.
glass	r. 17	B.E.: glȧss.
p<u>ar</u> ty	r. 6	For spelling, y says ĭ.
up on		
[tw<u>o</u>³ twin tw<u>ice</u> twel<u>ve</u>₂ twen ty b<u>e</u> tw<u>ee</u>n	 r. 6 r. 4	For spelling, say t w o͞o. (We probably once said *two* sounding the *w* as we still do in *twin, twice, twelve, twenty,* and *between,* each of which relates to *two*.) For spelling, say tĭ.
th<u>ey</u>²		
w<u>ou</u>l̤d		For spelling, say *w ou l d*. Underline *ou* twice because ŏŏ is an uncommon sound for *ou*. Underline l twice because it is silent. (The l came from *will*, the present tense of *would*.) For reading, say wŏŏd.
c<u>ou</u>l̤d		For spelling, say *c ou l d*. Underline *ou* twice because ŏŏ is an uncommon sound for *ou*. Underline l twice because l is silent. (The l was added to conform to *would* and *should*.) For reading, say cŏŏd.
<u>sh</u><u>ou</u>l̤d	r. 13	For spelling, say *sh ou l d*. The phonogram *sh* is used at the beginning of a base word to say *sh*. Underline *ou* twice because ŏŏ is an uncommon sound for *ou*. Underline l twice because it is silent. (The l comes from *shall*.) For reading, say shŏŏd.

Spelling Word	Rule(s)	Instructional Tips
<u>a</u>n y	r. 6	For spelling, say, *ăn ĭ*. Underline a twice because *ĕ* is an uncommon sound for a. For reading, say *ĕn ĭ*.
m<u>a</u>n y	r. 6	For spelling, say *măn ĭ*. For reading, say *mĕn ĭ*.
cit y	r. 6	For spelling, y says *ĭ*.
on ly	r. 19, 6	The base word is *one*. Normally the e would be retained, since the ending ly does not begin with a vowel (exception to rule 11). The o may say *ō* when followed by two consonants.
wh<u>e</u>re₅		For spelling and reading, say *wh*, not *w*. Write a one above the e to show it is not *er*.
w<u>ee</u>k		
w<u>ea</u>k		After children say the sounds for *weak*, say, "Use *ē, ĕ, ā*."
f<u>i</u>rst		After children say the sounds for *first*, say, "Use *er* of *first*."
sent		After children say the sounds for *sent*, say, "Use *s, z*."
cent		After children say the sounds for *cent*, say, "Use *k, s*."
m<u>i</u>l<u>e</u>		
s<u>ee</u>m		
<u>e</u> ven	r. 4	Be sure children say *vĕn*, not *vĭn*.
wi<u>th</u> <u>ou</u>t		Be sure children say *th*.
af t<u>er</u> n<u>oo</u>n		B.E.: <u>a</u>f t<u>er</u> n<u>oo</u>n.

Spelling Word	Rule(s)	Instructional Tips
Fri day	r. 26, 5, 18	In the writing lesson, explain that *Friday* was named for Frigga, the wife of Odin, in Norse mythology.
[hour [our		For spelling, say *h*. Underline h twice because it is silent.
wife		
state		
Ju ly	r. 26, 4, 5, 6	
head		
sto ry	r. 4, 6	For spelling, say *rĭ*.
o pen	r. 4	After children say the syllables, say, "Use *ĕ, ē*."
short	r. 13	The phonogram sh is used at the beginning of a base word to say *sh*.
la dy	r. 4, 6	For spelling, say, *dĭ*.
reach		After children say the sounds for *reach*, say, "Use *ē, ĕ, ā*."
bet ter	r. 29	For spelling, say both *t*'s. For reading, say *t* in the accented syllable *bet*.
wa ter		B.E.: The sound of a may be altered after *w*.
round		
cost		

Spelling Word	Rule(s)	Instructional Tips
pri<u>ce</u>		
b<u>e</u> com<u>e</u>₅	r. 4	
class	r. 17	B.E.: clăss.
h<u>orse</u>₅		
c<u>are</u>		
tr<u>y</u>	r. 5, 6	
mŏ<u>ve</u>₂		
d<u>e</u> la<u>y</u>	r. 4, 18	
p<u>ou</u>nd		
b<u>e</u> hind	r. 4, 19	
<u>a</u> r<u>ou</u>nd	r. 4	For spelling, say *ā round*. For reading, the a is not accented.
b<u>ur</u>n		After children say the sounds for *burn*, say, "Use *er* of *nurse*."
camp		
bĕ<u>a</u>r b<u>are</u>		After children say the sounds for *bear*, say, "Use *ē, ĕ, ā.*" B.E.: bĕ<u>a</u>r.
cl<u>ea</u>r		After children say the sounds for *clear*, say, "Use *ē, ĕ, ā.*"
cl<u>ea</u>n		After children say the sounds for *clean*, say, "Use *ē, ĕ, ā.*"
spell	r. 17	

Spelling Word	Rule(s)	Instructional Tips
p<u>oo</u>r		Say sounds separately.
fin i<u>sh</u>	r. 13	After children say the syllables, say, "Use the phonogram that says *sh* at the end of a syllable."
h<u>ur</u>t		After children say the sounds for *hurt*, say, "Use *er* of *nurse*."
m<u>ay</u> b<u>e</u>	r. 18, 4	
<u>a</u> cross	r. 4, 17	For spelling, say *ā cross*. For reading, the a is not accented.
t<u>o</u>³ ni<u>gh</u>t		After children say the sounds for *night*, say, "Use the three-letter *ī*."
ten<u>th</u>		
s<u>ir</u>		After children say the sounds for *sir*, say, "Use *er* of *first*."
th<u>e²s²e</u> th<u>o²s²e</u>		After children say the sounds for *these*, say, "Use *s, z*."
club		
s<u>ee</u>n s<u>ee</u>		Skip a space. Dictate the base word, *see*, first.
felt		
f<u>u</u>³ll	r. 17	
f<u>ai</u>l		

Spelling Word	Rule(s)	Instructional Tips
set ting set	r. 9	Skip a space. Dictate the base word, *set*, first. Before dictating the word *setting*, teach r. 9, the one-one-one rule (see chapter 1, page 59).
stamp		
light		After children say the sounds for *light*, say, "Use the three-letter *ī*."
com ing come₅	r. 11	Skip a space. Dictate the base word, *come*, first. Before dictating *coming* teach r. 11 (see chapter 1, page 63). After children say the syllable *come*, say, "Write *come* without the e before adding the ending *ing*, which begins with a vowel."
night		After children say the sounds for *night*, say, "Use the three-letter *ī*."
pass	r. 17	B.E.: pȧss.
shut	r. 13	The phonogram *sh* is used at the beginning of a base word.
eas y ease₅	r. 11, 6	Skip a space. Dictate the base word, *ease*, first. After children say the syllable, say, "Write *ease* without the e before adding the ending *ĭ*. Use *y, ĭ, ī*." After children say the sounds for *ease*, say, "Use *ē, ĕ, ā* and *s, z*."
bone		
cloud		
draw		
drink		Be sure children say *ĭ* correctly.

Spelling Word	Rule(s)	Instructional Tips
g<u>ar</u> den		After children say the syllables, say, "Use ĕ, ē."
g<u>oose</u>s		
[**hop p<u>ing</u>** [**hop**	r. 9	Skip a space. Dictate the base word, *hop*, first. (One-one-one rule.)
<u>kn</u>ife		After children say the sounds for *knife*, say, "Use the two-letter *n* that is used at the beginning of a base word."
m<u>ou</u>th		
<u>oa</u>k		After children say the sounds for *oak*, say, "Use ō of *boat*."
p<u>ea</u>ch		After children say the sounds for *peach*, say, "Use ē, ĕ, ā."
p<u>o</u>le		
qu<u>ee</u>n		
r<u>o</u>pe		
s<u>ea</u> s̆on		After children say the syllables, say, "In the first syllable, use ē, ĕ, ā." Be sure children say s̆ŏn, not s̆ŭn.
si<u>gn</u>	r. 19	After children say the sounds for *sign*, say, "Use the two-letter *n* that is used at the end of a word."
sp<u>ace</u>		
wag on		For spelling, say, ŏn, not ŭn.

Spelling Word	Rule(s)	Instructional Tips
wh**eat**		After children say the sounds for _wheat_, say, "Be sure to use _wh_ and _ē, ĕ, ā._"
win dŏw²		

Section L
133 Words for Spelling, Writing, and Reading

Spelling Word	Rule(s)	Instructional Tips
ca<u>tch</u> **ca<u>tch</u> <u>er</u>** **ki<u>tch</u> en** **bŭ̆<u>tch</u> <u>er</u>**		For spelling, say _t ch_ to keep children from putting _t_ in words like _much_ and _which_. The tch is an uncommon phonogram that always follows a single vowel that does not say _ā, ē, ī, ō, ū (cătch, ĕtch, wĭtch, bŏtch, clŭtch, bŭ̆tcher)._
bla<u>ck</u>	r. 25	
w<u>ar</u>m		For spelling, say _ar._ For reading, say _or._
un less	r. 17	
clŏ²<u>th</u> ing **clo²<u>the</u>s²** **clo²<u>the</u>**	r. 11	Skip two spaces. On the third line, write the base word, _clothe._ On the second line, write _clothes._ On the first line, write the Ayres word _clothing._ Write _clothe_ without the e before adding the ending _ing,_ which begins with a vowel.
b<u>e</u> gan **b<u>e</u> gin** **be gin <u>ning</u>**	r. 4 r. 4 r. 4, 10	Skip one space and write the base word, _begin._ On the first line, write _began._ Before dictating _beginning,_ teach rule 10 (see page 62). The accent is on _gin,_ which has one vowel, _ĭ,_ followed by one consonant, _n._ Write another n before adding the ending _ing,_ which begins with a vowel.

Spelling Word	Rule(s)	Instructional Tips
a̲ ble̲₄	r. 4	
[gone̲₅ **go̲**	r. 4	Skip a space. Dictate the base word, *go*, first.
[done̲₅ **do̊**		Skip a space. Dictate the base word, *do*, first. For spelling *done*, say ŏ.
su̲it		Say sounds separately.
tra̲c̲k	r. 25	
wåtc̲h		For spelling, say *t ch*. For reading, say *ch*. B.E.: The sound of a can be altered after w.
das̲h	r. 13	After children say the sounds for *dash*, say, "Use the phonogram that says *sh* at the end of a base word."
fell	r. 17	
fi̲g̲ht		
[buy̲ **by̲**	r. 5, 6 r. 5, 6	For spelling, say each sound *b ŭ ī*. For reading, say *bī*. The u is silent.
[*stop p̲ing* **stop**	r. 9	Skip a space. Dictate the base word, *stop*, first. (One-one-one rule.)
[wål̲k **tål̲k** **chål̲k**		For spelling, say *l*. For reading, say *wåk, tåk, chåk*. B.E.: The sound of a may be altered after w. B.E.: The sound of a may be altered when followed by an l.

Spelling Word	Rule(s)	Instructional Tips
grant		
s<u>oa</u>p		After children say the sounds in *soap*, say, "Use the ō of *boat*."
n<u>e</u>w<u>s</u> **n<u>e</u>w**		Skip a space. Dictate the base word, *new*, first.
sm<u>ǎll</u> *sm<u>ǎll</u> <u>er</u>* *sm<u>ǎll</u> est*	r. 17	B.E.: The sound of a may be altered when followed by an l.
w<u>ar</u>		For spelling, say *ar*. For reading, say *or*.
sum m<u>er</u>	r. 29	For spelling, say both *m*'s. For reading, say *m* in the accented syllable *sum*.
<u>a</u> bo<u>ve</u>₂	r. 4	For spelling, say *ā bove*. For reading, the a is not accented.
ex press	r. 20, 17	The letter s never follows x.
t<u>ur</u>n		After children say the sounds for *turn*, say, "Use *er* of *nurse*."
les son	r. 29	For spelling, say both *s*'s. For reading, say the s in the accented syllable *les*.
ha<u>l</u>f		For spelling, say *l*. For reading, say *haf*. B.E.: h<u>ǎl</u>f.
fa <u>ther</u>		
<u>an</u> y <u>thing</u>		For spelling, say *ǎn ǐ*. For reading, say *ěn ǐ*.
t<u>a</u> bl<u>e</u>₄	r. 4	
hi<u>gh</u>		

Spelling Word	Rule(s)	Instructional Tips
J<u>une</u>	r. 26	
[r<u>igh</u>t [<u>wri</u>te [wr<u>o</u>te		
d<u>ate</u>		
[r<u>oa</u>d [r<u>ode</u> [r<u>i</u>de		After children say the sounds for *road*, say, "Use the ō of *boat*."
[M<u>ar</u>ch [m<u>ar</u>ch	r. 26	
next		
in d<u>ee</u>d		
f<u>ou</u>r		After children say the sounds for *four*, say, "Use *ow, ō, ō̄ō, ŭ*." B.E.: For reading, say *faw*.
h<u>er</u> self		
p<u>ow</u> <u>er</u>		After children say the syllables, say, "In the first syllable, use *ow, ō*."
wi<u>sh</u>	r. 13	After children say the sounds for *wish*, say, "Use the phonogram that says *sh* at the end of a word."
[b<u>e</u> c<u>au</u>s<u>e</u>₅ [c<u>au</u>s<u>e</u>₅	r. 4	Skip a space. Dictate the base word, *cause*, first. After children say the sounds for *cause*, say, "Use the *au* that is not used at the end of a word."

Spelling Word	Rule(s)	Instructional Tips
w<u>or</u>ld	r. 8	
c<u>ou</u>n try	r. 6	For spelling, say *trĭ*.
[m<u>ee</u>t m<u>ea</u>t		After children say the sounds for *meet*, say, "Use the double *ee*."
an o<u>th</u> er		For spelling, say the syllables *ăn ŏth er*.
[*trip<u>pĕd</u>* trip	r. 9, 28	Skip a space. Dictate the base word, *trip*, first. (One-one-one rule.)
list		
p<u>eo</u> pl<u>e</u>₄		After children say the syllables, say, "In the first syllable, the uncommon phonogram eo says *ē*."
ev <u>er</u>		
held		
<u>ch</u>ur<u>ch</u>		After children say the sounds for *church*, say, "Use *er* of *nurse*."
[on<u>ce</u>₃ one		Skip a space. Dictate the base word, *one*, first. For spelling, say *o n s e*. For reading, say *wonce*. B.E.: For reading, say *wunce*.
<u>o</u>wn		
b<u>e</u> f<u>or</u>e	r. 4	Use of job 1 reinforces correct spelling.
[kn<u>o</u>w n<u>o</u>	 r. 4	

Spelling Word	Rule(s)	Instructional Tips
were₅ where₅ there₅ here		Although these four words have the same last three letters, they are not all alike. Each is phonetic. Put a one above the ĕ to show it is not *er*.
dĕad		
leave₂		After children say the sounds for *leave*, say, "Use ē, ĕ, ā."
ear ly	r. 6	For spelling, say *lĭ*.
clŏse *close*		
flow er *flour*		For spelling, say *r*, not *er*. The word is only one syllable.
noth ing		For spelling, say *nŏth*.
ground		
lead (the way) led (the way) lĕad (pencil)		Write *(the way)* after *lead*. Write *(the way)* after *led*. Write *(pencil)* after *lead*.
such		
morn ing		
how ev er		
mind	r. 19	

Spelling Word	Rule(s)	Instructional Tips
shall	r. 13, 17	
a l**one** ··	r. 4	For spelling, say $\bar{a}$. For reading, the a is not accented.
or d**er**		
third		
pŭ**sh**	r. 13	After children say the sounds for *push*, say, "Use the phonogram that says *sh* at the end of a base word."
p**oi**nt		
wi**th** in		
bod y	r. 6	For spelling, y says $\breve{\imath}$.
f**ie**ld	r. 12	After children say the sounds for *field*, say, "Use $\bar{e}, \bar{\imath}, \breve{\imath}$."
b̲e long̲s̲	r. 4	
*ch̲ees̲e̲*₅		
e̲a̲rn		
ed̲ge	r. 23	After children say the sounds for *edge*, say, "Use the three-letter *j* we use after an $\breve{e}$."
f̲e̲a̲t̲h̲ er		After children say the syllables, say, "In the first syllable, use $\bar{e}, \breve{e}, \bar{a}$. The phonogram *ea* saying $\breve{e}\bar{a}$ never ends a syllable."
*fen̲c̲e̲*₃		
fun n̲y	r. 9, 6	For spelling, say $n\breve{\imath}$.

Spelling Word	Rule(s)	Instructional Tips
go ing	r. 4	
hon ey		After children say the *syllables*, say, "In the last syllable, use the phonogram that says $\bar{a}$, $\bar{e}$, $\breve{i}$."
let ters	r. 29	For spelling, say both *t*'s. For reading, say the *t* in the accented syllable *let*.
or ange		For spelling, say $\breve{o}$, not *or*.
pock et	r. 25	For spelling, say $\breve{e}t$, not $\breve{i}t$.
shoes / shoe s	r. 13 / r. 13	Skip a space. Dictate the base word *shoe* first. Say, "Write *shoe* and add the ending $\bar{s}$." For reading, say *shŏs*.
stairs		
stream		After children say the sounds for *stream*, say, "Use $\bar{e}$, $\breve{e}$, $\bar{a}$."
talks		For spelling, say *l*. For reading, say *tåks*. B.E.: The sound of a may be altered when followed by an l.
ti ny	r. 5, 6	For spelling, say *tī nĭ*.
words	r. 8	

Section M
123 Words for Spelling, Writing, and Reading

Spelling Word	Rule(s)	Instructional Tips
trust		
ex tra	r. 20	

Spelling Word	Rule(s)	Instructional Tips
dress	**r. 17**	
b<u>e</u> s<u>ide</u>	**r. 4**	
t<u>ea</u>ch		After children say the sounds for *teach*, say, "Use $\bar{e}$, $\breve{e}$, $\bar{a}$."
hap pen	**r. 29**	For spelling, say both *p*'s. For reading, say only the *p* in the accented syllable *hap*.
b<u>e</u> gun	**r. 4**	
col lect	**r. 29**	For spelling, say both *l*'s. The letter c is often followed by a t at the end of a word (*direct, elect, protect*.) For spelling, sound each carefully.
f<u>i</u>l<u>e</u>		
pr<u>o</u> v<u>ide</u>	**r. 4**	
s<u>igh</u>t		
st<u>oo</u>d²		
[*fix<u>ed</u>*³] **[fix]**	**r. 28**	Skip a space. Dictate the base word, *fix*, first. Rule 9 does not apply to words ending in x (exception to r. 9) because x has two sounds, *ks* (*ox, oxen*).
b<u>o</u>rn		
[go<u>e</u>s²] **[g<u>o</u>]**	**r. 4**	Skip a space. Dictate the base word, *go*, first. Say, "Write *go* and add *es²*." For spelling and reading, say g <u>oe</u> s².
h<u>o</u>ld	**r. 19**	
drill	**r. 17**	

Spelling Word	Rule(s)	Instructional Tips
<u>ar</u> my	r. 6	For spelling, say ĭ.
pr<u>e</u>t ty	r. 29, 6	For spelling, say *prĕt tĭ*. For reading, say *prĭt ĭ*.
st<u>o</u>le		
in com<u>e</u>₅		
bo<u>u</u>ght		
[p<u>ai</u>d p<u>ay</u>	r. 18	Skip a space. Dictate the base word, *pay,* first.
en t<u>er</u>		
r<u>ai</u>l r<u>oa</u>d		
un <u>a</u> bl<u>e</u>₄	r. 4	
ti<u>ck</u> et	r. 25	For spelling, say *ĕt,* not *ĭt.*
ac c<u>ou</u>nt	r. 29	For spelling, say both *k*'s. For reading, say the *k* in the accented syllable *count.*
driv en	r. 11	In the writing lesson, discuss the base word, *drive,* and how rule 11 applies.
r<u>e</u> al	r. 4	This is a two-syllable word.
r<u>e</u> cov <u>er</u>	r. 4	
m<u>ou</u>n t<u>ai</u>n		For spelling, say *tain.* For reading, say *t'n.*
sp<u>ea</u>k		After children say the sounds for *speak,* say, "Use ē, ĕ, ā."
past		B.E.: pȧst.

Spelling Word	Rule(s)	Instructional Tips
m<u>igh</u>t		
con tract		For spelling, say *k t.*
d<u>ea</u>l		After children say the sounds for *deal,* say, "Use ē, ĕ, ā." This is a one-syllable word.
[ȧl most [ȧll	r. 21, 19 r. 17	Skip a space. Dictate the base word, *all,* first. After children say the syllable *al,* say, "Write one l when *all* is used as a prefix." B.E.: The sound of a may be altered when followed by an l.
[brou̅ght [brin<u>g</u>		Skip a space. Dictate the base word, *bring,* first.
less	r. 17	
<u>e</u> vent	r. 4	
[off [o<u>f</u>	r. 17	
[tru<u>e</u>₂ [*tru<u>th</u>*	 r. 19	For spelling, say ū. The silent final e is no longer needed.
t<u>o͞o</u>k		
<u>a</u> g<u>ai</u>n	r. 4	For spelling, say *gain.* For reading, say *gĕn.* B.E.: The pronunciation <u>a</u> g<u>ai</u>n is accepted.
in f<u>or</u>m		
bo<u>th</u>	r. 19	

Spelling Word	Rule(s)	Instructional Tips
h**ea**rt		For spelling, sound each phonogram *h ĕ ar t*. For reading, say *h**ar**t*. The e is silent.
mon**th**		
chil dren **ch**ild	r. 19	Skip a space. Dictate the base word, *child*, first. After children say the syllables, say, "Use ĕ, ē." (We often keep the base word in one syllable, but here we do not.)
b**ui**ld b**ui**lt		For spelling, say each phonogram *b ŭ ĭ l d*. For reading, say *bild*. For spelling, say each phonogram *b ŭ ĭ l t*. For reading, say *bilt*.
un d**er** stand		
fol l**o**w²	r. 29	For spelling, say both *l*'s. For reading, say *l* in the accented syllable *fol*.
charg**e**=3		
mem b**er**		
ca**s**e		
whil**e**		For spelling and reading, say *wh*, not *w*.
ăl s**o**³	r. 21, 4	After children say the syllables, say, "Write one l when *all* is used as a prefix." B.E.: The sound of a may be altered when followed by an l.
r**e** t**ur**n	r. 4	
of fi**ce**₃	r. 29	For spelling, say both *f*'s. For reading, say *f* in the accented syllable *of*.

Spelling Word	Rule(s)	Instructional Tips
gre$\overset{3}{\underline{a}}$t		After children say the sounds for *great*, say, "Use $\bar{e}, \breve{e}, \bar{a}$."
[Miss [miss	r. 26, 17 r. 17	
<u>wh</u>$\overset{3}{\text{o}}$		For spelling, say *wh* $\overset{3}{\text{o}}$. For reading, say *h*$\overset{3}{\text{o}}$.
[di$\overset{2\,2}{\underline{e}}$d [di$\overset{2}{\underline{e}}$	r. 28 r. 12	Skip a space. Dictate the base word, *die*, first. After children say the sounds for *die*, say, "Use $\bar{e}, \bar{\imath}, \breve{\imath}$." After children say the sounds for *died*, say, "Write *die* without the e and add the ending *ed, d, t*. The letters ie together say $\bar{\imath}$ and ed says $\overset{2}{e}d$."
[*chang ing* [*change*	r. 11	Skip a space. Dictate the base word *change*, first. After children say the syllables, say, "Write *change* without the e and add the ending *ing*, which begins with a vowel."
f$\overset{2}{\underline{ew}}$		
[ple$\overset{2}{\underline{a}}$$\overset{2}{\text{s}}$ ant [ple$\overset{2}{\underline{a}}\underset{5}{\underline{\text{se}}}$	r. 11	Skip a space. Dictate the base word, *please*, first. After children say the sounds for *please*, say, "Use $\bar{e}, \breve{e}, \bar{a}$, and *s, z*." Say, "Write *please* without the e and add the ending *ant*, which begins with a vowel."
[pic t$\underline{ure}$ [*pi<u>tch</u> <u>er</u>* [*pi<u>tch</u>*		For spelling, say *ture*, not *cher*. In the writing lesson, contrast pronunciation with *pitcher*. Skip a space. Dictate the base word, *pitch*, first. For spelling, say each sound *p $\breve{\imath}$ t ch*. For reading, the *t* is silent.

Spelling Word	Rule(s)	Instructional Tips
mon e͟y³		After children say the syllables, say, "Use *ā, ē, ĭ*."
rĕ͟ad y²	r. 6	For spelling, y says *ĭ*.
o͟ mit	r. 4	
a͟n y wa͟y	r. 18	For spelling, say *ăn ĭ*. For reading, say *ĕn ĭ*.
e͟ight		After children say the sounds for *eight*, say, "Use the four-letter *ā*."
brĕ͟ak fast²		B.E.: brĕ͟ak fȧst³. In the writing lesson, explain the meaning of *break* your *fast*.
c͟hanc͟e₃		
clim͟b	r. 19	For spelling, say *b*.
cof fe͟e	r. 29	For spelling, say both *f*'s. For reading, say *f* in the accented syllable *cof*.
col o͟r		Be sure children say *or*, not *er*. B.E.: Spelling is *col o͟ur²*.
con ta͟ins²		After children say the syllables, say, "Use the *ā* that we do not use at the end of a word."
[da͟i ly	r. 6	Skip a space. Dictate the base word, *day*, first. After children say the syllables in *daily*, say, "Use the *ā* that we do not use at the end of a word."
[da͟y	r. 18	
e͟a gl͟e₄		After children say the syllables, say, "Use *ē, ĕ, ā*."
fan cy	r. 6	For spelling, say *cĭ*.
fl͟y	r. 5, 6	

Spelling Word	Rule(s)	Instructional Tips
fŏr est		
frēeze₅		
gen tle₄		
grŏw		After children say the sounds for *grow*, say, "Use *ow, ō.*"
hŏles₅		
hǫ tel	r. 4	
į rǫn	r. 5	For spelling, say *ī ron.* For reading, say *ī ern.* B.E.: i ron.
liv ing live₂	r. 11	Skip a space. Dictate the base word, *live*, first. After children say the syllable *liv*, say, "Write *live* without the e before adding the ending *ing*, which begins with a vowel."
mon kĕy		After children say the syllables, say, "Use the phonogram that says *ā, ē, ĭ.*"
mӯ self	r. 5, 6	
nǫise₅		
pen cil		
pįe	r. 12	After children say the sounds for *pie*, say, "Use the phonogram that says *ē, ī, ĭ.*"
pŭll	r. 17	
sew (needle) sŏw (seeds) sǫ	r. 4	After children say the sounds for *sew*, say, "Use *ōo, ū.*" Write *(needle)* after *sew*. After children say the sounds for *sow*, say, "Use *ow, ō.*" Write *(seeds)* after *sow*.

Spelling Word	Rule(s)	Instructional Tips
st$\bar{ea}$m		After children say the sounds for *steam*, say, "Use $\bar{e}$, $\breve{e}$, $\bar{a}$."
thr$\overset{2}{\underline{ea}}$d		After children say the sounds for *thread*, say, "Use $\bar{e}$, $\breve{e}$, $\bar{a}$."
thun d$\underline{er}$		
[tr$\overset{2\ 2}{\underline{ie}}$d [tr$\underline{y}$	r. 24, 28 r. 5, 6	Skip a space. Dictate the base word, *try*, first. After children say the sounds for *tried*, say, "Use $\breve{i}$, $\bar{i}$, and add the ending *ed, d, t*. The letters ie together say $\bar{i}$ and the ending says $\overset{2}{e}d$.
v$\overset{2}{\underline{ei}}$n	r. 12	After children say the sounds for *vein*, say, "Use the phonogram that says $\bar{e}$, $\bar{a}$, $\breve{i}$."

Section N
110 Words for Spelling, Writing, and Reading

Spelling Word	Rule(s)	Instructional Tips
ex cept	r. 20	After children say the syllables, say, "Remember the letter s never follows the letter x. Use *ks*."
[$\underline{\underline{au}}$nt [ant		For spelling, say *aunt*.
cap t$\underline{ure}$		For spelling, say *ture*, not *cher*.
els$\underline{\underline{e}}_5$		
bri$\underline{dge}$	r. 23	After children say the sounds for *bridge*, say, "Which *j* may we use after $\breve{i}$?"
of f$\underline{er}$	r. 29	For spelling, say both *f*'s. For reading, say only the *f* in the accented syllable *of*.

Spelling Word	Rule(s)	Instructional Tips
suf f<u>er</u>	r. 29	For spelling, say both *f*'s. For reading, say only the *f* in the accented syllable *suf*.
cen t<u>er</u>		B.E.: Spelling is *cen tr<u>e</u>₄*.
front		For spelling, say ŏ.
[run n<u>ing</u> [run	r. 9	Skip a space. Dictate the base word, *run*, first. (One-one-one rule.)
r<u>u</u>l<u>e</u>		For spelling, say ū.
c<u>a</u>r ry	r. 29, 6	After children say the syllables, say, "The first syllable has three separate sounds." For spelling, say rĭ.
<u>ch</u><u>ai</u>n		
d<u>ea</u><u>th</u>		
l<u>ear</u>n		
won d<u>er</u>		B.E.: The sound of o may be altered after w.
[p<u>ai</u>r (two) [p<u>e</u>ar (eat) [p<u>a</u>r<u>e</u> (cut)		Write *(two)* after *pair*. Write *(eat)* after *pear*. B.E.: p<u>e</u>ar. Write *(cut)* after *pare*.
<u>ch</u>e<u>ck</u>	r. 25	
pr<u>o</u><u>ve</u>₂		
[h<u>ear</u>d [*h<u>ear</u>*		Skip a space. Dictate the base word, *hear*, first.

Spelling Word	Rule(s)	Instructional Tips
in spect		For spelling, say *k t.*
it self		For spelling, say *l f.*
ål way̆s̆	r. 21	After children say the syllables, say, "Write one l when *all* is a prefix." B.E.: The sound of a may be altered when followed by an l.
some thing		
ex pect	r. 20	After children say the syllables, say, "Remember *s* never follows an *x.*" For spelling, say *k t.*
need		
thus		
wo man	r. 4	For spelling, say *wō man.* For reading, say *wo͝o man.*
wo men	r. 4	For spelling, say *wō men.* For reading, say *wim en.*
young		
fair / **fare**		
dol lar	r. 29	For spelling, say both *l*'s. For reading, say only the *l* in the accented syllable *dol.* For spelling, say *lar.*
eve ning		
plan		
broke		

Spelling Word	Rule(s)	Instructional Tips
f<u>ee</u>l		
[<u>s</u>ure		For spelling, say *s*. For reading, say *sh*.
<u>s</u>ŭg <u>ar</u>		For spelling, say *s*. For reading, say *sh*.
l<u>ea</u>st		After children say the sounds for *least*, say, "Use ē, ĕ, ā."
sŏr ry	r. 29, 6	After children say the syllables, say, "The first syllable has three sounds." For spelling, say *rĭ*.
press	r. 17	
[God	r. 26	
god		
t<u>ea</u>ch <u>er</u>		
N<u>o</u> vem b<u>er</u>	r. 26, 4	In the writing lesson, explain that *novem* means "nine." *November* was the ninth month of the Roman calendar.
sub ject		For spelling, say *k t*.
<u>A</u> pril	r. 26, 4	
his t<u>o</u> ry	r. 4, 6	For spelling, say *rĭ*.
stud y	r. 6	For spelling, y says *ĭ*.
him self		For spelling, say *l f*.
mat t<u>er</u>	r. 29	For spelling, say both *t*'s.
<u>u</u>s̆e		
thouğht		

Spelling Word	Rule(s)	Instructional Tips
p<u>er</u> son		Be sure children say *sŏn*, not *sŭn*.
[n<u>or</u> <u>or</u>		
Jan <u>u</u> ăr y	r. 26, 4, 6	After children say the syllables, say, "The third syllable has two sounds." For spelling, y says *ĭ*. In the writing lesson, explain that *January* is named for the Roman god Janus.
m<u>ea</u>n		After children say the sounds for *mean*, say, "Use *ē*, *ĕ*, *ā*."
v<u>o</u>t<u>e</u>		
c<u>ou</u>rt		
cop y	r. 6	For spelling, y says *ĭ*.
act		
[b<u>ee</u>n b<u>e</u>	r. 4	Skip a space. Dictate the base word, *be*, first. For spelling, say *b<u>ee</u>n*. For reading, say *bĭn*. B.E.: b<u>ee</u>n.
yes t<u>er</u> d<u>ay</u>	r. 18	
<u>a</u> mon<u>g</u>	r. 4	
[ques <u>ti</u>on *quest*	r. 14	Skip a space. Dictate the base word, *quest*, first. For spelling, say *<u>ti</u>on*. For reading, say *<u>ch</u>on*.
doc t<u>or</u>		Be sure children say *or*, not *er*.

Spelling Word	Rule(s)	Instructional Tips
s<u>iz</u>e		The letter z is usually used at the beginning of a base word. (*Size, dozen, organize, realize,* and *citizen* are exceptions.)
De cem b<u>er</u>	r. 26, 4	In the writing lesson, explain that *decem* means "ten." *December* was the tenth month of the Roman calendar.
doz en		After children say the syllables, say, "In the first syllable, use ŏ, ō, o͞o. In the second syllable, use ĕ, ē."
<u>there</u>₅		
tax		
num b<u>er</u>		
Oc t<u>o</u> b<u>er</u>	r. 26, 4	In the writing lesson, explain that *octo* means "eight." *October* was the eighth month of the Roman calendar.
r<u>ea</u> son		After children say the syllables, say, "Use ē, ĕ, ā."
fif<u>th</u>		For spelling, say *f i f th* precisely.
bak <u>ing</u> b<u>ake</u>	r. 11	Skip a space. Dictate the base word, *bake*, first. After children say the syllables, say, "Write *bake* without the e before adding the ending *ing*, which begins with a vowel."
b<u>ow</u>l		After children say the sounds for *bowl*, say, "Use ow, ō."
<u>cheap</u>		After children say the sounds for *cheap*, say, "Use ē, ĕ, ā."

Spelling Word	Rule(s)	Instructional Tips
c̲h̲eer fŭl[3]	r. 22	After children say the syllables, say, "Write *ful* with one l when used as an ending (suffix)."
c̲h̲ick en	r. 25	
driv ing dr̲ive	r. 11	Skip a space. Dictate the base word, *drive*, first. After children say the syllables, say, "Write *drive* without the e before adding the ending *ing*, which begins with a vowel."
ec̲h̲[2] oe̅s[2] ec̲h̲[2] o̲	r. 4	Skip a space. Dictate the base word, *echo*, first. After children say the syllables, say, *ch, k, sh.*" After children say the syllables in *echoes*, say, "Write ō and add es̄ to form the plural. For spelling and reading, say o̲e̲s[2]."
f̲ai̲r y	r. 6	For spelling, y says ĭ.
kno̲c̲k̲	r. 25	After children say the sounds for *knock*, say, "Use two-letter *n* that we may use at the beginning of a word."
le̲a̲t̲h̲[2] er		The phonogram ea saying e̅a[2] never ends a syllable.
lin en		
mix t̲u̲r̲e	r. 20	For spelling, say *ture*, not *cher*.
na̲ t̲io̲n	r. 4, 14	After children say the syllables, say, "In the last syllable, use the phonogram *sh* that begins with a tall letter."
pau̲s̲e̲[2]5		
pe̲a̲c̲e̲3		After children say the sounds for *peace*, say, "Use ē, ĕ, ā."

Spelling Word	Rule(s)	Instructional Tips
_pe̲r_ mis _si̲on_	r. 14, 15	After children say the syllables, say, "In the last syllable, use the phonogram that says _sh, zh_."
rou̇̃gh		
_so̲_ _ci̲al_	r. 4, 14	After children say the syllables, say, "In the last syllable, use the phonogram _sh_ that begins with a short letter."
st_ea̲l_		After children say the sounds for _steal_, say, "Use ē, ĕ, ā."
stra_nge̲_		
tro̲ _ph̲y_	r. 4, 6	For spelling, say _ph̆ĭ_.
[v_oi̲c_ e̊š² v_oi̲ce̲_₃]	r. 11	Skip a space. Dictate the base word, _voice_, first. After children say the syllables, say, "Write _voice_ and add s to form the plural."

Section O
132 Words for Spelling, Writing, and Reading

Spelling Word	Rule(s)	Instructional Tips
[_eight_ _a̲te̲_]		
_a̲_ fr_ai̲d_	r. 4	
un cl_e̲_₄		
ra_th̲_ er²		B.E.: ra_th̲_³ er².
com f_or̲t_		

Spelling Word	Rule(s)	Instructional Tips
e lec tion e lect	r. 4, 14 r. 4	
a board	r. 4	After children say the syllables, say, "In the last syllable, use the *oa* of *boat*."
jail		B.E.: Spelling alternative is *ga ol*.
shed	r. 13	
re fuse	r. 4	
dis trict		Be sure children say *k t*.
re strain	r. 4	
roy al		Be sure children say *ăl*, not *ŭl*.
ob jec tion ob ject	r. 14	Skip a space. Dictate the base word, *object*, first. *(Continue to dictate the base word first throughout the section.)* Be sure children say *k t*.
pleas ure meas ure treas ure		After children say the syllables, say, "In the first syllable, use *ē*, *ĕ*, *ā*, and *s*, *z*. The phonogram ea saying *eă* never ends a syllable. The second syllable is *ū r ē*." Be sure children say *ūre*, not *er*.
na vy	r. 4, 6	For spelling, say *vĭ*.
for ty four teen fourth four	r. 6	Skip three spaces. On the fourth line, dictate the base word, *four*. On the third line, write *fourth*. On the second line, write *fourteen*. On the first line, write *forty*. For spelling *forty*, say *tĭ*.
pop u la tion	r. 4, 14	

Spelling Word	Rule(s)	Instructional Tips
prop <u>er</u>		
ju<u>dge</u>	r. 23	
[w<u>eath</u> <u>er</u> w<u>heth</u> <u>er</u>		After children say the syllables, say, "In the first syllable, use $\bar{e}$, $\breve{e}$, $\bar{a}$." The phonogram ea saying $e\overset{2}{a}$ never ends a syllable. Be sure children say *wh*, not *w*.
w<u>or</u>th	r. 8	
con t<u>ai</u>n		
fig <u>ure</u>		B.E.: For spelling, say *fig <u>ure</u>*.
sud den	r. 29	For spelling, say both *d*'s. For reading, say only the *d* in the accented syllable *sud*. *(Continue to require correct pronunciation for spelling and reading throughout the section.)*
in st<u>ea</u>d		
[thr<u>ow</u> *thr<u>ew</u>*		
p<u>er</u> son al		Be sure children say *ăl*, not *ŭl*.
ev <u>er</u> y thi<u>ng</u>		For spelling, y says *ĭ*.
r<u>ate</u>		
<u>chie</u>f	r. 12	
p<u>er</u> fect		Be sure children say *k t*.
sec ond		

Spelling Word	Rule(s)	Instructional Tips
sl**ide**		
far **ther**[2]		
d**u** ty	r. 4, 6	For spelling, say *tĭ*.
in tend		
com pan y	r. 6	For spelling, y says *ĭ*.
quite quit qui et	 r. 5	
non**e**₅		
kn**ew**[2] kn**ow**[2]		
r**e** m**ai**n	r. 4	
di rec **tion** di rect	r. 14	For spelling, say *dĭ*. Base word. Be sure children say *k t*.
ap p**ear**	r. 29	
lib **er** ty	r. 6	For spelling, say *tĭ*.
e no**u**gh[3]	r. 4	
fact		Be sure children say *k t*.
b**oar**d		After children say the sounds for *board*, say, "Use the *oa* in *boat*."
Sep tem b**er**	r. 26	

Spelling Word	Rule(s)	Instructional Tips
sta̲ tio̲n	r. 4, 14	
at tend	r. 29	
pub lic mu̲ s̆ic pic nic	r. 4	
fri̲e̲nds̆² fri̲e̲nd	r. 12 r. 12	Base word. After children say the sounds for *friend*, say, "Use the phonogram that says *ē, ī, ĭ*. The *ĕ* is an uncommon sound for ie."
du̇̆r ing̲		
po̲ li̲c̲e̲₃	r. 4	For spelling, say *pō l ĭ č̆² ē*. The French i says *ē*.
un til	r. 22	
tru̲ ly tru̲e̲₂	r. 6	The silent final e is no longer needed. For spelling, say *lĭ*. Base word.
w̲ho̲l̲e̲ ho̲l̲e̲		For spelling, say *wh*. For reading, say *h*.
ad dress	r. 29, 17	
re̲ qu̲est	r. 4	
rai̲s̲e̲₅²		
Au̲ gust	r. 26	
struc̲k	r. 25	

Spelling Word	Rule(s)	Instructional Tips
get ting get	r. 9	Base word.
don't = do not	r. 19	
Thurs day Sat ur day	r. 26, 18 r. 26, 18	In the writing lesson, explain that *Thursday* is *Thor's day* in Norse mythology. In the writing lesson, explain that *Saturday* is *Saturn's day* in Roman mythology.
ad mis sion	r. 29, 15	After children say the syllables, say, "In the last syllable, use *sh, zh*."
ca noe		
cap tain		For spelling, say *tain*.
cau tious *cau tion*	r. 14 r. 14	Base word.
cel lar	r. 29	Be sure children say *ar*, not *er*.
cov ered	r. 28	
crea ture		After children say the syllables, say, "In the first syllable, use $\bar{a}, \breve{e}, \bar{a}$." The second syllable says *ture*.
cur tain		For spelling, say *tain*.
de clared *de clare*	r. 4, 11, 28 r. 4	Base word.
dis tance *dis tant*		

Spelling Word	Rule(s)	Instructional Tips
ex pl<u>ai</u>n	r. 20	
fl<u>oat</u> <u>ed</u>	r. 28	
<u>g</u>host	r. 19	
hol i d<u>ay</u>	r. 24, 18	After children say the syllables, say, "In the second syllable, use ĭ, ī, instead of y."
h<u>o</u> ly	r. 4, 6	Base word. For spelling, say lĭ.
<u>knee</u>		
lem on		
l<u>y</u> ing	r. 5	After children say the syllables, say, "In the first syllable, use y, ĭ, ī."
l<u>ie</u>²	r. 12	Base word.
n<u>ai</u>l²s		
n<u>ee</u> dl<u>e</u>₄		
n<u>o</u> bod y	r. 4, 6	For spelling, y says ĭ.
<u>oar</u>		After children say the sounds for oar, say, "Use the oa of boat."
pal a<u>ce</u>₃		For spelling, say ă c ē.
pen ny	r. 29, 6	For spelling, say nĭ.
reg <u>u</u> l<u>ar</u>	r. 4	Be sure children say ar, not er.
r<u>e</u> p<u>ea</u>ts	r. 4	
<u>s</u><u>ai</u>l <u>or</u>		Be sure children say or, not er.
sen ten<u>ce</u>₃		

Spelling Word	Rule(s)	Instructional Tips
[shin ing shine]	r. 11	Base word.
sur face		For spelling, say *face*.
[sweep ing sweeps]		
thief	r. 12	
[waist waste]		
wait ing		
wea ry	r. 6	For spelling, say *rĭ*.
[writ ing writ er write]	r. 11 r. 11	Skip two spaces. On the third line, dictate the base word, *write*. On the second line, dictate *writer*. On the first line, dictate *writing*.

Section P
113 Words for Spelling, Writing, and Reading

Spelling Words	Rule(s)	Instructional Tips
spend		
en joy		Be sure children say *ĕn*, not *ĭn*.

Spelling Word	Rule(s)	Instructional Tips
a̲w fŭl³ a̲we̲₅	r. 22	Skip a space. Dictate the base word *awe*, first. *(Continue dictating the base word first throughout the section.)* In *awful*, the silent final e is not needed. After children say the syllables, say, "When *ful* is used as an ending (suffix), we write one l."
u s̆u̇² al	r. 4	Be sure children say *al*.
com pla̲int		
a̲u to̲	r. 4	
va̲ ca̲ t̲ion	r. 4, 14	
be̲au ti fŭl³ *be̲au ty*	r. 24, 22 r. 6	After children say the syllables, say, "In the last syllable, write one l when *ful* is used as a suffix." Base word. After children say the syllables, say, "In the first syllable, the uncommon (French) phonogram eau says *ū*."
fli̲g̲ht		
trav el		Be sure children say *el*, not *ul*.
rap id		
re̲ pa̲ir	r. 4	
trŏu⁴ bling trŏu⁴ ble̲₄	r. 11	Be sure children say only two syllables. Base word.
en tranc̲e̲₃		
im po̲r tanc̲e̲₃ im po̲r tant		

Spelling Word	Rule(s)	Instructional Tips
car ri̱e̱d	r. 29, 24, 28	After children say the syllables, say, "In the last syllable, use ĭ, ī, instead of y and add the past tense ending. The letters ie together say ĭ and the ending say e̋d."
car ry	r. 29, 6	Base word. For spelling, say both r's and rĭ. For reading, say r in the accented syllable cår. (*Continue to require correct pronunciation for spelling and reading throughout the section.*)
loss	r. 17	
fŏr tu̱ne		For spelling, say *tune*, not *chune*.
em pi̱re		
ma̱y o̱r		For spelling, say *or*. B.E: For reading, say ĕr.
wa̱it		
de̱ gre̱e̱	r. 4	
priš on		Be sure children say ŏn, not ŭn.
en gi̱ne̱₅		
viš it		
gu̱est		After children say the sounds for *guest*, say, "Use the two-letter *g*."
gu̱ess	r. 17	
de̱ på̱rt ment	r. 4	
ob ta̱in		
fam i ly	r. 6	

Spelling Word	Rule(s)	Instructional Tips
f<u>a</u> v<u>or</u>	r. 4	For spelling, say *or*. B.E.: Spelling is *f<u>a</u> v<u>ou</u>r*.
Mrs.	r. 26	Have children write the abbreviation. For reading, say *Mis us̆*. B.E.: Full stop (period) is not used. *Mrs* is the international alternative.
Mr. = <u>Mis</u> te<u>r</u>	r. 26	B.E.: Full stop (period) is not used. *Mr* is the international alternative.
Mi<u>ss</u>	r. 26, 17	
hu<u>s</u>² band		
<u>a</u> m<u>ou</u>nt	r. 4	
h<u>u</u> man	r. 4	
v<u>i</u><u>ew</u>²		For spelling, say each sound, *v ĭ ew̆*. For reading, say *vū*.
cl<u>er</u>k		B.E.: cl<u>er</u>k. For reading, say *clark*.
th<u>ou</u>²gh		
o'clo<u>ck</u> = o(f the) clock	r. 4, 25	
sup p<u>or</u>t	r. 29	
d<u>oe</u>²s̆		Write *do* and add *es̆*. For spelling, say each sound, *d oe s̆*. For reading, say *dŭs̆*.
d<u>o</u>³		Base word.
r<u>e</u> g<u>ar</u>d	r. 4	
es c<u>a</u><u>pe</u>		
sin<u>ce</u>₃		
wh<u>i</u>ch		Be sure children say *wh*, not *w*.

Spelling Word	Rule(s)	Instructional Tips
le_ng_th **lo_ng_** *stre_ng_th* *stro_ng_*		Be sure children say *ng* correctly. Base word. Be sure children say *ng* correctly. Base word.
de_ stro_y_	r. 4	
ne__ẘ_s̆ pa_ pe_r	r. 4	
dau_gh_ te_r *nau_gh_ ty* *cau_gh_t* *tau_gh_t*	 r. 6	After children say the syllables, say, "In the first syllable, the uncommon phonogram augh says *au*." For spelling *naughty*, say *tĭ*."
an sw_er__		For spelling, say *s w er*. For reading, say *ser*.
re_ ply_	r. 4, 5, 6	
sa_i_l *sa_le_*		
cit i̇_e_s̆ **cit y**	r.24 r.6	After children say the syllables, say, "In the last syllable, use *ĭ, ī* instead of y and add *e̊s̆*. The letters ie together say *ĭ* and s says *s̆*." Base word.
kno_̇w_n **kno_̇w_**		Base word.
sev er__ al		For spelling, say *al*, not *ul*.
de_ s̆i_r_e	r. 4	

Spelling Word	Rule(s)	Instructional Tips
n<u>ear</u> ly	r. 6	For spelling, say *lĭ*.
t<u>oo</u> tw<u>o</u>³ t<u>o</u>³		
an i mal		Be sure children say *măl*, not *mŭl*.
b<u>a</u> sin	r. 4	
br<u>eeze</u>₅		
but ton	r. 29	For spelling, say *tŏn*.
cab b<u>age</u>₌₃	r. 29	For spelling, say *ă g ē*.
c<u>are</u>³ fŭl	r. 22	
c<u>ou</u>⁴gh		
c<u>ou</u>⁴s² in		
dol l<u>ar</u>s²	r. 29	For spelling, say *ar*, not *er*.
ex c<u>use</u> ex c<u>use</u>²	r. 20 r. 20	After children say the syllables, say, "Remember s never follows x. Use *ks*."
i<u>s</u> land	r. 5, 19	For spelling, say *ĭ s land*.
gr<u>ie</u>f	r. 12	After children say the sounds for *grief*, say, "Use *ē, ī, ĭ*."
<u>gu</u>ard		
<u>gu</u>il ty	r. 6	
hun gry	r. 6	

Spelling Word	Rule(s)	Instructional Tips
lan guage		After children say the syllables, say, "The phonogram gu also says *gw*. The u says *w* as it does in qu (*kw*)."
laugh ter laugh		Base word. After children say the sounds for *laugh*, say, "The uncommon phonogram augh also says *ăf*." For reading, say *lăf*. B.E.: lăf.
lin ing line	r. 11	Base word.
o cean	r. 4	After children say the syllables, say, "In the last syllable, the uncommon phonogram ce says *sh*."
neph ew		
nine teen		
no ticed no tice₃	r. 4, 11, 28 r. 4	Base word.
pas sen gers	r. 29	
re mained	r. 4, 28	
re treat ing	r. 4	
style		
sub tract		Be sure children say *k t*.
tai lor		For spelling, say *or*, not *er*.
thumb		For spelling, say *b*.

Spelling Word	Rule(s)	Instructional Tips
trị al	r. 5	Be sure children say ăl, not ŭl.
voy age		
whis per		
wrong		

Section Q
127 Words for Spelling, Writing, and Reading

Spelling Words	Rule(s)	Instructional Tips
some₅ times²		
en gage		
fị nal	r. 5	
tĕr ri ble₄	r. 29	After children say the syllables, say, "The first syllable has three separate sounds." For spelling, say both *r*'s. For reading, say *r* only in the accented syllable *tĕr*. (*Continue to require correct pronunciation for spelling and reading throughout the section.*)
sur prise²		After children say the syllables, say, "In the first syllable, use *er* of *nurse*. In the second syllable, use *s, z*."
pe ri od	r. 4	
ad di tion	r. 29, 14	
em ploy		

Spelling Word	Rule(s)	Instructional Tips
prop **er** ty	r. 6	For spelling, say *tĭ*. (Continue to require precise pronunciation of vowels in unaccented syllables throughout the section.)
s**e** lect	r. 4	Be sure children say *k t*. (Continue to require precise pronunciation throughout the section.)
con nec **tion** con nect	r. 29, 14 r. 29	Skip a space. Dictate the base word, *connect*, first. (Continue to dictate the base word first throughout the section.)
f**i**rm		
r**e** **g**ion r**e** li **g**ion	r. 4 r. 4	After children say the syllables, say, "In the last syllable, the uncommon phonogram gi says *j*."
con vict		
pr**i** vat**e**₅	r. 5	
com mand	r. 29	
d**e** b**ate**	r. 4	
cr**ow**d		
fac t**o** ry	r. 4, 6	
pub li**sh**	r. 13	
rep r**e** ŝent	r. 4	After children say the syllables, say, "In the last syllable, use *s*, *z*."
t**er**m		
sec **tion**	r. 14	

Spelling Word	Rule(s)	Instructional Tips
rel <u>a</u> ti<u>v̲e̲</u>₂	r. 4, 11	
r<u>e</u> l<u>ate</u>	r. 4	Base word.
prog ress	r. 17	
pr<u>o</u> gress	r. 4, 17	
en ti<u>re</u>		
pre<u>s̆</u>² i dent	r. 11	After children say the syllables, say, "In the first syllable, use *s, z.*"
pre <u>s̆</u>²<u>ide</u>	r. 4	Base word.
f<u>a</u> m<u>ŏu</u>⁴s	r. 4, 11	
f<u>ame</u>		Base word.
s<u>er</u> v̲e̲₂		
es t<u>ate</u>		
r<u>e</u> mem b<u>er</u>	r. 4	
<u>ei</u>² <u>th</u>er	r. 12	After children say the syllables, say, "In the first syllable, use *ē, ā, ĭ.*"
ef f<u>or</u>t	r. 29	Be sure children say *or*, not *er*.
d<u>u̲e̲</u>₂		For spelling, say *ū* distinctly.
d<u>e̲w̲</u>²		
in cl<u>ude</u>		
al l<u>ow</u>	r. 29	

Spelling Word	Rule(s)	Instructional Tips
po̲ s̆i t̲ion	r. 4, 14	After children say the syllables, say, "In the second syllable, use *s, z*. In the third syllable, use *sh* that begins with a tall letter."
le<u>dg</u>e	r. 23	
cl<u>ai</u>m		
pri̦ ma̲ ry	r. 5, 4, 6	
re̲ s̆ult	r. 4	
ap p<u>oi</u>nt	r. 29	
in f<u>or</u> ma̲ t̲ion	r. 4, 14	
[wh<u>ŏ</u>m		For spelling, say *wh ŏ m*.
wh<u>ŏ</u>		For spelling, say *wh ŏ*.
ȧr rest	r. 29	
[<u>th</u>em selve̲s		After children say the syllables, say, "In the second syllable, use *v* instead of *f* and add *e̲s̆*."
self		Base word.
ca<u>l</u>ve̲s̆		After children say the sounds for *calves*, say, "Use *v* instead of *f* and add *e̲s̆*." B.E.: cȧ<u>l</u>ve̲s̆.
ca<u>l</u>f		Base word. B.E.: cȧ<u>l</u>f.
ha<u>l</u>ve̲s̆		After children say the sounds for *halves*, say, "Use *v* instead of *f* and add *e̲s̆*." B.E.: hȧ<u>l</u>ve̲s̆.
ha<u>l</u>f		Base word. B.E.: hȧ<u>l</u>f.

Spelling Word	Rule(s)	Instructional Tips
spē̄ cial	r. 14	After children say the syllables, say, "In the last syllable, use the *sh* that begins with a short letter."
preš ent pre šent	 r. 4	After children say the syllables, say, "In the first syllable, use *s, z*."
ac tion act	r. 14	After children say the syllables, say, "The base word tells you which phonogram to use." Base word.
jus tice₃ just		Base word.
gen tle₄ man gen tle₄		
en cloše		After children say the syllables, say, "In the last syllable, use *s, z*."
a wait	r. 4	
sup pože	r. 29	After children say the syllables, say, "In the last syllable, use *s, z*."
won der ful	r. 22	After children say the syllables, say, "In the last syllable, write one l when *ful* is a suffix."
for ward back ward to ward	 r. 25 r. 4	Be sure children say *ar*, not *or*. For spelling, say *to ward*. For reading, say *toard*. B.E.: For spelling, say *tŏ ward*. For reading, say *tŏ wawd*."

Spelling Word	Rule(s)	Instructional Tips
al though	r. 21	After children say the syllables, say, "When *all* is a prefix, write one l."
prompt		Be sure children say *p t*.
at tempt	r. 29	Be sure children say *p t*.
whose who		For spelling, say *wh ŏ s̄ e*. For reading, say *hōs̄*.
state ment state		Base word.
per haps		
their they	r. 12	After children say the sounds for *their*, say, "Use the phonogram that says, *ē, ā, ĭ*."
im pris on		After children say the syllables, say, "In the second syllable, use *s, z*."
writ ten writ	r. 9	One-one-one rule. Base word.
ar range	r. 29	After children say the syllables, say, "The last syllable has two separate consonants between the a and the silent e."
an kle		For spelling, say *ăn*.
ap pears	r. 29	
brace let brace		Base word.

Spelling Word	Rule(s)	Instructional Tips
breathe͟s̲ breath		Base word.
calm		For spelling, say c a l m.
cir cus		
con sent ed	r. 28	
con tin ued con tin ue₂	r. 11, 28	After children say the syllables, say, "Write *continue* without the *e* before adding the ending *ed*, which begins with a vowel. Base word.
dan ger ous		
debt		For spelling, say d ĕ b t.
dried dry	r. 24, 28 r. 5, 6	After children say the sounds for *dried,* say, "Use ĭ, ī, and add the past tense ending. The *ie* phonogram says ī and the ending says *ed*." Base word.
ex haust	r. 20	For spelling, say *h au s t.*
ex er cise	r. 20	After children say the syllables, say, "In the last syllable, use *s, z.*"
ex plo sion	r. 20, 4, 16	After children say the syllables, say, "In the last syllable, use *sh, zh.*"
gram mar	r. 29	For spelling, say *ar,* not *er.*
In di an	r. 26	

Spelling Word	Rule(s)	Instructional Tips
jour ney³ jour nal cour age		After children say the syllables, say, "In the first syllable, the uncommon phonogram *our* says *ur*." B.E.: For reading, say *cŭr age*.
laid lay	 r. 18	
pack age pack	r. 25 r. 25	Base word.
phys² i cal		Be sure children say *ăl*, not *ŭl*.
praise²₅		After children say the sounds for *praise*, say, "Use *s, z*."
prop er ly	r. 6	
searched³	r. 28	
smooth²		
thir teen		
throat		After children say the sounds for *throat*, say, "Use the *oa* of *boat*."
touch⁴		
tow el		
um brel la³	r. 29	
weap² on		The phonogram *ea* saying *ĕă* never ends a syllable.

Section R
125 Words for Spelling, Writing, and Reading

Spelling Words	Rule(s)	Instructional Tips
lōse̲₅ lo͞ose̲₅		
com bi nā tion com bīne	r. 11, 4, 14	Skip a space. Dictate the base word, *combine*, first. *(Continue dictating the base word first throughout the section.)*
av e̊ nue̲₂		
neigh bor		Be sure children say *or*, not *er*. B.E.: Spelling is *neigh bo̊ur*.
weight weigh		Base word.
we̊ar		After children say the sounds for *wear*, say, "Use ē, ĕ, ā." B.E.: we̱ar.
en ter tain		
sal a ry	r. 4, 6	For spelling, say *rĭ*. *(Continue to require precise pronunciation of vowels in unaccented syllables throughout the section.)*
viš i tor viš it		Be sure children say *or*, not *er*. Base word.
pub li cā tion	r. 4, 14	
ma chi̲ne̲₅		For spelling, say *c̆h ĭ n ē*. The French i says ē.

Spelling Word	Rule(s)	Instructional Tips
t**o** **w̲a̲r̲d**	r. 4	For spelling, say *to ward*. For reading, say *toard*. B.E.: For spelling, say *tŏ w̲a̲r̲d*. For reading, say *tŏ w̲a̲w̲d*.
suc cess	r. 17	
dr**o̲w̲**n		
a̲ dopt	r. 4	Be sure children say *p t*. (*Continue to require precise pronunciation throughout the section.*)
s**e̲** c**u̲r̲e̲**	r. 4	
h̲o̲n **o̲r̲**		For spelling, say *hŏn or*. Be sure children say *or*, not *er*. B.E.: Spelling is *h̲o̲n o̲u̲r*.
prom is**e̲**₅		
w̲r̲e**c̲k̲**	r. 25	
pr**e̲** p**a̲r̲e̲**	r. 4	
ves sel	r. 29	For spelling, say both *s*'s. For reading, say only the *s* in the unaccented syllable *ves*. (*Continue to require correct pronunciation for spelling and reading throughout the section.*)
b**u̲**s̆² y	r. 6	For spelling, say *bŭs̆ ĭ*. For reading, say *bĭs̆ĭ*.
*pref **e̲r̲** enc**e̲**₃*		In *preference*, we do not add another r because the accent shifts to the first syllable, *pref*.
pr**e̲** f**e̲r̲**	r. 4	Base word.

Spelling Word	Rule(s)	Instructional Tips
il lus tr<u>a</u> <u>ti</u>on	r. 29, 4, 11, 14	
il lus tr<u>ate</u>	r. 29	Base word.
dif f<u>er</u> ent	r. 29	
dif f<u>er</u>	r. 29	Base word.
pr<u>o</u> vi s̆ion	r. 4, 16	
pr<u>o</u> v<u>ide</u>	r. 4	Base word.
ac c<u>or</u>d <u>ing</u>	r. 29	
ȧl rĕ̄ad y	r. 21, 6	After children say the syllables, say, "In the second syllable, use ē, ĕ, ā. The phonogram ea saying eă̄ never ends a syllable."
at ten <u>ti</u>on	r. 29, 14	
ed <u>u</u> c<u>a</u> <u>ti</u>on	r. 4, 11, 14	
di rec t<u>or</u>		Be sure children say or, not er.
di rect		Base word.
p<u>ur</u> pos<u>e</u>₅		
com mon	r. 29	
di̯ <u>a</u> mond	r. 5, 4	
to geth̆ er		
con ven <u>ti</u>on	r. 14	

Spelling Word	Rule(s)	Instructional Tips
in creas̲e̲₅		After children say the syllables, say, "In the last syllable, use ē, ĕ, ā."
man ne̲r̲	r. 29	
fe̲a̲ tu̲r̲e		After children say the syllables, say, "In the first syllable, use ē, ĕ, ā."
a̲r̲ ti cl̲e̲₄		
[se̲r̲v ic̲e̲₃ se̲r̲v̲e̲₂	r. 11	Base word.
[*in ju̲ ry* in ju̲r̲e	r. 4, 11, 6	Base word.
ef fect	r. 29	
dis trib u̲te		
gen e̲r̲ al		
to̊³ mo̊r¹ ro̊w̲²	r. 29	Be sure children say each syllable precisely.
con sid e̲r̲		
[a̲ ga̲i̲nst a̲ ga̲i̲n	r. 4 r. 4	B.E.: May be a̲ ga̲i̲nst. Base word. For spelling, say *gain*. B.E.: May be a̲ ga̲i̲n.
com pl̲e̲t̲e̲		
s̲e̲a̲r̲c̲h̲		
tr̲e̲a̲s̲² u̲r̲e		

Spelling Word	Rule(s)	Instructional Tips
pop <u>u</u> l<u>ar</u>	r. 4	Be sure children say *ar*, not *er*.
[<u>Chris̆t</u> mas	r. 26	For spelling, say *Chrĭst mas*.
<u>Chris̆t</u>	r. 26, 19	Base word.
in t<u>er</u> est		
[ad v<u>ice</u>		
ad v<u>is̆e</u>		
[<u>A</u> mèr i can	r. 26, 4	
<u>A</u> mèr i c̊ȧ	r. 26, 4	
<u>bar</u> g<u>ai</u>n		
b<u>e</u> n<u>eath</u>	r. 4	After children say the syllables, say, "In the last syllable, use ē, ĕ, ā."
b<u>e</u> yond	r. 4	
[br<u>o</u> ken	r. 4, 11	
br<u>oke</u>		
br<u>ĕa</u>k		After children say the sounds for *break*, say, "Use ē, ĕ, ā."
c<u>o</u> c<u>oa</u>	r. 4	After children say the syllables, say, "In the last syllable, use the *oa* of *boat*."
col l<u>ar</u>	r. 29	Be sure children say *ar*, not *er*.
[com pàr i son	r. 11	
com p<u>are</u>		Base word.

Spelling Word	Rule(s)	Instructional Tips
con trolléd² con trŏl	r. 10, 19, 28	 Base word.
de<u>b</u>ts		For spelling, say *d ĕ b t s.*
diš² as t<u>er</u>		B.E.: diš² ås³ t<u>er</u>.
<u>ea</u> g<u>er</u>		After children say the syllables, say, "In the first syllable, use *ē, ĕ, ā.*"
en <u>e</u> my	r. 4, 6	
ex am pl<u>e</u>₄	r. 20	
ex c<u>ite</u> ment ex cit ing ex c<u>ite</u>	r. 20 r. 20, 11 r. 20	 Base word.
f<u>ier</u>c<u>e</u>₃	r. 12	
fl<u>ew</u> fl<u>ie</u>s² ² fl<u>y</u>	 r. 24 r. 5, 6	After children say the sounds for *flies,* say, "Use *ĭ, ī,* instead of y and add *es².* The ie together says *ī.*" Base word.
f<u>or</u> got t<u>en</u> f<u>or</u> got	r. 10 	 Base word.
g<u>i</u> gan tic g<u>i</u> ant	r. 5 r. 5	 Base word.
g<u>u</u>ide		

Spelling Word	Rule(s)	Instructional Tips
hur ry ing	r. 29	After children say the syllables, say, "Write *hurry* and add the ending *ing*. We don't change the y to i because we don't write two i's together."
hur ried	r. 29, 24, 28	After children say the syllables, say, "In the last syllable, use i instead of y and add the past tense ending. The ie together says *ĭ*."
hur ry	r. 29, 6	Base word.
knowl edge	r. 23	For spelling, say *kn ow l*.
know		Base word.
law yer		
par a graph	r. 4	
pa tient	r. 4, 14	
pa tience	r. 4, 14	
pi an ist		
pi an os		After children say the syllables, say, "Italian words ending in o add s to form plurals."
pi an o	r. 4	Base word. For spelling, say *pĭ*. The Italian i says *ē*.
pick les	r. 25	For spelling, say *l ĕ s*.
pick le	r. 25	Base word. For spelling, say *l ē*, not *ĕl*.
pris on er		
re lease	r. 4	After children say the syllables, say, "In the last syllable, use *ē*, *ĕ*, *ā*."
re sign	r. 4, 19	

Spelling Word	Rule(s)	Instructional Tips
re v**ea**l	r. 4	After children say the syllables, say, "In the last syllable, use $\bar{e}$, $\breve{e}$, $\bar{a}$."
sl**ee**v**e**$_2$		
sol d**ier**	r. 19	After children say the syllables, say, "In the last syllable, the uncommon phonogram di says *j*."
sum m**a** ry sum	r. 9, 4, 6	Base word.
s**w**_ord_		For spelling, say *s w or d*.
t**o** m**a** t**oe**^{2} t**o** m**a** t**o**	r. 4 r. 4	After children say the syllables, say, "In the last syllable, write *tō* and add *es*^{2}. The oe together says $\bar{o}$." Base word. B.E.: t**o** mȧ^3 t**o**.

Section S
125 Words for Spelling, Writing, and Reading

Spelling Words	Rule(s)	Instructional Tips
of t**e**n		For spelling, say $\breve{o}f$ $t\breve{e}n$. For reading, say $\breve{o}f$ $\breve{e}n$.
m**o** t**i**on	r. 4, 14	
th**e** **a** ter	r. 4	Accent is on the first syllable. B.E.: Spelling is th**e** **a** tr**e**$_4$.
im prŏ^{3}v**e**$_2$ment im prŏ^{3}v**e**$_2$		Skip a space. Dictate the base word, *improve*, first. (*Continue to dictate the base word first throughout the section.*)

Spelling Word	Rule(s)	Instructional Tips
cen tu ry cent	r. 4, 6	For spelling, say *rĭ*. *(Continue to require precise pronunciation of vowels in unaccented syllables throughout the section.)*
to tal	r. 4	
men tion	r. 14	
ar rive (1)	r. 29	For spelling, say both *r*'s. For reading, say only the *r* in the accented syllable *rive*. *(Continue to require correct pronunciation for spelling and reading throughout the section.)*
sup ply	r. 29, 5, 6	
as sist	r. 29	
dif fer ence₃	r. 29	
ex am i na tion ex am ine₅	r. 20, 11, 4, 14 r. 20	Base word. For spelling, say *ex am ĭnē*. For reading, say *eg zam in*.
par tic u lar	r. 4	
af fair	r. 29	
course₅ (2) coarse₅		After children say the sounds for *course*, say, "Use *ow, ō, ōō, ŭ*." After children say the sounds for *coarse*, say, "Use the *oa* of *boat*."
nei ther (2)	r. 12	After children say the syllables, say, "In the first syllable, use *ē, ā, ĭ*."
lo cal	r. 4	

Spelling Word	Rule(s)	Instructional Tips
mằr rìa̱ge̲	r. 29, 24	After children say the syllables, say, "In the last syllable, use ĭ, ī, instead of y and add the ending *age*."
mằr ry	r. 29, 6	Base word.
cằr rìa̱ge̲	r. 29, 24	After children say the syllables, say, "In the last syllable, use ĭ, ī, instead of y and add the ending *age*."
cằr ry	r. 29, 6	Base word.
fu̲r̃ t̲he̲r		
se̲ ri oũs	r. 4	After children say the syllables, say, "In the last syllable, use *ow, ō, ōo, ŭ*."
dou̲b̲t		Be sure children say *b t*. (*Continue to require precise pronunciation throughout the section*.)
con di t̲ion	r. 14	
gov e̲r̃n ment		Be sure children say *ern*, not *er*.
gov e̲r̃n		Base word.
o̲ pin i̲on	r. 4	For spelling, say *ĭ on*. For reading, say *yon*. The letter i says the consonant *y* sound. (Use this tip for the next four words.)
on i̲on		
ŭñ i̲on		
com pan i̲on		
mil l̲ion	r. 29	
be̲ hav i̲or	r. 4, 11	For spelling, say *i or*. For reading, say *yor*. B.E.: Spelling is *be̲ hav i̲õũr*.
be̲ lie̲ve̲₂	r. 4, 12	After children say the syllables, say, "In the last syllable, use *ē, ī, ĭ*."
sys tem		After children say the syllables, say, "In the first syllable, use *y, ĭ, ī*."

Spelling Word	Rule(s)	Instructional Tips
pos si bly *pos si ble₄*	r. 29, 11, 6 r. 29	Base word.
piece₃ *peace₃*	r. 12	After children say the sounds for *piece*, say, "Use $\bar{e}, \bar{\imath}, \breve{\imath}$." After children say the sounds for *peace*, say, "Use $\bar{e}, \breve{e}, \bar{a}$."
cer tain ly *cer tain*	r. 6	Base word.
wit ness	r. 17	
in ves ti gate		
there₅ fore *be fore*	 r. 4	
pleas ant		After children say the syllables, say, "In the first syllable, use $\bar{e}, \breve{e}, \bar{a}$. The phonogram *ea* saying $\overset{2}{ea}$ never ends a syllable."
a bil i ty	r. 4, 6	
ap pear ance₃	r. 29	After children say the syllables, say, "In the second syllable, use $\bar{e}, \breve{e}, \bar{a}$. Then add the ending *ance*."
at mos pher ic *at mos phere*	r. 11	Base word.
au tumn		
can vas		

Spelling Word	Rule(s)	Instructional Tips
c<u>ei</u>l <u>ing</u>	r. 12	After children say the syllables, say, "In the first syllable, use $\bar{e}$, $\bar{a}$, $\breve{i}$."
cel <u>er</u> y	r. 6	
sal <u>a</u> ry	r. 4, 6	
col <u>lege</u>₌₃	r. 29	
com m<u>u</u> ni t<u>ie</u>s [3 2]	r. 29, 4, 24	After children say the syllables, say, "In the last syllable, use $\breve{i}$, $\bar{i}$, instead of y and add e$\overset{2}{s}$. The ie together says $\breve{i}$."
com m<u>u</u> ni ty	r. 29, 4, 6	Base word.
cr<u>e</u> <u>a</u> <u>ti</u>on	r. 4, 14	
cr<u>e</u> <u>a</u> ti<u>ve</u>₂	r. 4, 11	
cr<u>e</u> <u>a</u> t<u>e</u>d	r. 4, 11, 28	
cr<u>e</u> <u>ate</u>	r. 4	Base word.
con c<u>er</u>t		
d<u>e</u> cid <u>ed</u>	r. 4, 11, 28	
d<u>e</u> c<u>ide</u>	r. 4	Base word.
d<u>e</u> $\overset{2}{s}$<u>ign</u>	r. 4, 19	
dic <u>ti</u>on àr y [1]	r. 14, 6	
el <u>e</u> <u>ph</u>ant	r. 4	
ev <u>er</u> y bod y	r. 6	
fr<u>ight</u> en<u>é</u>d [2]	r. 28	
fr<u>ight</u> en		
gr<u>o</u> c<u>er</u> y	r. 4, 6	

Spelling Word	Rule(s)	Instructional Tips
gr<u>ou</u>p [3]		After children say the sounds for *group*, say, "Use *ow, ō, ōo, ŭ*."
h<u>ea</u>lth [2]		After children say the sounds for *health*, say, "Use *ē, ě, ā*."
[lis <u>t</u>en<u>ed</u> [2]	r. 28	
lis <u>t</u>en		Base word.
ni<u>ck</u> el	r. 25	
ni<u>ece</u>₃	r. 12	After children say the sounds for *niece*, say, "Use *ē, ī, ǐ*."
[nor<u>th</u> [2] <u>ern</u>		
s<u>ou</u>th [4][2] <u>ern</u>		
<u>ea</u>st <u>ern</u>		
west <u>ern</u>		
[p<u>o</u> e [1] try	r. 4, 6	
p<u>o</u> et ic	r. 4	
p<u>o</u> et	r. 4	
p<u>o</u> em	r. 4	Base word.
[p<u>o</u> t<u>a</u> toe<u>s</u> [2]	r. 4	After children say the syllables, say, "In the last syllable, write *tō* and add *es* [2]. The oe together says *ō*."
p<u>o</u> t<u>a</u> t<u>o</u>	r. 4	Base word.
pres <u>sure</u>		For spelling, say *s ū r ē*.
[pr<u>o</u> d<u>uce</u>	r. 4	
prod uct		

Spelling Word	Rule(s)	Instructional Tips
pur chasĕd[3] pur chase	r. 11, 28	Base word.
quar rel	r. 29	
ra di o	r. 4	For spelling, say dĭ. The French i says ē.
re cess	r. 4, 17	
sau cer		
se cret	r. 4	
si mi lar		
sleigh		
so ci ĕ ty[1] so cial	r. 4, 5, 6 r. 4, 14	
so lu tion	r. 4, 14	
source[2,3]		After children say the sounds for source, say, "Use ow, ō, ōō, ŭ."
speech		
steak[3]		After children say the sounds for steak, say, "Use ē, ĕ, ā."
suc cess fŭl[3]	r. 22	
tails[2] tales[2]		
tear tear[3]		B.E.: teăr[2].

Spelling Word	Rule(s)	Instructional Tips
tel <u>e</u> phone	r. 4	
thro<u>ug</u>h out		
traf fic	r. 29	
[U nit <u>ed</u> States	r. 26, 4, 11, 28	
u n<u>ite</u>	r. 4	
u nit]	r. 4	Base word.
[val <u>u</u> <u>a</u> bl<u>e</u>₄	r. 4, 11	
val <u>ue</u>₂]		Base word.
[w<u>ore</u>		
w<u>or</u>n]		

Section T
125 Words for Spelling, Writing, and Reading

Spelling Words	Rule(s)	Instructional Tips
[c<u>ir</u> c<u>u</u> l<u>ar</u> c<u>ir</u> cl<u>e</u>₄]	r. 4	Skip a space. Dictate the base word, *circle*, first. (*Continue to dictate the base word first throughout the section.*) Be sure children say *ar*, not *er*. (*Continue to require precise pronunciation of vowels in unaccented syllables throughout the section.*)
[<u>ar</u> g<u>u</u> ment <u>ar</u> g<u>ue</u>₂]	r. 4	In *argument*, the silent final e is not needed. Base word.
vol <u>ume</u>		

Spelling Word	Rule(s)	Instructional Tips
or gan ize		After children say the syllables, say, "In the last syllable, use z. The letter z is usually used at the beginning of a base word." (*Size, dozen, organize, realize,* and *citizen* are exceptions.) B.E.: Spelling is <u>or</u> gan i<u>se</u>.
sum mon	r. 29	For spelling, say both *m*'s. For reading, say only the *m* in the accented syllable *sum*. (*Continue to require correct pronunciation for spelling and reading throughout the section.*)
of fi <u>c</u>ial	r. 29, 11	
of fi c<u>er</u>	r. 29, 11	
of fi<u>ce</u>₃	r. 29	Base word.
vic tim		
es ti m<u>ate</u>		
ac ci dent		After children say the syllables, say, "In the second syllable, *čĭ* has two separate phonogram sounds, *s, ĭ*."
in vi t<u>a</u> <u>t</u>ion	r. 11, 4, 14	
in v<u>ite</u>		Base word.
ac cept		For spelling, say *p t*. (*Continue to require precise pronunciation throughout the section.*)
im pos si bl<u>e</u>₄	r. 29	
con c<u>er</u>n		
<u>au</u> t<u>o</u> m<u>o</u> bil<u>e</u>₅	r. 4	

Spelling Word	Rule(s)	Instructional Tips
as s$\underline{o}$ ci $\underline{a}$ $\underline{ti}$on	r. 29, 4, 11, 14	After children say the syllables, say, "In the third syllable, $\overset{2}{\check{c}}\check{\imath}$ has two separate phonogram sounds, s, $\check{\imath}$."
as s$\underline{o}$ c$\underline{i}$ $\underline{ate}$	r. 29, 4, 14	Base word. After children say the syllables, say, "In the third syllable, use *sh* that begins with a short letter. The i has two functions: It forms the phonogram sh, and it provides the vowel sound for the syllable *shĭ*."
v$\overset{2}{\mathring{a}}$r i $\overset{4}{\underline{ou}}$s	r. 24	After children say the syllables, say, "In the second syllable, use $\check{\imath}$, $\bar{\imath}$, instead of y and add the ending $\overset{4}{ou}s$."
v$\overset{2}{\mathring{a}}$r y	r. 6	
v$\overset{1}{\mathring{e}}$r y	r. 6	Base word.
d$\underline{e}$ ci $\underline{s}\overset{2}{\underline{i}}$on	r. 4, 16	After children say the syllables, say, "In the second syllable, $\overset{2}{\check{c}}\check{\imath}$ has two separate phonogram sounds, s, $\check{\imath}$."
d$\underline{e}$ c$\underline{ide}$	r. 4	Base word.
en t$\underline{i}$ tl$\underline{\underline{e}}_4$	r. 5	
p$\underline{o}$ lit i cal	r. 4	
n$\overset{1}{\mathring{a}}$ $\underline{ti}$on al	r. 14	
n$\underline{a}$ $\underline{ti}$on	r. 4, 14	Base word.
r$\underline{e}$ cent	r. 4	
b$\underline{\underline{u}}\overset{2}{\underline{s}}$ i ness	r. 24, 17	After children say the syllables, say, "In the second syllable, use $\check{\imath}$, i, instead of y and add the ending *ness*.
b$\underline{\underline{u}}\overset{2}{\underline{s}}$ y	r. 6	Base word. For spelling, say $b\overset{2}{\check{u}}\overset{2}{\check{s}}$. For reading, say $b\overset{2}{\check{\imath}}\overset{2}{\check{s}}$.
r$\underline{e}$ f$\underline{er}$	r. 4	

Spelling Word	Rule(s)	Instructional Tips
min ut̲e̲₅		For spelling, say *ŭ t ē.*
mi̲ n̲u̲t̲e̲	r. 5	For spelling, say *n ū t ē.*
ou̅g̲ht		
ab sen̲c̲e̲₃		
ab sent		Base word.
con f̲e̲r enc̲e̲₃		In *conference,* we do not add another r because the accent moves to the first syllable, *con.*
con f̲e̲r		Base word.
Wed n̲e̲s̲ d̲a̲y	r. 26, 18	For spelling, say *Wed nes̊ day.* For reading, say *Wens̊ day.* In the writing lesson, explain that *Wednesday* is named for the German god Woden.
r̲e al ly	r. 4, 6	
r̲e al	r. 4	Base word. This is a two-syllable word.
cel e̲ br̲a ti̲on	r. 4, 14	
fo̲lks	r. 19	
fo̲l̲k	r. 19	Base word.
a̲c̲h̲es		
a̲c̲h̲e		Base word.
a̲ mu̲s̲e ment	r. 4	

Spelling Word	Rule(s)	Instructional Tips
an gri ly *an gry* *an g̲e̲r*	r. 24, 6 r. 6	After children say the syllables, say, "In the second syllable, use ĭ, ī, instead of y and add the ending *ly*." Base word. For spelling, say *an*. For reading, n before g, says *ng*.
ap prŏv al *ap prŏv̲e̲₂*	r. 29, 11 r. 29	Base word.
a̲ va̲i̲l a̲ bl̲e̲₄	r. 4	
a̲ vo̲i̲d	r. 4	
bă nan ả		B.E.: bả nản ả.
bis c̲u̲its		After children say the syllables, say, "In the last syllable, the uncommon phonogram cu says *k*."
bot tl̲e̲₄	r. 29	
bot tom	r. 29	
bru̲i̲s̲ĕ̲d *bru̲i̲s̲e̲₅*	r. 11, 28	Base word.
change a bl̲e̲₄ *change*	r. 4	After children say the syllables, say, "Write *change* with the e and add the ending *a ble*. We need the e to let the g say *j*." Base word.
c̲h̲ap ter		
c̲h̲im ně̲y̲		After children say the syllables, say, "In the last syllable, use ā, ē, ĭ."

Spelling Word	Rule(s)	Instructional Tips
<u>ch</u>oir		For spelling, say *ch oi r.* For reading, say *quire.*
com pete		
de ceive₂	r. 4, 12	After children say the syllables, say, "In the last syllable, use *k, s,* and ei."
de ter mi na tion	r. 4, 11, 14	
de ter minéd	r. 4, 11, 28	
de ter mine₅	r. 4	Base word.
dis cov er iés	r. 24	After children say the syllables, say, "In the last syllable, use ĭ, ī, instead of y and add eš. The ie together says ĭ."
dis cov er y	r. 6	
dis cov er		Base word.
e lec tric i ty	r. 4, 6	
e lec tri cian	r. 4, 14	
e lec tri cal	r. 4	
e lec tric	r. 4	Base word.
en teréd	r. 28	
ér ror	r. 29	For spelling, say *ér ror.*
err		Base word. For spelling, say *er r.* For reading, say *er.*
ex act	r. 20	
ex cep tions	r. 20, 14	
fa vor a ble₄	r. 4	B.E.: Spelling is *fa vour a ble₄.*
fa vor ite₅	r. 4	B.E.: Spelling is *fa vour ite₅.*
fa vor	r. 4	Base word. B.E.: Spelling is *fa vour.*

Spelling Word	Rule(s)	Instructional Tips
foúght		
fu̲ el	r. 4	
gen u̲ ine̲ₛ	r. 4	
grŏẘth		
hand fủl	r. 22	
ha̲rd ly	r. 6	
hym̲n̲		For spelling, say *h ĭ m n.*
in ves ti ga̲ t̲ion	r. 4, 11, 14	
[in volvĕd	r. 11, 28	
in volv̲e̲₂		Base word.
[lil i̲e̲s̆	r. 24	After children say the syllables, say, "In the last syllable, use ĭ, ī, instead of y and add es̆. The ie together says ĭ."
lil y	r. 6	Base word.
[mas siv̲e̲₂	r. 29	
mass	r. 17	Base word.
[med al		
met al		
med i cine̲ₛ		
ni̲ne̲ ty	r. 6	

Spelling Word	Rule(s)	Instructional Tips
re̱ al i̱ze	r. 4	The letter z is usually used at the beginning of a base word. (*Size, dozen, organize, realize,* and *citizen* are exceptions.) B.E.: re̱ al i̱se.
re̱ign	r. 12	
se̱ ve̱re̱	r. 4	
[slippe̱d	r. 9, 28	
slip]		Base word.
sneeze̱₅		
[sta̱ ti̱on ár y	r. 4, 14, 6	
sta̱ ti̱on ér y]	r. 4, 14, 6	In the writing lesson, have children relate this word to the paper for writing letters.
stom ac̲h		
straight		After children say the sounds for *straight,* say, "The uncommon phonogram aigh says ā."
suc ce̱ed		
tel e̱ vi si̱on	r. 4, 16	
tou̇gh		
[whis tling	r. 11	For spelling, be sure children say only two syllables (two vowel sounds) and pronounce the *t.* Base word. For spelling, say *tlē.*
whis tle̱₄]		
who̱le some̱₅		

Spelling Word	Rule(s)	Instructional Tips
wreath		
[wres tling wres tle₄	r. 11	Be sure children say only two syllables (two vowel sounds) and pronounce the _t_. Base word. For spelling, say _tlē_.

Section U
125 Words for Spelling, Writing, and Reading

Spelling Words	Rule(s)	Instructional Tips
[meant mean		Skip a space. Dictate the base word, _mean_, first. (_Continue to dictate the base word first throughout the section._)
[ear li est ear ly	r. 24 r. 6	After children say the syllables, say, "In the second syllable, use ĭ, ī, instead of y and add the ending _est_." Base word. For spelling, say _lĭ_. (_Continue to require precise pronunciation of vowels in unaccented syllables throughout the section._)
dis tin guish	r. 13	After children say the syllables, say, "In the last syllable, the phonogram gu says _gw_."
con sid er a tion	r. 4, 14	
[cŏ lo ni al col o nies col o ny	r. 4, 24 r. 4, 24 r. 4, 6	After children say the syllables, say, "In the third syllable, use ĭ, ī, instead of y and add the ending _ăl_." After children say the syllables, say, "In the last syllable, use ĭ, ī, instead of y and add _es_. The ie together says ĭ." Base word.

Spelling Word	Rule(s)	Instructional Tips
as <u>sure</u> _<u>sure</u>	r. 29	For spelling, say both _s_'s. For reading, say only the _s_ in the accented syllable _sure_. _(Continue to require correct pronunciation for spelling and reading throughout the section.)_ Base word. For spelling, say _s ū r ē_.
r<u>e</u> li<u>e</u>f	r. 4, 12	After children say the syllables, say, "In the second syllable, use _ē, ī, ĭ_."
oc cu̲ py̲	r. 29, 4, 5, 6	
prob <u>a</u> bly prob <u>a</u> bl<u>e</u>₄	r. 4, 11, 6 r. 4	Base word.
for e¹i<u>gn</u>³	r. 12	
ex pens<u>e</u>₅	r. 20	
r<u>e</u> spon si bl<u>e</u>₄ r<u>e</u> spons<u>e</u>₅	r. 4, 11 r. 4	Base word.
ap pli c<u>a</u> <u>ti</u>on ap pl<u>y</u>	r. 29, 24, 4, 14 r. 29, 5, 6	After children say the syllables, say, "In the second syllable, use _ĭ, ī_, instead of y." Base word.
dif fi cul ty dif fi cult	r. 29, 6 r. 29	Base word.

Spelling Word	Rule(s)	Instructional Tips
<u>sce</u>ne		After children say the sounds for *scene,* say, "The uncommon phonogram sc says *s.*"
<u>sc</u>en <u>er</u> y	r. 6	
<u>sc</u>i̊s̱ s̊oṟs̊	r. 29	
<u>sc</u>i en<u>ce</u>₃	r. 5	
d<u>e</u> <u>sc</u>end	r. 4	
d<u>e</u> <u>sc</u>ent	r. 4	
as cend	r. 29	Rule 29 holds here because s and c have the same sound.
as cent	r. 29	
fi̱ nal ly	r. 5, 6	
fi̱ nal	r. 5	Base word.
d<u>e</u> vel op	r. 4	
en vel op		For spelling, say *en vel op.*
en vel <u>ope</u>		For spelling, say *en vel <u>ope</u>.*
ci̱r cum stan<u>ce</u>₃		In the writing lesson, discuss how *circumstance* and *circumference* are related to *circle.*
ci̱r cum f<u>er</u> en<u>ce</u>₃		
ci̱r cl<u>e</u>₄		
i̱s̱ s<u>ue</u>₂	r. 29	For spelling, say *is sue.*
ti̱s̱ s<u>ue</u>₂	r. 29	For spelling, say *tis sue.*
mȧ t<u>e</u> ri al	r. 4	
sug gest		
m<u>ere</u>		

Spelling Word	Rule(s)	Instructional Tips
sen a̱ to̱ ri al	r. 4	
sen a̱ to̱r	r. 4, 11	
sen ate̱₅		Base word.
re̱ ceive̱₂	r. 4, 12	
re̱ spect fŭl ly	r. 4, 22, 6	
re̱ spect fŭl	r. 4, 22	
re̱ spect	r. 4	Base word. Be sure children say *c t*. (*Continue to require precise pronunciation throughout the section.*)
a̱ gre̱e ment	r. 4	
a̱ gre̱e	r. 4	Base word.
un fo̱r tu̱ nate̱₅	r. 4	
mă jŏr i ty	r. 6	
ma̱ jo̱r	r. 4	Base word.
e̱ lab o̱ rate̱₅	r. 4	
e̱ lab o̱ ra̱te	r. 4	
cit i zen	r. 24	After children say the syllables, say, "In the second syllable, use ĭ, ī, instead of y and in the last syllable, use z. The letter z is usually used at the beginning of a base word. (*Size, dozen, organize, realize,* and *citizen* are exceptions.)
cit y	r. 6	Base word.
nĕ ces si ty	r. 29, 6	
nec es săr y	r. 29, 6	Base word.

Spelling Word	Rule(s)	Instructional Tips
di v<u>i</u>d<u>e</u>		
<u>a</u> chieves[2]	r. 4, 12	
<u>a</u> chiev<u>e</u>₂	r. 4, 12	Base word. After children say the syllables, say, "In the second syllable, use *ē, ī, ĭ*."
ac q<u>ui</u>re		
ån c<u>i</u>ent [2]	r. 14	After children say the syllables, say, "In the last syllable, use *sh* that begins with a short letter."
<u>an</u> y one		
<u>a</u> p<u>ie</u>c<u>e</u>₃	r. 4, 12	After children say the syllables, say, "In the second syllable, use *ē, ī, ĭ*."
ap pr<u>oa</u>ch es[2]	r. 29	
at ta<u>ck</u>	r. 29, 25	
at t<u>or</u> ne<u>y</u>[3]	r. 29	For spelling, say *t<u>or</u>*. For reading, say *ter*.
bal an<u>ce</u>₃		
cal c<u>u</u> l<u>a</u> t<u>i</u>on	r. 4, 11, 14	
cal c<u>u</u> l<u>ate</u>	r. 4	Base word.
cen tral		
cér <u>e</u> m<u>o</u> ny[1]	r. 4, 6	
con c<u>ea</u>léd[2]	r. 28	
d<u>e</u> li c<u>iou</u>s[4]	r. 4, 14	After children say the syllables, say, "In the last syllable, use *sh* that begins with a short letter."

Spelling Word	Rule(s)	Instructional Tips
de scrib[2]ed	r. 4, 11, 28	
de scribe	r. 4	Base word.
dis ap pear	r. 29	
dropp[3]ed	r. 9, 28	
drop		Base word.
el e gant	r. 4	
em per or		
es tab lish ment	r. 13	
es tab lish[3]ed	r. 13, 28	
es tab lish	r. 13	Base word.
ex cel lent	r. 20, 10	In *excellent*, we write another l even though the accent moves to the first syllable.
ex cel	r. 20	Base word.
gath[2] er		
gen er al ly	r. 6	
grate f[3]ul	r. 22	
h[2]eir	r. 12	For spelling, say *h e[2]i r*.
in her[1] it		
hoarse[5]		B.E.: After children say the sounds for *hoarse*, say, "Use *oa* of *boat*."
i ci cle[4]	r. 5	After children say the syllables, say, "In the second syllable, use *k, s*."

Spelling Word	Rule(s)	Instructional Tips
[*i den ti fíed*	r. 5, 24, 28	After children say the syllables, say, "In the last syllable, use ĭ, ī, instead of y and add the past tense ending. The ie together says ī."
[*i den ti fy*	r. 5, 6	Base word.
[*ig no rance₃*	r. 4, 11	
ig no rant	r. 4, 11	
[*ig nore*		Base word.
[*in di ca tion*	r. 4, 11, 14	
[*in di cate*		Base word.
[*in ter fer ence₃*	r. 11	
[*in ter fere*		Base word.
[*lead er ship*	r. 13	
[*lead er*		Base word.
[*mes sen ger*	r. 29	
[*mes sage*	r. 29	Base word.
[*mu ši cian*	r. 4, 14	
[*mu šic*	r. 4	Base word.
pi geon		After children say the syllables, say, "In the last syllable, the uncommon phonogram ge says j."
[*plane*		
[*plain*		
prob lems		

Spelling Word	Rule(s)	Instructional Tips
re h<u>ear</u>s al	r. 4, 11	
re h<u>ear</u>se̲₅	r. 4	Base word.
re mŏv al	r. 4, 11	
re mŏvéd	r. 4, 11, 28	
re mŏv̲e̲₂	r. 4	Base word.
si<u>e</u>g<u>e</u>₃	r. 12	After children say the sounds for *siege*, say, "Use ē, ī, ĭ."
val lĕ<u>y</u>	r. 29, 6	After children say the syllables, say, "In the last syllable, use ā, ē, ĭ."
veg <u>e</u> t<u>a</u> bl<u>e</u>₄	r. 4	

Section V
125 Words for Spelling, Writing, and Reading

Spelling Words	Rule(s)	Instructional Tips
prin ci pal		After children say the syllables, say, "Use *k*, *s*." Be sure children say ăl, not ŭl. *(Continue to require precise pronunciation of vowels in unaccented syllables throughout the section.)*
prin ci pl<u>e</u>₄		
tes ti m<u>o</u> ny	r. 4, 6	
dis cus <u>sion</u>	r. 14, 15	Skip a space. Dictate the base word, *discuss*, first. *(Continue to dictate the base word first throughout the section.)*
dis cuss	r. 17	

Spelling Word	Rule(s)	Instructional Tips
$\lceil$ ár range ment	r. 29	
$\lfloor$ ár range	r. 29	Base word. For spelling, say both *r*'s. For reading, say *r* in the accented syllable *range*. *(Continue to require correct pronunciation for spelling and reading throughout the section.)*
$\lceil$ ref er ence₃		In *reference*, we do not write another r because the accent shifts to the first syllable, *ref*.
$\lfloor$ re fer	r. 4	Base word.
ev i dence₃		
ex pe ri ence₃	r. 20, 4	
ses sion	r. 14, 15	
sec re tár y	r. 4, 6	
as so ci a tion	r. 29, 4, 14	After children say the syllables, say, "The third syllable has two separate sounds, *s*, *ĭ*."
ca reer	r. 4	
$\lceil$ height		For spelling, say *h e igh t*.
$\lfloor$ high		Base word.
ap pár ent	r. 29	
as cend ing	r. 29	Rule 29 holds here because s and c have the same sound.
$\lceil$ ba si cal ly	r. 4, 6	
$\lfloor$ ba sic	r. 4	Base word.

Spelling Word	Rule(s)	Instructional Tips
[bo⁶u<u>gh</u> [b<u>ow</u> [b<u>o</u>²w		
cam p<u>ai</u><u>g</u>n		
[cap i tal [cap i tol		
c<u>e</u> r<u>e</u> al	r. 4	
<u>ch</u><u>oi</u>c<u>e</u>₃		
[<u>ch</u>o² <u>s</u>en [<u>ch</u>o²<u>s</u><u>e</u> [<u>ch</u>o<u>o</u>²<u>s</u><u>e</u>₅	r. 4, 11	We often keep the base word in one syllable, but here we do not. Base word.
c<u>oa</u>r<u>se</u>₅		B.E.: After children say the sounds in *coarse*, say "Use the *oa* of *boat*."
col um<u>n</u>²<u>s</u>		For spelling, say each sound in the second syllable.
co¹r rect	r. 29	For spelling, say *c t. (Continue to require precise pronunciation throughout the section.)*
c<u>ur</u> rent	r. 29	B.E.: c<u>u</u>¹r rent
[d<u>e</u>² <u>s</u>ir <u>a</u> bl<u>e</u>₄ [d<u>e</u>² <u>s</u>ir<u>e</u>	r. 4, 11 r. 4	Base word.
[di vi <u>si</u>²on [di v<u>ide</u>	r. 16	Base word.

Spelling Word	Rule(s)	Instructional Tips
Dr. = <u>D</u>oc to<u>r</u>	r. 26	B.E.: *Dr* is the international alternative.
dr<u>aw</u>n dr<u>ew</u> dr<u>aw</u>		 Base word.
<u>e</u> quip ment <u>e</u> quipp<u>ĕ</u>d <u>e</u> quip	r. 4 r. 4, 10, 28 r. 4	 Base word.
ex tr<u>eme</u> ly ex tr<u>eme</u>	r. 20, 6 r. 20	 Base word.
f<u>ear</u> fŭl f<u>ear</u>	r. 22	 Base word.
func <u>ti</u>on al func <u>ti</u>on	r. 14 r. 14	 Base word.
f<u>ur</u> ni t<u>ure</u>		
f<u>u</u> t<u>ure</u>	r. 4	
g<u>ath</u> <u>er</u> ing		
h<u>ea</u>v i ly h<u>ea</u>v i <u>er</u> h<u>ea</u>v y	r. 24 r. 24 r. 6	 Base word. The phonogram ea saying ĕ never ends a syllable.
hun dred		

Spelling Word	Rule(s)	Instructional Tips
im ag in̲e̲₅ *im a̲g̲e̲*	r. 11	Base word.
inch e̲s̲²		
in de̲ pen dent	r. 4	
in di vid u̲ al	r. 4	
in flu̲ en̲c̲e̲₃	r. 4	
in no̲ cent	r. 29, 4	
in stan̲c̲e̲₃		
in stru̲ men tal *in stru̲ ment*	r. 4 r. 4	Base word. For spelling, say *strū*.
le̲i̲ s̲ure²	r. 12	B.E.: *le̲i̲ s̲ure²*.
li̲ cen̲s̲e̲₅	r. 5	B.E.: Spelling for the noun is *li̲ cen̲c̲e̲₃*; verb is *li̲ cen̲s̲e̲₅*.
li qu̲id		
lo̲ ca̲ t̲ion *lo̲ cat e̲d̲* *lo̲ ca̲t̲e̲*	r. 4, 14 r. 4, 11, 28 r. 4	 Base word.
mag nif i cent		
ma̲i̲n		
min e̲r̲ al̲s̲²		
me̲t̲h̲ od		

Spelling Word	Rule(s)	Instructional Tips
mod _ern_		
[mys te̲ ri o̲us⁴ [mys te̲r y	r. 4, 24 r. 6	After children say the syllables, say, "In the third syllable, use ĭ, ī, instead of y and add the ending o̲us⁴. Base word. After children say the syllables, say, "In the first syllable, use y, ĭ, ī."
oc ca̲ si̲on²	r. 29, 4, 16	
[o̲r di nȧr¹ i ly [o̲r di nȧr¹ y	r. 24, 6 r. 6	After children say the syllables, say, "In the fourth syllable, use ĭ, ī, instead of y and add the ending _ly_." Base word.
pe̲r son al i ty	r. 6	
phy̲s² i cal ly	r. 6	
plan et		
[plen ti fu̇l³ [plen ty	r. 24, 22 r. 6	After children say the syllables, say, "In the second syllable, use ĭ, ī, instead of y and add the ending _ful_." Base word.
po̲w e̲r fu̇l³	r. 22	
prai̲ rie̲³	r. 12	
pre̲ pa̲re̲d²	r. 4, 11, 28	
pre̲ vent	r. 4	
[pro̲ tec _tion_ [pro̲ tec tiv̲e₂ [pro̲ tect	r. 4, 14 r. 4 r. 4	 Base word.

Spelling Word	Rule(s)	Instructional Tips
quar ter quart		Base word.
rec og ni tion	r. 14	
rec og nize		Base word. The letter z is usually used at the beginning of a base word. (*Size, dozen, organize,* and *citizen* are other exceptions.) B.E.: Spelling is *rec og nise*.
rec ords re cords	 r. 4	
re lieve	r. 4, 12	
re peat ed rep e ti tion	r. 4, 28 r. 4, 14	
re quired	r. 4, 11, 28	
sac ri fice		
sen si ble sense	r. 11	After children say the syllables, say, "Use the ending *ĭ ble.*" Base word.
shoul der	r. 13	
sit u a tion	r. 4, 14	
slight ly	r. 6	
sol emn		

Spelling Word	Rule(s)	Instructional Tips
spir it <u>u</u> al spir it	r. 4	Base word.
st<u>éad</u>²́ i ly st<u>éad</u>²́ y	r. 24, 6 r. 6	After children say the syllables, say, "In the second syllable, use ĭ, ī, instead of y and add the ending *ly*." Base word.
tem p<u>er</u> <u>a</u> t<u>ur</u>e	r. 4	
<u>thou</u> śand²́		
t<u>y</u> ing t<u>ie</u>²́	r. 5 r. 12	After children say the syllables, say, "In the first syllable, use y, ĭ, ī." Base word.
wiś²́ dom w<u>iśe</u>²́		Base word.

Section W
125 Words for Spelling, Writing, and Reading

Spelling Words	Rule(s)	Instructional Tips
<u>or</u> gan i z<u>a</u> <u>ti</u>on _or gan <u>ize</u>_	r. 11, 4, 14	Skip a space. Dictate the base word, *organize*, first. *(Continue to dictate the base word first throughout the section.)* B.E.: Spelling is <u>or</u> gan i śa²́ <u>ti</u>on. Base word. B.E.: Spelling is <u>or</u> gan <u>iśe</u>²́.
<u>e</u> m<u>er</u> gen cy	r. 4, 6	For spelling, y says ĭ. *(Continue to require precise pronunciation of vowels in unaccented syllables throughout the section.)*

Spelling Word	Rule(s)	Instructional Tips
ap pre ci a tive₂	r. 29, 4, 14, 11	
ap pre ci ate	r. 29, 4, 14	Base word. For spelling, say both *p*'s. For reading, say only the *p* in the accented syllable *pre. (Continue to require correct pronunciation for spelling and reading throughout the section.)* After children say the syllables, say, "In the third syllable, use *sh* that begins with a short letter. The i has two functions: It forms the phonogram that says *sh*, and it provides the vowel sound for the syllable *shĭ*."
sin cere ly	r. 6	
sin cere		Base word.
ath let ic	r. 11	
ath lete		Base word.
ex treme	r. 20	
prac ti cal		
pro ceed	r. 4	
cor dial ly	r. 6	B.E.: cor di al ly.
cor dial		Base word. After children say the syllables, say, "In the second syllable, the uncommon phonogram di say *j*." B.E.: cor di al.
char ac ter		
sep a rate	r. 4	

Spelling Word	Rule(s)	Instructional Tips
Feb ru̱ år y	r. 26, 4, 6	
[ac tiv i ti̱e̱s̱	r. 11, 24	
ac tiv i ty	r. 11, 6	
ac tiv̱e̱		
[ac tu̱ al	r. 4	
ac tu̱ al ly	r. 4, 6	
[an gu̱ la̱ṟ	r. 4	
an gḻe̱		Base word.
an ti̱q̱u̱e̱		For spelling, say *t ĭ qu ē*. The French i says *ē* and qu says *k*.
[an x̱i̱ e̊ ty	r. 5, 6	After children say the syllables, say, "In the second syllable, use the phonogram x saying *z*, an uncommon sound." For spelling, say *a n x ĭ o̱u̱s*; n followed by the sound *k* says *ng*.
anx io̱u̱s		
av e̱ṟ a̱g̱e̱		
bi̱ cy cḻe̱	r. 5	
bo̊u̱ q̱u̱e̱ṯ		After children say the syllables, say, "In the first syllable, use *ow, ō, ōo, ŭ*. In the second syllable, use qu to say *k* and et to say *ā* in this French word." B.E.: bo̊u̱ q̱u̱e̱ṯ.
cal en da̱ṟ		
[cen tu̱ ri̱e̱s̱	r. 4, 24	
cen tu̱ ry	r. 4, 6	Base word.

Spelling Word	Rule(s)	Instructional Tips
cl*i* m*ate*	r. 5	
com po$\overset{2}{s}$$\overset{2}{e}$d	r. 11, 28	
com p*o* $\overset{2}{s}$i *tion*	r. 4, 14	
con se *quence*$_{-=3}$	r. 4	
c*or* n*er*		
cot ton	r. 29	
c*ou*nt less	r. 17	
c*ou*nt		Base word.
d*e* pen dent	r. 4	
d*e* pend$\overset{2}{s}$	r. 4	
d*e* pend	r. 4	Base word.
di *a* gram	r. 5, 4	
di$\overset{2}{s}$ ea$\overset{2}{s}$*e*$_5$		
el *e* men t*a* ry	r. 4, 6	
el *e* ment	r. 4	Base word.
emp ty	r. 6	
en v*i* ron ment	r. 5	
e quiv *a* lent	r. 4	
e qual i ty	r. 4, 6	
e qual	r. 4	Base word.
ev *er* y one		

Spelling Word	Rule(s)	Instructional Tips
ev <u>er</u> y <u>wh</u>ère[1]₅		
ex cl<u>aim</u>éd[2]	r. 20, 28	
ex cl<u>a</u> m<u>a</u> <u>tion</u>	r. 20, 4, 14	
ex pèr[1] i men tal	r. 20	
ex pèr[1] i ment	r. 20	Base word.
ex pres <u>sion</u>	r. 20, 14, 15	
fac t<u>or</u>s[2]		
f<u>a</u>[1] t<u>ī gu ē</u>₂		For spelling, say *t ĭ gu ē*. The French i says *ē*.
for[1] <u>ei</u>[3] gn ers[2]	r. 12	
for[1] <u>ei</u>[3] gn	r. 12	Base word.
fre <u>quen</u> cy	r. 4, 6	
fre <u>quent</u>	r. 4	Base word.
grad <u>u</u> al ly	r. 4, 6	
grad <u>u</u> al	r. 4	
i<u>sth</u> mus		For spelling, say *i s th*.
lev el		
l<u>i</u> brȧr[1] y	r. 5, 6	
mod el		
m<u>o</u> ment	r. 4	

Spelling Word	Rule(s)	Instructional Tips
mos <u>qui</u> to̱	r. 4	For spelling, say *qu ĭ*. The phonogram qu says *k* and the Spanish i says *ē*.
mus cu̲ la̲r mus c̆le̲₄	r. 4 r. 29	Base word. After children say the syllables, say, "In the second syllable, use *k, s*." (Rule 29 holds here because s and c have the same sound.)
nắr rŏ̲w̲	r. 29	
nat u̲ ral ist nat u̲ ral ly nat u̲ ral na̲ tu̲r̲e	r. 4, 11 r. 4, 11, 6 r. 4, 11 r. 4	For spelling, say *nat u ral*. For reading, say *natch u ral*. Base word.
non sens̲e₅		
ob s̆er va̲ t̲ion ob s̆er̲v a̲ to̲ ry ob s̆er̲v̲e₂	r. 4, 11, 14 r. 4, 11, 6 	 Base word.
oc cu̲r̲ ren̲c̲e₃ oc cu̲r̲r̆ed oc cu̲r	r. 29, 10 r. 29, 10, 28 r. 29	B.E.: oc cŭr ren̲c̲e₃. Base word.
op po̲ s̆i t̲ion op po̲ s̆it̲e₅	r. 29, 4, 14 r. 29, 4	 Base word.
phra̎s̆e		
prac ti̲c̲e₃		B.E.: Spelling for the noun is *prac ti̲c̲e₃*; verb is *prac ti̲s̲e₅*.

Spelling Word	Rule(s)	Instructional Tips
proc ess	r. 17	B.E.: pr<u>o</u> cess.
⎡*pr<u>o</u> duc <u>tion</u>* |*pr<u>o</u> duc tiv<u>e</u>₂* ⎣*prod uct*	r. 4, 14 r. 4 	 Base word. Be sure children say *k t*. *(Continue to require precise pronunciation throughout the section.)*
pr<u>o</u> gram	r. 4	
⎡*r<u>e</u> s<u>ou</u>rc<u>e</u>₃ful* |*r<u>e</u> s<u>ou</u>rc e<u>s</u>* ⎣*r<u>e</u> s<u>ou</u>rc<u>e</u>₃*	r. 4, 22 r. 4 r. 4	
⎡*rhyme* |*rhythm* ⎣*rhyth mic*		After children say the sounds for *rhyme*, say, "Use the uncommon phonogram rh to say *r*." This is a one-syllable word.
r<u>ou</u>tes		B.E.: r<u>ou</u>tes.
s<u>afe</u> ty	r. 6	
sc<u>ale</u>		
⎡*sc<u>i</u> en tif ic* ⎣*sc<u>i</u> en tists*	r. 5 r. 5	After children say the syllables, say, "In the first syllable, use the uncommon phonogram sc to say *s*."
⎡*s<u>e</u> cr<u>e</u> cy* ⎣*s<u>e</u> cret*	r. 4, 6 r. 4	 Base word.
sec <u>tions</u>	r. 14	
s<u>qua</u>re		

Spelling Word	Rule(s)	Instructional Tips
stan d<u>ar</u>d		
struc tur al *struc t<u>ur</u>e*	r. 11	Base word.
sub stan <u>t</u>ial *sub stan<u>ce</u>₃*	r. 14	Base word.
ton<u>g</u>ue₌₂		For spelling, say *t ŏ ng ū ē.*
tr<u>i</u> an gl<u>e</u>₄	r. 5	
vár <u>i</u> ĕ ty	r. 5, 6	
v<u>e</u> hi cl<u>e</u>₄	r. 4	
vi cin i ty	r. 6	
vol un t<u>ee</u>r		
wel f<u>are</u>		
yà<u>ch</u>t		For spelling, say *y ằ ch t.*

Section X
125 Words for Spelling, Writing, and Reading

Spelling Words	Rule(s)	Instructional Tips
im m<u>e</u> di <u>ate</u>	r. 29, 4	For spelling, say both *m*'s. For reading, say only the *m* in the accented syllable *me.* (*Continue to require correct pronunciation for spelling and reading throughout the section.*)

Spelling Word	Rule(s)	Instructional Tips
con ven ient con vene	r. 11	Skip a space. Dictate the base word, *convene*, first. *(Continue to dictate the base word first throughout the section.)* For spelling, say ĭ ĕ n t. For reading, say *yent.* B. E.: con ve ni ent.
re ceipt	r. 4, 12	For spelling, say *p t.* *(Continue to require precise pronunciation throughout the section.)*
pre lim i nar y	r. 4, 6	For spelling, y says ĭ. *(Continue to require precise pronunciation of vowels in unaccented syllables throughout the section.)*
dis ap point	r. 29	
es pe cial ly spe cial	r. 14, 6 r. 14	Base word.
an nu al	r. 29, 4	
com mit tee com mit	r. 29, 10 r. 29	After children say the syllables, say, "In the third syllable, use the double *ee.*" Base word.
ad jec tive₂		
ad van tage		
af fect	r. 29	
Af ri ca	r. 26	
al ti tude		
an ces tors		

Spelling Word	Rule(s)	Instructional Tips
Ant arc ti că[3]	r. 26	
ap plied[2 2]	r. 29, 24, 28	
ap ply ing	r. 29, 5	
ap ply	r. 29, 5, 6	Base word.
ar chi[2] tec ture		
Arc tic O cean	r. 26, 4	
ar ti fi cial	r. 14	After children say the syllables, say, "In the fourth syllable, use *sh* that begins with a short letter."
A sia[2 3]	r. 26, 4, 16	
At lan tic O cean	r. 26, 4	
Aus trăl[2] iă[3]	r. 26	After children say the syllables, say, "In the first syllable, say *au s*. In the last syllable, say ĭ ă[3]." For reading, say *ya*. The letter i says the consonant *y* sound.
ben e fi cial	r. 4, 14	After children say the syllables, say, "In the last syllable, use the *sh* that begins with a short letter."
ben e fit	r. 4	
bound a riĕš[3 2]	r. 4, 24	After children say the syllables, say, "In the last syllable, use ĭ, ī, instead of y and add eš[2]. The ie together says ĭ."
bound a ry	r. 4, 6	Base word.
bril liant	r. 29	For spelling, say *l ĭ ă n t*. For reading, say *yant*. The letter i says the consonant *y* sound.
char[2] ac ter[1] is tics		
Chi[3] că go[3]	r. 26, 4	

Spelling Word	Rule(s)	Instructional Tips
<u>ch</u>oc <u>o</u> lat<u>e</u>₅		
civ i l<u>i</u> z<u>a</u> <u>t</u>ion	r. 5, 11, 4, 14	B.E.: Spelling is *civ i l<u>i</u> s<u>a</u> <u>t</u>ion.*
civ i l<u>i</u>z<u>e</u>d	r. 11, 28	B.E.: Spelling is *civ i l<u>i</u>s<u>e</u>d.*
civ i l<u>i</u>z<u>e</u>		B.E.: Spelling is *civ i l<u>i</u>s<u>e</u>.*
civ il		Base word.
col <u>o</u> nel	r. 4	For spelling, say *col ō nel.* For reading, say *kernel.*
con gress	r. 17	
con <u>ta</u> gi<u>ou</u>s	r. 4	The uncommon phonogram gi says *j.*
con ti nen tal		
con ti nent		Base word.
dep<u>th</u>		
d<u>e</u> scrip <u>t</u>ion	r. 4, 14	
d<u>e</u> scrip tiv<u>e</u>₂	r. 4	
d<u>e</u> vel op ment	r. 4	
d<u>e</u> vel op	r. 4	Base word.
d<u>i</u> ag <u>o</u> nal	r. 5, 4	
d<u>i</u> am e ter	r. 5	
ef fec tiv<u>e</u>₂	r. 29	
ef fect	r. 29	Base word.

Spelling Word	Rule(s)	Instructional Tips
em pl<u>oy</u> <u>ee</u> em pl<u>oy</u>		Base word.
E<u>ng</u> land E<u>ng</u> li<u>sh</u>	r. 26 r. 26, 13	
<u>e</u> n<u>or</u> m<u>o̊ů</u>s	r. 4	
es sen <u>ti</u>al	r. 29, 14	
<u>Eu</u> r<u>o</u>p<u>e</u>	r. 26	The uncommon phonogram eu says *u*.
<u>e</u> ven t<u>u</u> al ly	r. 4, 6	
ex cha<u>nge</u>	r. 20	
ex ist en<u>ce</u>₃ ex ist	r. 20 r. 20	Base word.
ex pl<u>o</u> r<u>a</u> <u>ti</u>on ex plor <u>er</u>š ex pl<u>ore</u>	r. 20, 4, 11, 14 r. 20, 11 r. 20	Base word.
ex qu<u>i</u> šit<u>e</u>₅	r. 20	
fam il i år i ty fam il <u>iar</u> fam i ly	r. 24, 6 r. 24 r. 6	After children say the syllables, say, "In the last syllable, use ĭ, ī, instead of y and add the ending *ar*." For spelling, say ĭ ar. The letter i says the consonant *y* sound. Base word.
f<u>or</u>th f<u>ou̇</u>rth		

Spelling Word	Rule(s)	Instructional Tips
⎡ frac <u>ti</u>on al	r. 14	
⎣ frac <u>ti</u>on	r. 14	Base word.
grav i ty	r. 6	
<u>g</u>uard		
hŏr i zon tal		
Il li n<u>oi</u>s	r. 26, 29	For spelling, say *n oi s*. The French s is silent.
im ag i n<u>a</u> <u>ti</u>on	r. 11, 4, 14	
in d<u>e</u> pen den<u>ce</u>₃	r. 4	
In di an <u>O</u> <u>c</u>ean	r. 26, 4	
⎡ in dus tri al	r. 24	
⎣ in dus try	r. 6	Base word.
in tel li gent	r. 29	
in t<u>e</u> ri <u>or</u>	r. 4	
⎡ in vent <u>ed</u>	r. 28	
⎣ in ven <u>ti</u>on	r. 14	
lat i t<u>ude</u>		
lat t<u>er</u>	r. 29	
Lin co<u>l</u>n	r. 26	For spelling, say *c ŏ l n*.
⎡ lon gi t<u>u</u> din al	r. 4, 11	
⎣ lon gi t<u>ude</u>		

Spelling Word	Rule(s)	Instructional Tips
[mā chĭn er y ma chĭne₅]	r. 11, 6	After children say the syllables, say, "Write *machine* without the e and add the endings *er, y.*" Base word. The French i says *ē*.
mag ă zĭne₅	r. 4	After children say the syllables, say, "In the third syllable, *zine*, use the French i saying *ē*."
mir rŏr	r. 29	
mis tak en	r. 11	
[mŏis tŭre mŏist]		Base word.
North Ā mĕr i că	r. 26, 4	
oc că sĭon al ly	r. 29, 4, 16, 6	
[op pŏr tŭ ni ty op pŏr tūne]	r. 29, 4, 11, 6 r. 29	Base word.
Pă cif ic Ō cean	r. 26, 4	
păr ents		
pĕ cŭl ĭar	r. 4	For spelling, say *ĭ ar*. For reading, say *yar*.
pĕr pen dic ŭ lar	r. 4	
pĕr sĕ vĕre	r. 4	
rĕ prŏachĕd	r. 4, 28	

Spelling Word	Rule(s)	Instructional Tips
rev <u>er</u> en<u>ce</u>₃	r. 11	
rev <u>er</u> ent	r. 11	
r<u>e</u> v<u>ere</u>	r. 4	Base word.
rins<u>ed</u>	r. 11, 28	
rins<u>e</u>₅		Base word.
s<u>e</u> <u>quence</u>₃	r. 4	
s<u>e</u> r<u>ie</u>s	r. 4, 12	
sim i l<u>ar</u> i t<u>ie</u>s	r. 24	After children say the syllables, say, "In the last syllable, use ĭ, ī, instead of y and add es. The ie together says ĭ."
sim i l<u>ar</u> i ty	r. 6	
sim i l<u>ar</u>		Base word.
S<u>ou</u>th <u>A</u> mer i ca	r. 26, 4	
tr<u>ea</u>ch <u>er</u> y	r. 6	The phonogram ea saying ĕa never ends a syllable.
ty pi cal		
t<u>ype</u>		Base word. After children say the sounds for *type*, say, "Use y, ĭ, ī."
v<u>er</u> ti cal		

Section Y
125 Words for Spelling, Writing, and Reading

Spelling Words	Rule(s)	Instructional Tips
d<u>e</u> ci <u>si</u>on	r. 4, 16	Skip a space. Dictate the base word, *decide*, first. (*Continue to dictate the base word first throughout the section.*)
d<u>e</u> c<u>ide</u>	r. 4	

Spelling Word	Rule(s)	Instructional Tips
prin ci ple₄		
ac com mo̱ da̱te̱	r. 29, 4	For spelling, say both *c*'s and *m*'s. For reading, say only the *c* and *m* in the accented syllable *com*. (*Continue to require correct pronunciation for spelling and reading throughout the section.*)
ac cu̱ ra̱ cy	r. 29, 4, 6	For spelling, *y* says *ĭ*. (*Continue to require precise pronunciation of vowels in unaccented syllables throughout the section.*)
ac cu̱ ra̱te̱	r. 29, 4	Base word.
ap prox i ma̱te̱	r. 29, 20	
ap prox i ma̱te̱₅	r. 29, 20	
com mence̱₃	r. 29	
com me̱r cial	r. 29, 11, 14	
com merce̱₃	r. 29	Base word.
com mu̱ ni ca̱ tion	r. 29, 4, 11, 14	
com mu̱ ni ca̱te̱	r. 29, 4	Base word.
com plex	r. 20	
con clu̱ ²sion	r. 4, 16	
con struc tion	r. 14	
con struct		Base word. Be sure children say *c t*. (*Continue to require precise pronunciation throughout the section.*)
con ve̱r sa̱ tion	r. 11, 4, 14	
con verse̱₅		Base word.

Spelling Word	Rule(s)	Instructional Tips
coun ter feit	r. 12	
cul tu ral cul ture	r. 4, 11	Base word.
cu ri os i ty cu ri ous	r. 4, 6 r. 4	
des ert des sert	 r. 29	
di gest i ble di gest di gest	 r. 5	Base word.
E gyp tian E gypt	r. 26, 4, 14 r. 26, 4	Base word. After children say the syllables, say, "In the second syllable, the phonogram y says ĭ."
e lec trons	r. 4	
e qua tor i al e qua tor e qua tion e quate	r. 4 r. 4, 11 r. 4, 11, 14 r. 4	The phonogram ti says the uncommon sound zh. Base word.
ex pen sive	r. 20, 11	
ex pla na tion	r. 20, 4, 14	

Spelling Word	Rule(s)	Instructional Tips
ex ten <u>sion</u>	r. 20, 14	
ex ten si<u>ve</u>₂	r. 20	
ex tent	r. 20	
ex tend	r. 20	Base word.
im men<u>se</u>₅	r. 29	
in tr<u>o</u> du<u>ce</u>d	r. 4, 11, 28	
in tr<u>o</u> duc <u>tion</u>	r. 4, 14	
in vi<u>s</u> i b<u>le</u>₄		
<u>leo</u> p<u>ar</u>d		For spelling, say lē. The uncommon phonogram eo says ĕ.
lit <u>er</u> al ly	r. 6	
lit <u>er</u> ar y	r. 6	
lit <u>er</u> <u>a</u> t<u>ure</u>	r. 4, 11	
lit <u>er</u> at<u>e</u>₅		Base word.
man <u>u</u> fac tur <u>ing</u>	r. 4, 11	
man <u>u</u> fac t<u>ure</u>	r. 4	Base word.
Med i t<u>er</u> r<u>a</u> n<u>e</u> an	r. 26, 29, 4	
mem <u>o</u> r<u>a</u> b<u>le</u>₄	r. 4	
mem <u>o</u> ri al	r. 4, 24	
mem <u>o</u> r<u>ize</u>	r. 4, 24	B.E.: Spelling is mem <u>o</u> ri<u>se</u>.
mem <u>o</u> ry	r. 4, 6	Base word.
men tal ly	r. 6	

Spelling Word	Rule(s)	Instructional Tips
mil l_ion aire̲₅	r. 29	After children say the syllables, say, "In the second syllable, the phonogram i says the consonant sound *y*."
mi̲ no̊r i ty mi̲ n<u>or</u>	r. 5, 6 r. 5	Base word.
neg a̲ tive̲₂ ne̲ g<u>ate</u>	r. 4, 11 r. 4	
nu̲ me̊r i cal nu̲ mer o̊us nu̲ m<u>er</u> al	r. 4 r. 4 r. 4	Base word.
op <u>er</u> a̲ t<u>ion</u> op <u>er</u> a̲ t<u>or</u> op <u>er</u> <u>ate</u>	r. 4, 11, 14 r. 4, 11	Base word.
o̊r ch̲es tr̊a		
o̲ rig i nal o̲ rig i nat <u>ed</u> o̊r i gin	r. 4 r. 4, 11, 28	Base word.
p<u>ar</u> li̲a ment		For spelling, say *l ĭ ă.*
p<u>er</u> ceiv̊ed p<u>er</u> c<u>eive</u>₂	r. 12, 11, 28 r. 12	Base word.
p<u>er</u> f<u>or</u>m ance̲₃ p<u>er</u> f<u>or</u>m		Base word.
p<u>er</u> m̊a nent		

Spelling Word	Rule(s)	Instructional Tips
$\overset{2}{pos}$ i tiv$\underline{\underline{e}}_2$		
[pr$\underline{e}$ cip i t$\overset{4}{\underline{ou}}$s	r. 4	
prec i pic$\underline{\underline{e}}_3$		
pr$\underline{e}$ vi $\overset{4}{\underline{ou}}$s	r. 4	
[pr$\overset{2}{es}$ enc$\underline{\underline{e}}_3$		
pr$\overset{2}{es}$ ents		
[prim i tiv$\underline{\underline{e}}_2$	r. 11	
pr$\underline{i}$ m$\underline{a}$ ri ly	r. 5, 4, 24, 6	
pr$\underline{i}$ m$\underline{a}$ ry	r. 5, 11, 4, 6	
pr$\underline{ime}$		Base word.
[pr$\underline{o}$ fes $\underline{si}$on al	r. 4, 15	
pr$\underline{o}$ fes $\underline{si}$on	r. 4, 15	
[pr$\underline{o}$ jec $\underline{ti}$on	r. 4, 14	
pr$\underline{o}$ jec t$\underline{or}$	r. 4	
pr$\underline{o}$ ject	r. 4	Base word.
[qu$\overset{3}{a}$l i ti$\overset{3}{\underline{e}}\overset{2}{s}$	r. 24	
qu$\overset{3}{a}$l i ty	r. 6	Base word.
[qu$\overset{3}{a}$n ti ti$\overset{3}{\underline{e}}\overset{2}{s}$	r. 24	
qu$\overset{3}{a}$n ti ty	r. 6	Base word.
r$\underline{e}$ s$\underline{ear}$ch	r. 4	

Spelling Word	Rule(s)	Instructional Tips
re šem blance₃ re šem ble₅	r. 4, 11 r. 4	Base word.
rec om mend	r. 29	
re la tion ship re la tion re late	r. 4, 14, 13 r. 4, 14 r. 4	Base word.
res tau rănt		
scarce ly	r. 6	
scheme		
seizĕd seize₅	r. 12, 11, 28 r. 12	Base word.
se lec tion	r. 4, 14	
sim pli ci ty sim pli fiĕd sim pli fy sim ple₄	r. 11, 6 r. 24, 28 r. 11, 5, 6 	Base word.
sub mă rine₅ mă rine₅		For spelling, say r ĭ n ē. The Latin i says ē.
su per in ten dent	r. 4	
sur geon		After children say the syllables, say, "The uncommon phonogram ge says j."
tel e scope	r. 4	

Spelling Word	Rule(s)	Instructional Tips
tĕr ri to ri al tĕr ri to ry	r. 29, 4, 24 r. 29, 4, 6	Base word.
thor ough ly	r. 6	After children say the syllables, say, "In the first syllable, use the phonogram or saying *er*, an uncommon sound."
tre men dŏus	r. 4	

Section Z
125 Words for Spelling, Writing, and Reading

Spelling Words	Rule(s)	Instructional Tips
judg ment judge	r. 23	Skip a space. Dictate the base word, *judge*, first. (*Continue to dictate the base word first throughout the section.*) B.E.: Spelling is *judge ment*.
rec om men dĕd rec om mend	r. 29, 28 r. 29	Base word. For spelling, say both *m*'s. For reading, say only the *m* in the accented syllable *mend*. (*Continue to require correct pronunciation for spelling and reading throughout the section.*)
al le giance al lege	r. 29, 4, 11 r. 29	After children say the syllables, say, "In the third syllable, add the endings *i ance*. The *gi* together says *j*." Base word.
a byss	r. 4, 17	After children say the syllables, say, "In the second syllable, use *y* to say *ĭ*."
ac quaint ance		

Spelling Word	Rule(s)	Instructional Tips
<u>a</u> pol <u>o</u> g<u>ize</u>	r. 4, 24	B.E.: Spelling is <u>a</u> pol <u>o</u> g$\overset{2}{i}$<u>s</u>e.
ap pr<u>o</u> pri <u>ate</u>	r. 29, 4	
ap pr<u>o</u> pri at<u>e</u>₅	r. 29, 4	
cant <u>a</u> l$\overset{2}{ou}$p<u>e</u>₅	r. 4	
c<u>au</u> li fl<u>ow</u> <u>er</u>		
cem <u>e</u> t$\overset{1}{e}$r y	r. 4, 6	For spelling, y says ĭ. *(Continue to require precise pronunciation of vowels in unaccented syllables throughout the section.)*
$\overset{3}{ch}$an d<u>e</u> l<u>ier</u>	r. 4, 12	
fin an c<u>ier</u>	r. 11	Exception to rule 12.
$\overset{3}{ch}$<u>auf</u> f<u>eur</u>	r. 29	For spelling, say $\overset{3}{ch}$ au f f ĕ ur. For reading, say $\overset{3}{ch}$ō fur.
com bus ti bl<u>e</u>₄		
con <u>sci</u> en t$\overset{4}{iou}$s	r. 14	After children say the syllables, say, "In the second syllable, use the uncommon phonogram sci. The i has two functions: It forms the phonogram that says *sh* and it provides the vowel sound for the syllable *shĭ*."
dis c<u>er</u>n i bl<u>e</u>₄	r. 29	
dis c<u>er</u>n	r. 29	Base word.
dis ci plin<u>e</u>₅	r. 29	
dis pens<u>e</u>₅		

Spelling Word	Rule(s)	Instructional Tips
dis sen <u>sion</u>	r. 29, 14	
dis sent	r. 29	Base word.
drȧ³ mat i cal ly	r. 6	
drȧ³ mat ic		
drȧ³ mȧ³		Base word.
e c<u>o</u> nom i cal	r. 4	
e c<u>o</u> nom ic	r. 4, 24	
e con <u>o</u> my	r. 4, 6	Base word.
e lim i n<u>ate</u>	r. 4	
ef fi <u>cien</u> cy	r. 29, 14	
ef fi <u>cient</u>	r. 29, 14	
em bȧr¹ rass ment	r. 29	
em bȧr¹ rass	r. 29, 17	Base word.
en dĕav² <u>or</u>		B.E.: Spelling is en dĕav² <u>ou</u>r.
en <u>thu</u>² ²si a²sm	r. 4	
ex tr<u>ao</u>r di nȧr¹ y	r. 20, 6	After children say the syllables, say, "In the second syllable, say t r ă or."
fȧ¹ ti <u>guing</u>	r. 11	
fȧ¹ <u>tigue</u>₂		Base word. For spelling, say t ĭ gu ē. The French i says ē.
<u>for</u> mal ly	r. 6	
<u>for</u> mal		Base word.

Spelling Word	Rule(s)	Instructional Tips
fron t<u>ie</u>r	r. 12	
g<u>u</u>ár an t<u>ee</u>		
<u>g</u>ui tar		
h<u>u</u> m<u>or</u> <u>ou</u>́s	r. 4	
h<u>u</u> m<u>or</u>	r. 4	Base word. B.E.: Spelling is h<u>u</u> m<u>ou</u>́r.
im pres s<u>ive</u>₌₂	r. 29	
im pres <u>s</u>ion	r. 15	
im press	r. 17	Base word.
in ces sant	r. 29	
Iš̆ r<u>ae</u> li	r. 26	For spelling, say r ā ē.
Iš̆ r<u>a</u> el	r. 26, 4	Base word.
l<u>ea</u>gue₌₂		
ma<u>th</u> <u>e</u> mat i cal	r. 4	
ma<u>th</u> <u>e</u> mat ics	r. 4	
mil i tár y	r. 6	
mi li t<u>ia</u>́	r. 14	
mis cel l<u>a</u> n<u>e</u> <u>ou</u>́s	r. 29, 4	
mis <u>chie</u>́ v<u>ou</u>́s	r. 12	B.E.: mis <u>chie</u>́ <u>v</u>oús
mis <u>chie</u>́f	r. 12	Base word.
m<u>or</u>t ga<u>ge</u>		

Spelling Word	Rule(s)	Instructional Tips
m*u* ni ci pal	r. 4	
[n*eu* tral *Eu* rope p*neu* mo ni *å*[3] l*ieu* ten ant	r. 26 r. 4	After children say the syllables, say, "In the first syllable, use the uncommon phonogram eu saying *ū*." After children say the syllables, say, "In the first syllable, use the uncommon phonograms pn saying *n* and eu saying *ū*." For spelling, say *l ĭ eu*. B.E.: Pronunciation varies.
oc c*ur* r*ence*[3]	r. 29, 10	B.E.: oc c*ŭr* ren*ce*[3].
p*år*[1] al lel	r. 29	
[p*er* cen t*age* p*er* cent		Base word.
[p*er* sis ten*ce*[3] p*er* sist		Base word.
p*hy*[2] *s̆i* cian	r. 14	
p*or* c*e* l*ai*n	r. 4	
priv i *lege*[3]		
[pr*o* fi *ci*en cy pr*o* fi *ci*ent	r. 4, 14, 6 r. 4, 14	Base word.
rec i p*e*	r. 4	
r*e* flect *ed*	r. 4, 28	Be sure children say *k t*. *(Continue to require precise pronunciation throughout the section.)*

Spelling Word	Rule(s)	Instructional Tips
ren dez v$\overset{3}{\underline{ou}}\underline{s}$		For spelling, say *rĕn dĕz v$\overset{3}{\underline{ou}}\underline{s}$*. For reading, say *ră̇n dā v$\overset{3}{\underline{ou}}$*. The French s is silent.
re$\overset{2}{}$ šist an<u>ce</u>₃ re$\overset{2}{}$ šist	r. 4 r. 4	 Base word.
<u>rh</u>ap s<u>o</u> dy <u>rh</u>i noc <u>er</u> os <u>rh</u>u b<u>ar</u>b	r. 4, 6 r. 5 r. 4	After children say the syllables, say, "In the first syllable, the uncommon phonogram rh says *r*."
sa<u>l</u>m on		For spelling, say *s ă l m*.
sat el l<u>ite</u>s	r. 29	
sat is fac <u>ti</u>on sat is fac t<u>o</u> ry sat is f$\overset{2\ 2}{\underline{ie}}$d sat is f<u>y</u>	r. 14 r. 4, 6 r. 24, 28 r. 5, 6	 Base word.
<u>sh</u>elv$\overset{2}{\underline{e}}$s <u>sh</u>elf	 r. 13	 Base word.
s<u>o</u> l<u>ar</u>	r. 4	
s$\overset{3}{\underline{ou}}$ v<u>e</u> n$\overset{1}{\underline{ir}}$	r. 4	
sov <u>er</u> $\overset{3}{\underline{eig}}$n	r. 12	
sp<u>e</u> c<u>ie</u>$\overset{2}{\underline{s}}$	r. 4, 14	

Spelling Word	Rule(s)	Instructional Tips
spe cif i cal ly	r. 4, 6	
spe ci fic	r. 4	
spec i fied	r. 24, 28	
spec i fy	r. 5, 6	Base word.
suf fi cient ly	r. 29, 14, 6	
syl la bles	r. 29, 4	
syl la ble	r. 29, 4	Base word.
tech nol o gy	r. 4, 6	
tech niques		For spelling, say *n ĭ qu ĕ s*. The French i says *ē*. The qu says *k*, an uncommon sound.
tech ni cal		
the o ry	r. 4, 6	
tor toise		
tran quil li ty	r. 10, 6	
tran quil		Base word.
u nique	r. 4	For spelling, say *n ĭ qu ĕ*. The French i says *ē*. The qu says *k*, an uncommon sound.
u ni ver si ty	r. 4, 11, 6	
u ni ver sal	r. 4, 11	
u ni verse	r. 4	Base word.
vac u um	r. 4	
vague ly	r. 6	
vague		

Spelling Word	Rule(s)	Instructional Tips
vic to̲ ri o̲u̲s	r. 4, 24	
vic to̲ ry	r. 4, 6	
vi̲ o̲ lenc̲e̲₃	r. 5, 4	
vi̲ o̲ lent	r. 5, 4	
xy̲ lo phone	r. 5, 4	After children say the syllables, say, "In the first syllable, use the phonogram x saying z, an uncommon sound."

EXTENDED AYRES WORD LIST: ALPHABETIZED

THE ALPHABETIZED Extended Ayres Word List is a handy reference for parents and teachers. Words can be located quickly when students ask questions about particular markings, spellings, or pronunciations. The list is also useful when words are needed to provide additional practice of specific rules or phonograms. Being able to find words quickly and easily conserves valuable instructional time.

Word	Section	Page
a	A–G	254
ability	S	343
able	L	290
aboard	O	312
about	H	266
above	L	291
absence	T	350
absent	T	350
abyss	Z	340
accept	T	348
accident	T	348
accommodate	Y	384
according	R	335
account	M	298
accuracy	Y	384
accurate	Y	384
ache	T	350
aches	T	350
achieve	U	359
achieves	U	359
acquaintance	Z	390
acquire	U	359
across	K	286
act	N, Q	308, 329
action	Q	329
active	W	371
activities	W	371
activity	W	371
actual	W	371
actually	W	371
add	I	274
addition	Q	325
address	O	315
adjective	X	377
admission	O	316
adopt	R	334
advantage	X	377
advice	R	337
advise	R	337
affair	S	341
affect	X	377
afraid	O	311
Africa	X	377
after	I	272
afternoon	K	283
again	M, R	299, 336
against	R	336
age	J	276
ago	A–G	257
agree	U	358
agreement	U	358
air	J	280
alike	I	273
all	A–G	258

Word	Section	Page
allege	Z	390
allegiance	Z	390
allow	Q	327
almost	M	299
alone	H, L	265, 295
along	J	280
already	R	335
also	M	300
although	Q	330
altitude	X	377
always	N	306
am	A–G	256
America	R	337
American	R	337
among	N	308
amount	P	321
amusement	T	350
an	A–G	256
ancestors	X	377
ancient	U	359
and	A–G	254
anger	T	351
angle	W	371
angrily	T	351
angry	T	351
angular	W	371
animal	P	323
ankle	Q	330
annual	X	377
another	L	293
answer	P	322
ant	N	304
Antarctica	X	378
antique	W	371
anxiety	W	371
anxious	W	371
any	K	283
anyone	U	359
anything	L	291
anyway	M	302
apiece	U	359
apologize	Z	391
apparent	V	363
appear	O	314
appearance	S	343
appears	Q	330
apple	H	267
application	U	356
applied	X	378
apply	U, X	356, 378
applying	X	378
appoint	Q	328
appreciate	W	370

Word	Section	Page
appreciative	W	370
approaches	U	359
appropriate	Z	391
approval	T	351
approve	T	351
approximate	Y	384
April	N	307
architecture	X	378
Arctic Ocean	X	378
are	A–G	259
argue	T	347
argument	T	347
army	M	298
around	K	285
arrange	Q, V	330, 363
arrangement	V	363
arrest	Q	328
arrive	S	341
article	R	336
artificial	X	378
as	H	265
ascend	U	357
ascending	V	363
ascent	U	357
Asia	X	378
ask	H	264
assist	S	341
associate	T	349
association	T, V	349, 363
assure	U	356
at	A–G	254
ate	H, O	267, 311
athlete	W	370
athletic	W	370
Atlantic Ocean	X	378
atmosphere	S	343
atmospheric	S	343
attack	U	259
attempt	Q	330
attend	O	315
attention	R	335
attorney	U	359
August	O	315
aunt	N	304
Australia	X	378
author	H	267
auto	P	319
automobile	T	348
autumn	S	343
available	T	351
avenue	R	333
average	W	371
avoid	T	351

Word	Section	Page
await	Q	329
away	I	271
awe	P	319
awful	P	319
baby	H	266
back	I	271
backward	Q	329
bad	A–G	257
bag	A–G	260
bake	N	309
baking	N	309
balance	U	359
ball	H	264
banana	T	351
band	J	276
bare	K	285
bargain	R	337
basic	V	363
basically	V	363
basin	P	323
be	A–G, N	257, 308
bear	K	285
beautiful	P	319
beauty	P	319
became	K	281
because	L	292
become	K	285
bed	A–G	255
been	N	308
before	L, S	293
beg	A–G	260
began	L	289
begin	L	289
beginning	L	289
begun	M	297
behavior	S	342
behind	K	285
believe	S	342
belong	H	263
belongs	L	295
beneath	R	337
beneficial	X	378
benefit	X	378
beside	M	297
best	I	273
better	K	284
between	K	282
beyond	R	337
bicycle	W	371
big	A–G	260
bill	J	278
bird	A–G	262
biscuits	T	351
black	L	289
block	I	269

Word	Section	Page
blow	I	269
blows	I	269
blue	A–G, J	257, 275
board	O	314
boat	J	276
body	L	295
bog	A–G	260
bone	K	287
book	A–G	259
born	M	297
both	M	299
bottle	T	357
bottom	T	357
bough	V	364
bought	M	298
boundaries	X	378
boundary	X	378
bouquet	W	371
bow	V	364
bowl	N	309
box	H	263
boy	A–G	259
brace	Q	330
bracelet	Q	330
brave	I	274
bread	H	267
break	R	337
breakfast	M	302
breath	Q	331
breathe	Q	331
breeze	P	323
bridge	N	304
brilliant	X	378
bring	H, M	264, 299
broke	N, R	306, 337
broken	R	337
brother	K	281
brought	M	299
brown	H	267
bruise	T	351
bruised	T	351
bug	A–G	260
build	M	300
built	M	300
burn	K	285
business	T	349
busy	R, T	334, 349
but	A–G	257
butcher	L	289
button	P	323
buy	L	290

Word	Section	Page
by	A–G, L	259, 290
cabbage	P	323
calculate	U	359
calculation	U	359
calendar	W	371
calf	Q	328
call	H	265
calm	Q	331
calves	Q	328
came	I	271
camp	K	285
campaign	V	364
can	A–G	254
cannot	J	277
canoe	O	316
cantaloupe	Z	391
canvas	S	343
capital	V	364
capitol	V	364
captain	O	316
capture	N	304
car	J	278
card	J	275
care	K	285
career	V	363
careful	P	323
carriage	S	342
carried	P	320
carry	N, P, S	305, 320, 342
case	M	300
cast	J	275
catch	L	289
catcher	L	289
caught	P	322
cauliflower	Z	391
cause	L	292
caution	O	316
cautious	O	316
ceiling	S	344
celebration	T	350
celery	S	344
cellar	O	316
cemetery	Z	391
cent	K, S	283, 341
center	N	305
central	U	359
centuries	W	371
century	S, W	341, 371
cereal	V	364
ceremony	U	359
certain	S	343

Word	Section	Page	Word	Section	Page	Word	Section	Page
certainly	S	343	clerk	P	321	confer	T	350
chain	N	305	climate	W	372	conference	T	350
chair	J	280	climb	M	302	congress	X	379
chalk	L	290	close	L	294	connect	Q	326
chance	A–G, M	257, 302	clothe	L	289	connection	Q	326
chandelier	Z	391	clothes	L	289	conscientious	Z	391
change	M, T	301, 351	clothing	L	289	consented	Q	331
changeable	T	351	cloud	K	287	consequence	W	372
changing	M	301	club	K	286	consider	R	336
chapter	T	351	coarse	S, V	341, 364	consideration	U	355
character	W	370				construct	Y	384
characteristics	X	378	cocoa	R	337	construction	Y	384
charge	A–G, M	257, 300	coffee	M	302	contagious	X	379
			cold	A–G	261	contain	O	313
chauffeur	Z	391	collar	R	337	contains	M	302
cheap	N	309	collect	M	297	continent	X	379
check	N	305	college	S	344	continental	X	379
cheerful	N	309	colonel	X	379	continue	Q	331
cheese	L	295	colonial	U	355	continued	Q	331
Chicago	X	378	colonies	U	355	contract	M	299
chicken	N	309	colony	U	355	control	R	338
chief	O	313	color	M	302	controlled	R	338
child	A–G, M	261, 300	columns	V	364	convene	X	377
			combination	R	333	convenient	X	377
children	M	300	combine	R	333	convention	R	335
chimney	T	351	combustible	Z	391	conversation	Y	384
chocolate	X	379	come	A–G, K	260, 287	converse	Y	384
choice	V	364				convict	Q	326
choir	T	352	comfort	O	311	cool	A–G	262
choose	V	364	coming	K	287	copy	N	308
chose	V	364	command	Q	326	cordial	W	370
chosen	V	364	commence	Y	384	cordially	W	370
Christ	R	337	commerce	Y	384	corn	I	274
Christmas	R	337	commercial	Y	384	corner	W	372
church	L	293	commit	X	377	correct	V	364
circle	T, U	347, 357	committee	X	377	cost	K	284
			common	R	335	cotton	W	372
circular	T	347	communicate	Y	384	cough	P	323
circumference	U	357	communication	Y	384	could	K	282
circumstance	U	357	communities	S	344	count	W	372
circus	Q	331	community	S	344	counterfeit	Y	385
cities	P	322	companion	S	342	countless	W	372
citizen	U	358	company	O	314	country	L	293
city	K, P, U	283, 322, 358	compare	R	337	courage	Q	332
			comparison	R	337	course	S	341
			compete	T	352	court	N	308
civil	X	379	complaint	P	319	cousin	P	323
civilization	X	379	complete	R	336	cover	J	276
civilize	X	379	complex	Y	384	covered	O	316
civilized	X	379	composed	W	372	create	S	344
claim	Q	328	composition	W	372	created	S	344
class	K	285	concealed	U	359	creation	S	344
clean	K	285	concern	T	348	creative	S	344
clear	K	285	concert	S	344	creature	O	316
			conclusion	Y	384	crowd	Q	326
			condition	S	342	cultural	Y	385

Word	Section	Page	Word	Section	Page	Word	Section	Page
culture	Y	385	determined	T	352	dollars	P	323
curiosity	Y	385	develop	U, X	357,	don't	O	316
curious	Y	385			379	done	L	290
current	V	364	development	X	379	door	H	263
curtain	O	316	dew	Q	327	doubt	S	342
cut	I	269	diagonal	X	379	down	J	278
daily	M	302	diagram	W	372	dozen	N	309
dance	I	274	diameter	X	379	Dr.	V	365
dangerous	Q	331	diamond	R	335	drama	Z	392
dark	J	276	dictionary	S	344	dramatic	Z	392
dash	L	290	did	A–G	258	dramatically	Z	392
date	L	292	die	M	301	draw	K, V	287,
daughter	P	322	died	M	301			365
day	H, M	263,	differ	R	335	drawn	V	365
		302	difference	S	341	dress	M	297
dead	L	294	different	R	335	drew	V	365
deal	M	299	difficult	U	356	dried	Q	331
dear	I	273	difficulty	U	356	drill	M	297
death	N	305	digest	Y	385	drink	K	287
debate	Q	326	digestible	Y	385	drive	N	310
debt	Q	331	dinner	I	274	driven	M	298
debts	R	338	direct	O, R	314,	driving	N	310
deceive	T	352			335	drop	U	360
December	N	309	direction	O	314	dropped	U	360
decide	S, T, Y	344,	director	R	335	drown	R	334
		349,	disappear	U	360	dry	Q	331
		383	disappoint	X	377	due	Q	327
decided	S	344	disaster	R	338	during	O	315
decision	T, Y	349,	discern	Z	391	duty	O	314
		383	discernible	Z	391	each	I	271
declare	O	316	discipline	Z	391	eager	R	338
declared	O	316	discover	T	352	eagle	M	302
deep	J	275	discoveries	T	352	earliest	U	355
degree	P	320	discovery	T	352	early	L, U	294,
delay	K	285	discuss	V	362			355
delicious	U	359	discussion	V	362	earn	L	295
department	P	320	disease	W	372	earth	A–G	262
depend	W	372	dispense	Z	391	ease	K	287
dependent	W	372	dissension	Z	392	east	J	276
depends	W	372	dissent	Z	392	eastern	S	345
depth	X	379	distance	O	316	easy	K	287
descend	U	357	distant	O	316	eat	H	263
descent	U	357	distinguish	U	355	eats	H	267
describe	U	360	distribute	R	336	echo	N	310
described	U	360	district	O	312	echoes	N	310
description	X	379	divide	U, V	359,	economic	Z	392
descriptive	X	379			364	economical	Z	392
desert	Y	385	division	V	364	economy	Z	392
design	S	344	do	A–G, L, P	254,	edge	L	295
desirable	V	364			290,	education	R	335
desire	P, V	322,			321	effect	R, X	336,
		364	doctor	N	308			379
dessert	Y	385	does	P	321	effective	X	379
destroy	P	322	dog	H	267	efficiency	Z	392
determination	T	352	doll	I	274	efficient	Z	392
determine	T	352	dollar	N	306	effort	Q	327

Word	Section	Page	Word	Section	Page	Word	Section	Page
egg	I	274	equip	V	365	explorers	X	380
Egypt	Y	385	equipment	V	365	explosion	Q	331
Egyptian	Y	385	equipped	V	365	express	L	291
eight	M, O	302, 311	equivalent	W	372	expression	W	373
			err	T	352	exquisite	X	380
either	Q	327	error	T	352	extend	Y	385
elaborate	U	358	escape	P	321	extension	Y	385
elect	O	312	especially	X	377	extensive	Y	385
election	O	312	essential	X	380	extent	Y	385
electric	T	352	establish	U	360	extra	M	296
electrical	T	352	established	U	360	extraordinary	Z	392
electrician	T	352	establishment	U	360	extreme	V, W	365, 370
electricity	T	352	estate	Q	327			
electrons	Y	385	estimate	T	348	extremely	V	365
elegant	U	360	Europe	X, Z	380, 394	eye	K	282
element	W	372				face	I	268
elementary	W	372	even	K	283	fact	O	314
elephant	S	344	evening	N	306	factors	W	373
eliminate	Z	392	event	M	299	factory	Q	326
else	N	304	eventually	X	380	fail	K	286
embarrass	Z	392	ever	L	293	fair	N	306
embarrassment	Z	392	every	J	279	fairy	N	310
emergency	W	369	everybody	S	344	fall	I	270
emperor	U	360	everyone	W	372	fame	Q	327
empire	P	320	everything	O	313	familiar	X	380
employ	Q, X	325, 380	everywhere	W	373	familiarity	X	380
			evidence	V	363	family	P, X	320, 380
employee	X	380	exact	T	352			
empty	W	372	examination	S	341	famous	Q	327
enclose	Q	329	examine	S	341	fancy	M	302
end	I	270	example	R	338	far	I	273
endeavor	Z	392	excel	U	360	fare	N	306
enemy	R	338	excellent	U	360	farther	O	314
engage	Q	325	except	N	304	fast	H	267
engine	P	320	exceptions	T	352	father	L	291
England	X	380	exchange	X	380	fatigue	W, Z	373, 392
English	X	380	excite	R	338			
enjoy	P	318	excitement	R	338	fatiguing	Z	392
enormous	X	380	exciting	R	338	favor	P, T	321, 352
enough	O	314	exclaimed	W	373			
enter	M	298	exclamation	W	373	favorable	T	352
entered	T	352	excuse	P	323	favorite	T	352
entertain	R	333	exercise	Q	331	fear	V	365
enthusiasm	Z	392	exhaust	Q	331	fearful	V	365
entire	Q	327	exist	X	380	feather	L	295
entitle	T	349	existence	X	380	feature	R	336
entrance	P	319	expect	N	306	February	W	371
envelop	U	357	expense	U	356	feed	A–G	262
envelope	U	357	expensive	Y	385	feel	N	307
environment	W	372	experience	V	363	feet	I	269
equal	W	372	experiment	W	373	fell	L	290
equality	W	372	experimental	W	373	felt	K	286
equate	Y	385	explain	O	317	female	K	281
equation	Y	385	explanation	Y	385	fence	L	295
equator	Y	385	exploration	X	380	few	M	301
equatorial	Y	385	explore	X	380	field	L	295

Word	Section	Page	Word	Section	Page	Word	Section	Page
fierce	R	338	fourth	O, X	312, 380	gone	L	290
fifth	N	309	fraction	X	381	good	A–G	256
fight	L	290	fractional	X	381	goose	K	288
figure	O	313	free	I	270	got	I	268
file	M	297	freeze	M	303	govern	S	342
fill	J	280	frequency	W	373	government	S	342
final	Q, U	325, 357	frequent	W	373	gradual	W	373
finally	U	357	Friday	K	284	gradually	W	373
financier	Z	391	friend	O	315	grammar	Q	331
find	I	272	friends	O	315	grand	J	275
fine	J	277	frighten	S	344	grant	L	291
finish	K	286	frightened	S	344	grateful	U	360
fire	J	276	from	J	279	gravity	X	381
firm	Q	326	front	N	305	great	M	301
first	K	283	frontier	Z	393	green	A–G	262
five	H	264	fruit	I	274	grief	P	323
fix	M	297	fuel	T	353	grocery	S	344
fixed	M	297	full	K	286	ground	L	294
flew	R	338	function	V	365	group	S	345
flies	R	338	functional	V	365	grow	M	303
flight	P	319	funny	L	295	growth	T	353
floated	O	317	fur	A–G	262	guarantee	Z	393
floor	H	263	furniture	V	365	guard	P, X	323, 381
flour	L	294	further	S	342			
flower	L	294	future	V	365	guess	P, J	280, 320
fly	M, R	302, 338	game	J	276			
folk	T	350	garden	K	288	guest	P	320
folks	T	350	gather	U	360	guide	R	338
follow	M	300	gathering	V	365	guilty	P	323
food	H	267	gave	I	273	guitar	Z	393
foot	I	269	general	R	336	had	A–G	259
for	H	266	generally	U	360	half	L, Q	291, 328
foreign	U, W	356, 373	gentle	M, Q	303, 329			
						halves	Q	328
foreigners	W	373	gentleman	Q	329	hand	A–G	260
forest	M	303	genuine	T	353	handful	T	353
forget	J	275	get	H, O	265, 316	hang	J	280
forgot	J, R	280, 338				happen	M	297
			getting	O	316	happy	J	275
forgotten	R	338	ghost	O	317	hard	J	276
form	I, J	273, 279	giant	R	338	hardly	T	353
			gigantic	R	338	has	H	266
formal	Z	392	girl	J	278	hat	A–G	261
formally	Z	392	girls	J	278	have	A–G	259
forth	X	380	give	I	272	he	A–G	255
fortune	P	320	glad	J	280	head	K	284
forty	O	312	glass	K	282	health	S	345
forward	Q	329	go	A–G, L, M	254, 290, 297	hear	N	305
fought	T	353				heard	N	305
found	J	278	god	N	307	heart	M	300
four	L, O	292, 312	God	N	307	heavier	V	365
			goes	M	297	heavily	V	365
fourteen	O	312	going	L	295	heavy	V	365
			gold	J	277	height	V	363
						heir	U	360
						held	L	293

Word	Section	Page	Word	Section	Page	Word	Section	Page
help	J	276	illustration	R	335	investigation	T	353
her	H, I	266, 273	image	V	366	invisible	Y	386
here	J, L	278, 294	imagination	X	381	invitation	T	348
herself	L	292	imagine	V	366	invite	T	348
high	L, V	291, 363	immediate	X	376	involve	T	353
him	A–G	258	immense	Y	386	involved	T	353
himself	N	307	importance	P	319	iron	M	303
his	H, I	267, 273	important	P	319	is	A–G	254
history	N	307	impossible	T	348	island	P	323
hoarse	U	360	impress	Z	393	Israel	Z	393
hold	M	297	impression	Z	393	Israeli	Z	393
hole	O	315	impressive	Z	393	issue	U	357
holes	M	303	imprison	Q	330	isthmus	W	373
holiday	O	317	improve	S	340	it	A–G	254
holy	O	317	improvement	S	340	it's	I	273
home	H	264	in	A–G	255	its	I	273
honey	L	296	incessant	Z	393	itself	N	306
honor	R	334	inches	V	366	jail	O	312
hop	K	288	include	Q	327	January	N	308
hope	J	280	income	M	298	journal	Q	332
hopping	K	288	increase	R	336	journey	Q	332
horizontal	X	381	indeed	L	292	judge	O, Z	313, 390
horse	K	285	independence	X	381			
hot	A–G	261	independent	V	366	judgment	Z	390
hotel	M	303	Indian	Q	331	July	K	284
hour	K	284	Indian Ocean	X	381	jump	H	267
house	H	265	indicate	U	361	June	L	292
how	H	266	indication	U	361	just	H, Q	264, 329
however	L	294	individual	V	366			
human	P	321	industrial	X	381	justice	Q	329
humor	Z	393	industry	X	381	keep	K	281
humorous	Z	393	influence	V	366	kill	A–G	260
hundred	V	365	inform	M	299	kind	J	278
hungry	P	323	information	Q	328	kitchen	L	289
hurried	R	339	inherit	U	360	knee	O	317
hurry	R	339	injure	R	336	knew	O	314
hurrying	R	339	injury	R	336	knife	K	288
hurt	K	286	innocent	V	366	knock	N	310
husband	P	321	inside	J	275	know	L, O, P, R	293, 314, 322, 339
hymn	T	353	inspect	N	306			
I	H, K	265, 282	instance	V	366			
			instead	O	313			
			instrument	V	366	knowledge	R	339
ice	A–G	261	instrumental	V	366	known	P	322
icicle	U	360	intelligent	X	381	lace	I	270
identified	U	361	intend	O	314	lady	K	284
identify	U	361	interest	R	337	laid	Q	332
if	H	266	interfere	U	361	lake	I	270
ignorance	U	361	interference	U	361	land	A–G	261
ignorant	U	361	interior	X	381	language	P	324
ignore	U	361	into	A–G	258	large	J	277
Illinois	X	381	introduced	Y	386	last	A–G	256
illustrate	R	335	introduction	Y	386	late	A–G	260
			invented	X	381	latitude	X	381
			invention	X	381	latter	X	381
			investigate	S	343	laugh	P	324

Word	Section	Page	Word	Section	Page	Word	Section	Page
laughter	P	324	location	V	366	meat	J, L	280, 293
law	H	264	lone	H	265	medal	T	353
lawyer	R	339	long	H, P	265, 322	medicine	T	353
lay	H, Q	267, 332	longitude	X	381	Mediterranean	Y	386
lead	L	294	longitudinal	X	381	meet	L	293
leader	U	361	look	A–G	258	member	M	300
leadership	U	361	looks	I	274	memorable	Y	386
league	Z	393	loose	R	333	memorial	Y	386
learn	N	305	lose	R	333	memorize	Y	386
least	N	307	loss	P	320	memory	Y	386
leather	N	310	lost	J	280	men	H	266
leave	L	294	lot	H	263	mentally	Y	386
led	H, L	294	love	H	265	mention	S	341
ledge	Q	328	low	A	263	mere	U	357
left	J	277	lying	O	317	message	U	361
leisure	V	366	machine	R, X	333, 382	messenger	U	361
lemon	O	317				metal	T	353
length	P	322	machinery	X	382	method	V	366
leopard	Y	386	made	J	279	might	M	299
less	M	299	magazine	X	382	mile	K	283
lesson	L	291	magnificent	V	366	military	Z	393
let	A–G	260	mail	K	281	militia	Z	393
letter	I	272	main	V	366	million	S	342
letters	L	296	major	U	358	millionaire	Y	387
level	W	373	majority	U	358	mind	L	294
liberty	O	314	make	A–G	259	mine	J	280
library	W	373	male	K	281	minerals	V	366
license	V	366	man	A–G, H	255, 266	minor	Y	387
lie	O	317				minority	Y	387
lieutenant	Z	394	manner	R	336	minute	T	350
life	J	278	manufacture	Y	386	mirror	X	382
light	K	287	manufacturing	Y	386	miscellaneous	Z	393
like	A–G	259	many	K	283	mischief	Z	393
lilies	T	353	March	L	292	mischievous	Z	393
lily	T	353	march	L	292	Miss	M, P	301, 321
Lincoln	X	381	marine	Y	389			
line	J, P	277, 324	marriage	S	342	miss	I, M, P	268, 301
linen	N	310	marry	S	342	mistaken	X	382
lining	P	324	mass	T	353	Mister	I, P	272
liquid	V	366	massive	T	353	mixture	N	310
list	L	293	material	U	357	model	W	373
listen	S	345	mathematical	Z	393	modern	V	367
listened	S	345	mathematics	Z	393	moist	X	382
literally	Y	386	matter	N	307	moisture	X	382
literary	Y	386	may	A–G, J	258, 277	moment	W	373
literate	Y	386				Monday	I	271
literature	Y	386	May	J	277	money	M	302
little	A–G	257	maybe	K	286	monkey	M	303
live	A–G, M	260, 303	mayor	P	320	month	M	300
			me	A–G	254	moon	I	271
living	M	303	mean	N, U	308, 355	more	J	279
local	S	341				morning	L	294
locate	V	366	meant	U	355	mortgage	Z	393
located	V	366	measure	O	312	mosquito	W	374

Word	Section	Page	Word	Section	Page	Word	Section	Page
most	J	279	nine	I	268	one	H, L	265, 293
mother	A–G	261	nineteen	P	324	onion	S	342
motion	S	340	ninety	T	353	only	K	283
mountain	M	298	no	A–G, L	255, 293	open	K	284
mouse	J	281				operate	Y	387
mouth	K	288	nobody	O	317	operation	Y	387
move	K	285	noise	M	303	operator	Y	387
Mr.	I, P	272, 321	none	O	314	opinion	S	342
			nonsense	W	374	opportune	X	382
Mrs.	P	320	noon	J	275	opportunity	X	382
much	H	264	nor	N	308	opposite	W	374
municipal	Z	394	north	I	268	opposition	W	374
muscle	W	374	North America	X	382	or	I, N	273, 308
muscular	W	374	northern	S	345			
music	O, U	315, 361	not	A–G	256	orange	L	296
			nothing	L	294	orchestra	Y	387
musician	U	361	notice	P	324	order	L	295
must	A–G	259	noticed	P	324	ordinarily	V	367
my	A–G	256	November	N	307	ordinary	V	367
myself	M	303	now	A–G	255	organization	W	369
mysterious	V	367	number	N	309	organize	T, W	348, 369
mystery	V	367	numeral	Y	387			
nails	O	317	numerical	Y	387	origin	Y	387
name	J	280	numerous	Y	387	original	Y	387
narrow	W	374	oak	K	288	originated	Y	387
nation	N, T	310, 349	oar	O	317	other	H	266
			object	O	312	ought	T	350
national	T	349	objection	O	312	our	J, K	279, 284
natural	W	374	observation	W	374			
naturalist	W	374	observatory	W	374	out	A–G	258
naturally	W	374	observe	W	374	outside	J	276
nature	W	374	obtain	P	320	over	A–G	259
naughty	P	322	occasion	V	367	own	L	293
navy	O	312	occasionally	X	382	Pacific Ocean	X	382
near	J	277	occupy	U	356	pack	Q	332
nearly	P	323	occur	W	374	package	Q	332
necessary	U	358	occurred	W	374	page	I	270
necessity	U	358	occurrence	W, Z	374, 394	paid	M	298
need	N	306				paint	A–G	262
needle	O	317	ocean	P	324	pair	N	305
negate	Y	387	o'clock	P	321	palace	O	317
negative	Y	387	October	N	309	paper	I	271
neighbor	R	333	of	A–G, M	267, 299	paragraph	R	339
neither	S	341				parallel	Z	394
nephew	P	324	off	M	299	pare	N	305
neutral	Z	394	offer	N	304	parents	X	382
never	J	278	office	M, T	300, 348	parliament	Y	387
new	I, L	272, 291				part	J	278
			officer	T	348	particular	S	341
news	L	291	official	T	348	party	K	282
newspaper	P	322	often	S	340	pass	K	287
next	L	292	oil	A–G	262	passengers	P	324
nice	I	270	old	A–G	257	past	M	298
nickel	S	345	omit	M	302	patience	R	339
niece	S	345	on	A–G	254			
night	K	287	once	L	293			

Word	Section	Page	Word	Section	Page	Word	Section	Page
patient	R	310, 339	play	A–G	261	primary	Q, Y	328, 388
pause	N	310	pleasant	M, S	301, 343	prime	Y	388
pay	J, M	277, 298	please	M	301	primitive	Y	388
peace	N, S	310, 343	pleasure	O	312	principal	V	362
			plentiful	V	367	principle	V, Y	362, 384
peach	K	288	plenty	V	367	print	J	279
pear	N	305	pneumonia	Z	394	prison	P	320
peculiar	X	382	pocket	L	296	prisoner	R	339
pencil	M	303	poem	S	345	private	Q	326
penny	O	317	poet	S	345	privilege	Z	394
people	L	293	poetic	S	345	probable	U	356
perceive	Y	387	poetry	S	345	probably	U	356
perceived	Y	387	point	L	295	problems	U	361
percent	Z	394	pole	K	288	proceed	W	370
percentage	Z	394	police	O	315	process	W	375
perfect	O	313	political	T	349	produce	S	345
perform	Y	387	pool	A–G	262	product	S, W	345, 375
performance	Y	387	poor	K	286			
perhaps	Q	330	popular	R	337	production	W	375
period	Q	325	population	O	312	productive	W	375
permanent	Y	387	porcelain	Z	394	profession	Y	388
permission	N	311	position	Q	328	professional	Y	388
perpendicular	X	382	positive	Y	388	proficiency	Z	394
persevere	X	382	possible	S	343	proficient	Z	394
persist	Z	394	possibly	S	343	program	W	375
persistence	Z	394	post	J	275	progress	Q	327
person	N	308	potato	S	345	project	Y	388
personal	O	313	potatoes	S	345	projection	Y	388
personality	V	367	pound	K	285	projector	Y	388
phone	J	281	power	L	292	promise	R	334
phrase	W	374	powerful	V	367	prompt	Q	330
physical	Q	332	practical	W	370	proper	O	313
physically	V	367	practice	W	374	properly	Q	332
physician	Z	394	prairie	V	367	property	Q	326
pianist	R	339	praise	Q	332	protect	V	367
piano	R	339	precipice	Y	388	protection	V	367
pianos	R	339	precipitous	Y	388	protective	V	367
pick	I	274	prefer	R	334	prove	N	305
pickle	R	339	preference	R	334	provide	M, R	297, 335
pickles	R	339	preliminary	X	377			
picnic	O	315	prepare	R	334	provision	R	335
picture	M	301	prepared	V	367	public	O	315
pie	M	303	presence	Y	388	publication	R	333
piece	S	343	present	Q	329	publish	Q	326
pigeon	U	361	presents	Y	388	pull	M	303
pitch	M	301	preside	Q	327	purchase	S	346
pitcher	M	301	president	Q	327	purchased	S	346
place	J	278	press	N	307	purpose	R	335
plain	U	361	pressure	S	345	push	L	295
plan	N	306	pretty	M	298	put	I	271
plane	U	361	prevent	V	367	qualities	Y	388
planet	V	367	previous	Y	388	quality	Y	388
plant	I	269	price	K	285	quantities	Y	388
planted	I	269	primarily	Y	388	quantity	Y	388

Word	Section	Page	Word	Section	Page	Word	Section	Page
quarrel	S	346	release	R	339	ring	A–G	260
quart	V	368	relief	U	356	rinse	X	383
quarter	V	368	relieve	V	368	rinsed	X	383
queen	K	288	religion	Q	326	river	I	269
quest	N	308	remain	O	314	road	L	292
question	N	308	remained	P	324	rode	L	292
quiet	O	314	remember	Q	327	room	J	280
quit	O	314	removal	U	362	rope	K	288
quite	O	314	remove	U	362	rough	N	311
race	J	276	removed	U	362	round	K	284
radio	S	346	rendezvous	Z	395	routes	W	375
railroad	M	298	repair	P	319	royal	O	312
rain	K	281	repeated	V	368	rule	N	305
raise	O	315	repeats	O	317	run	A–G,	255,
ran	H	266	repetition	V	368		H, N	266,
rapid	P	319	reply	P	322			305
rate	O	313	report	J	278	running	N	305
rather	O	311	represent	Q	326	sacrifice	V	368
reach	K	284	reproached	X	382	safety	W	375
read	J	277	request	O	315	said	J	279
ready	M	302	required	V	368	sail	P	322
real	M, T	298,	research	Y	388	sailor	O	317
		350	resemblance	Y	389	salary	R, S	333
realize	T	354	resemble	Y	389	sale	P	322
really	T	350	resign	R	339	salmon	Z	395
reason	N	309	resist	Z	395	same	J	280
receipt	X	377	resistance	Z	395	sang	I	270
receive	U	358	resource	W	375	satellites	Z	395
recent	T	349	resourceful	W	375	satisfaction	Z	395
recess	S	346	resources	W	375	satisfactory	Z	395
recipe	Z	394	respect	U	358	satisfied	Z	395
recognition	V	368	respectful	U	358	satisfy	Z	395
recognize	V	368	respectfully	U	358	Saturday	O	316
recommend	Y, Z	389,	response	U	356	saucer	S	346
		390	responsible	U	356	saw	J	277
recommended	Z	390	rest	J	276	say	A–G, J	260,
records	V	368	restaurant	Y	389			279
recover	M	298	restrain	O	312	says	J	279
red	A–G, J	257,	result	Q	328	scale	W	375
		277	retreating	P	324	scarcely	Y	389
refer	T, V	349,	return	M	300	scene	U	357
		363	reveal	R	340	scenery	U	357
reference	V	363	revere	X	383	scheme	Y	389
reflected	Z	394	reverence	X	383	school	H	263
refuse	O	312	reverent	X	383	science	U	357
regard	P	321	rhapsody	Z	395	scientific	W	375
region	Q	326	rhinoceros	Z	395	scientists	W	375
regular	O	317	rhubarb	Z	395	scissors	U	357
rehearsal	U	362	rhyme	W	375	sea	A–G	261
rehearse	U	362	rhythm	W	375	search	R	336
reign	T	354	rhythmic	W	375	searched	Q	332
relate	Q, Y	327,	rich	I	274	season	K	288
		389	ride	I, L	268,	second	O	313
relation	Y	389			292	secrecy	W	375
relationship	Y	389	rides	I	268	secret	S, W	346,
relative	Q	327	right	L	292			375

Word	Section	Page	Word	Section	Page	Word	Section	Page
secretary	V	363	similar	S, X	346, 383	sow	M	303
section	Q	326	similarities	X	383	space	K	288
sections	W	375	similarity	X	383	speak	M	298
secure	R	286	simple	Y	389	special	Q, X	329, 377
see	A–G, K	255, 265	simplicity	Y	389	species	Z	395
seem	K	283	simplified	Y	389	specific	Z	396
seen	K	286	simplify	Y	389	specifically	Z	396
seize	Y	389	since	P	321	specified	Z	396
seized	Y	389	sincere	W	370	specify	Z	396
select	Q	326	sincerely	W	370	speech	S	346
selection	Y	389	sing	I	270	spell	K	285
self	Q	328	sir	K	286	spend	P	318
senate	U	358	sister	J	275	spent	I	269
senator	U	358	sit	H	263	spirit	V	369
senatorial	U	358	sits	H	263	spiritual	V	369
send	H	265	situation	V	368	spring	I	269
sense	V	368	six	A–G	259	square	W	375
sensible	V	368	size	N	309	stairs	L	296
sent	K	283	sleep	H	268	stamp	K	287
sentence	O	317	sleeve	R	340	stand	H	264
separate	W	370	sleigh	S	346	standard	W	376
September	O	314	slide	O	314	stands	H	264
sequence	X	383	slightly	V	368	start	K	281
series	X	383	slip	T	354	state	K, Q	284, 330
serious	S	342	slipped	T	354	statement	Q	330
serve	Q, R	327, 336	small	L	291	station	O	315
service	R	336	smaller	L	291	stationary	T	354
session	V	363	smallest	L	291	stationery	T	354
set	K	287	smooth	Q	332	stay	J	275
setting	K	287	sneeze	T	354	steadily	V	369
seven	J	275	so	A–G, M	255, 303	steady	V	369
several	P	322				steak	S	346
severe	T	354	soap	L	291	steal	N	311
sew	M	303	social	N, S	311, 346	steam	M	304
shall	L	294	society	S	346	still	J	278
she	A–G	254	soft	H	263	stole	M	298
shed	O	312	solar	Z	395	stomach	T	354
shelf	Z	395	sold	I	273	stone	I	270
shelves	Z	395	soldier	R	340	stood	M	297
shine	O	318	solemn	V	368	stop	L	290
shining	O	318	solution	S	346	stopping	L	290
ship	J	277	some	H	266	store	J	281
shoe	L	296	something	N	306	story	K	284
shoes	L	296	sometimes	Q	325	straight	T	354
short	K	284	son	J	276	strange	N	311
should	K	282	song	I	270	stream	L	296
shoulder	V	368	soon	I	271	street	A–G	260
show	I	271	sorry	N	307	strength	P	322
shut	K	287	source	S	346	strong	P	322
sick	I	268	south	J	275	struck	O	315
side	J	278	South America	X	383	structural	W	376
siege	U	362	southern	S	345	structure	W	376
sight	M	297	souvenir	Z	395	study	N	307
sign	K	288	sovereign	Z	395	style	P	324

Word	Section	Page	Word	Section	Page	Word	Section	Page
subject	N	307	telescope	Y	389	tire	J	276
submarine	Y	389	television	T	354	tissue	U	357
substance	W	376	tell	H	264	to	H, P	265, 323
substantial	W	376	temperature	V	369	today	A–G	258
subtract	P	324	ten	A–G	255	toe	J	281
succeed	T	354	tenth	K	286	together	R	335
success	R	334	term	Q	326	told	I	273
successful	S	346	terrible	Q	325	tomato	R	340
such	L	294	territorial	Y	390	tomatoes	R	340
sudden	O	313	territory	Y	390	tomorrow	R	336
suffer	N	305	testimony	V	362	ton	A–G	255
sufficiently	Z	396	than	I	272	tongue	W	376
sugar	N	307	thank	I	273	tonight	K	286
suggest	U	357	that	H	267	too	P	323
suit	L	290	the	A–G	255	took	M	299
sum	R	340	theater	S	340	tooth	A–G	262
summary	R	340	their	Q	330	top	A–G	255
summer	L	291	them	H	266	tortoise	Z	396
summon	T	348	themselves	Q	328	total	S	341
sun	J	276	then	H	265	touch	Q	332
Sunday	I	271	theory	Z	396	tough	T	354
sung	I	270	there	L, N	294, 309	toward	Q, R	329, 334
superintendent	Y	389	therefore	S	343	towel	Q	332
supper	J	281	these	K	286	town	J	275
supply	S	341	they	K, Q	282, 330	track	L	290
support	P	321				traffic	S	347
suppose	Q	329	thief	O	318	train	J	277
sure	N, U	307, 356	thing	I	272	tranquil	Z	396
			think	J	275	tranquillity	Z	396
surface	O	318	third	L	295	travel	P	319
surgeon	Y	389	thirteen	Q	332	treachery	X	383
surprise	Q	325	this	A–G	257	treasure	O, R	312, 336
sweeping	O	318	thoroughly	Y	390			
sweeps	O	318	those	K	286	tree	I	268
sword	R	340	though	P	307, 321	tremendous	Y	390
syllable	Z	396				trial	P	325
syllables	Z	396	thought	N	307	triangle	W	376
system	S	342	thousand	V	369	tried	M	304
table	L	291	thread	M	304	trip	L	293
tailor	P	324	three	A–G	261	tripped	L	293
tails	S	346	threw	O	313	trophy	N	311
take	I	272	throat	Q	332	trouble	P	319
tales	S	346	through	J	281	troubling	P	319
talk	L	290	throughout	S	347	true	M, O	299, 315
talks	L	296	throw	O	313			
tan	A–G	255	thumb	P	324	truly	O	315
taught	P	322	thunder	M	304	trust	M	296
tax	N	309	Thursday	O	316	truth	M	299
teach	M	297	thus	N	306	try	K, M	285, 304
teacher	N	307	ticket	M	298			
tear	S	346	tie	V	369	turn	L	291
technical	Z	396	time	A–G	257, 258	twelve	L	282
techniques	Z	396				twenty	K	282
technology	Z	396	tin	A–G	256	twice	K	282
teeth	A–G	262	tiny	L	296			
telephone	S	347						

EXTENDED AYRES WORD LIST: PARTS OF SPEECH

THE EXTENDED AYRES Word List is a quick reference for lesson planning when categorized by parts of speech. Parts of speech are the building blocks of language structure. They are tools for teaching children to analyze and discuss language. Skillful use enables students to write creatively.

When primary students have written A–G words in their spelling notebooks, introduce the parts of speech using these words (see chapter 2, pages 94–96, for detailed instructions). Sections A–G provide 37 nouns, 11 pronouns, 33 verbs, 26 adjectives, 8 adverbs, 9 prepositions, and 2 conjunctions to use for teaching the attributes of *simple* sentences. Children can already spell and read these words; therefore, they can concentrate on sentence structure and meaning. Older disabled readers usually have a limited vocabulary and insufficient knowledge of sentence or text structure. These words provide a basic, nonthreatening word bank for teaching language structure.

Words are listed under each part of speech in the order of instruction in the Extended Ayres Word List. Multiple-meaning words are listed under the part(s) of speech commonly used by students in that grade level. If students' oral speaking vocabulary is limited, teach the most common meaning first, and then introduce the less familiar meaning in a later lesson.

PARTS OF SPEECH: SECTIONS A–G

Nouns	Pronouns	Verbs	Adjectives	Adverbs	Prepositions	Conjunctions
can	me	do	a	so	at	and
run	it	go	the	no	on	but
man	she	is	ten	now	in	
ten	he	can	tan	up	up	
tin	you	see	tin	not	of	
ton	we	run	top	ago	out	
bed	my	will	an	out	into	
top	us	am	last	today	by	
time	this	be	good		over	
chance	your	time	blue			
today	him	have	little			
six		charge	old			
boy		are	bad			
book		be	red			
street		may	this			
hand		look	all			
ring		did	six			
bag		like	live			
bog		had	late			
bug		must	big			
mother		make	three			
three		say	cold			
land		come	hot			
hat		hand	ice			
child		ring	cool			
ice		live	green			
play		kill				
sea		let				
bird		beg				
earth		land				
fur		play				
oil		feed				
paint		paint				
pool						
tooth						
teeth						
worm						

PARTS OF SPEECH: SECTION H

Nouns	Pronouns	Verbs	Adjectives	Adverbs	Prepositions	Conjunctions
day	I	eat	low	yes	to	if
lot	some	sit	soft	just	about	as
box	her	sits	five	must	for	
school	them	belong	much	then		
door	other	stand	long	as		
floor	that	stands	alone	how		
yard	his	bring	lone	well		

PARTS OF SPEECH: SECTION H

Nouns	Pronouns	Verbs	Adjectives	Adverbs	Prepositions	Conjunctions
five		tell	one	fast		
ball		ask	some			
law		get	other			
way		call	that			
home		love	brown			
love		send	fast			
house		has	yellow			
year		ran				
one		was				
baby		led				
well		lay				
men		ate				
apple		eats				
author		jump				
bread		sleep				
dog		wash				
food						
sleep						
wash						

PARTS OF SPEECH: SECTION I

Nouns	Pronouns	Verbs	Adjectives	Adverbs	Prepositions	Conjunctions
nine	each	miss	nine	north	after	after
face	what	ride	sick	back		than
ride	its	rides	north	away		or
tree		got	white	soon		
north		spent	free	yet		
foot		blow	nice	after		
feet		blows	each	very		
block		plant	new	west		
spring		planted	dear			
river		cut	west			
plant		sing	best			
cut		sang	far			
song		sung	alike			
winter		lace	brave			
stone		end	rich			
lake		fall				
lace		went				
page		put				
end		came				
fall		show				
paper		find				
Sunday		give				
show		take				
Monday		thank				
moon		sold				

PARTS OF SPEECH: SECTION I

Nouns	Pronouns	Verbs	Adjectives	Adverbs	Prepositions	Conjunctions
letter		told				
Mister = Mr.		form				
thing		gave				
west		add				
form		dance				
corn		looks				
dance		pick				
dinner		zip				
doll						
egg						
fruit						
zoo						
zero						

PARTS OF SPEECH: SECTION J

Nouns	Pronouns	Verbs	Adjectives	Adverbs	Prepositions	Conjunctions
seven	our	forget	seven	south	inside	when
noon	mine	think	happy	inside	outside	
sister		cast	south	outside	near	
cast		stay	deep	east	down	
card		rest	grand	near	under	
south		help	dark	down	from	
post		race	east	why	along	
town		cover	hard	still	with	
band		fire	gold	never	through	
game		wire	fine	here		
boat		tire	left	most		
rest		read	large	more		
east		line	still	when		
son		left	kind			
sun		ship	every			
help		train	most			
race		saw	more			
cover		pay	lost			
fire		want	same			
wire		part	glad			
tire		place				
age		report				
gold		found				
May		made				
line		said				
ship		says				
train		work				
saw		wind				
pay		print				
bill		fill				
girl		lost				

PARTS OF SPEECH: SECTION J

Nouns	Pronouns	Verbs	Adjectives	Adverbs	Prepositions	Conjunctions
girls		name				
part		hope				
place		glad				
report		forgot				
side		guess				
kind		hang				
life		store				
car						
word						
work						
wind						
print						
air						
name						
room						
hope						
chair						
guess						
meat						
mouse						
phone						
store						
supper						
toe						

PARTS OF SPEECH: SECTION K

Nouns	Pronouns	Verbs	Adjectives	Adverbs	Prepositions	Conjunctions
brother	they	became	two	twice	upon	
rain	any	keep	twin	where	between	
start	many	start	twelve	first	without	
mail	these	mail	twenty	even	behind	
male	those	would	any	behind	around	
female		could	many	around	across	
eye		should	only	without		
glass		sent	weak	maybe		
party		seem	first	tonight		
two		state	even			
twin		open	afternoon			
twelve		reach	open			
twenty		water	short			
city		cost	better			
week		become	round			
cent		care	bare			
mile		try	clear			
afternoon		move	clean			
Friday		delay	poor			
hour		pound	hurt			

PARTS OF SPEECH: SECTION K

Nouns	Pronouns	Verbs	Adjectives	Adverbs	Prepositions	Conjunctions
wife		burn	tenth			
state		camp	these			
July		clean	those			
head		spell	full			
story		finish	easy			
lady		hurt				
water		seen				
cost		felt				
price		fail				
class		set				
horse		setting				
care		stamp				
move		light				
delay		coming				
pound		pass				
burn		shut				
camp		draw				
bear		drink				
finish		hop				
tonight		hopping				
sir		sign				
club		space				
set						
setting						
stamp						
light						
night						
pass						
ease						
bone						
cloud						
drink						
garden						
goose						
knife						
mouth						
oak						
peach						
pole						
queen						
rope						
season						
sign						
space						
wagon						
wheat						
window						

PARTS OF SPEECH: SECTION L

Nouns	Pronouns	Verbs	Adjectives	Adverbs	Prepositions	Conjunctions
catch	anything	catch	black	indeed	above	unless
catcher	herself	warm	warm	ever	before	because
kitchen	another	clothe	able	once	within	however
butcher	one	began	new	there		
clothing	nothing	begin	small	early		
clothes		beginning	smaller	close		
suit		gone	smallest	alone		
track		done	high	third		
watch		suit	right	within		
dash		track	next	nothing		
fight		watch	four	no		
walk		dash	another			
chalk		fell	dead			
grant		fight	early			
soap		buy	close			
news		stop	such			
war		stopping	many			
summer		walk	no			
turn		talk	third			
lesson		grant	funny			
half		express	orange			
father		turn	tiny			
table		write				
June		wrote				
date		rode				
road		ride				
ride		march				
March		wish				
march		cause				
four		meet				
power		trip				
wish		tripped				
cause		list				
world		held				
country		own				
trip		know				
list		were				
people		leave				
church		close				
flower		flour				
flour		lead				
nothing		mind				
ground		shall				
lead		order				
morning		push				
mind		point				
order		belongs				
point		earn				
body		going				
field		talks				

PARTS OF SPEECH: SECTION L

Nouns	Pronouns	Verbs	Adjectives	Adverbs	Prepositions	Conjunctions
cheese						
edge						
feather						
fence						
honey						
letters						
orange						
pocket						
shoe						
shoes						
stairs						
stream						
words						

PARTS OF SPEECH: SECTION M

Nouns	Pronouns	Verbs	Adjectives	Adverbs	Prepositions	Conjunctions
trust	all	trust	extra	past	beside	while
dress	both	dress	pretty	almost	past	
file	who	teach	unable	all		
sight	few	happen	real	less		
hold	myself	begun	past	off		
drill		collect	less	again		
army		file	true	also		
income		provide	both	please		
railroad		sight	great	anyway		
ticket		stood	few	daily		
account		fix	pleasant			
mountain		fixed	ready			
past		born	eight			
might		goes	daily			
contract		hold	fancy			
deal		drill	gentle			
event		stole	so			
truth		bought				
heart		paid				
month		enter				
children		account				
member		driven				
case		recover				
office		speak				
change		might				
picture		contract				
pitcher		deal				
pitch		brought				
money		took				
eight		inform				
breakfast		build				

PARTS OF SPEECH: SECTION M

Nouns	Pronouns	Verbs	Adjectives	Adverbs	Prepositions	Conjunctions
climb		built				
coffee		understand				
color		follow				
eagle		return				
fancy		die				
fly		died				
forest		change				
freeze		changing				
holes		please				
hotel		picture				
iron		pitch				
living		omit				
monkey		climb				
noise		color				
pencil		contains				
pie		fancy				
steam		fly				
thread		freeze				
thunder		grow				
vein		iron				
		live				
		living				
		pull				
		sew				
		sow				
		steam				
		thread				
		thunder				
		tried				

PARTS OF SPEECH: SECTION N

Nouns	Pronouns	Verbs	Adjectives	Adverbs	Prepositions	Conjunctions
aunt	itself	capture	else	else	except	except
ant	himself	bridge	front	always	among	nor
capture		offer	young	something		
bridge		suffer	fair	thus		
offer		center	sure	sure		
center		running	least	yesterday		
front		rule	sorry	fifth		
rule		carry	mean			
chain		chain	dozen			
death		learn	fifth			
wonder		wonder	cheap			
pair		pair	cheerful			
pear		pare	leather			
check		check	linen			
something		prove	rough			

PARTS OF SPEECH: SECTION N

Nouns	Pronouns	Verbs	Adjectives	Adverbs	Prepositions	Conjunctions
need		hear	social			
woman		heard	strange			
women		inspect				
fare		expect				
dollar		need				
evening		plan				
plan		broke				
sugar		feel				
press		press				
God		study				
god		matter				
teacher		use				
November		thought				
subject		mean				
April		vote				
history		copy				
study		act				
matter		been				
use		question				
thought		tax				
person		number				
January		reason				
vote		bake				
court		baking				
copy		drive				
act		driving				
yesterday		echo				
question		echoes				
quest		knock				
doctor		pause				
size		steal				
December						
dozen						
tax						
number						
October						
reason						
fifth						
bowl						
chicken						
drive						
echo						
echoes						
fairy						
knock						
leather						
linen						
mixture						
nation						
pause						

PARTS OF SPEECH: SECTION N

Nouns	Pronouns	Verbs	Adjectives	Adverbs	Prepositions	Conjunctions
peace						
permission						
rough						
social						
trophy						
voice						
voices						

PARTS OF SPEECH: SECTION O

Nouns	Pronouns	Verbs	Adjectives	Adverbs	Prepositions	Conjunctions
uncle	everything	comfort	afraid	rather	aboard	whether
comfort	none	elect	royal	aboard	during	
election	nobody	jail	forty	fourth	until	
jail		shed	fourteen	instead		
shed		refuse	fourth	farther		
district		restrain	four	quite		
objection		object	proper	none		
object		measure	worth	truly		
pleasure		treasure	sudden			
measure		weather	personal			
treasure		judge	perfect			
navy		contain	second			
forty		figure	farther			
fourteen		throw	quiet			
population		threw	direct			
judge		rate	enough			
weather		slide	public			
worth		intend	true			
figure		quit	whole			
throw		knew	cautious			
rate		remain	distant			
chief		direct	holy			
second		appear	regular			
slide		board	waste			
duty		station	weary			
company		attend				
direction		picnic				
liberty		police				
fact		address				
board		request				
September		raise				
station		struck				
public		getting				
music		caution				
picnic		covered				
friend		declare				
friends		declared				

PARTS OF SPEECH: SECTION O

Nouns	Pronouns	Verbs	Adjectives	Adverbs	Prepositions	Conjunctions
police		explain				
hole		floated				
address		lying				
request		lie				
raise		repeats				
August		sentence				
Thursday		shine				
Saturday		shining				
admission		sweeping				
canoe		sweeps				
captain		waste				
caution		waiting				
cellar		writing				
creature		write				
curtain						
distance						
ghost						
holiday						
knee						
lemon						
lie						
nails						
needle						
oar						
palace						
penny						
sailor						
sentence						
shine						
surface						
thief						
waist						
waste						
writer						

PARTS OF SPEECH: SECTION P

Nouns	Pronouns	Verbs	Adjectives	Adverbs	Prepositions	Conjunctions
awe	which	spend	awful	o'clock	since	though
complaint	several	enjoy	usual	since		since
auto		travel	beautiful	nearly		
vacation		repair	rapid	too		
beauty		trouble	important	wrong		
flight		troubling	which			
travel		carried	strong			
repair		wait	naughty			
trouble		visit	several			
entrance		guess	two			

PARTS OF SPEECH: SECTION P

Nouns	Pronouns	Verbs	Adjectives	Adverbs	Prepositions	Conjunctions
importance		obtain	careful			
loss		favor	guilty			
fortune		view	hungry			
empire		support	nineteen			
mayor		does	wrong			
wait		regard				
degree		escape				
prison		destroy				
engine		caught				
visit		taught				
guest		answer				
guess		reply				
department		sail				
family		known				
favor		desire				
Mrs.		button				
husband		cough				
amount		excuse				
human		guard				
view		laugh				
clerk		lining				
support		notice				
regard		noticed				
escape		remained				
length		retreating				
strength		subtract				
newspaper		tailor				
daughter		thumb				
answer		whisper				
reply						
sail						
sale						
cities						
desire						
animal						
basin						
breeze						
button						
cabbage						
cough						
cousin						
dollars						
excuse						
island						
grief						
guard						
language						
laughter						
laugh						
lining						

PARTS OF SPEECH: SECTION P

Nouns	Pronouns	Verbs	Adjectives	Adverbs	Prepositions	Conjunctions
ocean						
nephew						
nineteen						
notice						
passengers						
style						
tailor						
thumb						
trial						
voyage						
whisper						

PARTS OF SPEECH: SECTION Q

Nouns	Pronouns	Verbs	Adjectives	Adverbs	Prepositions	Conjunctions
surprise	either	engage	final	sometimes	toward	either
period	whom	surprise	terrible	due		although
addition	themselves	employ	firm	forward		
property	whose	select	private	backward		
connection	their	connect	relative	perhaps		
firm	they	convict	entire	properly		
region		command	famous			
religion		debate	either			
convict		crowd	due			
command		publish	primary			
debate		represent	special			
crowd		section	gentle			
factory		relate	wonderful			
term		progress	prompt			
section		preside	calm			
relative		serve	dangerous			
progress		remember	dry			
president		include	physical			
fame		allow	smooth			
estate		position	thirteen			
effort		claim				
due		appoint				
dew		arrest				
position		present				
ledge		enclose				
claim		await				
primary		suppose				
result		prompt				
information		attempt				
arrest		imprison				
self		written				
calves		arrange				
calf		appears				

PARTS OF SPEECH: SECTION Q

Nouns	Pronouns	Verbs	Adjectives	Adverbs	Prepositions	Conjunctions
halves		brace				
present		breathe				
action		calm				
justice		consented				
gentleman		continue				
prompt		continued				
attempt		dry				
statement		dried				
writ		exhaust				
ankle		exercise				
bracelet		journey				
brace		laid				
breath		package				
calm		pack				
circus		praise				
debt		searched				
exhaust		smooth				
exercise		touch				
explosion						
grammar						
Indian						
journey						
journal						
courage						
package						
pack						
praise						
thirteen						
throat						
touch						
towel						
umbrella						
weapon						

PARTS OF SPEECH: SECTION R

Nouns	Pronouns	Verbs	Adjectives	Adverbs	Prepositions	Conjunctions
combination		lose	loose	already	against	
avenue		combine	secure	together	beneath	
neighbor		weigh	busy	tomorrow	beyond	
weight		wear	different	again		
salary		entertain	common	beneath		
visitor		drown	general	beyond		
publication		adopt	complete			
machine		secure	popular			
success		honor	eager			
honor		promise	fierce			
promise		wreck	gigantic			

PARTS OF SPEECH: SECTION R

Nouns	Pronouns	Verbs	Adjectives	Adverbs	Prepositions	Conjunctions
wreck		prepare	giant			
vessel		busy	patient			
preference		prefer				
illustration		illustrate				
provision		differ				
attention		according				
education		increase				
director		feature				
purpose		injure				
diamond		effect				
convention		distribute				
increase		consider				
manner		complete				
feature		search				
article		treasure				
service		interest				
injury		advise				
effect		bargain				
general		broken				
tomorrow		break				
search		compare				
treasure		control				
Christmas		controlled				
Christ		excite				
interest		exciting				
advice		fly				
American		flies				
America		flew				
bargain		forgotten				
cocoa		guide				
collar		hurry				
comparison		hurried				
debts		hurrying				
disaster		pickle				
enemy		release				
example		resign				
excitement		reveal				
fly		sum				
flies						
giant						
guide						
knowledge						
lawyer						
paragraph						
patient						
patience						
piano						
pianos						
pianist						
pickle						

PARTS OF SPEECH: SECTION R

Nouns	Pronouns	Verbs	Adjectives	Adverbs	Prepositions	Conjunctions
pickles						
prisoner						
release						
sleeve						
soldier						
summary						
sum						
sword						
tomato						
tomatoes						

PARTS OF SPEECH: SECTION S

Nouns	Pronouns	Verbs	Adjectives	Adverbs	Prepositions	Conjunctions
motion	neither	motion	total	often	throughout	neither
theater	everybody	improve	particular	further		
improvement		total	coarse	possibly		
century		mention	local	certainly		
total		arrive	further	therefore		
supply		supply	serious	throughout		
difference		assist	million			
examination		examine	possible			
affair		marry	certain			
course		further	atmospheric			
marriage		doubt	autumn			
carriage		govern	creative			
doubt		believe	northern			
condition		piece	southern			
government		witness	eastern			
opinion		investigate	western			
onion		canvas	poetic			
union		create	secret			
companion		created	similar			
million		decide	successful			
behavior		decided	valuable			
system		design	worn			
piece		frighten				
witness		frightened				
ability		group				
appearance		listen				
atmosphere		listened				
autumn		pressure				
canvas		produce				
ceiling		purchase				
celery		purchased				
college		quarrel				
community		radio				
communities		recess				

PARTS OF SPEECH: SECTION S

Nouns	Pronouns	Verbs	Adjectives	Adverbs	Prepositions	Conjunctions
creation		tear				
concert		telephone				
design		traffic				
dictionary		unite				
elephant		value				
grocery		wore				
group		worn				
health						
nickel						
niece						
poem						
poet						
poetry						
potato						
potatoes						
pressure						
produce						
product						
purchase						
quarrel						
radio						
recess						
saucer						
secret						
sleigh						
society						
solution						
source						
speech						
steak						
tails						
tales						
tear						
telephone						
traffic						
United States						
unit						
value						

PARTS OF SPEECH: SECTION T

Nouns	Pronouns	Verbs	Adjectives	Adverbs	Prepositions	Conjunctions
circle		circle	circular	really		
argument		argue	official	angrily		
volume		organize	impossible	hardly		
officer		summon	various	straight		
victim		estimate	political			

PARTS OF SPEECH: SECTION T

Nouns	Pronouns	Verbs	Adjectives	Adverbs	Prepositions	Conjunctions
estimate		invite	national			
accident		accept	recent			
invitation		concern	minute			
concern		associate	absent			
automobile		vary	folk			
associate		entitle	angry			
association		refer	available			
decision		ought	changeable			
business		absent	determined			
minute		confer	electric			
absence		ache	electrical			
conference		aches	exact			
Wednesday		anger	favorable			
celebration		approve	favorite			
folk		avoid	genuine			
folks		bruise	massive			
ache		bruised	ninety			
aches		change	severe			
amusement		compete	stationary			
anger		deceive	straight			
approval		determine	tough			
banana		determined	wholesome			
biscuits		discover				
bottle		entered				
bottom		err				
bruise		fought				
chapter		fuel				
chimney		involve				
choir		involved				
determination		realize				
discovery		reign				
discoveries		slip				
electricity		slipped				
electrician		sneeze				
error		succeed				
exceptions		whistle				
fuel		whistling				
growth		wrestle				
handful		wrestling				
hymn						
investigation						
lily						
lilies						
mass						
medal						
metal						
medicine						
ninety						
reign						

PARTS OF SPEECH: SECTION T

Nouns	Pronouns	Verbs	Adjectives	Adverbs	Prepositions	Conjunctions
sneeze						
stationary						
stationery						
stomach						
television						
whistle						
wreath						

PARTS OF SPEECH: SECTION U

Nouns	Pronouns	Verbs	Adjectives	Adverbs	Prepositions	Conjunctions
consideration	anyone	meant	earliest	probably		
colony		distinguish	colonial	finally		
colonies		assure	probable	respectfully		
relief		occupy	foreign	generally		
expense		apply	responsible			
response		descend	difficult			
application		ascend	mere			
difficulty		develop	senatorial			
scene		envelop	respectful			
scenery		circle	unfortunate			
scissors		issue	major			
science		suggest	elaborate			
descent		receive	necessary			
ascent		respect	ancient			
envelope		agree	apiece			
circumstance		major	central			
circumference		elaborate	delicious			
circle		divide	elegant			
issue		achieve	excellent			
tissue		achieves	grateful			
material		acquire	hoarse			
senator		approaches	ignorant			
senate		attack	plain			
respect		balance				
agreement		calculate				
major		concealed				
majority		describe				
citizen		described				
necessity		disappear				
approaches		drop				
attack		dropped				
attorney		establish				
balance		established				
calculation		excel				
central		gather				
ceremony		inherit				
drop		identity				

PARTS OF SPEECH: SECTION U

Nouns	Pronouns	Verbs	Adjectives	Adverbs	Prepositions	Conjunctions
emperor		identified				
establishment		ignore				
heir		indicate				
icicle		interfere				
ignorance		rehearse				
indication		remove				
interference		removed				
leader						
leadership						
message						
messenger						
musician						
pigeon						
plane						
plain						
problems						
rehearsal						
removal						
siege						
valley						
vegetable						

PARTS OF SPEECH: SECTION V

Nouns	Pronouns	Verbs	Adjectives	Adverbs	Prepositions	Conjunctions
principal		discuss	principle	basically		
principle		refer	apparent	extremely		
testimony		experience	ascending	heavily		
discussion		ascending	basic	ordinarily		
arrangement		bow	choice	physically		
reference		campaign	capital	slightly		
evidence		choose	correct	steadily		
experience		chose	current			
session		chosen	desirable			
secretary		correct	extreme			
career		drawn	fearful			
height		drew	functional			
bough		equip	heavy			
bow		equipped	heavier			
campaign		fear	hundred			
capital		function	independent			
capitol		gathering	individual			
cereal		imagine	innocent			
choice		inches	instrumental			
columns		influence	liquid			
current		license	magnificent			
division		locate	main			
Dr.		located	modern			

PARTS OF SPEECH: SECTION V

Nouns	Pronouns	Verbs	Adjectives	Adverbs	Prepositions	Conjunctions
equipment		prepared	mysterious			
fear		prevent	ordinary			
function		protect	plentiful			
furniture		quarter	powerful			
future		recognize	protective			
hundred		records	repeated			
image		relieve	required			
inches		repeated	sensible			
individual		required	solemn			
influence		sacrifice	spiritual			
instance		sense	steady			
instrument		shoulder	thousand			
instrumental		steady	wise			
leisure		tie				
license		tying				
liquid						
location						
main						
minerals						
method						
mystery						
occasion						
ordinary						
personality						
planet						
plenty						
prairie						
protection						
quart						
quarter						
recognition						
records						
repetition						
sacrifice						
sense						
shoulder						
situation						
spirit						
spiritual						
temperature						
thousand						
tie						
wisdom						

PARTS OF SPEECH: SECTION W

Nouns	Pronouns	Verbs	Adjectives	Adverbs	Prepositions	Conjunctions
organization	everyone	appreciate	appreciative	sincerely		
emergency		proceed	sincere	cordially		
athlete		separate	athletic	actually		
character		angle	extreme	everywhere		
February		average	practical	gradually		
activity		bicycle	cordial	naturally		
activities		composed	separate	opposite		
angle		corner	active			
anxiety		count	actual			
bicycle		depend	angular			
bouquet		depends	antique			
calendar		diagram	anxious			
centuries		empty	average			
climate		equal	countless			
composition		exclaimed	dependent			
consequence		experiment	elementary			
corner		fatigue	empty			
cotton		factors	equal			
dependent		frequent	equivalent			
diagram		level	experimental			
disease		model	foreign			
element		muscle	frequent			
environment		narrow	gradual			
equality		observe	level			
exclamation		occur	model			
experiment		occurred	muscular			
expression		phrase	narrow			
factors		practice	natural			
fatigue		process	opposite			
foreigners		program	process			
frequency		rhyme	productive			
isthmus		routes	resourceful			
level		scale	rhythmic			
library		sections	scientific			
model		square	secret			
moment		structure	square			
mosquito		volunteer	structural			
muscle			substantial			
nature			volunteer			
naturalist						
nonsense						
observation						
observatory						
occurrence						
opposite						
opposition						
phrase						
practice						
process						
production						

PARTS OF SPEECH: SECTION W

Nouns	Pronouns	Verbs	Adjectives	Adverbs	Prepositions	Conjunctions
program						
resource						
resources						
rhyme						
rhythm						
routes						
safety						
scale						
scientists						
secret						
secrecy						
sections						
square						
standard						
structure						
substance						
tongue						
triangle						
variety						
vehicle						
vicinity						
volunteer						
welfare						
yacht						

PARTS OF SPEECH: SECTION X

Nouns	Pronouns	Verbs	Adjectives	Adverbs	Prepositions	Conjunctions
receipt		convene	immediate	especially		
preliminary		disappoint	convenient	eventually		
annual		commit	preliminary	forth		
committee		affect	annual	fourth		
adjective		applied	adjective	occasionally		
advantage		applying	artificial			
Africa		benefit	beneficial			
altitude		civilize	brilliant			
ancestors		civilized	chocolate			
Antarctica		exchange	civil			
architecture		exist	civilized			
Arctic Ocean		explore	contagious			
Asia		invented	continental			
Atlantic Ocean		mirror	descriptive			
Australia		mistaken	diagonal			
benefit		persevere	effective			
boundary		reproached	enormous			
boundaries		revere	essential			
brilliant		rinse	exquisite			
characteristics		rinsed	familiar			

PARTS OF SPEECH: SECTION X

Nouns	Pronouns	Verbs	Adjectives	Adverbs	Prepositions	Conjunctions
Chicago		sequence	fractional			
chocolate		type	horizontal			
civilization			industrial			
colonel			intelligent			
congress			interior			
continent			latter			
depth			longitudinal			
description			mistaken			
development			moist			
diagonal			opportune			
diameter			peculiar			
employee			perpendicular			
England			reverent			
English			typical			
Europe			vertical			
exchange						
existence						
explorers						
exploration						
familiarity						
fraction						
gravity						
horizontal						
Illinois						
imagination						
independence						
Indian Ocean						
industry						
interior						
invention						
latitude						
Lincoln						
longitude						
machinery						
magazine						
mirror						
moisture						
North America						
opportunity						
Pacific Ocean						
parents						
perpendicular						
reverence						
rinse						
sequence						
series						
similarity						
similarities						
South America						
treachery						

PARTS OF SPEECH: SECTION X

Nouns	Pronouns	Verbs	Adjectives	Adverbs	Prepositions	Conjunctions
type						
vertical						

PARTS OF SPEECH: SECTION Y

Nouns	Pronouns	Verbs	Adjectives	Adverbs	Prepositions	Conjunctions
accuracy		accommodate	accurate	literally		
commerce		approximate	approximate	mentally		
commercial		commence	commercial	primarily		
communication		communicate	complex	scarcely		
complex		construct	converse	thoroughly		
conclusion		converse	counterfeit			
construction		counterfeit	cultural			
conversation		culture	curious			
counterfeit		desert	desert			
culture		digest	digestible			
curiosity		equate	equatorial			
desert		extend	expensive			
dessert		introduced	extensive			
digest		manufacture	immense			
Egypt		manufacturing	invisible			
Egyptian		memorize	literate			
electrons		minor	literary			
equation		negate	memorable			
equator		operate	minor			
explanation		originated	negative			
extent		perceive	numerous			
extension		perceived	numerical			
introduction		perform	original			
leopard		project	permanent			
literate		research	positive			
literature		resemble	precipitous			
manufacturing		recommend	previous			
Mediterranean		scheme	primitive			
memory		seize	prime			
memorial		seized	professional			
millionaire		simplify	quality			
minor		simplified	simple			
minority		telescope	marine			
negative			territorial			
numeral			tremendous			
operator						
operation						
orchestra						
origin						
original						
parliament						
performance						

PARTS OF SPEECH: SECTION Y

Nouns	Pronouns	Verbs	Adjectives	Adverbs	Prepositions	Conjunctions
permanent						
positive						
precipice						
presence						
presents						
prime						
primary						
primitive						
profession						
professional						
projector						
projection						
quality						
qualities						
quantity						
quantities						
research						
resemblance						
relation						
relationship						
restaurant						
scheme						
selection						
simplicity						
marine						
submarine						
superintendent						
surgeon						
telescope						
territory						

PARTS OF SPEECH: SECTION Z

Nouns	Pronouns	Verbs	Adjectives	Adverbs	Prepositions	Conjunctions
judge		judge	appropriate	dramatically		
judgment		recommended	combustible	formally		
allegiance		allege	conscientious	percent		
abyss		apologize	discernible	specifically		
acquaintance		appropriate	dramatic	sufficiently		
cantaloupe		chauffeur	economical	vaguely		
cauliflower		discern	economic			
cemetery		discipline	economy			
chandelier		dispense	efficient			
financier		dissent	extraordinary			
chauffeur		eliminate	formal			
discipline		embarrass	humorous			
dissent		endeavor	impressive			
dissension		fatiguing	incessant			

PARTS OF SPEECH: SECTION Z

Nouns	Pronouns	Verbs	Adjectives	Adverbs	Prepositions	Conjunctions
drama		guarantee	mathematical			
economy		humor	military			
efficiency		impress	miscellaneous			
embarrassment		mortgage	mischievous			
endeavor		persist	municipal			
enthusiasm		reflected	neutral			
formal		rendezvous	lieutenant			
frontier		resist	parallel			
guarantee		satisfy	percent			
guitar		satisfied	proficient			
humor		specify	satisfactory			
impression		specified	solar			
Israel		vacuum	sovereign			
Israeli			specific			
league			technical			
mathematics			tranquil			
militia			unique			
military			universal			
mischief			vacuum			
mortgage			vague			
Europe			victorious			
pneumonia			violent			
lieutenant						
parallel						
percent						
percentage						
persistence						
physician						
porcelain						
privilege						
proficiency						
recipe						
rendezvous						
resistance						
rhapsody						
rhinoceros						
rhubarb						
salmon						
satellites						
satisfaction						
shelf						
shelves						
souvenir						
sovereign						
species						
syllables						
syllable						
technology						
techniques						
theory						

PARTS OF SPEECH: SECTION Z

Nouns	Pronouns	Verbs	Adjectives	Adverbs	Prepositions	Conjunctions
tortoise						
tranquillity						
universe						
university						
vacuum						
victory						
violence						
xylophone						

RECOMMENDED LANGUAGE ARTS SCOPE AND SEQUENCE

THE LANGUAGE ARTS scope and sequence provides recommended grade-level objectives to be mastered in spelling, writing, and reading lessons from kindergarten through eighth grade. Each day's lessons include objectives from spelling, writing, and reading because the content and skills are interrelated and interdependent. *Each objective that addresses a skill will be applied to grade-appropriate content (e.g., language rules applied to grade-level spelling words).* At each successive grade, teachers pretest to determine where instruction should begin. (See *Spelling Assessment Manual.*) Previously introduced skills are reviewed and applied to new, grade-appropriate content. Teacher judgment determines the amount of review necessary to maintain mastery throughout the grades. (Labels for concepts taught need not be used initially.)

Code

I/P: *Introduce* and *practice*, but automaticity (mastery) by a majority of students is not expected.

P: *Practice* to achieve automaticity (mastery).

M: *Mastery* means accurate and automatic recall of grade-appropriate content and application of grade-appropriate skills.

R: *Review* to *reinforce* (1) previously introduced content and (2) application of skills to new, grade-appropriate content.

C: *Challenge* for students who have achieved mastery of grade-level content and skills.

SPELLING SCOPE AND SEQUENCE

Grade-Level Objectives

CODE
I/P: Introduce/Practice
P: Practice
M: Mastery
R: Review/Reinforce
C: Challenge

Phonograms with Handwriting The student will . . .	K	1	2	3	4	5	6	7	8
segment spoken words into sounds/syllables.	I/P	M	R	R	R	R	R	R	R
blend spoken sounds into words.	I/P	M	R	R	R	R	R	R	R
explain the purpose for learning phonograms.	I/P	M	R	R	R	R	R	R	R
explain the purpose for precise handwriting.	I/P	M	R	R	R	R	R	R	R
precisely read phonograms (1–70).	I/P	M	R	R	R	R	R	R	R
precisely say and write phonograms (1–70).	C	M	R	R	R	R	R	R	R

Language Rules and Concepts The student will . . .	K	1	2	3	4	5	6	7	8
1. write qu (a two-letter consonant sound) to say /kw/.	I/P	M	R	R	R	R	R	R	R
2. read c before e, i, and y as /s/.	I/P	M	R	R	R	R	R	R	R
3. read g before e, i, and y as /j/.	I/P	M	R	R	R	R	R	R	R
4. read/mark /ā/, /ē/, /ī/, /ō/, and /ū/, at the end of open syllables.	I/P	M	R	R	R	R	R	R	R
5. read/mark i and y at the end of a syllable as appropriate.	I/P	M	R	R	R	R	R	R	R
6. write y, not i, at the end of a word.	I/P	M	R	R	R	R	R	R	R
7. read/mark/explain jobs of silent e's.	I/P	M	R	R	R	R	R	R	R
8. read /or/ as /er/ after a w.	I/P	M	R	R	R	R	R	R	R
9. explain/apply the 1-1-1 rule to one-syllable words (hop).	C	I/P	P	M	R	R	R	R	R
10. explain/apply the 2-1-1 rule to multisyllable words (begin).	C	I/P	P	P	M	R	R	R	R
11. explain/apply r. 11 to final silent e words (hope/hoping).	C	I/P	P	M	R	R	R	R	R
12. write ie except after c if we say /ā/ or in exceptions.	-	I/P	P	M	R	R	R	R	R
13. write sh to say /sh/ at the beginning/end of words and at the end of syllables.	I/P	M	R	R	R	R	R	R	R
14. write ti, si, and ci to say /sh/ in syllables after the first one.	-	I/P	P	M	R	R	R	R	R
15. write si to say /sh/ if the preceding syllable/base word ends in s.	-	I/P	P	M	R	R	R	R	R
16. read/mark and explain that si may also say /zh/.	-	I/P	P	M	R	R	R	R	R
17. write two l's, f's, or s's after one vowel in one syllable.	I/P	M	R	R	R	R	R	R	R
18. write ay to say /ā/ at the end of a word.	I/P	M	R	R	R	R	R	R	R
19. read /ī/ and /ō/ before two consonants when appropriate.	I/P	M	R	R	R	R	R	R	R
20. explain/apply r. 20 (s never follows the letter x).	C	I/P	P	M	R	R	R	R	R
21. write all with one l when used as a prefix.	C	I/P	P	M	R	R	R	R	R
22. write till and full with one l when used as a suffix.	C	I/P	P	M	R	R	R	R	R
23. write dge to say /j/ after one vowel saying its first sound.	C	I/P	P	M	R	R	R	R	R
24. write i, instead of y, when adding vowel endings.	C	I/P	P	M	R	R	R	R	R
25. write ck to say /k/ after one vowel saying its first sound.	I/P	P	M	R	R	R	R	R	R

SPELLING SCOPE AND SEQUENCE

Grade-Level Objectives

CODE
I/P: Introduce/Practice
P: Practice
M: Mastery
R: Review/Reinforce
C: Challenge

Language Rules and Concepts The student will . . .	K	1	2	3	4	5	6	7	8
26. capitalize names and titles.	I/P	**M**	R	R	R	R	R	R	R
27. write *z* to say /z/ at the beginning of words (*zoo*).	I/P	**M**	R	R	R	R	R	R	R
28. read ending *ed* as /ed/ if the base word ends in *d* or *t* (*grad ed*). read ending *ed* as /d/ after a voiced consonant (*lived*). read ending *ed* as /t/ after an unvoiced consonant (*stopped*).	C	I/P	**M**	R	R	R	R	R	R
29. read double consonants in both syllables for spelling (*lit tle*). read only the consonant in the accented syllable for reading (*lit le*).	-	I/P	P	**M**	R	R	R	R	R
Extended Ayres Word List The student will . . .	K	1	2	3	4	5	6	7	8
explain the purpose for spelling dictation.	I/P	**M**	R	R	R	R	R	R	R
precisely say, write, read words in sections A–G.	I/P	**M**	R	R	R	R	R	R	R
precisely say, write, read words in section H.	C	**M**	R	R	R	R	R	R	R
precisely say, write, read words in section I.	C	**M**	R	R	R	R	R	R	R
precisely say, write, read words in section J.	-	**M**	R	R	R	R	R	R	R
precisely say, write, read words in section K.	-	I/P	**M**	R	R	R	R	R	R
precisely say, write, read words in section L.	-	I/P	**M**	R	R	R	R	R	R
precisely say, write, read words in section M.	-	I/P	**M**	R	R	R	R	R	R
precisely say, write, read words in section N.	-	I/P	**M**	R	R	R	R	R	R
precisely say, write, read words in section O.	-	C	I/P	**M**	R	R	R	R	R
precisely say, write, read words in section P.	-	-	I/P	**M**	R	R	R	R	R
precisely say, write, read words in section Q.	-	-	I/P	**M**	R	R	R	R	R
precisely say, write, read words in section R.	-	-	C	I/P	**M**	R	R	R	R
precisely say, write, read words in section S.	-	-	-	I/P	**M**	R	R	R	R
precisely say, write, read words in section T.	-	-	-	I/P	**M**	R	R	R	R
precisely say, write, read words in section U.	-	-	-	C	I/P	**M**	R	R	R
precisely say, write, read words in section V.	-	-	-	-	I/P	**M**	R	R	R
precisely say, write, read words in section W.	-	-	-	-	I/P	**M**	R	R	R
precisely say, write, read words in section X.	-	-	-	-	C	I/P	**M**	R	R
precisely say, write, read words in section Y.	-	-	-	-	-	I/P	**M**	R	R
precisely say, write, read words in section Z.	-	-	-	-	-	I/P	**M**	R	R

WRITING SCOPE AND SEQUENCE
Grade-Level Objectives

CODE
I/P: Introduce/Practice
P: Practice
M: Mastery
R: Review/Reinforce
C: Challenge

Capitalization The student will capitalize . . .	K	1	2	3	4	5	6	7	8
first words of sentences.	I/P	**M**	R	R	R	R	R	R	R
single-word proper nouns and titles (Mr., etc.).	I/P	**M**	R	R	R	R	R	R	R
abbreviations.	-	I/P	**M**	R	R	R	R	R	R
multiword proper nouns.	C	I/P	P	**M**	R	R	R	R	R
titles of books, poems, short stories.	C	I/P	P	**M**	R	R	R	R	R
informal letter components.	-	I/P	P	**M**	R	R	R	R	R
first words of direct quotations.	-	C	I/P	**M**	R	R	R	R	R
familial titles, races, nationalities.	-	-	C	I/P	**M**	R	R	R	R
course titles, religious terms, periods of time.	-	-	-	-	C	I/P	**M**	R	R
formal letter components.	-	-	-	-	C	I/P	**M**	R	R

Punctuation The student will use . . .	K	1	2	3	4	5	6	7	8
periods (full stops) . . .									
at the end of declarative sentences.	I/P	**M**	R	R	R	R	R	R	R
with abbreviations.	-	I/P	**M**	R	R	R	R	R	R
question marks.	I/P	P	**M**	R	R	R	R	R	R
exclamation points.	I/P	P	**M**	R	R	R	R	R	R
apostrophes in contractions and possessives.	-	I/P	P	**M**	R	R	R	R	R
commas . . .									
in series, dates, addresses, friendly letters.	-	I/P	P	**M**	R	R	R	R	R
in compound sentences.	-	I/P	P	P	**M**	R	R	R	R
with introductory phrases and clauses.		I/P	P	P	**M**	R	R	R	R
with appositives, direct address, interrupters, quotations.	-	I/P	P	P	P	**M**	R	R	R
after closing a business letter.	-	-	C	I/P	P	**M**	R	R	R
to avoid confusion.	-	-	-	C	I/P	P	**M**	R	R
underlining for titles of books within texts.		I/P	P	**M**	R	R	R	R	R
quotation marks . . .									
with direct quotations.	-	C	I/P	P	**M**	R	R	R	R
with titles of short works within text.	-	C	I/P	P	**M**	R	R	R	R
colons . . .									
in time.	I/P	P	**M**	R	R	R	R	R	R
in lists, after the saluation in business letters.	-	-	C	I/P	P	**M**	R	R	R
hyphens . . .									
in syllabication.	-	C	I/P	P	**M**	R	R	R	R
in words that designate compound numbers, fractions.	-	C	I/P	P	**M**	R	R	R	R
in compound adjectives.	-	-	C	I/P	**M**	R	R	R	R
semicolons . . .									
in compound sentences.	-	-	-	-	C	I/P	**M**	R	R
in a series that is already punctuated.	-	-	-	-	-	C	I/P	**M**	R
joining closely associated sentences.						C	I/P	**M**	R

WRITING SCOPE AND SEQUENCE
Grade-Level Objectives

CODE
I/P: Introduce/Practice
P: Practice
M: Mastery
R: Review/Reinforce
C: Challenge

Sentence Construction The student will . . .	K	1	2	3	4	5	6	7	8
explain the attributes of a *simple* sentence.	I/P	**M**	R	R	R	R	R	R	R
compose *simple* declarative sentences that include . . .									
subject nouns with present tense regular action verbs.	C	I/P	**M**	R	R	R	R	R	R
subject pronouns with present tense regular action verbs.	C	I/P	**M**	R	R	R	R	R	R
subject noun plurals and action verbs.	C	I/P	**M**	R	R	R	R	R	R
adjectives, nouns, and present tense regular action verbs.	C	I/P	**M**	R	R	R	R	R	R
subject nouns/pronouns linking verbs with adjectives.	C	I/P	**M**	R	R	R	R	R	R
subject nouns/pronouns linking verbs with nouns.	C	I/P	**M**	R	R	R	R	R	R
subject nouns/pronouns with past tense regular verbs.	C	I/P	**M**	R	R	R	R	R	R
subject nouns/pronouns with past tense irregular verbs.	C	I/P	**M**	R	R	R	R	R	R
subject nouns/pronouns with main and helping verbs.	C	I/P	**M**	R	R	R	R	R	R
subject nouns/pronouns, action verbs, and object nouns.	C	I/P	**M**	R	R	R	R	R	R
subject nouns/pronouns, action verbs, and object pronouns.	C	I/P	**M**	R	R	R	R	R	R
subject nouns/pronouns, action verbs, and adverbs.	C	I/P	**M**	R	R	R	R	R	R
irregular noun plurals and action, linking, or helping verbs.	C	I/P	**M**	R	R	R	R	R	R
compound subjects with action/linking helping verbs.	C	I/P	**M**	R	R	R	R	R	R
subject nouns/pronouns with compound action verbs.	C	I/P	**M**	R	R	R	R	R	R
subject nouns with action verbs and compound object nouns/pronouns.	C	I/P	**M**	R	R	R	R	R	R
subject nouns with action verbs with prepositional phrases.	C	I/P	**M**	R	R	R	R	R	R
explain the attributes of a question (interrogative sentence).	C	I/P	**M**	R	R	R	R	R	R
compose questions that include . . .									
subject nouns/pronouns with action/linking/helping verbs.	C	I/P	**M**	R	R	R	R	R	R
explain the attributes of an *exclamatory* sentence.	C	I/P	**M**	R	R	R	R	R	R
compose exclamations that include . . .									
subject nouns/pronouns with action verbs.	C	I/P	**M**	R	R	R	R	R	R
explain the attributes of a *command* (imperative sentence).	C	I/P	**M**	R	R	R	R	R	R
compose commands that include . . .									
subject nouns/pronouns with action/linking/helping verbs.	C	I/P	**M**	R	R	R	R	R	R
explain the attributes of a *compound* sentence.	C	I/P		**M**	R	R	R	R	R
compose *compound* sentences that include . . .									
subject nouns/pronouns and conjunctions *and, or,* and *but.*	C	I/P	**M**	R	R	R	R	R	R
subject nouns/pronouns and conjunctions *for, nor,* and *yet.*	-	C	I/P	**M**	R	R	R	R	R
explain the attributes of a *complex* sentence.	C	I/P	P	**M**	R	R	R	R	R
compose *complex* sentences that include . . .									
subject nouns/pronouns and conjunctions *if, after,* and *when.*	C	I/P	P	P	**M**	R	R	R	R
subject nouns and conjunctions *than, unless, because,* and *however.*	C	I/P	P	P	**M**	R	R	R	R

Parts of Speech—Nouns The student will . . .	K	1	2	3	4	5	6	7	8
explain the concept *noun.*	I/P	M	R	R	R	R	R	R	R
identify nouns as persons, places, or things.	I/P	M	R	R	R	R	R	R	R
explain/identify nouns that are *concepts.*	I/P	P	M	R	R	R	R	R	R
explain the concepts *plural* and *ending* (suffix).	I/P	M	R	R	R	R	R	R	R
use the ending *s* or *es* to form noun plurals.	I/P	M	R	R	R	R	R	R	R
explain the concept *irregular* plural.	I/P	M	R	R	R	R	R	R	R
write irregular noun plurals.	I/P	M	R	R	R	R	R	R	R
explain the concept *subject* noun.	I/P	P	M	R	R	R	R	R	R
identify subject nouns in simple sentences.	I/P	P	M	R	R	R	R	R	R
explain the concept *object* noun.	C	I/P	M	R	R	R	R	R	R
identify object nouns in simple sentences.	C	I/P	M	R	R	R	R	R	R
explain the concepts *common* and *proper* nouns.	C	I/P	M	R	R	R	R	R	R
identify common and proper nouns in sentences.	C	I/P	M	R	R	R	R	R	R
explain the concept *compound* noun.	C	I/P	M	R	R	R	R	R	R
identify compound nouns in simple sentences.	C	I/P	M	R	R	R	R	R	R
explain the concept *prefix.*	-	I/P	P	P	M	R	R	R	R
identify prefixes that express number.	-	I/P	P	P	M	R	R	R	R
explain the concept *suffix* (ending).									
identify suffixes that form nouns.	-	I/P	P	P	M	R	R	R	R
form nouns by adding suffixes.	-	I/P	P	P	M	R	R	R	R
explain/identify verbs used as nouns (verbals).	-	-	-	C	I/P	M	R	R	R
use nouns in sentences (see Sentence Construction).	I/P	M	R	R	R	R	R	R	R

Part of Speech—Verbs The student will . . .	K	1	2	3	4	5	6	7	8
explain the concept *action* verb.	I/P	M	R	R	R	R	R	R	R
identify *action* verbs in sentences.	I/P	M	R	R	R	R	R	R	R
add the ending *s* or *es* to third-person singular action verbs.	C	I/P	M	R	R	R	R	R	R
explain the concept *linking* verb.	C	I/P	M	R	R	R	R	R	R
identify *linking* verbs in sentences.	C	I/P	M	R	R	R	R	R	R
explain the concept of *tense* (time) . . .									
present tense.	C	I/P	M	R	R	R	R	R	R
past tense of *regular* verbs.	C	I/P	M	R	R	R	R	R	R
add the past tense ending *ed* to regular action verbs.	C	I/P	M	R	R	R	R	R	R
explain the concept of *irregular* verbs.	C	I/P	M	R	R	R	R	R	R
write the past tense of irregular verbs.	C	I/P	M	R	R	R	R	R	R
explain the concept of *future* tense.	C	I/P	M	R	R	R	R	R	R
write verb phrases that express future action.	C	I/P	M	R	R	R	R	R	R
explain the concept of *action happening now.*	C	I/P	M	R	R	R	R	R	R
write verb phrases to express action happening now.	C	I/P	M	R	R	R	R	R	R
explain the concept of *principal parts* of verbs.	-	I/P	P	M	R	R	R	R	R
identify principal parts of verbs in sentences.	-	I/P	P	M	R	R	R	R	R
write verb phrases that use principal parts of verbs.	-	-	I/P	P	M	R	R	R	R

WRITING SCOPE AND SEQUENCE
Grade-Level Objectives

CODE
I/P: Introduce/Practice
P: Practice
M: Mastery
R: Review/Reinforce
C: Challenge

Part of Speech—Verbs The student will . . .	K	1	2	3	4	5	6	7	8
explain the concepts *main* and *helping* verbs.	C	I/P	**M**	R	R	R	R	R	R
write main and helping verb phrases.	C	I/P	**M**	R	R	R	R	R	R
explain the concept *compound* verb.	C	I/P	**M**	R	R	R	R	R	R
identify *compound* verbs in sentences.	C	I/P	**M**	R	R	R	R	R	R

Part of Speech—Verbs The student will . . .	K	1	2	3	4	5	6	7	8
explain the concept *prefix*.	C	I/P	**M**	R	R	R	R	R	R
identify prefixes that express time and place.	-	-	I/P	P	**M**	R	R	R	R
identify prefixes that express negation/reversal.	-	-	I/P	P	**M**	R	R	R	R
identify suffixes that form verbs.	-	I/P	P	P	**M**	R	R	R	R
form verbs by adding suffixes.	-	I/P	P	P	**M**	R	R	R	R
explain the concepts *transitive* and *intransitive* verbs.	-	C	I/P	P	P	**M**	R	R	R
categorize transitive and intransitive verbs	-	C	I/P	P	P	**M**	R	R	R
use verbs in sentences (see Sentence Construction).	C	I/P	**M**	R	R	R	R	R	R

Parts of Speech—Pronouns The student will . . .	K	1	2	3	4	5	6	7	8
explain the concept *pronoun*.	C	I/P	**M**	R	R	R	R	R	R
explain the concept *subject* pronoun.	C	I/P	**M**	R	R	R	R	R	R
substitute subject pronouns for subject nouns:									
she, he, we, you, it, I, they.	C	I/P	**M**	R	R	R	R	R	R
explain the concept *object* pronoun.	C	I/P	**M**	R	R	R	R	R	R
substitute object pronouns for object nouns:									
me, him, us, you, it, her, them.	C	I/P	**M**	R	R	R	R	R	R
explain subject/pronoun agreement.	-	I/P	**M**	R	R	R	R	R	R
identify subject/pronoun agreement in sentences.	-	I/P	**M**	R	R	R	R	R	R
explain the concept of *possession* (belonging to).	-	I/P	**M**	R	R	R	R	R	R
identify possessive pronouns in sentences:									
my, your, yours, her, hers, his, its, our, ours, their, theirs.	-	I/P	**M**	R	R	R	R	R	R
explain the concept *interrogative* pronoun.	-	I/P	**M**	R	R	R	R	R	R
identify interrogative pronouns in sentences:									
what, who, which, whose, whom.	-	I/P	**M**	R	R	R	R	R	R
explain the concept *demonstrative* pronoun.	-	I/P	**M**	R	R	R	R	R	R
identify demonstrative pronouns in sentences:									
this, that, these, those.	-	I/P	**M**	R	R	R	R	R	R

Parts of Speech—Pronouns The student will . . .	K	1	2	3	4	5	6	7	8
explain the concept *reflexive* pronoun.	-	I/P	**M**	R	R	R	R	R	R
identify reflexive pronouns in sentences:									
herself, myself, himself, itself, themselves.	-	I/P	**M**	R	R	R	R	R	R
explain the concept *indefinite* pronoun.	-	I/P	**M**	R	R	R	R	R	R
identify indefinite pronouns in sentences:	-								
other, some, each, more, most, any, many.	-	I/P	**M**	R	R	R	R	R	R
another, anything, one, nothing, both, few.	-	I/P	**M**	R	R	R	R	R	R
all, something, none, nobody, everyone.	-	I/P	P	P	**M**	R	R	R	R
everything, several, either, everybody, neither.	-	I/P	P	P	**M**	R	R	R	R
use pronouns in sentences (see Sentence Construction).	-	I/P	**M**	R	R	R	R	R	R
Parts of Speech—Adjectives The student will . . .	K	1	2	3	4	5	6	7	8
explain the concept *adjective.*	I/P	P	**M**	R	R	R	R	R	R
explain the concept *noun signal* (article).	I/P	P	**M**	R	R	R	R	R	R
use *a, the,* and *an* with *appropriate* nouns.	I/P	P	**M**	R	R	R	R	R	R
explain the purpose for using adjectives.	I/P	P	**M**	R	R	R	R	R	R
identify adjectives in sentences.	I/P	P	**M**	R	R	R	R	R	R
write *appropriate* adjectives with nouns.	C	I/P	**M**	R	R	R	R	R	R
write phrases with multiple adjectives and commas.	C	I/P	P	**M**	R	R	R	R	R
explain the concept of *comparative* adjectives.	C	I/P	**M**	R	R	R	R	R	R
add the ending *er* to adjectives.	C	I/P	P	**M**	R	R	R	R	R
add the ending *est* to adjectives.	C	I/P	P	**M**	R	R	R	R	R
use *more/most* with two- to three-syllable adjectives.	-	C	I/P	**M**	R	R	R	R	R
explain the concept *proper* adjective.	-	-	C	I/P	**M**	R	R	R	R
write phrases including proper adjectives.	-	-	C	I/P	**M**	R	R	R	R
identify suffixes that form adjectives:									
ed, al, en, ish, ant, ent, ous, able, ible, ful, less.	-	I/P	P	P	**M**	R	R	R	R
form adjectives by adding suffixes.	-	I/P	P	P	**M**	R	R	R	R
use adjectives and phrases in sentences (see Sentences Construction).	C	I/P	**M**	R	R	R	R	R	R
Parts of Speech—Adverbs The student will . . .	K	1	2	3	4	5	6	7	8
explain the concept *adverb.*	I/P	P	**M**	R	R	R	R	R	R
explain the purpose for using adverbs.	I/P	P	**M**	R	R	R	R	R	R
identify adverbs in sentences.	I/P	P	**M**	R	R	R	R	R	R
write adverbs that express extent/when/where/how:									
so, no, now, up, not, ago, out, yes, just, then.	I/P	P	**M**	R	R	R	R	R	R
as, how, well, fast, back, away, soon, yet, after.	C	I/P	**M**	R	R	R	R	R	R
very, south, inside, outside, east, near, down.	C	I/P	**M**	R	R	R	R	R	R
why, still, never, here, when, twice, where, first.	C	I/P	**M**	R	R	R	R	R	R
even, behind, around, without, maybe, tonight.	C	I/P	**M**	R	R	R	R	R	R
indeed, ever, once, where, there, here, early.	C	I/P	**M**	R	R	R	R	R	R
close, alone, third, within, nothing, past, almost.	C	I/P	**M**	R	R	R	R	R	R
all, less, off, again, also, please, anyway, daily.	C	I/P	**M**	R	R	R	R	R	R

WRITING SCOPE AND SEQUENCE
Grade-Level Objectives

CODE
I/P: Introduce/Practice
P: Practice
M: Mastery
R: Review/Reinforce
C: Challenge

Parts of Speech—Adverbs The student will . . .	K	1	2	3	4	5	6	7	8
explain the concept of *adverb phrases*.	C	I/P	P	**M**	R	R	R	R	R
write adverb phrases that express extent/when/where/how.	C	I/P	P	**M**	R	R	R	R	R
identify suffixes that form adverbs (*ily, ly*).	-	I/P	P	P	**M**	R	R	R	R
form adverbs by adding suffixes.	-	I/P	P	P	**M**	R	R	R	R
use adverbs/adverb phrases in sentences (see Sentence Construction).	C	I/P	**M**	R	R	R	R	R	R

Parts of Speech—Conjunctions The student will . . .	K	1	2	3	4	5	6	7	8
explain the concept *conjunction*.	I/P	P	**M**	R	R	R	R	R	R
use *and/or* to join compound nouns.	I/P	P	**M**	R	R	R	R	R	R
use *and/or* to join compound verbs.	I/P	P	**M**	R	R	R	R	R	R
use *and/or* to join adjective phrases.	I/P	P	**M**	R	R	R	R	R	R
use *and/or* to join adverb phrases.	I/P	P	P	**M**	R	R	R	R	R
use *and/or* to join sentences.	I/P	P	**M**	R	R	R	R	R	R
use *but* to contrast nouns.	I/P	P	**M**	R	R	R	R	R	R
use *but* to contrast verbs.	C	I/P	**M**	R	R	R	R	R	R
use *but* to contrast sentences.	C	I/P	**M**	R	R	R	R	R	R
use conjunctions with complex sentences:									
if, as, after, than, when.	C	I/P	**M**	R	R	R	R	R	R
unless, because, however, while.	C	I/P	P	**M**	R	R	R	R	R
whether, though, since, although.	-	-	C	I/P	**M**	R	R	R	R
either . . . or, neither . . . nor.	-	-	C	I/P	**M**	R	R	R	R
use conjunctions in sentences (see Sentence Construction).	C	I/P	**M**	R	R	R	R	R	R

Parts of Speech—Prepositions The student will . . .	K	1	2	3	4	5	6	7	8
explain the concept *preposition*.	C	I/P	**M**	R	R	R	R	R	R
use prepositions with nouns/pronouns (phrases):									
at, on, in, up, of, out, into, by, over, to, about, for.	C	I/P	**M**	R	R	R	R	R	R
after, inside, outside, near, under, from, along, with.	C	I/P	**M**	R	R	R	R	R	R
through, upon, between, without, behind, around, across.	C	I/P	**M**	R	R	R	R	R	R
by, above, before, within, beside, past.	C	I/P	P	**M**	R	R	R	R	R
except, among, aboard, during, until, since, toward.	-	C	I/P	P	**M**	R	R	R	R
against, beneath, beyond, throughout.	C	I/P	P	P	**M**	R	R	R	R
write adjective prepositional phrases.	C	I/P	**M**	R	R	R	R	R	R
write adverb prepositional phrases.	C	I/P	P	**M**	R	R	R	R	R
use prepositions in sentences (see Sentence Construction).	C	I/P	**M**	R	R	R	R	R	R

Related Sentences The student will . . .	K	1	2	3	4	5	6	7	8
explain the concept *topic*.	C	I/P	**M**	R	R	R	R	R	R
explain the concept *related* sentences.	C	I/P	**M**	R	R	R	R	R	R
distinguish between related and unrelated sentences.	C	I/P	**M**	R	R	R	R	R	R
compose two or three related sentences that include . . .									
previously introduced language skills.	C	I/P	**M**	R	R	R	R	R	R

Paragraph Construction The student will . . .	K	1	2	3	4	5	6	7	8
explain attributes of paragraphs.	C	I/P	**M**	R	R	R	R	R	R
explain paragraph conventions (margins/indents).	C	I/P	**M**	R	R	R	R	R	R
explain stages in the writing process.	C	I/P	**M**	R	R	R	R	R	R
use the writing process to compose . . .									
first-person informative-narratives.	C	I/P	**M**	R	R	R	R	R	R
third-person informative-narratives.	C	I/P	**M**	R	R	R	R	R	R
informative paragraphs.	C	I/P	**M**	R	R	R	R	R	R
first-person narrative paragraphs.	C	I/P	**M**	R	R	R	R	R	R
third-person narrative paragraphs.	C	I/P	**M**	R	R	R	R	R	R
summarize informative-narratives.	-	C	I/P	**M**	R	R	R	R	R
summarize informatives.	-	C	I/P	**M**	R	R	R	R	R
summarize narratives.	-	C	I/P	**M**	R	R	R	R	R

Composition The student will . . .	K	1	2	3	4	5	6	7	8
use the writing process to compose . . .									
first-person informative-narratives.	C	I/P	**M**	R	R	R	R	R	R
third-person informative-narratives.	C	I/P	**M**	R	R	R	R	R	R
informatives.	C	I/P	**M**	R	R	R	R	R	R
first-person narratives.	C	I/P	**M**	R	R	R	R	R	R
third-person narratives.	C	I/P	**M**	R	R	R	R	R	R
informal communications.	C	I/P	**M**	R	R	R	R	R	R
formal communications.	-	-	I/P	P	**M**	R	R	R	R
expository essays with references/bibliography.	-	-	-	-	I/P	P	**M**	R	R
persuasive essays.	-	-	-	-	-	C	I/P	**M**	R
summarize informative-narratives.	-	C	I/P	**M**	R	R	R	R	R
summarize informatives.	-	C	I/P	**M**	R	R	R	R	R
summarize narratives.	-	C	I/P	**M**	R	R	R	R	R

READING SCOPE AND SEQUENCE

Grade-Level Objectives

CODE
I/P: Introduce/Practice
P: Practice
M: Mastery
R: Review/Reinforce
C: Challenge

Literary Appreciation The student will . . .	K	1	2	3	4	5	6	7	8
explain the concept *attributes* of imaginative literature.	C	I/P	**M**	R	R	R	R	R	R
identify attributes in imaginative literature:									
descriptive language, emotional appeal.	C	I/P	**M**	R	R	R	R	R	R
content, insight, and universality.	C	I/P	P	P	**M**	R	R	R	R
reflect on author's use of attributes:									
descriptive language, emotional appeal.	C	I/P	P	**M**	R	R	R	R	R
content, insight, and universality.	C	I/P	P	P	P	**M**	R	R	R
compare use of attributes across selections/cultures:									
descriptive language, emotional appeal.	C	I/P	P	**M**	R	R	R	R	R
content, insight, and universality.	C	I/P	P	P	P	**M**	R	R	R
identify elements in imaginative literature:									
characters (main and supporting).	I/P	P	**M**	R	R	R	R	R	R
settings (integral and backdrop).	I/P	P	**M**	R	R	R	R	R	R
plots (order, types of conflict, patterns of action).	I/P	P	**M**	R	R	R	R	R	R
point of view (first and third).	C	I/P	**M**	R	R	R	R	R	R
theme (main idea).	C	I/P	**M**	R	R	R	R	R	R
style:									
imagery, figurative language, hyperbole.	C	I/P	P	**M**	R	R	R	R	R
onomatopoeia, rhythm, alliteration.	C	I/P	P	**M**	R	R	R	R	R
allusion, symbolism, understatement.	-	-	-	-	-	C	I/P	P	**M**
connotation, denotation.	-	-	-	-	-	C	I/P	P	**M**
assonance, consonance.	-	-	-	-	-	C	I/P	P	**M**
tone.	-	-	-	-	-	C	I/P	P	**M**
reflect (evaluate) author's use of elements:									
characters, setting, plot.	C	I/P	**M**	R	R	R	R	R	R
point of view, theme (main idea).	C	I/P	P	P	**M**	R	R	R	R
style, tone.	-	-	-	-	-	C	I/P	P	**M**
compare elements across selections/cultures:									
characters, setting, plot.	C	I/P	**M**	R	R	R	R	R	R
point of view, theme (main idea).	C	I/P	P	P	**M**	R	R	R	R
style, tone.	-	-	-	C	I/P	P	P	P	**M**
explain elements of fluent, expressive reading.	C	I/P	**M**	R	R	R	R	R	R
read fluently and expressively.	C	I/P	**M**	R	R	R	R	R	R

Text Structure The student will . . .	K	1	2	3	4	5	6	7	8
explain the concept *author's purpose.*	I/P	P	**M**	R	R	R	R	R	R
explain/identify author's purpose in narratives.	I/P	P	**M**	R	R	R	R	R	R
explain the concept *narrative elements.*	I/P	P	**M**	R	R	R	R	R	R
identify narrative elements in paragraphs.	I/P	P	**M**	R	R	R	R	R	R

Text Structure The student will . . .	K	1	2	3	4	5	6	7	8
explain/identify author's purpose in informatives.	I/P	P	**M**	R	R	R	R	R	R
explain the concept *informative elements*.	I/P	P	**M**	R	R	R	R	R	R
identify informative elements in paragraphs.	I/P	P	**M**	R	R	R	R	R	R
explain/identify author's purpose in informative-narratives.	I/P	P	**M**	R	R	R	R	R	R
explain the concept *informative-narrative elements*.	I/P	P	**M**	R	R	R	R	R	R
identify both narrative and informative elements in paragraph.	I/P	P	**M**	R	R	R	R	R	R
use elements to identify types of writing.	I/P	P	**M**	R	R	R	R	R	R
use elements to vary reading rate.	I/P	P	**M**	R	R	R	R	R	R

Mental Actions The student will . . .	K	1	2	3	4	5	6	7	8
explain the concept *mental actions*.	I/P	P	**M**	R	R	R	R	R	R
explain the purpose for *consciously* using mental actions.	I/P	P	**M**	R	R	R	R	R	R
monitor comprehension of . . .	I/P	P	**M**	R	R	R	R	R	R
words.	I/P	P	**M**	R	R	R	R	R	R
phrases.	I/P	P	**M**	R	R	R	R	R	R
sentences.	I/P	P	**M**	R	R	R	R	R	R
make connections with prior knowledge and text to . . .	I/P	P	**M**	R	R	R	R	R	R
infer word meanings, topic, cause and effect.	I/P	P	**M**	R	R	R	R	R	R
elaborate on topic, main idea, outcomes.	I/P	P	**M**	R	R	R	R	R	R
make predictions of . . .	I/P	P	**M**	R	R	R	R	R	R
type of writing, main idea, actions, events, behavior.	I/P	P	**M**	R	R	R	R	R	R
topic, topic sentence, main idea, outcomes.	I/P	P	**M**	R	R	R	R	R	R
reformat/categorize information to . . .									
identify essential and additional information.	I/P	P	**M**	R	R	R	R	R	R
identify elements of types of writing.	I/P	P	**M**	R	R	R	R	R	R
mentally summarize:	I/P	P	**M**	R	R	R	R	R	R
retell narratives in correct sequence.	I/P	P	**M**	R	R	R	R	R	R
restate information in correct sequence.	I/P	P	**M**	R	R	R	R	R	R
identify stated main ideas in text.	I/P	P	**M**	R	R	R	R	R	R
derive implied main ideas in text.	I/P	P	**M**	R	R	R	R	R	R
use mental actions to comprehend print.	I/P	P	**M**	R	R	R	R	R	R

FRAMEWORK FOR PLANNING INTEGRATED LANGUAGE ARTS LESSONS

Two- to Three-Hour Instructional Setting

SPALDING LANGUAGE ARTS instruction is composed of spelling, writing, and reading lessons divided into three or four periods a day. Instructional objectives in this framework are sequenced from easiest to hardest. Each day, add specific phonograms, words, and so forth, as appropriate. For example, after introduction of the first four phonograms on day 1, the oral phonogram review objective would be, "The students will read phonograms *a, c, d, and f.*" On day 2, "The students will read phonograms *a, c, d, f, g, o, s, and qu.*" Each day, review the new and previously introduced phonograms. (See chapter 1, pages 39–42.)

Teach *only* one objective at a time. For example, when dictating Ayres words, do not introduce vocabulary development of unfamiliar words. Word meanings are taught in the writing lesson.

Model each *new* objective, then coach, scaffold, and fade (see the Collins model, in chapter 4). Ensure that students are at the accurate level before introducing a new objective that requires accuracy of the previous objective. For example, do not begin spelling dictation in the notebook until students can accurately say and write the first forty-five phonograms, because these are needed to spell the Ayres words. During those first three weeks, spend more time on literary appreciation and text-structure lessons as explained in chapters 2 and 3.

The recommended times are approximations to help balance integrated language arts instruction. When students can automatically say and write seventy phonograms, plan more time for writing and reading lessons.

Time allotments are adjusted for one-hour special education resource room and tutorial settings (see chapter 5, pages 168–169).

The Spelling Lesson (See pages 9–72.)
(twenty to forty minutes depending on grade level)

Oral Phonogram Review (See page 39.)
(two to ten minutes at a time with a maximum of thirty phonograms)
The students will automatically read . . .

- clock letters (*a, c, d, f, g, o, s, qu*).
- line letters (*b, e, h, i, j, k, l, m, n, p, r, t, u, v, w, x, y, z*).
- selected phonograms 1–45.
- selected phonograms 1–70.

Written Phonogram Review (See pages 40–42.)
(five to ten minutes at a time with a maximum of thirty phonograms)
   The students will automatically say and write . . .

- clock letters (*a, c, d, f, g, o, s, qu*).
- line letters (*b, e, h, i, j, k, l, m, n, p, r, t, u, v, w, x, y, z*).
- selected phonograms 1–45.
- selected phonograms 1–70.

Spelling Dictation and Rule Application (See pages 42–72.)
(twelve to twenty minutes at a time)
   The students will . . .

- precisely say, write, and read Extended Ayres (EA) words . . .
   __(word)__ to __(word)__ in section _____.
- explain pronunciation of selected EA words in section _____.
- explain spelling of selected EA words in section _____.
- read selected EA words for spelling and reading in sections _____ and _____.

The Writing Lesson (See pages 73–120.)
(twenty to sixty minutes depending on grade level)

Sentence Construction (See pages 74–104.)
(integrated spelling/writing lessons ranging from twenty to thirty minutes)
   The students will . . .

- compose oral/written simple sentences that demonstrate meaning and usage of selected EA words in section _____ and include grade-appropriate capitalization and punctuation.
- compose compound sentences that demonstrate meaning and usage of selected EA words in section _____ and include grade-appropriate capitalization and punctuation.
- compose complex sentences that demonstrate meaning and usage of selected EA words in section _____ and include grade-appropriate capitalization and punctuation.
- identify parts of speech of selected EA words in section _____.

Paragraph Construction (See pages 107–120.)
(integrated paragraph lessons ranging from twenty to thirty minutes)
   The students will use the writing process to compose . . .

   • related sentences using content-area and EA words through section _____.
   • informative/narrative paragraphs.
   • informative paragraphs.
   • narrative paragraphs.

Composition (See pages 105–120.)
(integrated composition lessons ranging from twenty to thirty minutes)
   The students will use the writing process to compose . . .

   • informative/narratives.
   • informatives (reports).
   • narratives.
   • informal/formal communications.
   • poetry.
   • speeches/presentations.
   • expository/persuasive essays with references and bibliography.

   The students will use the writing process to . . .

   • summarize informative-narratives.
   • summarize informatives.
   • summarize narratives.

The Reading Lesson (See pages 121–147.)
(twenty to sixty minutes depending on grade level)

Literary Appreciation (See pages 122–133.)
(literary appreciation lessons ranging from ten to thirty minutes)
   The students will . . .

   • identify the attributes of literature appropriate to grade level.
   • identify the elements of narratives appropriate to grade level.
   • reflect on author's use of the attributes of literature.
   • reflect on author's use of the elements of narratives.
   • read fluently and expressively.

Text Structure (See pages 133–141.)
(text-structure lessons ranging from ten to thirty minutes)
  The students will . . .

- identify and label the elements of narrative paragraphs appropriate to grade level.
- identify and label the elements of an informative paragraph appropriate to grade level.
- identify and label the elements of an informative-narrative appropriate to grade level.
- distinguish between informative, narrative, and informative-narrative paragraphs.
- use the elements to predict author's purpose, type of writing, topic.
- vary reading rate and focus appropriate to text structure.

Mental Actions (See pages 141–147.)
(mental action lessons ranging from ten to thirty minutes)
  The students will . . .

- monitor comprehension while listening to paragraphs read.
- make connections with prior knowledge and text to . . .
  - infer word meanings, topic, main idea, cause and effect.
  - elaborate on topic, main idea, outcomes, behaviors.
- make predictions of type of writing, topic, main idea, behaviors.
- reformat/categorize information.
- retell simple paragraphs, including essential information.
- use underlining/note-taking to confirm a stated main idea.
- use note-taking to derive an implied main idea.
- use five mental actions to demonstrate comprehension.

RESOURCES

For the Teacher

The Writing Road to Reading, fifth edition
Phonogram sounds CD
Phonogram Cards, 4¼-by-6-inch (10.8-by-15.2-cm) classroom set
or 3-by-4¼-inch (7.6-by-10.8-cm) individual student set
Word Builder Cards, 3-by-5-inch (7.6-by-12.7-cm) class set
Spelling Assessment Manual
The Comprehension Connection, User's Guide for McCall-Harby
and *McCall-Crabbs Book A with Passage Analyses and Answer
Keys* (kindergarten through second grade)
*The Comprehension Connection, User's Guide for McCall-Crabbs
Standard Test Lessons in Reading Books B–E with Passage Analyses and Answer Keys* (third grade and above)
Primary or intermediate Spelling/Vocabulary notebook
Comprehension/Writing Poster Set
Mental Action Sentence Strips
Optional: Primary and Intermediate Instructional Videos and a
Spelling Instructional Video*

For Each Student in Kindergarten through Second Grade

One six-sided, No. 2 pencil, ⅝-inch (1.6-cm) lined paper, and one
4-inch (10.2-cm) ruler
One primary Spelling/Vocabulary notebook, ⅝-inch (1.6-cm) lines,
34 leaves
One *McCall-Harby Test Lessons in Primary Reading* (kindergarten/first grade)
One *McCall-Crabbs Standard Test Lessons in Reading, Book A*
(second grade)
Children's literature books (see recommended titles in "Instructional Materials")

*Contact SEI for catalog. To order resources, please use one of the following:
Mail: Spalding Education International, 2814 West Bell Road, Suite 1405, Phoenix, AZ
85053; Phone: Metro Phoenix (602) 866-7801; toll-free 1-877-866-7451;
Fax: (602) 866-7488;
Online: www.spalding.org

For Each Student in Third Grade and Above

One six-sided, No. 2 pencil, one red pencil, and one 4-inch (10.2-cm) ruler
One intermediate Spelling/Vocabulary notebook, ⅜-inch (1.0-cm) lines, 50 leaves
One *McCall-Crabbs Standard Test Lessons in Reading, Book B, C, D, or E*
Children's literature books (see recommended titles in "Instructional Materials")

References

Adams, M. J. 1990. *Beginning to read: Thinking and learning about print.* A summary prepared by S. A. Stahl, J. Osborn, and F. Lehr. Champaign, Ill.: Office of Public Affairs/Office of Publications for the Center for the Study of Reading.

Adams, M. J., and M. Bruck. 1995. Resolving the "great debate." *American Educator* 19:7, 10–20.

Anderson, R. C., E. H. Hiebert, J. A. Scott, and I. A. Wilkinson. 1985. *Becoming a nation of readers: The report of the Commission on Reading.* Contract No. 400-83-0057. Washington, DC: National Institute of Education.

Auckerman, R. C. 1984. *Approaches to beginning reading.* 2nd ed. New York: John Wiley and Sons.

Ball, E. W., and B. A. Blachman. 1991. Does phoneme awareness training in kindergarten make a difference in early word recognition and developmental spelling? *Reading Research Quarterly* 26: 49–66.

Barzun, J. 1975. *Simple and direct: A rhetoric for writers.* New York: Harper & Row.

Beck, I. L., and C. Juel. 1995. The role of decoding in learning to read. *American Educator* 19:8, 21–25.

Biemiller, A. J. 1970. The development of the use of graphic and contextual information as children learn to read. *Reading Research Quarterly* 6:75–96.

Blachman, B. 1996. Preventing early reading failure. In S. C. Cramer and W. Ellis, eds., *Learning disability: Lifelong issues.* Baltimore, Md.: Paul C. Brookes and Company.

Byrne, B., and R. Fielding-Barnsley. 1993. Evaluation of a program to teach phonemic awareness to young children: A one-year follow-up. *Journal of Educational Psychology* 85: 104–111.

Byrne, B., and R. Fielding-Barnsley. 1995. Evaluation of a program to teach phonemic awareness to young children: A two- and three-year follow-up and a new preschool trial. *Journal of Educational Psychology* 87: 488–503.

Chall, J. S. 1983a. *Stages of reading development.* New York: McGraw-Hill.

———. 1983b. *Learning to read: The great debate.* 2nd ed. New York: McGraw-Hill.

———. 1996a. *Learning to read: The great debate.* 3rd ed. Harcourt Brace College Publications.

———. 1996b. *Stages of reading development.* 2nd ed. New York: Harcourt Brace College Publications.

Collins, A., J. S. Brown, and S. E. Newman. 1989. Cognitive apprenticeship: Teaching the crafts of reading, writing, and mathematics. In L. B. Resnick, ed., *Knowing, learning, and instruction: Essays in honor of Robert Glaser.* Hillsdale, N.J.: Lawrence Erlbaum Associates.

Ehri, L. C., and L. S. Wilce. 1987. Does learning to spell help beginners learn to read words? *Reading Research Quarterly* 22: 47–63.

Every Child Reading: An Action Plan of the Learning First Alliance. 1998. In *American Educator* 22: 52–63.

Farnham-Diggory, S. 1987. From theory to practice in reading. Paper presented at the annual meeting of the Reading Reform Foundation, San Francisco (July).

———. 1990. *Schooling.* Cambridge, Mass.: Harvard University Press.

———. 1992. *Cognitive processes in education.* New York: HarperCollins.

Fletcher, J. M., and G. R. Lyon. 1998. Reading: A research-based approach. In W. M. Evers, ed., *What's gone wrong in America's classrooms?* Stanford, Calif.: Hoover Institution Press.

Foorman, B. R., D. F. Francis, S. E. Shaywitz, B. A. Shaywitz, and J. M. Fletcher. 1997. The case for early reading intervention. In B. A. Blachman, ed., *Foundations of reading acquisition and dyslexia: Implications for early intervention.* Mahwah, N.J.: Lawrence Erlbaum Associates.

Goodman, K. S., and Y. Goodman. 1979. Learning to read is natural. In L. B. Resnick and P. A. Weaver, eds. *Theory and practice of early reading.* Vol. 1. Hillsdale, N.J.: Lawrence Erlbaum Associates.

Gough, P. 1972. One second of reading. In J. Kavanagh and I. Mattingly, eds., *Language by ear and by eye.* Cambridge, Mass.: MIT Press.

Groff, P. 1977. The new anti-phonics. *The Elementary School Journal* (March).

Hatcher, P. J., C. Hulme, and A. W. Ellis. 1994. Ameliorating early reading failure by integrating the teaching of reading and phonological skills: The phonological linkage hypothesis. *Child Development* 65: 41–57.

Hoerl, M. F., and D. Koons. 1995. Effect of Spalding multisensory phonics instruction on the literacy skills of high school special education students. In C. W. McIntyre and J. P. Pickering, eds., *Clinical studies of multisensory structured language education.* Salem, Ore.: International Multisensory Structured Language Education Council.

Hohn, W. E., and L. C. Ehri. 1983. Do alphabet letters help prereaders acquire phonemic segmentation skill? *Journal of Educational Psychology* 75: 752–762.

Koerner, J. D. 1959. *The case for basic education.* Boston: Little, Brown and Company.

Liberman, I. Y., and A. Liberman. 1992. Whole language versus code emphasis: Underlying assumptions and their implications for reading instruction. In P. B. Gough, L. C. Ehri, and R. Treiman, eds., *Reading acquisition.* Hillsdale, N.J.: Lawrence Erlbaum and Associates.

Lukens, R. J. 1976. *A critical handbook of children's literature.* Glenview, Ill.: Scott Foresman and Company.

———. 1995. *A critical handbook of children's literature.* New York: HarperCollins College Publishers.

Lyon, G. R. 1995. Toward a definition of dyslexia. *Annals of Dyslexia* 45: 3–27.

———. 2001. Statement before the House Committee on Education and the Workforce. Available from www.house.gov/ed and workforce/hearings/oeri5400/lyons.htm.

Mitchell, R. 1979. *Less than words can say.* Boston: Little, Brown and Company.

Moats, L. C. 2000. *Speech to print: Language essentials for teachers.* Baltimore, Md.: Paul H. Brooks Publishing Company.

North, M. E. 1991. The writing road to reading: From theory to practice. *Annals of Dyslexia* 42: 110–123.

———. 1995. The effects of Spalding instruction on special education students. In C. W. McIntyre and J. P. Pickering, eds., *Clinical studies of multisensory structured language education.* Salem, Ore.: International Multisensory Structured Language Education Council.

Pinker, S. 1999. Foreword in D. McGuinness, *Why our children can't read and what we can do about it.* New York: Simon & Schuster.

Potter, B. *The Tale of Peter Rabbit.* New York: Penguin Group.

Report of the National Reading Panel. 2000. National Institute of Health Publication No. 00-4769 (April).

Rieben, L., and C. A. Perfetti. 1991. Learning to read: Basic research and its implications. Hillsdale, N.J.: Lawrence Erlbaum and Associates.

Rumelhart, D. E. 1977. Toward an interactive model of reading. In S. Dornic and P. M. A. Rabbitt, eds., *Attention and performance.* Vol. 4. Hillsdale, N.J.: Lawrence Erlbaum and Associates.

Rumelhart, D. E., and J. L. McClelland. 1986. Interactive processing through spreading activation. In A. M. Lesgold and C. A. Perfetti, eds., *Interactive processes in reading.* Hillsdale, N.J.: Lawrence Erlbaum Associates.

Russell, W. F. 1984. *Classics to read aloud to your children.* New York: Crown Publishers. Quoting H. C. Andersen, *The ugly duckling.* 13–18.

Smith, C. L., and H. Tager-Flusberg. 1982. Metalinguistic awareness and language development. *Journal of Experimental Child Psychology* 34: 449–468.

Smith, F. 1971. *Understanding reading.* New York: Holt, Rinehart & Winston.

Share, D., and K. Stanovich, 1995. Cognitive processes in early reading development: Accommodating individual differences into a model of acquisition. In J. Carlson, ed., *Issues in education: Contributions from education psychology.* 1:1–57.

Snow, E., M. S. Burns, and P. Griffin, eds. 1998. *Preventing reading difficulties in young children.* Washington, D.C.: National Academy Press.

Stanovich, K. E. 1986. Mathew effects in reading: Some consequences of individual differences in the acquisition of literacy. *Reading Research Quarterly* 21: 360–407.

———. 1993. Does reading make you smarter? Literacy and the development of verbal intelligence. In H. Reese, ed. *Advances in child development and behavior* 24: 133–180. San Diego, Calif.: Academic Press.

———. 1994. Romance and reality. *Reading Teacher* 4: 280–290.

Treiman, R. 1985. Phonemic awareness and spelling: Children's judgments do not always agree with adults.' *Journal of Experimental Child Psychology* 39: 182–201.

———. 1993. *Beginning to spell: A study of first-grade children.* New York: Oxford University Press.

Treiman, R., and J. Baron. 1983. Phonemic-analysis training helps children benefit from spelling-sound rules. *Memory & Cognition* 11: 382–389.

Vellutino, F. R., and D. M. Scanlon. 1991. The effects of instructional bias on word identification. In L. Rieben and C. A. Perfetti, eds., Learning to read: Basic research and its implications. Hillsdale, N.J.: Lawrence Erlbaum Associates.

Vellutino, F. R., D. M. Scanlon, and M. S. Tanzman. 1994. Components of reading ability: Issues and problems in operationalizing word identification, phonological coding, and orthographic coding. In G. R. Lyon, ed., *Frames of reference for the assessment of learning disabilities: New views on measurement issues.* Baltimore, Md.: Paul H. Brookes Publishing Co.

Index

Page numbers in *italics* refer to illustrations.

Romalda Bishop Spalding, 1899–1994

Romalda Spalding was a remarkably gifted teacher, but more than that, she was a remarkable woman. Finding that professional preparation was not adequate to the task of helping all students learn to read and write, she embarked on a path that ultimately led to instructing teachers across the globe.

In New York City in 1938, her search for a better way to teach language led her to the eminent neurologist Dr. Samuel T. Orton. Under Orton's direction, she taught students who found reading and writing difficult. At Dr. Orton's invitation, she attended his course for pediatricians at the Columbia College of Physicians and Surgeons at the New York Academy of Medicine. For two and a half years, Dr. Orton taught Mrs. Spalding principles of learning and specific tutoring techniques for struggling students. She learned from Orton that the method of teaching determines which pathways develop in the brain, and that every phonetic language develops from speech, to letters that represent speech sounds, and then to words and sentences. She soon realized that the techniques that worked so well with children having difficulty also often prevented reading problems—a concept that is now validated by research.

"With a good phonics system, the student says the sound he hears, writes the letter or letters which represent it, and sees this representation as he reads it," Mrs. Spalding said. She understood that *how* spelling is taught is of great importance and that it should be "taught as scientifically as possible," from the spoken word to the written form. Applying Dr. Orton's principles, she developed her multisensory method of language arts instruction. His direction to her, "When a problem is presented, divide it into its component parts, build them sequentially, and talk about each part," guided her every step.

Mrs. Spalding's formal work with Dr. Orton ended in 1941 with the advent of World War II and her navy commander husband's assignment to Boston. However, she continued to perfect and expand on the method taught her by Dr. Orton while teaching children with language problems, working with physicians at Harvard Children's Hospital, and later serving as a consultant in reading to the superintendent of the Catholic schools in Hawaii.

Recent medical studies into the way the brain works and reading research have validated principles of learning and instruction used by Dr. Orton. These principles, enriched by Mrs. Spalding's classroom experience and her intense study of how children learn, were incorporated in The Spalding Method.

In 1957, with her husband's help and encouragement, she put her knowledge and experience into her book, *The Writing Road to Reading*. She devoted the rest of her life to teaching her method to teachers and parents and to tutoring students of all ages. Many honors were accorded her in recognition of her contributions to literacy. Among these, she was awarded an honorary Doctor of Humane Letters by Chaminade University of Honolulu in 1975. She served as advisor to the International Montessori Society and on the Orton Dyslexia Society (now International Dyslexia Association) Council of Advisors until her death. Thousands of teachers and tens of thousands of children have benefited from Mrs. Spalding's tireless dedication to literacy. We at Spalding Education International take pride in carrying her legacy forward.